Japanese/Korean Linguistics

Volume 27

Japanese/Korean Linguistics

Volume 27

edited by
Michael Barrie

Published for the Stanford Linguistics Association by

CSLI PUBLICATIONS
Center for the Study of
Language and Information
Stanford, California

CSLI Publications
Center for the Study of Language and Information
Leland Stanford Junior University
Printed in the United States
21 20 19 18   1 2 3 4 5

Library of Congress Cataloging-in-Publication Data

Conference on Japanese/Korean Linguistics
(1st : 1989 : University of Southern California)
Japanese/Korean Linguistics / edited by Hajime Hoji.
Volume 27 / edited by Michael Barrie

p.   cm.

Includes bibliographical references and index.
ISBN-13: 978-1-68400-067-8
ISBN-13: 978-1-68400-066-1 (pbk.)
eISBN-13: 978-1-68400-068-5 (electronic)
1. Japanese language—Congresses. 2. Korean language—Congresses.
3. Japanese language—Grammar, Comparative—Korean—Congresses.
4. Korean language—Grammar, Comparative—Japanese—Congresses.
5. Linguistics—Congresses. I. Hoji, Hajime. II. Stanford Linguistics Association. III. Center for the Study of Language and Information (U.S.) IV. Title.
PL503.C6 1989
495.6–dc20   90-2550

CIP

∞ The acid-free paper used in this book meets the minimum requirements of the American National Standard for Information Sciences—Permanence of Paper for Printed Library Materials, ANSI Z39.48-1984.

CSLI was founded in 1983 by researchers from Stanford University, SRI International, and Xerox PARC to further the research and development of integrated theories of language, information, and computation. CSLI headquarters and CSLI Publications are located on the campus of Stanford University.

Visit our website at
http://cslipublications.stanford.edu/
for comments on this and other titles, as well as for changes and corrections by the author and publisher. For the Japanese/Korean

Linguistic Cumulative table of contents, please visit:
https://web.stanford.edu/group/cslipublications/cslipublications/ja-ko-contents/jako-collective-toc.shtml/

Contents

POSTER PRESENTATIONS
(Alphabetical by Author's Last Name)

Invited Speakers

The Parallel Route the Japanese- and Korean-Acquiring Children Take to Attain the Adult Grammar: An Implication for the Minimalist Theory

KEIKO MURASUGI

1 Introduction*

How varied can human language be? Greenberg's typological research, for example, suggests that languages are divided into some major groups. Then, investigation into language variation can be of two kinds. One concerns the major divisions among languages. In this paper, we will consider the presence/absence of φ-feature agreement and discuss its

* I would like to thank Michael Barrie, Mamoru Saito and Kensuke Takita for the comments and suggestions for this paper. Sincere thanks go to the organizers, participants and anonymous reviewers of JK 27 and the series of workshops at Center for Linguistics, Nanzan University and NINJAL. Part of the research presented here is based on the joint works with Chisato Fuji, Tomoko Hashimoto, Tomomi Nakatani and Naoko Sawada, and is supported by Nanzan University Pache Research Grant I-A (2019, 2020) and by JSPS Grant-in-Aid (#17K02752).

Japanese/Korean Linguistics 27
Edited by Michael Barrie.

implications for the theory of language acquisition. The other kind has to do with the variations within a specific language group. The comparative work on Japanese and Korean obviously belongs to this. Before moving into the main topic, we will briefly mention an example of this type of research.

As is well known, Japanese and Korean share considerable similarity in their syntax and morphology. They are synthetic languages with morphology that employs agglutination, and the stem of the verbal elements cannot stand bare. They are languages with rich Case marking, and allow scrambling and (referential) *pro*.

(1) a. *tabe- 'to eat'
b. (watasi-ga) (ringo-o) tabe-ru/ta
I -NOM apple-ACC eat-PRES/-PAST
'(I) eat/ (an apple)'
c. ringo-o watasi-ga tabe-ru/ta
apple-ACC I -NOM eat-PRES/-PAST
'As for the apple, I eat/ate.' (Japanese)

The arguments (the subject noun phrase *watasi-ga* (I) and the object *ringo-o* (an apple)) in (1b), for example, can be phonetically null, and the object *ringo-o* can be scrambled to the sentence-initial position as shown in (1c).

Despite such commonalities, however, there are differences found between them as well: The phonetic and lexical resemblances are not large in those languages, and the degree of grammaticalization in auxiliary verbs, for instance, is different. Furthermore, as Saito and An (2014) point out, there is a syntactic difference between the two languages. Japanese and Korean contrast with respect to N'-ellipsis: Japanese has N'-ellipsis as argued in Saito and Murasugi (1990), but Korean does not. Relevant examples are shown in (2)-(3).

(2) [Taroo-no kenkyuu-nitaisuru taido]-wa yoi-ga, (Japanese)
T-gen research-toward attitude-top good-though
[Hanako-no ___]-wa yoku-nai
H-gen -top good-not
'Taroo's attitude toward research is good, but Hanako's isn't.'

(3) * [Chelswu-uy yenkwu-eytayhan thayto]-nun coh-cimen, (Korean)
C-gen research-toward attitude-top good-though
[Swuni-uy ___]-nun cohci ahnta
S-gen -top good not
'Chelswu's attitude toward research is good, but Swuni's isn't.'

They propose a parameterization of the modifier insertion rule in Noun Phrases (NPs) as shown in (4), and argue that it accounts for the difference between the two languages with respect to N'-ellipsis.

(4) Mod Insertion
$[_{YP} \ldots XP\ Y^n] \rightarrow [_{YP} \ldots XP\text{-}Mod\ Y^n]$
(Mod = *no* in Japanese and *uy* in Korean.)
where (i) Y = N or D, X is [-V], and
(ii) Y is overt. (Only in Korean.)

To restate the analysis, languages lacking φ-feature agreement have a modifier insertion rule in the structure of NPs, but the rule is (micro-) parameterized, and the parametric difference would account for the difference between the two languages with respect to N'-ellipsis. This is a typical example of a formal analysis of language variation. What appears to be an outstanding difference between two languages is explained by a small difference in the formulation of a common rule.

The (micro-) parameter in (4) is based on the premise that Japanese and Korean share a major property, the lack of φ-feature agreement. The typological difference with respect to φ-feature agreement raises a number of questions. What is the function of φ-feature agreement in languages that have it? How is the function achieved in languages without it? And finally, how does the acquisition proceed in languages with and without φ-feature agreement? The last question is the main topic of this paper.

In the following section, we will introduce Chomsky's (2013) Labeling Algorithm in which φ-feature agreement plays an important role, and Saito's (2016) proposal that suffixal Case performs this role in languages without φ-feature agreement. With this background, we will examine the very early utterances produced by the young children (around 2 years of age) acquiring English, Japanese and Korean in Section 3. We will show that the "erroneous" strings such as Root Infinitive (Analogues) (RI(A)s) that children produce are essentially similar across languages with and without φ-feature agreement. They are without φ-feature agreement and suffixal Case. Based on analysis of RIAs in Murasugi (in press), I will conclude that the early stage of acquisition can be characterized as the period in which children are trying to figure out the Labeling Algorithm of the target language. This supports the hypothesis that there is a major parameter in Labeling; some languages appeal to φ-feature agreement and others to suffixal Case. Section 4 concludes the paper.

2 Parameterization in Minimalist Program

In Chomsky's (1994, 2013) minimalist approach to syntax, Merge is proposed as the most fundamental operation that combines two elements, α and β, into a constituent containing α and β as shown in (5).

(5) α, β → γ = {α, β}

This operation accompanies a Labeling Algorithm (LA) that specifies the nature of the formed object, and it is this LA that largely dictates the distribution of nominal phrases and the application of movement (Internal Merge). The idea is that the nature of the syntactic object Merge forms must be specified. For example, the interpretive components need to know whether γ = {D(P), V(P)} is verbal (VP) or nominal (DP). Chomsky (2013) presents a concrete proposal for the Labeling Algorithm, as summarized in (6).

(6) a. α determines the label of γ = {α, β} if
(i) α is a head and β is a phrase or (ii) γ fully contains α but not β.
b. The label of γ = {α, β} is <F, F> if
α, β are both phrases and their heads share a significant feature F.

In the Minimalist Program, Merge and Labeling are considered to be part of Universal Grammar (UG), but questions arise here. How are linguistic variations explained? Are Merge and Labeling absolutely universal or relatively universal? Chomsky (2013) argues that a finite clause is labeled through the sharing of φ-features between the subject DP and Tense (T), and that this is the reason language requires φ-feature agreement. Then, how are languages lacking φ-feature agreement explained?

Addressing these questions, Saito (2016) presents an analysis that suffixal Case markers make it possible to label finite clauses in languages that lack φ-feature agreement. More precisely, Saito (2016) proposes that suffixal Cases in those languages serve as anti-labeling devices. That is, in those languages, βP provides the label for the constituent γ in (7).

(7) γ = {αP-Case, βP}, where Case is suffixal.

This proposal accounts for the Labeling not only of simple tensed clauses but also of multiple nominative subject sentences, exemplified by (8) from Kuno (1973).

(8) [$_{TP}$ Bunmeikoku-ga [$_{TP}$ dansei-ga [$_{TP}$ heikin-zyumyoo-ga
civilized.country-NOM male-NOM average-life.span-NOM
[$_{TP}$ mizikai]]]]
short
'It is in civilized countries that it is the male population whose average life-span is short.'

As the subjects accompany the nominative Case marker *-ga*, their sister TPs provide the label for γ = {DP-*ga*, TP}.

The proposal also explains why scrambling sentences such as (1c) are possible in languages with suffixal Case markers. In (9), the matrix clause is labeled by the lower TP because the scrambled object accompanies the accusative Case marker *-o*.

(9) [$_{TP}$ Sono hon-o [$_{TP}$ Taroo-ga katta]] (koto)
that book-ACC Taroo-NOM bought fact
'(the fact that) Taroo bought that book'

If the proposal illustrated above is correct, φ-feature agreement is indispensable for Labeling in English-type languages, and Case markers play crucial roles for Labeling in Japanese/Korean-type languages. Given the analysis, the cross-linguistic variations with respect to multiple subjects and scrambling, for example, are explained by the differences in the mechanism of Labeling. In other words, the system of Labeling is parameterized, and those children acquiring languages lacking φ-features agreement would attain the adult system of anti-labeling devices, while those children acquiring languages with φ-features agreement would not. The universality of Labeling can be considered, therefore, to be relative, not absolute.

Murasugi (in press) provides some pieces of supportive evidence for Saito's (2016) proposal of the parameterization of Labeling based on the well-known "erroneous" strings that very young children produce. In the following section, we will review the argument and show that children indeed need to acquire the Labeling system of the target language on the basis of the data presented to them.

1 Root Infinitive (Analogue) Stage and the Acquisition of Labeling

Children do not always produce strings identical to those of adults. Among the examples are sentences with the so-called Root Infinitives (RIs). RIs are typically the infinitival verb forms used by children around two years of age in matrix (root) clauses, where they cannot appear in adult grammar. (Phillips, 1995, among others) It is well known that there are some morpho-syntactic and semantic properties common to RIs.

(10) a. RIs are tenseless verbs in root contexts.
b. At the RI stage, no T-related/C-related items are found.
c. RIs are produced to describe events in real time, that is, as an ongoing activity in the past, present, or future that the child is involved in.
d. RIs occur in modal contexts (the Modal Reference Effects (MREs)).
e. RIs are restricted to event-denoting predicates (the Eventivity Constraint).
f. Head Merger is not available during the RI stage.
(Deen 2002, among others)

The Tense- and Complementizer-related items do not co-occur with RIs. Also, RIs are typically produced as a result of children's intention, desire, or volition, in various irrealis modal contexts. This is termed the Modal Reference Effects as shown in (10d) (Hoekstra and Hyams 1998).

Schütze and Wexler (1996), among others, raise the question why young children produce such non-target-consistent or incomplete strings as RIs, and propose the Agreement/Tense Omission Model (ATOM). According to ATOM, there is a RI stage during which the features of Tense (including the φ-features) may be underspecified. This results in children optionally using non-finite verb forms (RIs) in contexts in which finite verb forms would be obligatory in adult grammar, producing "erroneous" strings such as those in (11).

(11) a. That go in there
b. Daddy going to the shops
c. Mummy gone to work

The ATOM explains, in addition, the Case "errors," exemplified in (12). Children sometimes use non-nominative pronouns such as *me*, *my*, *him*, and *her* in contexts in which nominative pronouns are required. (See Rispoli 1994, 1999 and Wexler 1998, among many others.)

(12) a. My go in there
b. Me went home
c. Him going to the shops
d. Her gone to work

These "errors," according to Schütze and Wexler, are related to the deficiency of the feature specification of Tense or failure to phonetically realize the Case feature value properly.

How can the insights of ATOM be reformulated in the recent framework of generative grammar? Under the Minimalist Program, the Root-Infinitive (RI) stage can be analyzed as the stage where the φ-feature agreement is "underspecified" or more plausibly, absent. And related to this is the question regarding how sentences with RIs are labeled. Although it remains a possibility that children at the RI stage postulate abstract Tense with unvalued φ-features and successfully label RI sentences as <φ, φ>, this does not seem to be viable unless φ-feature agreement is a universal property of human language that is encoded in UG. As noted in Section 2, there are languages like adult Japanese and adult Korean that lack φ-feature agreement.

Then, do the RI sentences produced by children acquiring English lack φ-feature agreement just as in adult Japanese and adult Korean? Discussing this question, Murasugi (in press) points out that the absence of Tense and erroneous Case are not the only phenomena observed in the very early utterances of English-acquiring children. The subject not only can be erroneously Case-marked but also can be null. And interestingly enough, when the subject is missing, the object sometimes appears in front of the verbal element as if the object is "scrambled" to the sentence-initial position. Radford (1990), for instance, cites Bowerman (1973) and reports that Kendall, just before two years of age, produced verb phrases in both Verb-Object (henceforth, VO) order as in (13) and Object-Verb (henceforth, OV) order as in (14).

(13) a. Look Kendall (VO) 'Look at Kendall' (1;10-1;11)
b. Writing book (VO) (1;10-1;11)
c. Break Fur-Book (VO) (1;10-1;11)
name of book
d. Bite…finger (VO) (1;10-1;11)

(14) a. Doggie sew (OV) 'Sew a doggie' (1;10-1;11)
b. Kimmy kick (OV) 'Kick Kimmy' (1;10-1;11)
c. Kendall pick-up (OV) 'Pick up Kendall' (1;10-1;11)
d. Doggie lookit (OV) 'Look at the doggie' (1;10-1;11)

Radford (1990: 249) further reports that the same pattern is found with structures containing both an overt subject and an overt complement. The order Subject-Verb-Object (e.g., *Mommy… sew doggie*) and the order Object-Verb-Subject (*Mommy hit Kendall*, meaning Kendall hit Mommy) are both found.

The word order variation exemplified above is significant especially because the head parameter is set quite early at the two-word stage. Radford (1990: 70-72) himself observes that the word order in Prepositional Phrases (PP), for example, is adult-like even at the stage where functional categories are missing. He states that children clearly "know" from a very young age that P can be projected to P-bar by the addition of a following complement just like N and V, as shown in (15).

(15) a. Paula play with ball. In there, mummy. Put in there. Go in there. Hat on baby.
b. Paula play with ball. Open box. Go in. Get out. (Paula, 1;06)

The head Ps in (15a), *with*, *in* and *on*, are placed before their complements just like the head Vs of VPs in (15b). In this case, the word order is strict and consistent with the target language, and no PO-OP alternation is observed in contrast with VO-OV.

The consistent PO order indicates that the basic word order of the target language is acquired at a very early stage as the hypothesis of Very Early Parameter Setting (VEPS) advanced by Wexler (1998) suggests. Murasugi (in press) argues that given VEPS and the consistency of the word order in the two-word stage in Japanese and English, the operation of head-complement Merger must already be acquired at an earliest observable stage of grammar acquisition. This is so because a child needs to distinguish heads and complements in order to consistently produce head-initial or head-final structures. This in turn indicates that head-complement Merger, together with the accompanying Labeling Algorithm, is an absolute universal.

Now, if the children who produce the OV examples in (14) already set the head parameter as head-initial, then those examples are derived by preposing the object with a scrambling-like movement operation. And this is not expected under the assumption that children at this stage have the adult grammar with functional categories and φ-feature agreement. This is because the adult grammar of English does not allow OV order or scrambled sentences.

The task, at this point, is to characterize the early child grammar that exhibits the RI phenomenon, "erroneous" Case realization, and occasional OV order. There seem to be two possibilities. If the RI sentences lack φ-feature agreement and are still labeled, then it may be that children at this stage have Japanese/Korean-type grammar with null suffixal Case. This would predict as well that scrambling, and hence, OV order are possible at the stage in question. The other possibility is that there is neither φ-feature agreement nor suffixal Case at the RI stage. That is, children compose sentences with Merge, the head parameter and semantics, but are yet to discover how a constituent fully containing two phrases, {αP, βP}, is labeled in the target language.

Murasugi (in press) argues for the latter possibility: During the RI stage, the target system of labeling is under construction because φ-feature agreement and Case are not target-grammar-like.[1] Suppose, on the contrary, that English-speaking children at the RI stage have an adult Japanese/Korean-type grammar with null suffixal Case markers. As noted above, this would make it possible for (14) to be labeled~~,~~ and predict that English-speaking children produce utterances with OV order. However, this hypothesis encounters a serious learnability problem. If English-acquiring children assume null suffixal Case, how do they find out that the assumption is wrong? The fact that adult English allows neither multiple nominative subjects nor scrambling would lead to the desired conclusion. But this would require negative evidence.

Furthermore, RIs and RI Analogues (RIAs) are in fact attested in very young children's speech across a wide variety of languages.[2] Importantly, in child Japanese and child Korean, the RIAs are also found, as exemplified in (16a) and (16b).

(16) a. *Tii si-ta (Sumihare, 1;07: Murasugi and Fuji 2010)
pee do-PAST
'I want to pee.'
b. *Ayki pwo-a (Jiyoung, 2;02-2;03; Kim and Phillips 1998)
baby look-DECL
'Baby (I) will look at it.'

Murasugi and Fuji (2011), among others, and Kim and Phillips (1998) examine ~~the~~ child Japanese and child Korean respectively. They arrive at

---

1 See Murasugi (in press) for the detailed analysis.

2 Although the use of tense-less verbs in root contexts by very young children is a universal phenomenon, there are morphological variations associated with the different verbal systems in the target languages. That is, the form of RIs is not always infinitive. Murasugi, Nakatani and Fuji (2010) argue that there are three types of RIs in world languages; the infinitive forms (e.g., Dutch, French, German, among others), the bare verbal forms (e.g., English, Chinese, ASL, among others), and the surrogate forms (e.g., Japanese, Korean, Arabic, Turkish, among others). Due to the limit of the available pages, we do not illustrate the RIs in other languages here, but see Murasugi, Nakatani and Fuji (2010) for the details.

similar conclusions; (i) there is an RIA stage that corresponds to the early stage of RI in other languages, (ii) the form in question is the past-tense form V-*ta* and/or mimetics(-*ta*/-*sita*) in Japanese, and V-*e* in Korean, (iii) there are no C- or T-related elements at the time. During the RIA stage, verbs and adjectives do not indicate tense, and Case markers are not observed.

Let us briefly overview-Kim and Philips (1998). They report that a Korean-acquiring child used the declarative V-*e* form in some ungrammatical contexts at 2;02 through 2;03, as shown in (17).

(17) *mek-e emma (adult form: *mek-ca* (PROPOSITIVE))
eat-DECL. mommy
'Let's eat, Mommy.'

In (17), the default mood marker *–e (-a)* is "erroneously" used in contexts where the specific propositive marker *-ca* should be employed in adult Korean. Kim and Phillips (1998) analyzes the V-*e* form in (17) as an RIA form, as this and other examples of this kind bear some typical RIA properties. As noted above, the V-*e* form in this stage is not marked for tense. In adult Korean, the tense morpheme *-ess* is obligatory to express completive events as the contrast between (18a) and (18b) indicates. The Korean-acquiring child, however, did not use the past-tense morphemes even in the obligatory contexts from 2;02 through 2;03, as exemplified in (19).

(18) a. mek-ess-ta (Past)
eat-PAST-DECL. 'I ate.'
b. mek-e (Present)
eat-DECL. 'I eat.'

(19) enni ka-Ø-(a) (2 years)
sister go-(PAST)-(QUESTION)
'Intended meaning: Did sister go?'

Second, the V-*e*-form did not co-occur with a nominative Case marker, a tense-related item, in the child's utterances. In adult Korean, nominative Case markers can be dropped in discourse-licensed contexts as in (20a), but this is not totally free. For example, they cannot be omitted in scrambled sentences as shown in (20b).

(20) a. emma-(ka) pap-ul mek-ess-e (SOV)
mom-NOM meal-ACC eat -PAST-DECL.
'Mommy ate the meal.'
b. pap-ul emma-*(ka) mek-ess-e (OSV)
meal-ACC mom-NOM eat-PAST-DECL.
'Mommy ate the meal.'

The child, however, dropped the nominative Case marker even in scrambled sentences and other obligatory contexts. According to Kim and Phillips (1998), her mother used the nominative Case marker 50% of the time in non-obligatory contexts and 96% in the grammatically required contexts. On the other hand, the child used it in only 1% of the time in optional contexts and 0% in grammatically required contexts.

Murasugi, Nakatani and Fuji (2010), Murasugi and Fuji (2011), Murasugi (2015), among others, independently report findings parallel to those in Kim and Phillips (1998). They note that the stage is found earlier than in European languages, i.e., even at one year of age. They also point out that the typical properties of the Root Infinitives are found in the Japanese RIAs as well. That is, the V-*ta* and/or mimetics(*-ta/-sita*) are used to express children's intention of request or volition, as (16a) shows.[3]

Based on the empirical study of the RIAs attested in young children's utterances in Japanese and Korean, Murasugi (in press) argues that the learnability issue also arises with Japanese/Korean-acquiring children in the surrogate RI stage. If the children–successfully label (16a) and (16b) because they assume null suffixal Case, how do they discover that suffixal Case markers cannot be null in contexts where they are obligatory? This too would require negative evidence.

Then, given Saito's (2016) hypothesis that tensed clauses are labeled differently depending on the language, a more plausible possibility seems to be that children go through a stage when they try to discover the Labeling Algorithm of their target language. Merge is a necessary part of a language, and it requires that every constituent be labeled. It is also universal that the head determines the label of a head-complement structure, {H, XP}.[4] However, the way an {XP, YP} structure is labeled can vary among languages, as discussed in Section 2. Chomsky (2013) proposes that a tensed clause in

[3] The difference found between the form of Japanese RIA and that of Korean RIA maybe due to the fact that the past-tense morpheme in adult Japanese appears in the verb-final position but the one in adult Korean does not. Korean past-tense morpheme *-ess* appears in a word-medial position with phonetic variation. This suggests that the surrogate RIAs in the agglutinative languages include a verb-ending suffixal element.

[4] Chomsky (2015) proposes that there are weak heads, for example, T in English, which cannot contribute to labeling. If one adopts this, the statement in the text holds for strong heads.

English, {DP, TP}, is labeled <φ, φ> because D and T share the same φ-features. This is made possible by φ-feature agreement. Saito (2016), on the other hand, suggests that the same structure in Japanese, {DP-NOM, TP}, is labeled by TP because suffixal Case markers in the language function as "anti-labeling devices." If this parametric variation indeed exists, a child must acquire the knowledge, on the basis of positive experience, on how her/his language accomplishes the labeling of {XP, YP} structure.

Then, what would work as a trigger for the children, who initially produce non-target-consistent strings, to attain the adult grammar? Murasugi (in press) argues that the acquisition of the labeling of clauses becomes possible only after Tense is introduced into the clausal structure as a head, in both English-type languages and Japanese/Korean-type languages.[5] Given ATOM, and even if there is a small clause stage without functional categories, as Radford (1990) proposes, there is no φ-feature agreement between Tense and the external argument at this stage. In Japanese/Korean type languages, the external argument cannot appear in nominative because there is no Tense in the structure to value this Case. In fact, Murasugi (in press) shows that consistent nominative marking of the subject and the emergence of Tense in the structure coincide. Given this, again, the development of children's grammar starting with the RI(A) stage can be viewed as a process of acquiring how the labeling of {XP, YP} is accomplished in the target language.

4 Conclusion and Implications

In this paper, we have discussed the well-known "erroneous" strings that very young children produce and their analysis under the Minimalist Program (Chomsky 2015, among others). The RI(A)s, which are essentially similar across even distantly related languages are produced because the target grammar, including the system of Labeling, is under construction. The analysis supports the idea in Saito (2016) that the way {XP, YP} structure is labeled varies among language. To summarize the analysis, the acquisition process can be schematized as in (20).

---

[5] Murasugi (in press) suggests that predicate-argument structure as well as the topic and comment relationship would put together or "glue" the "erroneous" strings produced at the stage where the Labeling is under construction.

(20) Merge, Labeling of {H, XP}
(knowledge of predicate-argument structure and the topic-comment relation)
→ Introduction of Tense, φ-feature agreement, and Case valuation
→ Labeling of {XP, YP} structure

Children are equipped with the operation Merge and the knowledge that the structure formed by Merge needs to be labeled. They also know that H provides the label for {H, XP}. They form {XP, YP} structures as demanded by the predicate-argument structure. They probably interpret them using the knowledge of the topic-comment relation, but are yet to discover how they are labeled. Only after the RI(A) stage is over and Tense consistently appear in the structure, they gain knowledge of φ-feature agreement and Case, and discover how {XP, YP} structures are labeled inn their target language.

This paper also suggests that Japanese- and Korean-acquiring children take parallel routes to attain the target grammar. They go through the RIA stage. During the stage, they produce the surrogate non-finite forms as the RIAs, because the target language is agglutinative whether it is Japanese or Korean. This in turn suggests that not only the basic word order, but also the morphological properties of the mother tongue are part of VEPS.

Child Japanese and child Korean are like twins. In fact, similarities are found not only in the acquisition stages children go through (e.g., babbling, one-word stage, two-word stage, RIA stage, etc.) but also in other "erroneous" strings children voluntarily produce. The overgeneration of a complementizers *no* (Japanese) and *kes* (Korean), for example, are well documented in both languages at around the age of two to four.

(21) a. gohan tabeteru *no butasan
rice eating Comp piggy
'the piggy that is eating rice'
(Nagisa 3;02; Murasugi 1991:14)

b. Acessi otoopai tha-nun *ke soli ya.
man motorbike ride-ADNOM Comp sound is
'It is the sound of a man riding a motorbike.'
(Polam 2;03; Y-J. Kim 1987:20)

Despite the fact that a complementizer never appears in the adult complex NPs, *no* (Japanese) and *kes* (Korean), which are homophonous with the head of the presuppositional phrase in cleft sentences, "erroneously" appear as the head of the sentential modifiers. A possible analysis for the overgeneration of a complementizer would be that the structure of relative clauses is parameterized (TP or CP) among languages, and children acquiring Japanese and Korean, at one point of grammar acquisition, commonly choose the "wrong" value of CP structure for the relative clauses, (Murasugi 1991). Likewise, children acquiring Japanese and Korean often "erroneously" produce unaccusative verbs in place of transitive verbs (**aite* 'open (unaccusative)' (the intended verb form: *akete* 'open (transitive)' (Murasugi and Hashimoto 2004; Murasugi, Hashimoto and Fuji 2007)) and **ol-la-gada* 'go up' (the intended verb form: *ol-li-da* 'raise') (Lee and Kodner 2019)).

Within the Continuity Hypothesis, the process of the first language acquisition can be viewed as the process of choosing the exact parametric value of the target language among the several possibilities restricted by UG. If the "erroneous" strings children produce are parallel in distinct languages, then, the target grammars of the languages would share the common values of the core parameters. Evidence that the two languages, Korean and Japanese, are similar syntactically and typologically is obtained even from the errors very tiny children voluntarily produce.

References

Bowerman, M. 1973. Structural relationships in children's utterances: Semantic or syntactic? In *Cognitive development and the acquisition of language*, ed. by M. Timothy, 197-213. New York: Academic Press.

Chomsky, N. 1994. Bare phrase structure. *MIT Occasional Papers in Linguistics 5*, MIT, Cambridge, Mass.

Chomsky, N. 2013. Problems of projection. *Lingua* 130: 33-49.

Chomsky, N. 2015. Problems of projection: Extensions. In *Structures, strategies, and beyond*, ed. by E. Di Domenico, C, Hamann and S. Matteini, 1-16. Amsterdam: John Benjamins.

Deen, K. 2002. The omission of inflection prefixes in the acquisition of Nairobi Swahili. Ph.D. dissertation. UCLA.

Harris, T. and K. Wexler. 1996. The optional-infinitive stage in child English. In *Generative perspectives in language acquisition*, ed. by Harald Clahsen, 1-42. Philadelphia: John Benjamins.

Hoekstra, T. and N. Hyams. 1998. Aspects of root infinitives. *Lingua* 106: 91-112.

Kim, M. and C. Phillips. 1998. Complex verb construction in child Korean: Overt markers of covert functional structure. *Boston University Conference on Language Development* 22: 430-441.

Kuno, S. 1973. *The structure of the Japanese language.* Cambridge, MA: MIT Press.

Lee, S. J and J. Kodner, 2019. Acquiring the Korean Causatives. https://www.ling.upenn.edu/~jkodner/CLS2019.pdf#search=%27Lee%2C+Kodner%2C+Korean%2C+transitive%27

Murasugi, K. 1991. Noun phrases in Japanese and English: A study in syntax, learnability and acquisition. Ph.D. dissertation. University of Connecticut.

Murasugi, K. 2015. Root infinitive analogues in child Japanese. In *Handbook of Japanese psycholinguistics*, ed. by Mineharu Nakayama, 117-147. Berlin: De Gruyter Mouton.

Murasugi, K. (in press) Parameterization in labeling: Evidence from child language. *The Linguistic Review*. De Gruyter Mouton.

Murasugi, K. and C. Fuji. 2011. Root infinitives: The parallel routes the Japanese- and Korean-speaking children step in. *Japanese/Korean Linguistics* 18: 1-15.

Murasugi, K. and T. Hashimoto. 2004. Three pieces of acquisition evidence for the *v*-VP Frame. *Nanzan Linguistics* 1: 1-19.

Murasugi, K., T. Hashimoto and C. Fuji. 2007. VP-shell analysis for the acquisition of intransitive verbs, transitive verbs, and causatives. *Linguistics* 45: 615-651.

Murasugi, K., T. Nakatani and C. Fuji. 2010. The roots of root infinitive analogues: The surrogate verb forms common in adult and child grammars. *Boston University Conference on Language Development 34 Proceedings Online Supplement*: 1-10.

Noji, J. 1973-1977. *Youji no Gengoseikatu no Jittai* I-IV [A longitudinal study of Japanese language acquisition]. Tokyo: Bunka Hyoron Shuppan.

Phillips, C. 1995. Syntax at age two: Cross-linguistic differences. In *Papers on language processing and acquisition, MIT Working Papers in Linguistics* 26: 325-382.

Poeppel, D. and K. Wexler. 1993. The full competence hypothesis of clause structure in early German. *Language* 69: 1-33.

Radford, A. 1990. *A syntactic theory and the acquisition of English syntax.* Oxford: Blackwell.

Rispoli, M. 1994. Pronoun case overextensions and paradigm building. *Journal of Child Language* 21: 157-172.

Rispoli, M. 1999. Case and agreement in language development. *Journal of Child Language* 26: 357-372.

Saito, M. 2016. (A) case for labeling: Labeling in languages without φ-feature agreement. *The Linguistic Review* 33: 129-176.

Saito, M. and D. An. 2010. A comparative syntax of ellipsis in Japanese and Korean. *Proceedings of the Sixth Workshop on Altaic Formal Linguistics, MIT Working Papers in Linguistics* 61: 287-307.

Saito, M. and K. Murasugi. 1990. N'-deletion in Japanese: A Preliminary Study. *Japanese/Korean Linguistics* 1: 258-301.

Schütze, C. and K. Wexler. 1996. Subject case licensing and English root infinitives. *Boston University Conference on Language Development* 20: 670-681.

Wexler, K. 1998. Very early parameter setting and the unique checking constraint: A new explanation of the optional infinitive stage. *Lingua* 106: 23-79.

Intervention Effects in Japanese Revisited: Gradable Acceptability and its Theoretical Consequences

SATOSHI TOMIOKA

YOSHIHISA KITAGAWA

KATSUO TAMAOKA

1 Intervention Effects – Introduction

What has come to be known as "intervention effect" (IE) in wh-interrogative sentences appears to be a well-defined problem. When a certain group of expressions, called interveners, occupy syntactic positions that c-command in-situ wh-phrases, these wh-phrases cannot be associated with the C^0s that are placed beyond the interveners. This phenomenon is reported from a number of typologically unrelated languages including Japanese, Korean, German, Chinese, Malayalam, Turkish among others.

Japanese/Korean Linguistics 27.
Edited by Michael Barrie.

(1) a. *Wer hat niemanden **wo** angetroffen?
who has nobody where met
'Who has nobody meet where?' (German)

b. *Daremo **dare-o** sasow-anak-atta-no
anyone who-Acc invite-Neg-Past-Q
'Who did nobody invite?' (Japanese)

c. *Amwuto **nwukwu-lul** chotayha-ci ahn-ass-ni?
anyone who-Acc invite-Comp not do-Past-Q
'Who did nobody invite?' (Korean)

d. *Aarum **eetə pustakam-aan**ə waayikk-aa-te irunn-atə?
anyone which book-be read-Neg-Aug Aux-Nmz
'Which book did nobody read?' (Malayalam)

e. *Kimse **nereye** git-me-di?
anyone where go-Neg-Past
'Where did nobody go?' (Turkish)

The ill-effects of intervention are removed if the order of the intervener and the in-situ wh-phrase is reversed.

(2) a. Wer hat **wo** niemanden angetroffen?
who has where nobody met
'Who has nobody meet where?' (German)

b. **Dare-o** daremo sasow-anak-atta-no
who-Acc anyone invite-Neg-Past-Q
'Who did nobody invite?' (Japanese)

c. **Nwukwu-lul** amwuto chotayha-ci ahn-ass-ni?
who-Acc anyone invite-Comp not do-Past-Q
'Who did nobody invite?' (Korean)

d. **Eetə pustakam-aan**ə aarum waayikk-aa-te irunn-atə?
which book-be anyone read-Neg-Aug Aux-Nmz
'Which book did nobody read?' (Malayalam)

e. **Nereye** kimse git-me-di?
Where anyone go-Neg-Past
'Where did nobody go?' (Turkish)

The clarity of this initial portrayal of IEs is deceiving, however. First and foremost, it is not easy to define what counts as an intervener. The most common interveners across languages are negative quantifiers and other downward entailing quantifiers (e.g., *few*, *less than N*), NPIs, and focused phrases with *only*. Apart from those, languages can differ. Universal quantifiers, disjunctive phrases, focused phrases with *also, even* are included in the intervener repertoires of some languages but not all.

This cross-linguistic variation in the intervener inventory is one of the major issues that make it hard to define potential interveners. The 'Universalist' approach, represented by S-S. Kim 2002, Beck 2006, Kotek 2019 among others, attempts to pinpoint an attribute that binds (at least) the most common interveners across languages and find the right label for that attribute, which is, hopefully, flexible enough to allow some variability across languages. There are more language-specific approaches. In Tomioka 2007, for instance, the primary goal is to explain IEs within the target languages (i.e., Japanese and Korean). The obvious advantage of this type of approach is that the categorization of interveners is more precise and finer-tuned. Needless to say, there is a serious drawback associated with it as well. We may end up with a collection of different criteria for interveners (and different analyses of IEs), missing an important typological generalization.

This problem is commonly acknowledged, and its urgency cannot be underestimated. However, the focus of the current study is on a different kind of variability which is not as frequently discussed in the literature: gradable judgement and/or variable judgment within one language. Within this category of variation, inter-personal variability is frequently mentioned. It is a coded way of expressing the fact that native speakers disagree in acceptability judgments. While this issue does arise with respect to IEs, it is not central to the discussions that we offer in the paper. We will concentrate on the gradability and variability issues that are fairly consistent across speakers.

2 Strong and Weak Interveners

It has been noted that some languages exhibit gradable strength of IEs: In Korean and Japanese, for instance, the universal quantifiers *nwuku-na* and *da're-mo* (accented), 'everyone' are weak interveners in the sense that their ill-effects are noticeably weaker compared to the NPI interveners, such as *amwuto* or *dare-mo* (unaccented) 'anyone'.

(3) a. ??**Nwukuna-ka** onu kyosu-lul chonkyongha-ni?
everyone-Nom which professor-Acc respect-Q
'Which professor does everyone respect?' (Korean)
(Beck and Kim 1997, (75a))

b. ??**Da'remo-ga** nani-o yon-da-no?
everyone-Nom what-Acc read-Past-Q
'What did everyone read?' (Japanese)
(Tomioka 2007, (5a))

The relative strength of ill effect is not the only domain where the strong–weak contrast is relevant. In Korean, *-man* 'only' is an intervener whose effects are considered fairly strong but can vary depending on linguistic environments. The effects become much weaker, for instance, if a *-man* phrase is a non-subject. For the NPI intervener, the weakening effect of non-subjects is minimal. The following are some examples with dative-marked interveners.

(4) a. Chelswu-nun **Sunhee-eykey-man** nwuku-lul cwu-ess-ni?
Chelswu-Top Sunhee-Dat-only what-Acc give-Past-Q
'What did Chelswu give only to Sunhee?'

b. *Chelswu-nun **amwu-eykey-to** nwuku-lul cwu-ess-ni?
Chelswu-Top anyone-Dat-also what-Acc give-Past-Q
'What didn't Chelswu give to anyone?'

The strong–weak contrast is problematic. One possible and reasonable line of explanation for the contrast is (5).

(5) There is a common explanation for both weak and strong intervention effects. Strong effects come about due to some additional factors that only apply to strong interveners.

Tomioka's (2007) account for the strong–weak contrast is an example of this approach. Tomioka suggests that an NPI intervener has an additional prosodic constraint that requires an NPI to be in the same phonological phrase as its licensor (V+negation), and the intervention configuration violates this requirement in addition to the information structural constraint that Tomioka proposes (see Tomioka (2007, section X). Tomioka's analysis is in accordance with Hirotani's (2005) experimental fundings. One challenge of this approach is that (5) aims to find a common explanation for both weak and strong IEs, but we cannot ignore the fact that strong interveners tend to be the most consistent interveners across languages. For instance, the Chinese *mei(-ge)*, the Chinese counterpart of the universal quantifiers in (3) is not an intervener at all. Therefore, (5) deepens the mystery of cross-linguistic variations in the inventories of potential interveners. Another issue with (5) is the nature of the relevant constraint or regulation on IEs. If strong IEs are due to some additional factor(s) that can be independent of IEs, the main target of the explanation is the weak IEs. Generally speaking, a generative-theoretical account is categorical (ungrammatical vs ungrammatical), and such an approach is not suited for explaining weak effects if (5) is to be adopted. There are a few alternative options to (5). (6) is a mirror image of (5):

(6) There is a common explanation for both weak and strong intervention effects. Weak effects come about due to some ameliorating factors that only apply to weak interveners.

While (6) is a logical possibility, generative linguists are not used to this line of reasoning, especially when the explanation relies on a categorical factor that polarizes the status either as grammatical or ungrammatical. So far, no attempts of this kind have been made. Another possible approach is (7).

(7) There are different explanations for weak and strong intervention effects.

This is the path that Kobayashi 2017 advocates. Kobayashi argues that Tomioka's (2007) explanation of the strong status of NPIs in Japanese based on phonological phrasing is inadequate, as not only NPIs but also Positive Polarity Items (PPIs), such as *dareka*, are also strong interveners. PPIs do not require any licensors, which makes the issue of phonological phrasing irrelevant.[1] Although not based on the weak-strong distinction, Law and Li 2016 also endorse non-uniform explanations for intervention effects (based on Mandarin Chinese). Their distinction is between focus intervention and quantificational intervention. The biggest challenge of this approach is the question fo how two different explanations converge in such a way that both strong and weak interveners seem sensitive to the same linguistic environment.

There is yet another possibility:

(8) The relevant explanation for IEs itself is gradable.

Although there has not been any concrete proposal of this nature for the strong-weak distinction of interveners, the spirit of Tomioka's 2009 account of IEs in *why*-questions closely follows (8). As we will see in the next section, *why*-questions in Japanese and Korean present a gradability problem of a different kind, but we face the same challenge of how to account properly for gradable acceptability judgments.

---

[1] Tomioka (in preparation), however, casts doubt on Kobayashi's characterization of the strong interveners based on an experiment conducted by but not included in Kitagawa et al 2013, which indicates that PPIs are not true interveners as the scrambled word order (the 'intervener–wh' order) does not show statistically significant improvement from the intervention order. Tomioka further points out that this fact is consistent with the 'epistemic indefinite' status of the PPIs that Kobayashi uses (see Sudo 2010 and Alonso-Ovalle and Shimoyama 2013 for discussion on *wh-ka* as an epistemic indefinite). In addition to its usual existential meaning, the use of an epistemic indefinite gives rise to the inference that the speaker does not know who or what the indefinite refers to. Tomioka reports that a German wh-interrogative sentence with the epistemic indefinite *irgend-* is highly dubious even when the configuration does not fit the intervention structure. This observation strongly suggests that the ill-effects generated by epistemic indefinites are independent of intervention effects.

3 Strong and Weak Linguistic Environments

It has been observed that in some languages, the strength of IEs varies based on linguistic environments. Tomioka (2007) notes that when the intervener is the matrix subject, it elicits the strongest effects in Japanese and Korean.[2] We have seen a case of dative *-man* 'only' in Korean. Eilam 2011 notes many instances of improvement when the context makes it clear that the relevant interveners are regarded as given. His examples include alternative questions in English, negative wh-in-situ questions in French and Chinese wh-questions with 'only'.

As a case study of gradable judgments based on linguistic environments, we examine *why*-questions in Japanese. According to Kuwabara 1996, Kuwabara 1998, and Ko Ko (2005), intervention effects disappear in *why*–questions in Japanese and Korean. In the following examples, the NPIs can precede *naze/way* 'why' without generating IEs.

(9) a. Taroo-sika **naze** sono hon-o yoma-nakat-ta-no?
Taroo-except why that book-Acc read-not-Past-Q
'Why did only Taroo read that book?'
(Ko 2005, (9a), originally from Kuwabara 1996)
b. Amwuto **way** ku chayk-ul ilk-ci-anh-ass-ni?
Anyone why that book-Acc read-CI-not-Past-Q
'Why did no one read that book?'
(Ko 2005, (8a))

While acknowledging the relevant improvement in (9)), Tomioka (2009) objects to the characterization of the phenomenon as the disappearance of IEs, based on the observation that the (scrambled) word order, shown below, is still preferred.

(10) a. **Way** amwuto ku chayk-ul ilk-ci-anh-ass-ni?
Why anyone that book-Acc read-CI-not-Past-Q
'Why did no one read that book?'
b. **Naze** Taroo-sika sono hon-o yoma-nakat-ta-no?
Why Taroo-except that book-Acc read-not-Past-Q
'Why did only Taroo read that book?'

Exactly how to characterize the judgment patterns is extremely important, as it determines what kind of explanation is to be sought after. Those who focus on the first contrast propose 'categorical' solutions. Ko (2005), for instance, offers the following explanation.

---

[2] This observation was inspired by Hagstrom's 1998 discovery that IEs are weaker within some syntactic islands.

(11) a. The source of IEs is LF movement of a wh-phrase over an intervener, as argued by Beck (1996) and Beck and Kim (1997).
b. In an 'intervener-argument wh' configuration, the wh-phrase moves to the relevant Spec CP at LF, crossing over the intervener. Hence, ungrammatical.
c. On the other hand, *why* can be generated directly in a Spec CP. Thus, an 'intervener-*why*' structure is created by a surface movement (scrambling) of the intervener over *why*. Since there is no LF wh-movement, no IEs arise.

Under this account, IEs are either present or absent, and in a *why*-question, there is no IE, whether the structure is '*why-intervener* or *intervener-why*. Therefore, if there is a contrast in acceptability between (9) and (10), it is rather inconvenient for a categorical explanation like Ko's. Ko herself acknowledges (Ko 2006, footnote 7) that one reviewer pointed out this contrast as a potential problem but does not incorporate it into her proposal, as, according to to her and her consultants' judgments, it is weak or non-existent.

A dramatically different view is presented in Tomioka (2009), who considers the contrast between (9) and (10) to be part of IEs. Tomioka's account is based on the information structure of wh-questions. A wh-question elicits an IE when there is a gap between the information structure required for the wh-question and its ideal linguistic realization. The non-wh portion of a wh-question should be confined within the background of the question, and for Japanese, the ideal position for such material is either the topic position (with the particle *-wa* in Japanese and *-(n)un* in Korean) or the sequence following a wh-phrase, which is prosodically reduced due to the post–focus reduction process of the focus intonation (cf. Kori 1989, Maekawa 1991, and Sugahara 2003, among others). Since potential interveners are anti-topical in the sense that they resist the topic-marking, the post wh portion of the sequence is the most suitable place they can appear in. That is why the 'wh-intervener' order is always preferred. What makes *why*-questions special, on the other hand, is their presuppostional property. In a *why*-question, the proposition that excludes *why* must be presupposed. For instance, the question 'why did no one attend the meeting?' presupposes that no one attended the meeting.

This contrasts sharply with an argument-wh question, such as 'what did no one buy?', for which a comparable presupposition is not definable.[3] This special presuppositional property of a *why*-question helps the intervener be confined within the background of the question, and this is the reason for the improvement in *why*-questions. Nevertheless, the '*why*-intervener order is still considered a better option because the prosody and the required information structure are completely in sync.

It is easy to see the origin of the difference between the two accounts. It lies in the interpretation of the acceptability judgment pattern, an issue so fundamental that discussing the theoretical merits of the two accounts becomes a rather moot point. In the following section, we report the experiments we conducted on IEs in *why*-questions. The main objective was to investigate from an experimental point of view the controversial judgment issues of IEs with *why*-questions. Specifically, we aim to answer the following questions.

(12) a. Do *why*-questions in Japanese and Korean show weaker IEs than other types of wh-questions?

b. Is there any difference in acceptability between the '*why*–intervener' and 'intervener–*why*' orders?

A categorical account, such as Ko's, would expect 'yes' to the first question and 'no' to the second, while with the Tomioka's account, the expected answer is 'yes' to both.

4 Gradable Acceptability of *Why*-questions

4.1 Experiment 1

Materials: For the stimulus sentences in our experiment, we paired an IE-sentence with an argument wh-phrase with one with *why*. Two of the three tested interveners were non-NPIs (*dake* 'only' and *izyoo* 'more than', and the other was an NPI (*daremo* 'anyone'). The sentences in (13) are argument questions, and (14) are *why*-questions.

[3] First of all, it is hard to define the proposition that excludes the wh-phrase. The best candidate would be the proposition that no one did buying, but this proposition is certainly not presupposed in the question. The other plausible presupposition candidate is the existentially quantified one: There is something that no one bought. While some have claimed (e.g., Katz and Postal , Comorovski 1996 that this type of proposition is indeed presupposed, there are many who doubt, including Groenendijk and Stokhof 1984. Tomioka (2009) assumes, following Romero and Han 2004, that the existentially quantified proposition is an 'epistemic bias' on the speaker's part. Crucially, the speaker's bias is not guaranteed to be shared by the hearer, and, unlike a presupposition, it does not become a part of the common ground.

(13) a. **Junko-dake-ga** nani-o tyuumon-sita-no?
Junko-only-Nom what-Acc order-did-Q
'What did only Junko order?'

b. **San-nin-izyoo-no-hito-ga** nani-o
thee-CL-more than-Gen-person-Nom what-Acc
tyuumon-sita-no?
order-did-Q
'What did more than three people order?'

c. **Daremo** nani-o tyuumon-si-nakat-ta-no?
anyone what-Acc order-do-neg-Past-Q
'What did no one order?'

(14) a. **Junko-dake-ga** naze Kyooko-o izimeru-no?
Junko-only-Nom why Kyoko-Acc bully-Q
'Why does only Junko bully Kyoko?'

b. **Nizyuu-nin-izyoo-no-syain-ga** naze
twenty-CL-more.than-Gen-employee-Nom why
kubi.ni.natta-no?
got.fired-Q
'Why did more than twenty employees get fired?'

c. **Daremo** naze ko-nakat-ta-no?
anyone why come-neg-Past-Q
'What did no one come?'

Participants: Fifty-eight native Japanese speakers (31 males and 27 females), who were either undergraduate or graduate students at a Japanese University, participated in the experiment conducted in October, 2008. Ages ranged from 19 years and 8 months to 26 years and 2 months, with the average age being 22 years and 1 month with a standard deviation of 1 year and 10 months on the day of testing. They were all non-linguists and were paid for their participation.

Procedure: The subjects were asked to silently read the printed example sentences one by one at their own paces, and to provide an acceptability rating for each sentence by selecting one of the six options: As a Japanese sentence, 5 = entirely appropriate, 4 = quite appropriate, 3 = somewhat appropriate, 2 = somewhat inappropriate, 1 = quite inappropriate, 0 = entirely inappropriate.

Results: The mean acceptability score of each sentence pattern is shown in Table 1 (argument wh) and Table 2 (*why*).

TABLE 1 Intervention with Argument Wh

Intervener	Mean	SD
dake 'only'	3.15	1.26
N-izyoo 'more than N'	3.84	1.09
daremo 'anyone'	1.52	1.43

TABLE 2 Intervention with *Why*

Intervener	Mean	SD
dake 'only'	4.24	0.73
N-izyoo 'more than N'	4.79	0.45
daremo 'anyone'	3.62	1.13

There were two missing values of acceptability scores in Experiment 1. Thus, a 2 (wh-type: argument and *naze*) x 3 (intervener-type: *dake*, *izyoo*, *daremo*) ANOVA with repeated measures (of both variables) was conducted on acceptability scores judged by 56 participants. The main effect of wh-type was highly significant [$F(1,55)=152.237$, $p<.001$], suggesting that sentences with argument wh-phrases (Mean(M)=2.84) were significantly less acceptable than those with *naze* (M=4.21). The main effect of intervener-type was also highly significant [$F(2,110)=98.483$, $p<.001$], indicating differences in acceptability among the three interveners. Simple contrasts were conducted between the argument wh stimuli and the why-stimuli in regard to each of the three interveners. In each case, the contrast was highly significant – for the *dake*–pairs [$F(1,55)=46.523$, $p<.001$], the *izyoo*–pairs [$F(1,55)=48.968$, $p<.001$], and *daremo*–pairs [$F(1,55)=103.739$, $p<.001$]. Thus, the acceptability contrast between the argument whs and *why* in the IE-sentences (the intervener–wh order) has been confirmed with respect to all three interveners taken up in our experiment.

Discussion: The results of Experiment 1 confirmed some of the recurring patterns in the acceptability judgments reported in the previous studies. First of all, there is a contrast in acceptability between argument wh-questions and *why*-questions, as claimed by Kuwabara (1998), Miyagawa (1997), and Ko (2005). While this contrast was present with all three interveners we have examined, a clear distinction among the three was found in terms of the strength of IEs they elicit. The ranking was consistently daremo > dake > izyoo, and the effect of the NPI intervener (daremo) was most dramatic both with argument whs and *why*. The result, in other words, was consistent with Tomioka's (2007) observation that NPIs make the strongest interveners.

4.2 Experiment 2

Materials: In this experiment, each of the IE sentences with *why*, shown in (14) above, is compared with the sentences in the non-IE order (i.e., 'why–intervener' order) in (15).

(15) a. Naze **Junko-dake-ga** Kyooko-o izimeru-no?
Why Junko-only-Nom Kyoko-Acc bully-Q
'Why does only Junko bully Kyoko?'

b. Naze **nizyuu-nin-izyoo-no-syain-ga**
why twenty-CL-more.than-Gen-employee-Nom
kubi.ni.natta-no?
got.fired-Q
'Why did more than twenty employees get fired?'

c. Naze **daremo** ko-nakat-ta-no?
why anyone come-neg-Past-Q
'What did no one come?'

Participants and Procedure: The same as Experiment 1.

Results: The mean acceptability score of each sentence pattern is shown in Table 3 (Non IE order; *why*–intervener) and Table 4 (IE order; intervener–*why*).

TABLE 3 Non-IE order

Intervener	Mean	SD
naze–dake	4.74	0.48
naze–N-izyoo	4.84	0.40
naze daremo	4.86	0.36

TABLE 4 IE order

Intervener	Mean	SD
dake–naze	4.24	0.74
N-izyoo–naze	4.79	0.45
daremo–naze	3.62	1.12

There were no missing values of acceptability scores in Experiment 2. Thus, a 2 (IE vs. non-IE) x 3 (intervener-types) ANOVA with repeated measures (of both variables) was conducted on acceptability scores judged by all 58 participants. The main effect of word order was highly significant [$F(1,57)=87.613$, $p<.001$], suggesting that the *why*–initial stimuli ($M=4.81$) are significantly more acceptable than the why second stimuli ($M=4.21$). The main effect of intervener-type was also highly significant [$F(2,114)=29.793$,

$p<.001$], indicating differences in acceptability among the three interveners. Furthermore, the interaction of these two variables was also highly significant [$F(2,114)=43.406$, $p<.001$], suggesting that word order and intervener-type synagistically had some additive effect on acceptability scores.

Although the main effect of the *why*-position was significant, further analyses of simple contrasts were conducted to confirm differences in acceptability among different interveners. The results indicated that the difference of 0.52 (4.74 vs. 4.24) with *dake* was significant [$F(1,57)=43.182$, $p<.001$], and the difference of 1.24 (4.86 vs. 3.62) was also significant [$F(1,57)=75.902$, $p<.001$], but the difference of 0.05 with *izyoo* [$F(1,57)=1.498$, $p=.226$, *ns*] was not. Therefore, the effect of *why*-position was apparent in *daremo* and *dake*, but not in *izyoo*.

Discussion: In addition to the much discussed contrast in IEs between argument wh-questions and why-questions, our results also confirmed the presence of the other contrast, namely the one between the intervener–*why* order and *why*–intervener order. While the contrast was ignorable with *izyoo* 'more than', it was statistically significant with the other two interveners. In particular, with the NPI intervener *daremo*, the preference for the *why*–intervener order over the other was quite strong. Given that the NPI is probably the only reliable intervener of the three, we will focus on the result with *daremo*. While Ko (2005) considered the second contrast minimal or non-existent, she was aware that some speakers find it significant. She speculated that this contrast is essentially 'stylistic', due to the scrambling of an intervener over *why*. In her proposal, *why* is (or at least can be) directly generated in Spec CP, which makes the '*why*–subject' order the base order. The other order is created by scrambling of the subject, which is stylistically less preferred. However, our experimental data are not compatible with Ko's explanation. If the scrambling of the subject is causing the degradation, the effects should be observable with all the potential interveners. While all the three interveners received near perfect scores in the '*why*–intervener' order, the other order shows different patterns. The acceptability with the NPI intervener lowered significantly. On the other hand, *dake* 'only' showed weaker effects, and with *-izyoo*, the degradation was not significant. Ko's stylistics-based account cannot explain this pattern. A much more plausible scenario is that the degradation is a manifestation of IEs. It is expected that the stronger effects are found with the strong interveners, such as the NPI *daremo*.

4.3 General Discussion on the Two Experiments

While the gradability of grammatical judgments has been occasionally acknowledged in the past it is often shelved into footnotes and rarely receives formal and systematic explanations. The two experimental studies reported above took up intervention effects (IEs) with *why*–questions in Japanese and confirmed the long-suspected gradability in judging sentences that induce IEs. The gradability is multi-faceted, and the multiple factors involved in it are inter-connected. First, we observed a consistent ranking in the strength of IE-inducing interveners among the three tested in our experiments; the NPI daremo 'anyone' is the strongest and the most consistent of the three items that we tested. This pattern was consistent in all types of IE-sentences. Second, the contrast between argument wh-questions and *why*-questions was experimentally proved significant. Specifically, the IEs in *why*-questions are much weaker than those in argument wh-questions with all three types of interveners (but particularly noticeable with the NPI, the strongest intervener). This result was predicted by many of the previous theoretical researchers. Importantly, however, it was also revealed that *why*-questions are not devoid of IEs. Our study showed that the 'intervener-*why*' order is still worse than the other order, verifying Tomioka's (2009) assumption that the IEs in *why*-questions involve gradable judgment. IEs are weakened in *why*-questions but do not disappear, contrary to the assumption on which a categorical explanation is based. The account advocated in Tomioka (2009) correctly predicts the judgment pattern, but the IEs in *why*-questions may be even more intricate than the two contrasts examined in the experiment.

5 More on *Why*-questions: Focus Sensitivity

There is another factor that separates *why*-questions from other wh-questions. Bromberger (1992) observes that, unlike other wh-interrogative sentences, the interpretation of a *why*-question is affected by focus whereas other Wh-questions do not show comparable variability.[4]

(16) a. Why did JOHN buy beer? (A: Because he was the only one who had his ID)
 b. Why did John buy BEER? (A: Because it was on sale)

(17) a. When did ANNA visit Kyoto? (A: Last month)
 b. When did Anna visit KYOTO? (A: Last month)

[4] The core presuppositional property of a *why*-question remains the same, regardless of the location of focus. In both (16a) and (16b), the question still presupposes that John bought beer.

Japanese can employ a similar prosodic strategy to express the focus sensitivity of *why*–questions, as illustrated below.

(18) a. NAZE Anna-wa Kyooto-de Mana-ni atta-no?
why Anna-Top Kyoto-Loc Mana-Dat met-Q
'Why did Anna meet Mana in KYOTO?'
b. NAZE Anna-wa MANA-ni Kyooto-de atta-no?
why Anna-Top Mana-Dat Kyoto-Loc met-Q
'Why did Anna meet MANA in Kyoto?'

In these examples, the causal wh-phrases are placed sentence-initially and receive focal accents. The focalization of the causal wh-phrases is not surprising at all, as wh-phrases are assigned focal accents in Japanese wh-questions. Their focus associates are not adjacent to the wh-phrases, and they are also focalized prosodically. For many speakers, however, this strategy is rather a marked option to express the focus sensitivity of *why*-questions. The more common method is what Tomioka 2017 calls the adjacency strategy, in which a causal wh-phrase is placed immediately before its focus associate. In (19ab) below, for example, the phrases immediately following the causal wh-phrase (underlined) are regarded as the focus-associates.[5]

(19) a. Anna-wa NAZE <u>Kyooto-de</u> Mana-ni atta-no?
Anna-Top why Kyoto-Loc Mana-Dat met-Q
'Intended: Why did Anna meet Mana in KYOTO?'
b. Anna-wa NAZE <u>Mana-ni</u> Kyooto-de atta-no?
Anna-Top why Mana-Dat Kyoto-Loc met-Q
'Intended: Why did Anna meet MANA in Kyoto?'

Let us now examine what happens with focus sensitive *why*-questions with interveners. Suppose that one wishes to ask the question, 'Why didn't anybody buy souvenirs in KYOTO?', where it is expected to get such an answer as 'Because they were told that Osaka is better for souvenir shopping'. The following are three possible varieties of this question:

[5] Interestingly, the focus associates in (19) need not be assigned any prosodic prominence. In other words, by virtue of immediately following *why*, a phrase can be regarded as the focus associate, and prosodic marking is unnecessary. See Tomioka 2017 for more discussion.

(20) a. NAZE daremo Kyooto-de(-wa) omiyage-o
Why anyone Kyoto-Loc(-Top) souvenir-Acc
kaw-anak-atta-no?
buy-Neg-Past-Q
'Why did nobody buy souvenirs in KYOTO?'

b. Daremo NAZE Kyooto-de(-wa) omiyage-o
Anyone why Kyoto-Loc(-Top) souvenir-Acc
kaw-anak-atta-no?
buy-Neg-Past-Q
'Why did nobody buy souvenirs in KYOTO?'

c. NAZE Kyooto-de(-wa) daremo omiyage-o
Why Kyoto-Loc(-Top) anyone souvenir-Acc
kaw-anak-atta-no?
buy-Neg-Past-Q
'Why did nobody buy souvenirs in KYOTO?'

It turns out that choosing one over the others in (20) is not an easy task. (20a) is a non-IE structure where the intervener *daremo* is placed in the domain of post focal reduction. However, the focus associate *Kyooto* is not adjacent to *naze*, so this sentence employs the prosodic association, which is arguably less preferred strategy. (20b) uses the more common adjacency strategy for focus association, but this structure is an IE configuration, as the intervener precedes *naze*. Possibly (20c) is the best candidate since it is a non-IE structure that uses the adjacency method of association. One blemish of this version is, however, that it creates a lengthy string of rhythmically monotonic and tonally compressed material, as post focal reduction applies to the whole sentence except the wh-phrase. Such a long monotonic prosody is generally dispreferred in natural language (Selkirk 1984, Kubozono 1993, Kitagawa and Fodor 2006).

While the observation remains impressionistic, it highlights the complexity of acceptability judgment of IEs in *why*-questions. The IE configuration is an important but not a deterministic factor that shapes our judgment of *why*-questions, and it interacts with other considerations. All of them are collectively responsible for materializing the syntax-information structure synchronization.

6 Final Remarks

The majority of the existing analyses of IEs are based on the belief that relevant data are categorized either as grammatical/acceptable or ungrammatical/unacceptable. There have been some concerns raised for the categorical approach to IEs, however, and the data reported in this paper further support the idea that a proper analysis of IEs, at least in Japanese and Korean, should start with the assumption that native speakers' judgments on IE sentences are gradient.

For a possible model of explanation for IEs, we would like to offer the following. First, there are two different tiers in the analysis: a general guideline and concrete and specific factors. The general guideline can be phrased as in (21).

(21) How close is an expression, α, to the ideal linguistic realization of the information-structural properties of α?

Second, the distance from the ideal form is measured or evaluated by a set of specific factors which themselves can but need not be gradient. As a matter of fact, most of the known factors are categorical and translatable into a bunch of polar questions. Here are some examples.

(22) a. Is the intervener in the post focal reduction portion of the sentence?
b. Is the intervener the matrix subject?
c. Is the intervener a part of a presupposition of the sentence?
d. Does the intervener require a structural licensor, such as negation?

We believe that the two-tier idea makes the gradability problem more manageable. We need not invent a gradient scale that directly applies to IEs. The second tier of the analysis consists mostly of a series of categorical elements that are close to the traditional generative theorizing. They are different from typical grammatical constraints, however, as none of these factors single-handedly makes the sentence ungrammatical. We also hypothesize that this model is well-suited for accounting for cross-linguistic variations in IEs. It is conceivavskip10ptble that languages can differ in the choice of the factors on the second tier while all the languages have (21) as the common general guideline.

References

Alonso-Ovalle, Luis and Junko Shimoyama. 2013. Expressing ignorance in the nominal domain: Japanese *wh-ka*. In *Proceedings of the 31st West Coast Conference on Formal Linguistics*.

Beck, Sigrid. 2006. Intervention effects follow from focus interpretation. *Natural Language Semantics* 14(1):1–56.

Beck, Sigrid and Shin-Sook Kim. 1997. On WH- and operator scope in Korean. *Journal of East Asian Linguistics* 6:339–384.

Bromberger, Sylvain. 1992. *On What We Know We don't Know: Explanation, Theory, Linguistics, and How Questions Shape them*. University of Chicago Press.

Comorovksi, Ileana. 1996. *Interrogative Phrases and the Syntax-Semantics Interface*, vol. 59 of *Studies in Linguistics and Philosophy*. Dordrecht: Kluwer Academic Publishers.

Eilam, Aviad. 2011. *Explorations in the Informational Component*. Ph.D. thesis, University of Pennsylvania.

Groenendijk, Jeroen. and Martin Stokhof. 1984. *Studies on the Semantics of Questions and the Pragmatics of Answers*. Ph.D. thesis, University of Amsterdam, Amsterdam.

Hagstrom, Paul. 1998. *Decomposing Questions*. Ph.D. thesis, Massachusetts Institute of Technology. Distributed by MIT Working Papers in Linguistics, Cambridge, Mass.

Kim, Shin-Sook. 2002. Intervention effects are focus effects. *Japanese/Korean Linguistics* 10:615–628.

Kitagawa, Yoshihisa and Janet Dean Fodor. 2006. Prosodic influence on syntactic judgments. In G. e. a. Fanslow, ed., *Gradience in grammar: Generative perspectives*, pages 336–358. Oxford University Press.

Kitagawa, Yoshihisa, Katsuo Tamaoka, and Satoshi Tomioka. 2013. Prosodic matters in intervention effects in japanese: An experimental study. *Lingua* 124:41–63.

Ko, Heejeong. 2005. Syntax of why-in-situ: Merge into [spec, cp] in the overt syntax. *Natural Language & Linguistic Theory* 23(4):867–916.

Kobayashi, Ryoichiro. 2017. Is it syntactic or pragmatic? *Language and Linguistics* 18(2):228–253.

Kori, Shiro. 1989. Kyocho-to intoneshon (emphasis and intonation). In M. Sugito, ed., *Koza Nihongo-to Nihongo-kyoiku 2: Nihongo-no OnseiOn'in Vol. 1,*, pages 316–342. Tokyo, Japan: Meiji Shoin.

Kotek, Hadas. 2019. *Composing Questions*. MIT Press.

Kubozono, Haruo. 1993. *The organisation of Japanese prosody.*. Tokyo, Japan: Kuroshio Publishers.

Kuwabara, Kazuki. 1996. Multiple wh-phrases in elliptical clauses and some aspects of clefts with multiple foci. In M. K. et al, ed., *Formal Approaches to Japanese Linguistics 2: MITWPL 29*, pages 97–116. MITWPL.

Li, Haoze and Jess H-K Law. 2016. Alternatives in different dimensions: a case study of focus intervention. *Linguistics and philosophy* 39(3):201–245.

Maekawa, Kikuo. 1991. Perception of intonation characteristics of wh and non-wh questions in tokyo japanese. In *Proceedings of the XXIInd International Congress of Phonetic Science*, vol. 4, pages 202–205.

Miyagawa, Shigeru. 1998. WH chains and quantifier induced barriers. Ms., MIT.

Romero, Maribel and Chung-Hye Han. 2004. On negative *Yes/No* questions. *Linguistics and Philosophy* 27(5):609–658.

Selkirk, Elizabeth O. 1984. *Phonology and Syntax: The Relation between Sound and Structure*. Cambridge, MA: MIT Press.

Sudo, Yasutada. 2010. *Wh-Ka* pronouns in japanese and the semantics of indeterminate pronouns. Handout for talk at the *Workshop on Epistemic Indefinites*, University of Goettingen.

Sugahara, Mariko. 2003. *Downtrends and Post-Focus Intonation in Tokyo Japanese*. Ph.D. thesis, University of Massachusetts at Amherst.

Tomioka, Satoshi. 2007. Pragmatics of lf intervention effects: Japanese and korean wh-interrogatives. *Journal of Pragmatics* 39(9):1570–1590.

Tomioka, Satoshi. 2009. *Why* questions, presuppositions, and intervention effects. *Journal of East Asian Linguistics* 18:253–271.

Tomioka, Satoshi. 2017. Focus–prosody mismatch in japanese why-questions. In T. Y. C'eleste Guillemot and S. J. Lee, eds., *Proceedings of WAFL 13*. MITWPL.

Oral Presentations

Part I

Discourse Analysis / Corpus Linguistics

Playful Frames of Interaction in Korean: Designs of Teasing and Banter

TYLER MIYASHIRO

University of Hawaii at Manoa

1 Introduction

Playful frames of interaction rely upon non-serious interpretations to construct humorous exchanges (Dynel, 2008) and associated phenomena include, but are not limited to, teasing, banter, irony, and ritual insults. In order to explain such ostensibly provocative acts, researchers have built upon the principles of influential scholars such as Grice and Leech by analyzing the sociopragmatic and pragmalinguistic characteristics of interlocutors' utterances in conversations. This has enabled us to account for pragmatic connotations in addition to literal meanings, something that is necessary to demystify the putatively equivocal nature of utterances produced in playful frames of interaction. The various design features implemented for such playful frames of interaction work in combination to invoke a sense of lightheartedness ascribed to what has been described as "playful talk" (Coates, 2007).

Teasing has been described as a type of playful talk that involves the "presence of an element of criticism in the interaction" (Attardo, 1994), thereby placing it within a category of "adversarial" humor types (Veale, Feyaerts, & Brône, 2006). When teasing sequences are expanded into a series of witty exchanges known as "banter," (Leech, 1983; Norrick, 2003; Dynel, 2008; Haugh, 2014), the ostensible provocativeness of the teases themselves can escalate within the play frame, depending on what type of verbal and non-verbal devices interlocutors employ in the conversation. The fact that teasing incorporates the act of criticism within a playful frame of

Japanese/Korean Linguistics 27.
Edited by Michael Barrie.

interaction provides an interesting area of research for exploring the interactional mechanizations and environments that are conducive to the act of teasing itself, which has led to an increasing number of studies over the years (Davies, 1984; Drew, 1987; Attardo, 1994; Boxer & Cortes-Conde, 1997; Norrick, 2003; Holmes, 2006; Coates, 2007; Kotthoff, 2007; Dynel, 2008, 2009; Haugh, 2010, 2014, 2016; Haugh & Bousfield, 2012; Robles, 2019). Indeed, it is safe to assume that the act of criticizing someone or something is universal in any language community, although the array of (para)linguistic devices employed to carry out a criticism will likely vary between cultures as emic perspectives unavoidably influence a language community's pragmalinguistic and sociopragmatic conceptualizations. Thus, an all-encompassing elucidation of teasing practices that can apply in a cross-cultural context is of critical importance. However, literature about the iterations of teasing in languages other than English still remains relatively scarce. When we consider the fact that teasing's multi-layered nature not only involves combinations of non-seriousness and ostensible provocation (Haugh, 2017) but can also reflect differences between cultures in terms of preferences for how and when playful frameworks are constructed (Culpeper, Haugh, & Sinkeviciute, 2017), the necessity for studies with a cross-cultural perspective becomes more apparent.

This paper looked at a particularly underexplored version of teasing that takes place during the initial interactions between interlocutors who are unfamiliar with one another. Thought to only occur between family or close friends, teasing and banter can take place even between strangers (Haugh & Pillet-Shore, 2018). Blind dates are particularly interesting contexts since interlocutors must inquire about each other while assessing degrees of compatibility between themselves. Blind date participants formulated teasing utterances that indicated aspects of their target as problematic, which seems to be a risky social action of impropriety to take against someone who they have just met. And yet, this practice was found to occur frequently, indicating a propensity towards utilizing teasing utterances as a strategy to fulfill some kind of interactional goal such as enhancing rapport (Norrick, 2003) or inviting "intimate interaction" (Coates, 2007; Haugh & Pillet-Shore, 2018). Indeed, inter-speaker solidarity seems to be more than just a coincidental result; conversational participants make collaborative efforts to "recognize that a play frame has been invoked and then have to choose to maintain it" (Coates, 2007).

Section 2 of this paper provides background information about the data and methods of this study, while Section 3 contains a detailed analysis of the conversations within which the design and reception patterns of teasing utterances were sorted according to varying degrees in structural complexity (combinations of lexical, syntactic, and discursive items) and the ways in which the teases were oriented to by the interlocutors. Lastly, Section 4 summarizes the findings of the study and reflects on future implications.

2 Methodology and Data

Utilizing conceptual frameworks rooted in the disciplines of interactional sociolinguistics, this paper has incorporated the concept of contextualization cues (Gumperz, Cook-Gumperz, 1982) that help to situate the implications of conversational participants' actions and utterances. Serving as global levels of inference that help to channel "what topics can be brought up, what is wanted by way of a reply, as well as what can be put in words and what is to be left implied," (Gumperz, Cook-Gumperz, 2012, p. 69) contextualization cues normalize teasing utterances by framing the ongoing interaction as taking place within a jocular environment, which prompts any recipient of a tease to defer to a non-serious interpretation for any ostensible display of criticism or derision. The jocular frame established by these contextualization cues can be perpetuated or concluded by the participants themselves, as frames have been described by Goffman as "definitions of a situation [. . .] built up in accordance with principles of organization which govern events" that unavoidably depend on the subjective involvement of agentive entities (1986, p. 10). Haugh (2017) has provided a detailed list of both linguistic and paralinguistic devices that serve as contextualization cues, which include but are not limited to extreme case formulations, idioms, allusions, compressed pitch range, laughter, and smiling.

Applying Haugh's summary of what types of devices constitute contextualization cues, this study analyzed the teases for salient usage patterns of (para)linguistic devices that helped to encode a playful frame of interaction. To check for the sequential environment of the teases, preceding utterances were analyzed for what have been deemed as "teasables" (actions of the tease target that warrant a tease) while subsequent utterances were analyzed to check for what kind of uptake tease recipients displayed in response to the teasing utterance, with mutual ratification of the non-seriousness of the tease occurring frequently to construct a moment of affiliation between interlocutors (Haugh & Pillet-Shore, 2018). By analyzing both the form and location of the teasing utterances, this study prioritized a systematic explication of how and when interlocutors produce teases of one another in initial interactions. The conversations were transcribed through a simplified version of Jefferson's transcription conventions, for which an explanatory chart has been provided in the Appendix. This also includes an explanatory list for the morpheme by morpheme gloss that has been created for all data sets.

The data set consists of conversations between unacquainted Korean speakers ranging in age from their early 20s to mid 30s, participating in blind dates. Recorded by two Korean reality programs (*2 Face Date* on YouTube and *My Friend's Blind Date* on MBN), the meetings were prearranged but all of the dialogues were spontaneous without any outside guidance or instruction, which guaranteed for candid interactions and extemporaneously constructed utterances. Out of 40 conversations spanning approximately eight hours, 20 contained instances of teasing or banter.

3 Analysis

One of the most salient contextualization cues of teasing within a playful frame of interaction is the overt display of exaggerated behavior or overstatements (Boxer & Cortes-Conde; Norrick, 2003; Coates, 2007; Dynel, 2008; Haugh 2014). This sense of exaggeration is accomplished through various verbal (lexical items, formulaicity, register clash) and non-verbal (laughter, phonetic practices, facial cues) elements (Drew, 1987; Lampert & Ervin-Tripp, 2006; Dynel, 2009; Haugh, 2014), which allows for an abundant inventory of contextual cues for both the producer as well as the recipient of the tease. This paper has organized four examples of teasing, which have been arranged according to two criteria: the complexity of the teasing utterances themselves, and whether the teases involve "ridicule" or "reprimand." The term "ridicule" refers to instances in which the target of the teasing utterance is also clearly indicated as the recipient of ostensibly insulting remarks. A typical example of a "ridicule" tease involves the speaker orienting toward the tease recipient as a "mocker" by making an insinuation that the recipient possesses undesirable qualities that can be relegated into a certain category of person based on sanctionable behavior that is prototypically associated with that particular group (Drew, 1987). This type of phenomenon has also been referred to as "negative category attributions" or "NCAs" (Korobov & Laplante, 2013). Meanwhile, the term "reprimand" tease refers to a situation in which the speaker orients toward the tease recipient as a "disciplinarian" by accusing them of committing an interactional transgression that warrants a form of admonishment.

3.1 Ridicule Teases

The first two excerpts illustrate teases that involve the speaker blatantly ridiculing the tease recipient, who is presumed to possess an undesirable quality. Excerpt 1 is an instance in which the tease designer focalizes and appropriates specific lexical items previously uttered by the tease target.

Excerpt 1: "Music"

(J had asked S about how much she usually allows for her boyfriend in terms of meeting friends of the opposite gender, especially for outings that might involve drinking or going to nightclubs)

1	*S:*	*khullep cohahay-yo? hoksi?*
		club like-POL by any chance
		"Do you like clubs, by any chance?"
2	*J:*	*aytul: chinkwu-tul-ilang icey moi-myen:*
		kids friend-PL-with now assemble-when
		"When I get together with my friends"

3 S: *um: ((nodding))*
"Mmmhmm"

4 J: *e: (.) umak: (0.1)* ((smiles as he hesitates))
uh music
"Uh, the music"

5 S: *um[ak:::?* ((slightly bobbing head, smiling with eye contact))
music
"The music?"

6 J: *[tul-ule=*
listen-in order to
"To listen to (the music)"

7 S: *=tul-ule:::? hhhhh* ((smiles and laughs loudly))
listen-in order to
"To listen to (the music) eh?"

8 J: ((takes a bite of food while gazing off to the side and smiling))

The compositions of S's teases in line 5 and 7 are quite simple and short; S merely repeats words from J's explanation for going to clubs: "music" and "listen." However, she incorporates undulations in pitch (line 5) to impart a playful sensibility to her words, and the other paralinguistic cues of her smiles and laughter also help to contextualize her utterance as taking place within a jocular framework. Such a combination of appropriating J's words with playful phonetic practices gives the effect of putting air quotes around J's justification for clubbing, which is "to listen to the music." Air quotes involve the speaker making quotation symbols with their pointer and middle finger while uttering the words that they find to be ironic or unacceptable to be taken at face value, which reflects the fact that "to listen to the music" is a common euphemism utilized to underplay other practices in nightclubs, practices that would be considered less than wholesome. Such practices might include consuming large amounts of alcohol, flirting, or partying all night, which S effectively associates with J through her teases in lines 5 and 7. Within this highly contextualized sub-cultural background, the phrase "to listen to the music" is thus exploited by S as a vehicle for making a "scripted NCA" (Korobov & Laplante, 2013) that compels both interlocutors to not only retrieve the scripted associations with "clubbing subculture," but it also allows them to realize that they have a mutual understanding of clubbing as an extant sub-culture itself. By doing so, S has attributed to J a characteristic that is prototypical of the persona category of "clubber" or "partier," which could be construed as an inappropriate insult but is framed as a light-hearted remark that is followed by laughter or smiling from both the tease designer and recipient. S and J's mutual understanding of the conventions associated with the "clubbing subculture" allowed for the successful formulation and uptake of teasing with reference to a highly enriched global environment that extended beyond the immediate confines of the current conversation, despite the fact that the teasing remarks by S do not extend beyond the phrase level.

Excerpt 2 demonstrates how the intensity of teasing utterances can be calibrated depending on the speaker's choice of morpho-syntactic structures and lexical items.

Excerpt 2: "Don't Cry"

(K has talked about a past experience in which he was cheated on by a girlfriend, despite the fact that he always tried to be considerate of her feelings, and says that he must have been too boring)

1 K: *cey chinkwu-lang¿ (.) palam-i na-ss-ko: heyeci-n kyengwu-to iss-ess-ko*
my friend-with have.affair.PST-and split-ATTR case-also exist-PST-and
"There was also a case when we broke up after (she) cheated with my friend,"

2 Y: *caymi-ka eps-nun key ani-la maum-i eps-nun ke-yey-yo.* [*hhhh*
fun-NOM not:exist-ATTR thing not-COP heart-NOM not:exist-ATTR thing-COP-POL
"It's not that you were boring, she just wasn't being sincere."

3 K: [°*ayu*°] *maum-i aphu-ta kuke-nun*
Ahhh heart-NOM hurt-IPFV:DEC that-TOP
"Ahhh, that's heart-breaking"

4 Y: *hhhh wul-ci ma-sey-yo. hhhhhh* ((laughs and smiles))
cry-NOM do:not-SH-POL
"Don't cry."

5 K: *a an wul(h)-eyo* [*hhhh*] *nemwu yeys[nal yayki-la-se*
NEG cry-POL very old story-COP-CONN
"I'm not crying, it was such a long time ago so"

6 Y: [**hhhh**] [**wu-l ke kath-**untay****? ((points at A's eyes while laughing))
cry-ATTR thing seem-but
"It looks like you're going to cry **though**"

7 K: *>an-yo an-yo [ani-ntey?<*
no-POL no-POL not-but
"No, no, I'm not!"

8 Y: [***kulssengkulsseng**ha-**ntey***?
tears:brim-but
"You're **brimming with tears though**"

9 K: *a<u>ni</u>e-<u>yo</u>.*
not:be-POL
"I'm not."

Y's initial tease in line 1 indicates that rather than K being a boring person, his girlfriend just did not have sincere feelings for him, which on the surface would seem like a form of consolation that presupposes K's ex-girlfriend as being the source of the problem. However, this implies that K's ex-girlfriend never sincerely liked K, thus prompting K's response in line 3 of "that's heart-breaking." K's comment gives the impression of someone still recovering from the tragedy of being exploited in a one-sided relationship, creating an interactionally delicate moment in the ongoing conversation. A preferred response might be a no-prefaced answer to repair the tease from line 2, but Y instead constructs another tease in line 4. Y tells K to not cry, which functions as an apparently incongruous presupposition of K being unable to contain his sadness and prompts a denial interpolated with laughter from K in line 5. After K's denial, Y escalates the tease by utilizing a challenging rejoinder encoded with *-nuntey* in her statement of "It looks like you're going to cry though!" in line 6, which reflects the observation of *-nuntey's* ability to encode the speaker's "territory of knowledge or experience" while invoking a prospect that is tangential (in this case, the prospect of K crying in a heartbroken state) to the current interaction (Kim, 2018). In response, K utilizes his own challenging rejoinder with *-nuntey* in line 7 to increase the intensity of his denial, after which Y counters with another teasing rebuttal of "You're brimming with tears though" in line 8. This continuous exchange of challenging rejoinders vividly demonstrates the ability of *-nuntey* to invite the addressee to engage in the process of turn co-construction while "co-leveraging the current course of action within the terms that the [*nuntey*-speaker] has proposed ostensibly on the basis of his/her epistemic supremacy or membership knowledge" (Kim, 2018). This also reflects the sequential propensity for *-nuntey* to be used in a secondary position, making it an ideal vehicle for tease designers who seek to make an ostensibly critical assessment of the teasing target's previous utterance or actions while still allowing for the respondent to make some kind of counterargument. More interestingly, due to its ability to connect two clauses, *-nuntey* can saliently mark a transition relevant place by signaling to the interlocutor that something needs to be accounted for or addressed (Kim, 2018). It should be noted that Y's teases become increasingly unmitigated through her subsequent turn after line 6, where she initially inserted within her *-nuntey* rejoinder the periphrastic *-kes kath* construction which roughly translates to "seems" and is used pragmatically to dilute the forcefulness of the speaker's assessment (Kim, 2011). In line 8, Y uses the *-nuntey* rejoinder without *-kes kath*, thereby eliminating any sense of speculation or conjecture. Thus, Y constructs an unequivocal assertion that K is actually crying. Y's use of the highly formulaic, duplicative ideophone of *kulssengkulsseng* in line 8 also adds to the sense of exaggeration and heightens the intensity of the tease. This shows the potential for challenging rejoinders to not only serve as linguistic codes of dispreferred responses, but also the opportunities for circumventing prescriptive moralities and enhancing unreserved exchanges of opinion.

3.2 Reprimand Teases

The next two examples illustrate the speaker ostensibly reprimanding the addressee for an interactional transgression. By doing so, the speaker puts the addressee "on the spot," thus allowing for humorous exchanges.

Excerpt 3: "Winter Cow"

(M had asked Y how old he was, to which he responded that he was 34 years old. The conversation then delves into a discussion about what Y's Chinese zodiac animal sign is, which is the Cow)

1 M: *myech wel sayng-i-sey-yo?*
what month birth-COP-SH-POL
"What month were you born in?"

2 Y: *sipilwel-i-yo.*
November-COP-POL
"November."

3 M: *kyewul-uy so-kwuna.*
winter-GEN cow-APP
"You're a winter cow (I see)."

4 Y: *kyewul-uy so-yo?*
winter-GEN cow-POL
"A winter cow?"

5 M: *ney. hhhh*
"Yes."

6 Y: *keyilu-ta?*
lazy-IPFV:DEC
"(Meaning) I'm lazy?"

7 M: *hhhhhhhhhh* ((leans back with back of hand placed in front of mouth while stretching the other hand in front of her to slightly wave it in denial while laughing))

8 Y: *hhhhh* ((smiles while gazing at Y, then gazes downward))

9 M: *icey (.) so-ka ilha-l cwun(h)pi ha-nun ke-c-yo. hhh*
now cow-NOM work-ATTR prepare-ATTR thing-COMM-POL
"Cows are now getting ready to work (of course)."

After M finds out Y's birth year and subsequently his Chinese zodiac animal sign, M proceeds to ask about the month in which Y was born in line 1, which turns out to be November. The fact that Y was born in the year of the cow and in the season of autumn makes him a "winter cow," which M points out in line 3. In line 4, Y initiates a repair by repeating M's utterance, thereby indicating something problematic. M then laughs in line 5, to which Y responds by uttering the word "lazy" (line 6) with a rising intonation and effectively paraphrasing M's utterance in line 5 as an insult. An interesting contrast exists between Y's question in line 5, which utilizes the *-yo* suffix that is indicative of the polite speech level and his next question in line 6, which utilizes the plain speech level as indicated by the *-ta* suffix. As this is Y and M's first encounter with one another, convention would dictate that both interlocutors adhere to the usage of the polite speech level in order to show respect for one another. However, Y's abrupt but noticeable shift to the plain speech level in line 6 indicates a departure from this convention, as the plain declarative form inherently lacks any linguistic marker for politeness towards the addressee. But rather than taking umbrage to Y's question in line 6, M produces a significant amount of laughter as she leans back, smiling extremely widely. There is no apparent evidence of interactional difficulty, which indicates that Y's deviation from his use of the polite speech style might actually be a discursive strategy rather than a conversational impropriety. The discursive strategy in question involves the use of an audience-blind form (ABF), which has been defined as a type of sentence-ender in Korean that "lack(s) interactional and intersubjective features" but can be intended by the speaker to be "overheard" by the listener which results in manipulation of the form as well as the delivery of the utterance (Rhee & Koo, 2017). Since the plain declarative form used by Y in line 6 is putatively non-interactional, the comment itself is presented as being undirected at a particular addressee, and is more of a "feigned monologual question" through which Y can display his disaffiliative stance towards M's previous comment, albeit to the exclusion of M as a direct addressee (Rhee & Koo, 2017). However, Y still maintains eye contact with M and since the structure of the conversation is inherently dyadic, Y expects some form of uptake from M. Therefore, the intentionality of Y's audible ABF question in line 6 prevents it from being a truly rhetorical question. Another layer of complexity is added by both M's and Y's laughter and smiles interspersed throughout their utterances (lines 5 to 9), with joint laughter taking place immediately after line 6. Such moments can indicate shared affiliation between both interlocutors.

3.3 Banter

The fourth and final excerpt not only offers an example of "reprimand" style teases, but it also exemplifies a conversation in which a one-turn tease can develop into a series of exchanges (i.e. banter) after both interlocutors indicate a willingness to participate in a humorous frame. Banter has also been referred to as a type of confrontational language game known as "trumping," which can involve a type of conversational "expropriation" that arises through either the mirroring or warping of "the linguistic-conceptual construal of [the addressee's] utterances" (Veale et. al, 2006). The excerpt below opens with an instance in which a conversational participant undermines the speaker's own words as part of utilizing them towards accomplishing a "contrary communicative goal" (Veale et. al 2006).

Excerpt 4: "A Pretty Name"
(H and S had discussed whether they use alternate names for their jobs)

1 H: ilum-i toykey yeyppu-sye-kaciko
name-NOM very pretty-SH-CONN
"Your name is very pretty,"

2 S: ilum-man-yo?
name-just-POL
"Just my name?"

3 H: ney?
yes
"Huh?"

4 S: ani-eyyo. hhhhh
not-COP:POL
"No, never mind."

5 H: a ette-n taytap-ul tut-ko siph-usi-n ke-ciyo?
ah what:kind-ATTR answer-ACC hear-want-SH-ATTR thing-COMM:POL
"Ah yes, what kind of answer do you want to hear?"

ce-nun cal molu -keyss -[sup-ni-ta!
I-TOP well not:know-CONJ-AH-IND-DEC
"I'm not sure!"

6 S: [ceng-hay-cye iss-nun ku taytap-i mac-sup-ni-ta!
set-do:AUX-CONN exist-ATTR that answer-NOM correct-AH-IND-DEC
"That pre-determined answer is the right one!"

In line 2, S's use of the delimiter *-man* (translates to "only" in English) qualifies H's utterance in line 1 as problematic. By adding *-man*, S has characterized what was originally a compliment by H in line 1 as an insult that insinuates the only thing pretty about S is her name. S has also structured her utterance in line 2 as a polar yes or no question, which not only deviates from a preferred response of acknowledging or denying the compliment (Leech, 2014), but also has a "de-automizing" effect (Veal et. al, 2006) that prevents the completion of the basic compliment-denial adjacency pair and extends the exchange of turns between the interlocutors by warranting an immediate response from H that must operate within the question's parameters. In response to S's question in line 2, H expresses his surprise by using the affective token *ney?* in line 3, which further demonstrates that S's question in line 2 acts as a source of trouble to the extent that it has somewhat flustered H. Upon seeing how taken aback H is, S prefaces her utterance in line 4 with *ani-* 'no, not' in order to disavow her previous question in line 2 as non-serious, which reflects the utility of "no-prefaced claims" to non-serious intent (Haugh, 2016). S's use of turn-final laughter as an immanent design feature of her tease also contributes to signaling her talk as playful. Upon his apparent realization of the non-serious nature of S's question in line 2, H extends the playful interaction by saying that he does not know what answer S would like to hear while using modulated pitch ranges in line 5. This incorporates superfluous elements that exhaustively verbalize H's lack of knowledge as to what kind of answer would satisfy S, which when coupled with the modulated pitch ranges helps to form a purposefully overreactive caricature of a response to S's question in line 2 (Korobov & Laplante, 2013). In line 6, S uptakes H's teasing utterance by responding with a formulaic catch phrase that has developed into a nonce word: '*tapcengne*,' which translates to "The answer is set, you just have to say it." S's response to H's non-serious utterance utilizes the same type of register clash which extends the playful interaction and results in exchanges of teasing utterances.

4 Conclusion

By investigating types of topic teases (i.e. ranging from being more local to global) as well as the usage patterns of (para)linguistic devices for constructing teasing sequences within a playful frame of interaction, this study intended to add to the breadth of literature that addresses the pragmalinguistic implications of teasing between unfamiliar interlocutors. Two seemingly different situations of teasing coined as "ridicule" teasing and "reprimand" in this study were observed, with ridicule teases occurring approximately five times more than reprimand teases (48 to 11), which could be related to the differing levels of ostensible aggression that is built into the type of tease itself. Reprimand teases involve the display of umbrage or even anger by the speaker, especially if they are delivered in an ostensibly serious manner (Haugh, 2016) which has the potential to pro-offer antagonistic exchanges. It is through these types of teasing sub-categories that the spectrum of the "nipping versus biting" nature of teases as initially proposed by Boxer & Cortés-Conde (1997) is more vividly demonstrated. However, the interactional effect of both teasing types in the blind date settings served as a vehicle for two main purposes: to express the speaker's stance in regard to an interactional impropriety or sanctionable attribute ascribed to the tease recipient, as well as purposefully creating an interactionally delicate situation that prods the recipient to respond in a way that circumvents perfunctory pleasantries in order to provide an opportunity for more candid, intimacy-enhancing exchanges between interlocutors (Davies, 1984).

In terms of the construction patterns for the teasing utterances, a variety of morpho-syntactic constructions combined with paralinguistic devices to serve as contextual cues of non-serious interaction frames. The linguistic devices varied between lexical (word choice), syntactic (clausal connectives such as *-nuntey* or ABF forms such as *-ta*), and discursive levels (no-prefaced responses) which is indicative of the various linguistic levels that the speaker can utilize for the purpose of teasing (Brône, 2008).

In terms of paralinguistic devices, not just laughter but smiling as well as modulated pitch all combined to provide non-verbal cues to blatant exaggeration and jocular frames of interpretation. Leaning forward or backward and excessive clapping of one's hands further added to a humorous setting that discouraged the expression of sincere offense at a tease, thereby upholding the image of someone who does not take themselves too seriously

(Goddard, 2009). This has been brought up when discussing the interactions of English speakers, but the data in this study suggest that such conclusions can potentially be true for the conversations of Korean speakers as well. Playful frames of interaction need to be studied in an analytic frame with cross-cultural considerations, and through the analysis of differential patterns for design teases amongst Korean speakers, this study has attempted to provide a more detailed basis of comparison with other languages that also remain unexplored in the realm of playful interactions.

5 Appendix

Transcription Conventions

[ ]	overlapping talk
=	contiguous talk
(.)	micro pause
(0.0)	timed pause represented in tenths of a second
:	extension of the sound or the syllable it follows
_:	up-down pitch contour starting from underlined portion
:̲	start of rising pitch
.	stopping that results in falling intonation
,	continuing intonation
?	questioning that results in rising intonation
!	exclamation with slightly rising intonation before and then slightly falling intonation after
°	portions quieter than the surrounding talk
*	portions louder than the surrounding talk
-	cut-off or self-interruption
> <	compressed or rushed talk
hhh	laughter
(( ))	transcriber's comments

Abbreviations

ACC	accusative
AH	addressee honorific
APP	apperceptive
ATTR	attributive
AUX	auxiliary
COMM	committal
CONJ	conjecture
CONN	connective
COP	copula
DEC	declarative
GEN	genitive
IND	indicative mood
IPFV	imperfective
NOM	nominative
POL	polite speech level
PL	plural
RESUL	resultative
SH	subject honorific
TMP	temporal
TOP	topic marker

References

Attardo, S. 1994. *Linguistic Theories of Humor*. New York: Mouton.

Boxer & Cortés-Conde. 1997. From Bonding to Biting: Conversational Joking and Identity Display. *Journal of Pragmatics* 27(3): 275-294.

Brône, Geert. 2008. Hyper- and Misunderstanding in Interactional Humour. *Journal of Pragmatics* 40: 2027–2061.

Coates, J. 2007. Talk in a Play Frame: More on Laughter and Intimacy. *Journal of Pragmatics* 39: 29–49.

Culpeper, J., Haugh, M., & Sinkeviciute, V. 2017. (Im)politeness and Mixed Messages. In *The Palgrave Handbook of Linguistic (Im)politeness*, pp. 323-355. Palgrave Macmillan.

Davies, C. 1984. Joint Joking: Improvisational Humorous Episodes in Conversation. *Proceedings of the Tenth Annual Meeting of the Berkeley Linguistics Society*, pp. 360-371.

Drew, P. 1987. Po-faced Receipts of Teases. *Linguistics* 25(1): 219-253.

Dynel, M. 2008. No Aggression, Only Teasing: The Pragmatics of Teasing and Banter. *Lodz Papers in Pragmatics* 4(2): 241-261.

Dynel, M. 2009. Beyond a Joke: Types of Conversational Humour. *Language and Linguistics Compass* 3(5): 1284-1299.

Goddard, C. 2009. Not Taking Yourself Too Seriously in Australian English: Semantic Explications, Cultural Scripts, Corpus Evidence. *Intercultural Pragmatics* 6(1): 29–53.

Goffman, E. 1986. Frame Analysis. New York: Harper & Row.

Haugh, M. 2010. Jocular Mockery, (Dis)affiliation and Face. *Journal of Pragmatics* 42(8): 2106–2119.

Haugh, M., and Bousfield, D. 2012. Mock Impoliteness, Jocular Mockery and Jocular Abuse in Australian and British English. *Journal of Pragmatics* 44(9): 1099–1114.

Haugh, M. 2014. Jocular Mockery as Interactional Practice in Everyday Anglo-Australian Conversation. *Australian Journal of Linguistics* 34(1): 76-99.

Haugh, M. 2016. "Just Kidding": Teasing and Claims to Non-Serious Intent. *Journal of Pragmatics* 95: 120-136.

Haugh, M. 2017. Teasing. In *Salvatore Attardo (ed.), Handbook of Language and Humour*, pp. 204-218. Routledge, London.

Haugh, M. and Pillet-Shore, D. 2018. Getting to Know You: Teasing as an Invitation to Intimacy in Initial Interactions. *Discourse Studies* 20(2): 246-269.

Holmes, J. 2006. Sharing a Laugh: Pragmatic Aspects of Humour and Gender in the Workplace. *Journal of Pragmatics* 38: 26–50.

Kim, H. 2011. An Interactional Analysis of the Meanings and Functions of -nun kes kathta '(I) think' in Korean Conversation. *Language and Linguistics* 52: 25-52.

Kim, K. 2018. Enhancing Solidarity through Dispreferred Format: The nuntey-clause in Korean Conversation as a Normative Basis for Leveraging Action. *East Asian Pragmatics* 3(1): 27-57.

Korobov, N. and Laplante, J. 2013. Using Improprieties to Pursue Intimacy in Speed-Dating Interactions. *Studies in Media and Communication* 1(1): 15–33.

Kotthoff, H. 2007. Oral Genres of Humor: On the Dialectic of Genre Knowledge and Creative Authoring. *Pragmatics* 12: 263–296.

Lampert, M. and Ervin-Tripp, S. 2006. Risky Laughter: Teasing and Self-Directed Joking among Male and Female Friends. *Journal of Pragmatics* 38: 51-72.

Leech, Geoffrey. 1983. *Principles of Pragmatics*. London: Longman.

Norrick, N. 2003. Issues in Conversational Joking. *Journal of Pragmatics* 35: 1333-1359.

Park, Y. 1999. The Korean Connective nuntey in Conversational Discourse. *Journal of Pragmatics* 31: 191-218.

Rhee, S. and Koo, H. 2017. Audience-Blind Sentence-Enders in Korean: A Discourse-Pragmatic Perspective. *Journal of Pragmatics* 120: 101-121.

Robles, J. 2019. Building Up by Tearing Down. *Journal of Language and Social Psychology* 38*(1):* 85-105.

Ryshina-Pankova, M. (2018). Discourse Moves and Intercultural Communicative Competence in Telecollaborative Chats. *Language Learning & Technology,* 22(1): 218-239.

Schegloff, E. (2001). Getting Serious: Joke→Serious 'No.' *Journal of Pragmatics* 33: *1947-1955*.

Veale, T., Feyaerts, K., & Brône, G. (2006). The Cognitive Mechanisms of Advers arial Humor. *Humor – International Journal of Humor Research* 19(3): 305-339.

Expressive and Innovative Ideophones in Japanese and Korean: A Corpus-Based Approach

JIYEON PARK*

Nagoya University/JSPS Research Fellow

1 Introduction

The aim of the current paper is to investigate the usage of new ideophones (also known as mimetics or sound symbolic words; e.g., *kirakira* 'twinkle twinkle' (J), *panccak panccak* 'twinkle-twinkle' (K)) in everyday language. It is well-known that ideophones are words full of creativity (Dingemanse 2014; Nuckolls 2001, 2004; Nuckolls et al. 2016). Over the past decade, there has been an increase in the creation of new ideophones in Japanese and Korean. However, most studies have only focused on their creative usage in literary works such as novels or cartoons (Inoue 2009, 2013; Nasu 2004; Tamori 2011; Yun 2003) rather than in spoken language.

In this paper, I attempt to show how Japanese and Korean native speakers create new ideophones in their daily lives and the principles that

* This study is supported by JSPS Research Fellowships for Young Scientists (no.18J12559). I appreciate the insightful comments at the 27th Japanese/Korean Linguistics Conference that I received from the audiences. I am deeply indebted to Kimi Akita for his ingenious suggestions for an early version (Park 2019a) of the paper.

Japanese/Korean Linguistics 27.
Edited by Michael Barrie.

production is based on. Based on these investigations, I argue that unconventional ideophones can be divided into two types: "Expressiveness" and "Innovativeness". Second, there is an inverse relationship between expressiveness and morphosyntactic integration. Third, Korean ideophones exhibit more preference for conventionalization than Japanese ideophones do. Finally, in the process of creating new words, the two languages use different strategies based on the internal and external factors of their language. Japanese ideophones tend to use expressiveness over innovativeness whereas Korean ideophones tend to use innovativeness over expressiveness.

The organization of this paper is as follows. Section 2 overviews previous studies on unconventional ideophones. Section 3 offers information regarding the data and explains methodology. Section 4 reports the frequency of new ideophones and the syntactic realization. Section 5 discusses the relationship between expressiveness, innovativeness and syntactic realization while addressing internal and external factors that affect the creation of new words. Section 6 concludes the paper.

2 Previous Studies

To date, previous studies have described phonological (Inoue 2007, 2009; Nasu 2004), morphological (Inoue 2007, 2009), syntactic (Tamori 2011) and semantic features (Inoue 2013) of unconventional ideophones of Japanese in literary works. In addition, Nastume (2013) addressed the specific writing system in Japanese cartoons. In Korean ideophones, Park (2006, 2007) investigated morphological features of unconventional ideophones in Internet websites, lyrics and novels (see also Yun 2003).

On the other hand, Dingemanse & Akita (2017) examined a corpus of interviews with victims and rescuers from the 2011 Great East Japan Earthquake for expressive prosodic and morphological features in Japanese ideophones. Furthermore, the authors found an inverse relationship between expressiveness and morphosyntactic integration; ideophones that are more expressive tend to be deeply integrated into a sentence. Although previous studies have investigated several features of unconventional ideophones, a closer look is required to understand how new words are created in everyday language use.

3 Methods

Data was collected using spoken corpora in the Basic Transcription System for Japanese (BTSJ) for Japanese and the 21st Century Sejong Corpus for Korean. To examine daily language use, I only used 99 informal conversations (48,152 sentences) from BTSJ and 77 informal conversations (100,381 sentences) from Sejong Corpus. All speakers were students or office workers in their 20's or 30's. BTSJ consists of 198 speakers and the Sejong Corpus consists of 595 speakers.

To label unconventional ideophones, I referred to five dictionaries in Japanese and two dictionaries and three vocabulary lists from previous studies in Korean. Ideophones were judged unconventional if they were not listed at all in dictionaries or vocabulary lists or if they were only listed from one of the used references.

In this paper, unconventional ideophones were divided into two types in terms of expressiveness and innovativeness. The expressive category was defined by foregrounded prosodic, expressive morphological features such as vowel lengthening (e.g., *ba:t* (J), *hwa:k* (K)), partial reduplication (e.g., *kirakira**kira*** (J), *pwulul**ulu*** (K)), mora augmentation (*ni**k**koniko* (J)) and stem repetition (*hurahura**hurahura*** (J), *challangchallang**challangchallang*** (K)) (Dingemanse & Akita 2017). All of these types were present in Japanese; however, I could not find any mora augmentation words in Korean. The innovative category was measured by noncanonical phonological features such as alternation of consonants/vowels. Furthermore, creative usage of meanings is also considered an innovative feature where ideophones express different meanings from how they are defined in dictionaries. The criteria of unconventional ideophones are set out in Table 1.

		Innovativeness	
		○	×
Expressiveness	○	J *washa:t*	J *ba:t* (the original form: *bat*)
		K *ttatatatatatatatatatata*	K *hwa:k* (the original form: *hwak*)
	×	J *jobojobo*	J *chirahora*
		K *syak*	K *tetumtetum*

Table 1. The criteria for classification of unconventional ideophones

It should be noted that there are several words that have two types of features of expressiveness and innovativeness together. Therefore, unconventional ideophones can be divided into four types: both features, either feature or neither feature as shown above in Table 1.

To examine the relationship between expressiveness or innovativeness and morphosyntactic integration, the syntactic category was categorized into five sections: holophrase, adverbial, verbal, adjectival and others. The categories of holophrase and adverbial are classified as non-predicative form while the categories of verbal and adjectival are classified as predicative form.

4 Results

4.1 The token frequency in the corpora

In the results, I have obtained 585 ideophones in Japanese and 645 ideophones in Korean. As Figure 1 shows, Japanese tends to use unconventional words more than Korean ($\chi^2(1) = 13.48, p < .001$).

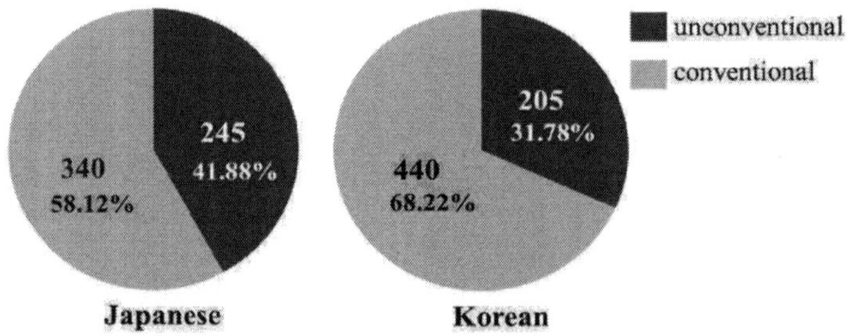

Figure 1. The token frequency of ideophones in spoken corpora

Table 2 below presents the summary of classified expressiveness and innovativeness in Japanese and Korean respectively.

		Innovativeness		sum
		○	×	
Expressiveness	○	46 (7.86%)	175 (29.91%)	221
	×	24 (4.10%)	340 (58.12%)	364

Table 2. Expressive and innovative ideophones in Japanese

		Innovativeness		sum
		○	×	
Expressiveness	○	20 (3.10%)	120 (18.60%)	140
	×	65 (10.08%)	440 (68.22%)	505

Table 3. Expressive and innovative ideophones in Korean

Below, I illustrate some example sentences of Japanese ((1) to (3)) and Korean ((4) to (6)).

(1) *Kusuri* *non-de* ***gussuri,*** *a:* *ku-jikan* *ne-tara, ...*
medecine get-CONJ IDEO EXCL nine-hour sleep-COND
a: *yoku* ***sukkiri**-si-ta.*
EXCL well IDEO-do-DEC
'I took medicine and I slept *soundly* for 9 hours, I *felt fine*.'
(Conventional, Adverbial/Verbal)

(2) ... ***baribaribaribari*** *ya-tte* *ru-kara,* *hontoni.*
IDEO do-CONJ NPST-because really
'[He] really *energetically* works.'
(Unconventional: expressiveness, Adverbial)

(3) *Nanka* *asi-ni* ***jobojobo*** *tamaru-desho.*
something feet-LOC IDEO drench-guess
'[Are your] feet *drenched* with something.'
(Unconventional: innovativeness, Adverbial)

(4) *Na-lul* ***hilkkum*** *chyetapo-teni,* *mak.*
I-ACC IDEO glance-and continuously
'[He] was to *glance* at me continuously.'
(Conventional, Adverbial)

(5) *Kokay-lo* ***kkutekkkutekkkutek**-hay* *kaci-kwu talla-ko*
head-INS IDEO-do have-and give-COMP
ha-ci *anh-na.*
do-COMPL NEG-CONJ
'[She] was *nodding* and asking [me] to give it.'
(Unconventional: expressiveness, Verbal)

(6) *Ttak sihemci cwu-myen* ***tatatatatatatata*** *ssu-ko.*
IDEO paper give-COND IDEO write-CONJ
'[A teacher] gives a paper, [students] are writing [answers] on it *very quickly*.'
(Unconventional: expressiveness and innovativeness, Adverbial)

In the following sections, I will show the syntactic distribution of ideophones that I obtained in my data and the relationship between expressiveness/innovativeness and syntactic realization.

4.2 The syntactic realization of expressiveness/innovativeness

Tables 4 and 5 show the overview of syntactic distribution in each category of Japanese and Korean ideophones based on the classification from Table 1.

	exp/ino	exp/non-ino	non-exp/ino	non-exp/ non-ino	sum
predicative	2 (4.35%)	25 (14.28%)	5 (20.83%)	112 (32.94%)	144
non-predicative	23 (50.30%)	102 (58.29%)	12 (50.30%)	171 (50.30%)	308
others	21 (45.65%)	48 (27.43%)	7 (29.17%)	57 (16.76%)	133
sum	46 (100%)	175 (100%)	24 (100%)	340 (100%)	585

Note: exp = expressiveness, ino = innovativeness

Table 4. The syntactic distribution of Japanese ideophones

	exp/ino	exp/non-ino	non-exp/ino	non-exp/ non-ino	sum
predicative	4 (20.00%)	5 (4.16%)	21 (32.31%)	153 (34.77%)	183
non-predicative	12 (60.00%)	104 (86.67%)	43 (66.15%)	265 (60.23%)	424
others	4 (20.00%)	11 (9.17%)	1 (1.54%)	22 (5.00%)	38
sum	20 (100%)	120 (100%)	65 (100%)	440 (100%)	645

Note: exp = expressiveness, ino = innovativeness

Table 5. The syntactic distribution of Korean ideophones

As shown in Tables 4 and 5, it is remarkable that Japanese has more numbers than Korean in the category of others. This result suggests that Japanese ideophones are more likely to show unconventional syntactic structures than Korean ideophones.

Next, the results of the relationship between expressiveness and syntactic realization in Japanese and Korean are presented in Figures 2 and 3 respectively.

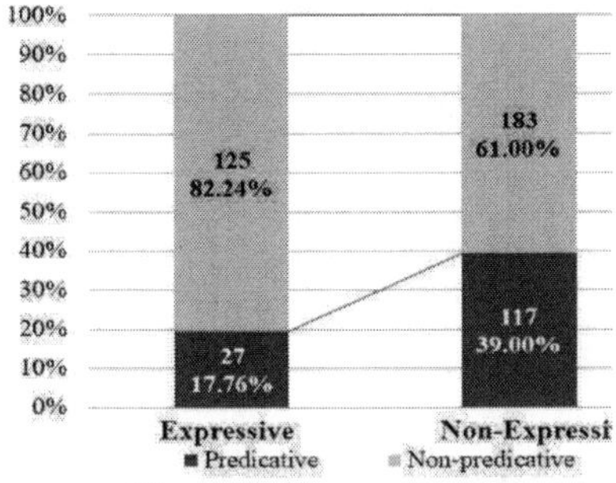

Figure 2. Expressiveness and syntactic realization in Japanese ($\chi^2(1) = 20.95, p < .001$)

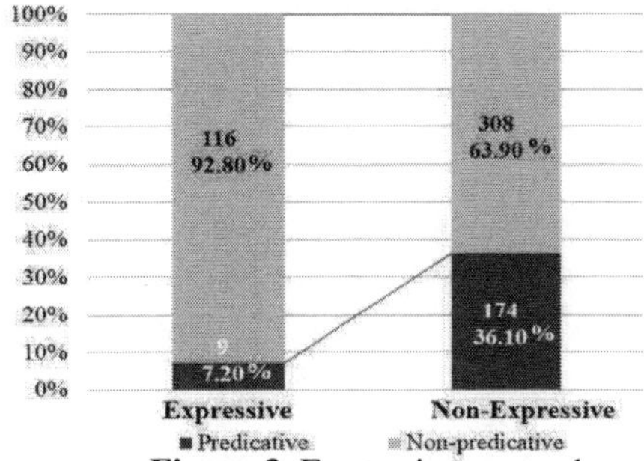

Figure 3. Expressiveness and syntactic realization in Korean ($\chi^2(1) = 39.36, p < .001$)

As shown in Figures 2 and 3, I found that there is a significant inverse association between expressiveness and morphosyntactic integration in both Japanese and Korean; the more expressive, the more likely it is to be in a non-predicative form, such as holophrases or adverbials. The result of this paper has confirmed the findings of Dingemanse & Akita (2017), who found an inverse relationship between expressiveness and morphosyntactic integration (see also Fawcett 2018; Ibarretxe-Antuñano 2017).

On the other hand, there is no significant statistical association between innovativeness and morphosyntactic integration as in Figures 4 and 5.

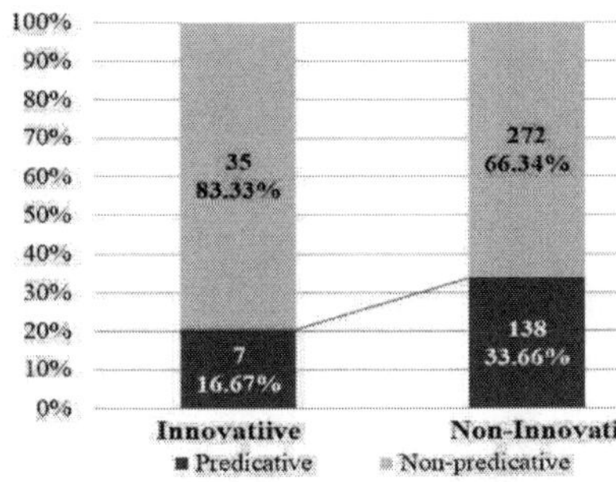

Figure 4. Innovativeness and syntactic realization in Japanese ($\chi^2(1) = 5.04, p = 0.02$)

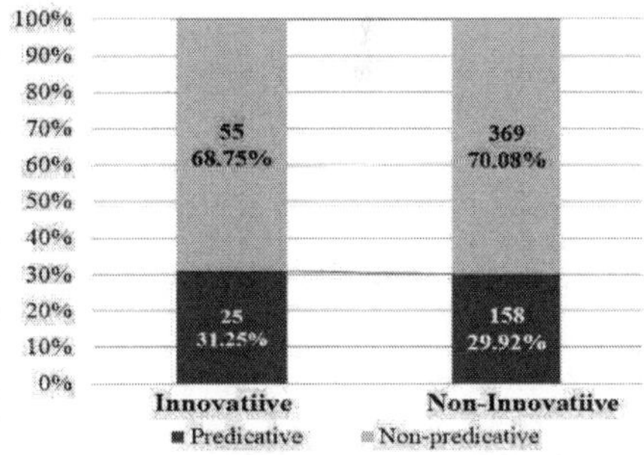

Figure 5. Innovativeness and syntactic realization in Korean ($\chi^2(1) = 0.05, p = 0.81$)

Based on the above results, in the next section, I will discuss the relationship of expressiveness, innovativeness and morphosyntactic integration (section 5.1), conventionalization and the actual use of new ideophones (section 5.2) and the differences of new ideophones creation in Japanese and Korean (section 5.3).

5 Discussion

5.1 Expressiveness/innovativeness and morphosyntactic integration

The above Figures 2 and 3 show ideophones that have more expressive features and are more likely to appear as non-predicative forms, such as holophrases and adverbials or vice versa. This result is in accord with recent studies indicating an inverse relationship between expressiveness and morphosyntactic integration. For example, Dingemanse & Akita (2017) argued that expressive features signal a switch from the descriptive mode of representation to the depictive, setting them apart as words that "show" rather than "tell". Thus, this representative mode of depictive status is reinforced by grammatical independence.

On the other hand, no significant correlation was found between innovativeness and morphosyntactic integration as in Figures 4 and 5 above. A possible explanation for this might be that even though innovativeness is one way to represent an event in depictive mode, it has features that are closer to conventional ideophones. In this paper, I defined innovativeness as noncanonical phonological variants created by alternation of consonants/vowels as in (7) and unusual meaning that gives ideophones a new sense as in (8).

(7) ***Kkwucilkkwucil****:-hay* *kac-kwu.*
IDEO-be have-CONJ
'It is *dirty*.'

A Korean ideophone *kkwucilkkwucil* is assumed that a vowel alternating from the ideophone *kkocilkkocil*. In general, the original form *kkocilkkocil* does not have its counterpart which alternated consonants or vowels in the dictionary (*Standard of Korean Dictionary*). In (7), *kkwucilkkwucil* expresses a state of clothes or a body being extremely dirty. The vowel *wu* /u/ emphasizes the meaning of dirtiness more than the vowel *o* /o/.

Korean ideophones have a system that displays systematic vowel alternation. Vowels in Korean ideophones are divided into three groups; dark, bright and neutral vowels. The dark vowels include *e* /ə/, *ey* /e/, *wu* /u/, *u* /ɨ/, the bright vowels include *a* /a/, *ay* /ɛ/, *o* /o/ and the neutral vowel is *i* /i/. In general, the dark vowels connote largeness, heaviness or thickness, while the bright vowels connote smallness, lightness, tenuity, force, and goodness (Aoyama 1977; Kim 1977; Kim-Renaud 1976). This new word creation by vowel alternation is based on a language-specific symbolism system, which makes it easier for native speakers to understand newly created words.

In the following example, (8) is a Japanese ideophone that takes an existing word and gives it a new meaning by creatively working.

(8) ***Do:n do:n**-tte* *dekai-kara,* *demo, un,* *sarani* *kinniku*
IDEO IDEO-QUOT big-because but EXCL furthermore muscle
tui-tan-yarona.
get-PST-I.guess
'Because [his] body is *big*, [I guess his] muscles developed more.'

In the dictionary (Hida & Hideko 2004), the word *don* is defined as a word that expresses a sound caused by a gun or an object hitting a hard surface. However, in (8), the word *don* expresses a person that has big body. It is assumed that the meaning of a loud noise and a strong impact are metaphorically extended to describe a state being a condition of having a big body size.

The above examples clarify that innovativeness tends to rely on an individual language's specific properties. It thus assumed that ideophones that have innovative features are more likely to be closer to conventional ideophones. Hence, it can be suggested that there is a spectrum of a representation mode, and expressiveness is posited near the end of the depictive mode while innovativeness is posited in between the depictive and the descriptive mode.

5.2 Conventionalization and the use of new ideophones

From Table 1 and Tables 4 and 5 above we can see that Japanese ideophones exhibit more preference for unconventional words and syntactic structures. I found that there are more unconventional words and syntactic structures in Japanese than Korean. In the syntactic distribution of both ideophones in my data, Japanese has more numbers in a category of others (22.73% (133/585)) than Korean (5.89% (38/645)).

I illustrate the examples of the category of others in the below. In the following examples (9) (Japanese) and (10) (Korean) are the types that omit the main verb.

(9) *Porugo-de* *sono-ba-de* ***ba:t**-te.*
portuguese-INS that-place-LOC IDEO-QUOT
'[He] [explained] something *speedily* in Portuguese.'

(10) *Han sikan* *issta pi* ***ccwak**.*
one hour later rain IDEO
'It will be [rain] *heavily* one hour later.'

Ideophones that omit the main verb occupied the largest number in the category of others in both Japanese (55/133) and Korean (30/38). Besides this type, there are various unconventional structures found in Japanese ideophones. I found nominal expressions (13/133), ideophone endings (12/133), and ambiguous expressions (15/133)[1]. Below (11) is the example of nominal expression[2].

(11) *De, dondon tama-tte,* ***iraira**-ga.*
so IDEO build.up-CONJ IDEO-NOM
'So, I am getting more and more *stressed out*.'

There are two possible language-internal and external explanations for this result. The first explanation is the differences between "expression structure" in the Japanese and Korean languages. The term "expression structure" is defined for native speakers of the language and it asks whether it seems natural for the language or not (Lim 2003: 206[3]). To date, a number of studies have found that Japanese exhibits a preference for a noun-oriented structure, while Korean exhibits a preference for a verb-oriented structure. Second, in Japanese, pragmatic inference plays a significant role in interpreting linguistic items (Kim 2003; Ogoshi 2002).

The nature of the Japanese language using a noun-oriented structure and pragmatic inferencing might be one of the main reasons why various unconventional usages are found in Japanese ideophones.

Another possible explanation for this result is the policies of the Korean language and the strong socio-cultural tendency towards conventionalization in Korean. In Korea, the National Institute of Korean Language is responsible for conducting research for the standard Korean language such as Hangeul orthography, standard Korean regulation, loanword orthography and the romanization of Hangeul. In general, it is considered desirable to be in accordance with the standard in Korea in areas such as education, broadcasting, newspapers, official documents, and so on. In Japan, there is also a national institution of the Japanese language that is called the National Institute for Japanese Language and Linguistics (NINJAL). However, there are no regulations and there is a lack of a strong socio-cultural tendency to construct standard Japanese.

Taken together, the properties of the Japanese language and the language external factor of Korean might explain why Japanese ideophones exhibit more preference for unconventionalization while Korean ideophones exhibit more preference for conventionalization.

[1] There is also a type in the category of others that with a predicative *-naru* 'become' (e.g., *Honttoni moo zikken-toka zenzen kankei-naku, un,* ***wa:t**-te na-tte*. 'Everyone *laughed loudly* regardless of we were in an experiment').

[2] Park (2019b) has investigated that nominal expressions of Japanese ideophones can be divided into two types: representing an object and an entire event.

[3] The original Japanese sentences were translated into English by the author.

5.3 Strategies for new ideophones creation

As mentioned above in chapter 1, compared to Korean in new words creation, Japanese tends to use more expressiveness than innovativeness ($\chi^2(1) = 11.37, p < .001$). Table 6 is a table that is calculated based on above Table 2 and 3.

	Expressiveness	Innovativeness	sum
Japanese	221 (75.95%)	70 (24.05%)	291 (100%)
Korean	140 (62.22%)	85 (37.78%)	225 (100%)

Table 6. The distribution of expressiveness and innovativeness

These differences can be explained by three factors that include semantic specificity of suffixes, broad range of using final-consonants and the elaborate systematic sound symbolism system in Korean ideophones.

Korean ideophones have four suffixes; *-kelita*, *-tayta,* *-ita* and *-hata.* The suffix *-hata* expresses 'do' or 'be' (e.g., *Ku-nun kokay-lul* ***kkutekkkutek****-hay-ss-ta.* 'He was *nodding* his head.'), on the other hand, the other three suffixes *-kelita*, *-tayta* and *-ita* express 'keep going' (e.g., *Ku-nun kokay-lul* ***kkutek****-{kely-ess/tay-ss/y-ess}-ta.* 'He was *nodding* his head.'). Thus, it is not necessary to form reduplication or repetition forms to express durativity in many Korean ideophones[4]. It is not ungrammatical if a reduplication form is combined with suffixes *-kelita*, *-tayta* and *-ita*; however, it bears a nuance of redundancy. Thus, it is assumed that Korean ideophones have less of a need to make new ideophones with a stem repetition form than Japanese ideophones do. I found 28 words with a stem repetition form in Japanese, whereas I only found 4 words in Korean.

Another possible explanation for the results of this paper is a broad range of using final-consonants in Korean ideophones. A study by Kim (1995) found that 93.28% of Korean ideophones have final-consonants such as a velar plosive consonant *-k* (e.g., *kkamppa****k****kkamppa****k*** 'blink blink') and a velar nasal consonant *-ŋ* (e.g., *telkhe****ŋ****telkhe****ŋ*** 'rattling'). Therefore, these final consonants make it difficult to insert an additional consonant between syllables to make a mora augmentation form. I found 15 words with a mora augmentation form in Japanese, whereas I could not find the form in Korean. In summary, expressiveness that is represented by expressive morphology is difficult to realize in Korean ideophones due to the existence of suffixes and final-consonants.

On the other hand, in Korean ideophones, instead of using expressive morphology for creating new words, Koreans are more likely to use sound symbolism such as alternation of consonants and vowels as in (7). As I

[4] However, there are a few exceptional words that can function as a verb combined with a suffix *-hata* 'do' that express emotions (e.g., ***meng****-hata* 'dazed', ***ccing****-hata* 'choked up'; Park 1994: 16).

mentioned in chapter 5.1, Korean ideophones are well known for the rich use of sound symbolism to form variant items. Besides the vowel system that was explained earlier the chapter, Korean ideophones have a three-way contrast in initial consonants. There are three types of consonants: plain *p* /p/, *t* /t/, *s* /s/, *c* /tɕ/, *k* /k/), tense (*pp* /p'/, *tt* /t'/, *ss* /s'/, *cc* /tɕ'/, *kk* /k'/), and aspirated (*ph* /pʰ/, *th* /tʰ/, *ch* /tɕʰ/, *kh* /kʰ/, *h* /h/). A plain consonant connotes slowness, softness, and gentleness, an aspirated consonant connotes elasticity, crispness, swiftness, and intensity, and a tense consonant connotes compactness, tightness, and solidness (e.g., *pasakpasak* /pasakpasak/ : *ppasakppasak* /p'asakp'asak/ 'biting a hard object gently': 'biting a hard object strongly').

Taken together, these are assumed to be the reasons why Korean ideophones are more likely to use innovativeness than expressiveness than Japanese ideophones.

6 Conclusion

This paper has argued that unconventional ideophones in Japanese and Korean can be divided into two types in terms of expressiveness and innovativeness. Moreover, I found that there is an inverse relationship between expressiveness and morphosyntactic integration. Furthermore, the study suggested that the language specific and language external factors could explain how new ideophones are created and used in everyday language use.

To develop a full picture of the everyday language use of ideophones, additional studies will be needed to examine prosodic features and body gestures while using unconventional ideophones. Moreover, further studies should be carried out to establish the pragmatic function by using new ideophones in discourse.

References

Aoyama, H. 1977. Tyoosengo-no onsei-syootyo (Sound symbolism of Korean). *Gengo* (Linguistis) 6, 10: 26-33.

Atoda, M. & Kazuko, H. 1995. *Giongo/gitaigo Tukaikata-ziten* (A Dictionary of the Usage of Mimetics). Tokyo: Sotakusha.

Dingemanse, M. 2014. Making new ideophones in Siwu: Creative depiction in conversation. *Pragmatics and Society* 5, 3: 384-405.

Dingemanse, M. & Akita, K. 2017. An inverse relation between expressiveness and grammatical integration: On the morphosyntactic typology of ideophones, with reference to Japanese. *Journal of Linguistics* 53: 501-532. https://doi.org/10.1017/S002222671600030X

Fawcett, A. 2018. Ideophone integration and expressiveness in Wao Terero. *Presentation presented at the SSILA 2018*, Salt Lake City, Utah.

Hida, Y. & Hideko, A. 2004. *Gendai Giongo/gitaigo Yoohoo-ziten* (A Dictionary of the Usage of Current Mimetics). Tokyo: Tokyodo.

Ibarretxe Antuñano, I. 2017. Basque ideophones from a typological perspective. *The Canadian Journal of Linguistics* 62, 2: 196-220.

Inoue, K. 2007. Sinzoo-onomatope-no on'in/keitaiteki tokutyoo: Hindo-no kooka-no kanten-kara (Morphophonological characteristics of coined onomatopoeia: From the perspective of frequency effect). *Gengo-bunka Kyoodoo-kenkyuu Puroziekuto 2006: Bunka-to Retorikku* (A Project of Language and Culture Collaboration 2006: Culture and Rhetoric). 73-82.

Inoue, K. 2009. Onomatopoeic Neologisms in Japanese Comics. *Osaka University Journal of Language and Culture* 18: 69-85.

Inoue, K. 2013. Onomatope-no tagisei-to sozosei (The polysemy and creativity of ideophones), In Shinohara, K. & Uno, R., eds., *Onomatope-kenkyuu-no Syatei: Tikazuku Oto-to Imi* (Sound Symbolism and Mimetics: Rethinking the Relationship between Sound and Meaning in Language), 101-115. Tokyo: Hituzi Syobo.

Kim, I. H. 1995. *Hyentay Hankwuke-uy Umsengsangcinge Yenkwu* (A study on the Lexicon Exhibiting Phonetic Sound Symbolism in Modern Korean), PhD dissertation, Ehwa Womans Universiy.

Kim, K. O. 1977. Sound symbolism in Korean. *Journal of Linguistics* 13, 1: 67-75.

Kim, H. B. 1995. *Hankwuke-uy Sangcinge Yenkwu* (A Study of Symbolic Words of Korean). PhD dissertation, Yonsei University.

Kim-Renaud, Y. K. 1976. Semantic features in phonology: Evidence from vowel harmony in Korean. In *Papers from the Regional Meeting* 12: 397-412.

Kim, U. H. 2003. Nihongo-no meisi-sikoo-koozoo-to kankokugo-no-doosi-sikoo-koozoo (The nominal-oriented structure of Japanese and the verbal-oriented structure of Korean). *Tyoosen Gakuhoo* (Journal of the Academic Association of Koreanology in Japan) 188: 1-83.

Lim, P. Y. 2003. Hyoogen-koozoo Ronkoo (A study of the expression structure). *Nihon Kenkyuu* (Journal of Japanese Studies) 46: 205-219.

Mastumura, A. 1995. *Daijirin* (Great Forest of Words). Tokyo: Sansido.

National Institute of Korean Language. *Phyocwun Kwuke Taysacen* (Standard Korean Dictionary). (http://stdweb2.korean.go.kr)

Natsume, H. 2013. Manga-ni okeru onomatope (Japanese ideophones in cartoons). In Shinohara, K. & Uno, R., eds., *Onomatope-kenkyuu-no Syatei: Tikazuku Oto-to Imi* (Sound Symbolism and Mimetics: Rethinking the Relationship between Sound and Meaning in Language). 217-241. Tokyo: Hituzi Syobo.

Nasu, A. 2004. Sinzoo-onomatope-no on'in-koozoo-to bunsetu-no muhyoosei (Phonological structure of mimetic neologisms and segmental unmarkedness). *Japanese Linguistics* 16: 69-91.

Nuckolls, J. 2001. Ideophones in pastaza quechua. *In Voeltz & Kilian-Hatz., eds., Ideophones (Typological studies in language 44). 271-286. Amsterdam/Philadelphia: John Benjamins.*

Nuckolls, J. 2004. To be or to be not ideophonically impoverished. *Proceedings of the 11th Annual Symposium about Language and Society*, 131-42.

Nuckolls, J., Nielsen, E., Stanley, J. A., & Hopper, R. 2016. The systematic stretching and contracting of ideophonic phonology in Pastaza Quichua. *International Journal of American Linguistics* 82, 1: 95-116.

Ogoshi, N. 2002. Nihongo/kankokugo-ni okeru rentai-syuusyoku-hyoogen-no tukaware-kata: "Kireina-hana!" taipu-no bun-wo tyuusin-ni (The usage of relative clause expressions in Japanese and Korean: The type of "A beautiful flower"). *Taisyoo Gengogaku* (Comparative Linguistics). 75-98.

Ono, M. 2007. *Giongo/gitaigo 4500: Nihongo Onomatope Ziten* (Mimetics 4500: A Dictionary of Japanese Onomatopoeia). Tokyo: Shogakukan.

Park, C. J. 2006. Sinco kamthansa mich uysenge-ey tayhan piphancek kochal (A Study of interjection and phenomimes neologisms). *Kwuke Kyoyuk* (The Korean Language Education) 121: 275-315.

Park, C. J. 2007. Sinco uythaye-uy silthay-wa mwuncey (The Realities and Problem of the Newly-coined Mimic Word). *Hankwuke-hak* (Korean Linguistics) 35: 305-333.

Park, D. G. 1994. '-Hata, -tayta, -kelita, -ita' yenkwu (1): Hwungnaymal-kwauy hyengthay/thonge-lon-cek thukseng-ey ttalun kyelhap kyuchik (A Study on '-hada, -taeda, -korida, -ida': Word formation rules with symbolic words by their morphosyntactic properties). *Kenkwuk-tayhakyo Tayhakwen Nonmwuncip* (Bulletin of the Graduate School of Konkuk University) 38: 9-22.

Park, D. G. 2015. Hankwuke uysenge-wa uythaye-uy umwun pikyo (A phonological comparison between onomatopoetic and imitative words of Korean). *Hanmal Yenkwu* 37: 177-203.

Park, J. Y. 2019a. *Nik-kan Ryoo-gengo ni okeru Onomatope-no Gengo-teki Toogoosei-ni kansuru Taisyoo-kenkyuu* (A Contrastive Study of the Linguistic Integration of Ideophones in Japanese and Korean). PhD dissertation. Nagoya University.

Park, J. Y. 2019b. Nihongo-onomatope-nomeisi-yoohoo-nikansuru imi-teki kenkyuu : Hukusi/doosi/keiyoosi-ga meisi-yoohoo-tosite kinoo suru-baai (A semantic study of the nominal expressions in Japanese ideophones: The types of adverbial, verbal and adjectival ideophones). *Nihongaku Kenkyuu* (The Journal of Japanese Studies) 58: 201-223.

Shon, D. I. 2012. *Hyentaykwuke Uysenguythaye-uy Hyengthay-wa Umwun Yenkwu* (A Study on the Morphological and Phonological Characteristics of Onomatopoeia in Modern Korean). PhD dissertation, Ehwa Womans University.

Tamori, I. 2011. Miyazawakenji tokuyu-no onomatope: Kenji dokuji-no hikanshuteki-yoho (Kenji Miyazawa's unique onomatopoeia: His own unconventional usage). *Kobeshoka-daigaku Jimbun-ronshu* (Journal of Cultural science) 46: 15-30.

Yamaguchi, N. 2003. *Kurasi-no Kotoba: Gion-/gitaigo Ziten* (Language of Life: A Dictionary of Mimetics). Tokyo: Kodansha.

Yonsei Institute of Language and Information Studies 1998. *Yensey Hankwuke Sacen* (Yonsei Korean Dictionary). Seoul: Dusan Donga.

Yun, P. H. 2003. Honpwul-uy sangcinge kochal (A study on symbolic words in Honbul). *Hyentay Mwunhak Ilon Yenkwu* (The Study of Modern Literary Theory) 20: 1-46.

Corpus: Basic Transcription System for Japanese (BTSJ) vol. 2018. Usami Mayumi Laboratory, Tokyo university of Foreign Studies (Tokyo, Japan).

Corpus: 21st Century Sejong Corpus. Korean Ministry of Culture and Tourism (Seoul, South Korea).

Politeness in Japanese and Korean Disaster Warnings

EUNHYE KIM HESS

AMY IVES TAKEBE

Oklahoma State University

1 Introduction

Two rhetorical moves are observed in Japanese disaster warnings: constatives for hazard information and directives for evacuation instructions (Yamori 2016). Since the consequence of hazards is often influenced by what people are informed at the preparedness stage of a disaster (Lindell and Perry 2004), how the latter move is realized with linguistic features within contexts is an important area to examine. From a speech act theory point of view, previous studies suggest the use of direct requests in warnings (Arai 2013; Brown and Levinson 1987). Brown and Levinson (1987) demonstrated that direct imperatives are used in English in urgent situations. Similar to Brown and Levinson (1987), Arai (2013) argued that the polite expressions

Japanese/Korean Linguistics 27.
Edited by Michael Barrie.

should not be used in Japanese disaster warnings because they inhibit the sense of emergency.

However, their arguments raise a question about polite requests in disaster warning discourse from cross-cultural pragmatic perspectives. Japanese and Korean are generally known as honorific languages in which the speakers' politeness and the relationship with the interlocutors are encoded in the languages (Kim-Renaud 2012; Matsumoto 1993). Previous studies have also found the pragmatic differences of polite requests in Japanese and in Korean (Kawamura 1999; Suh 2017). However, to our knowledge, there is a real dearth of cross-linguistic studies focusing on the polite requests in disaster warnings discourse.

Thus, this study aims to examine the use of polite requests in Japanese and Korean disaster warnings from a usage-based approach (Bybee 2006). The usage-based linguistics view that language is emergent and is shaped based on usage-events, in which token and type frequency play a significant role in the entrenchment and schematicity of constructions. Furthermore, the usage-events are context-dependent. Therefore, in order to investigate the conventionalized directives in Japanese and Korean disaster warnings, we analyzed naturally-occurring data from Twitter postings. We examined the frequency of the direct request constructions in Japanese and Korean disaster warning postings and attempted to examine whether the contextual information indexes the politeness.

2 Previous Studies

2.1 Directives in Disaster Warnings

Disaster researchers define disaster warnings as a statement that initiates protective actions among the warning recipients (Lindell and Perry 2004). Such communicative purpose corresponds with directive speech acts (Searle 1976).

In Japanese disaster warning, Yamori (2016) points out two main types of utterances in disaster warnings: constatives and performatives. In speech act theory, although there are some overlaps, statements that describe or report are generally identified as constatives whereas performatives are performances or actions that are done by uttering the words (Austin 1962). In disaster warnings, the hazard information is delivered in constatives while the evacuation instructions are delivered in performatives. Furthermore, they seem to occur as rhetorical moves. This is illustrated in an example Twitter post from Hokuto City Disaster Preparedness Information (2018).

(1) Hokuto shi nai ni ooame keihou, boufu
Hokuto city inside DAT heavy rain warning strong wind
keihou kouzui chuihou, kaminari chuihou ga hatsurei
warning flooding watch, thunder watch NOM announce
s-are-te i-masu[1].
do-PASS-te exit POL-NONPST
kongo no kishou jyouhou ni jyuubun
in the future GEN weather information DAT thoroughly
chui shi-te kudasai.
pay attention do please
'A heavy rain warning, a strong wind warning, a flooding warning, and a thunder warning is been issued to areas within Hokuto city. Please thoroughly attention to the future weather information'

Based on the communicative purpose, the first sentence in (1) is perceived as constative as it reports the issuance of warnings. On the other hand, the next sentence functions as a performative as it instructs people to pay attention to the future weather information. In disaster and hazard literature, the instructions or guidance in disaster warnings, as shown in the last sentence of Example (1), is usually called Call-to-Action (CTA) statements (Farley 2007); it instructs people what to do, CTAs can function as directives.

Disaster warnings in other languages also seem to follow similar rhetorical moves. Example (2) below is the emergency text message from Korean Meteorological Administration when the Phohang earthquake took place in November 15th, 2017 (Chosun Media 2017).

(2) kyengpwuk phohang-si pwuk-kwu pwuk-ccok 6km ciyek
Kyengbwuk Phohang-city North-gu North-side 6km area
kyumo 5.5 cicin-palsayng/
scale 5.5 earthquake-occurrence/
yecin tung ancen-ey **cwuuy-pala-pni-ta**.
aftershock etc satefy-to caution hope-DEF-DEC
'The occurrence scale 5.5 earthquake in 5 km north of the northern district of Kyengbuwk Phonhang. Hope (you) be cautious to safety such as aftershock.'

[1] The current paper follows Hasegawa's (2015) grammar abbreviations. *s-are-te i-masu* is the polite passive form of the *V-te iru* construction, which expresses progressive aspect of the action. With the passive form of verb *suru* 'do' (*s-areru*), the progressive form V-*te iru*, and the addressee polite form of the existential verb *iru* (*i-masu, non-past*), we have a polite passive progressive form, *s-are-te i-masu*.

Here, the two moves are clearly found: the earthquake information in constative and the protective guidance in performative. In English, the same moves are also observed. Consider the following English disaster warning from University of Oklahoma Department of Campus Safety's (2019) Twitter post:

(3) Severe thunderstorm warning until 1130pm. **Stay indoors** until these storms pass through! #OUSafe

It is important to note that the directive in the above examples are realized by using requests. However, different linguistic features are observed in each example. In the Japanese and Korean examples, a polite form is used (i.e., *chui shite kudasai* and *cwuuy palapnita*) while imperatives are used in the English example (i.e. *Stay indoors*).

The use of imperatives in Example (3) supports Brown and Levinson's (1987) claim that bald imperatives are expected in urgent situations since maximum efficiency of communication[2] is expected in such cases. In their politeness theory, Brown and Levinson proposed that the intention behind one's linguistic behavior is to maintain the interlocutor's public image or positive or negative face. Thus, the use of polite expressions in conversation is motivated by the speaker's intention to avoid face-threatening acts (FTA). Urgent situations are cases where the speaker's FTA is not avoided because "doing the FTA is primarily in H's interest" (Brown and Levinson 1987:98), and therefore bald-on-records strategies (e.g., imperatives) are used in such cases.

However, Arai (2013) who investigated disaster warnings that were released by local governments during the 2011 Great East Japan Earthquake reports frequent use of a polite request form, *kudasai,* in the CTA statement of disaster warnings. Similarly, a polite request form in the CTA statement is also found in Korean. Although there is no known literature about the frequency of polite request forms in the CTA statement in Korean disaster warnings, example (2) above shows that the use of the deferential speech ending *-(n)pnita* indicates the polite expression in Korean.

Such findings raise a question of Brown and Levinson's politeness theory in relation to the linguistic realization of directives in honorific languages in urgent situations such as disaster warnings.

---

[2] e.g., *Don't say more than required* (Grice 1975)

2.2 *Kudasai* as an imperative direct request

With an imperative morpheme *i*, in *kudasai*, the *te* form of a verb with *kudasai* 'give' (hereafter, V-*te kudasai* construction) belongs to imperative polite direct requests (Makino and Tsutsui 1986; Narrog 2009). It has a sense of politeness because *kudasai* is derived from the honorific verb, *kudasaru*, which is used when the subject is an honored person (Hasegawa 2015). However, V-*te kudasai* construction is considered less polite compared to a syntactically similar request construction, o-V*stem kudasai* construction, which includes the honorific prefix, *o*- or its variant *go*- before the verb.

Previous studies on requests observed that the pragmatic difference between these two constructions are that V-*te kudasai* is used when the speakers expect the hearers to comply with the request and indicate benefit transfer to the hearer or the public. In the meantime, *o*-V*stem kudasai* is used when the speaker intends to be humble yet needs to give an order or command because of their occupation (Ohso 1974, 1983; Makino 2008). Consider example sentences (4) and (5) recited from Ohso (1975, 1983).

(4) A lecturer is telling students about an assignment (Ohso 1983:143)
repooto wa raishuu no kinyoubi made ni
Report TOP next week GEN Friday until GEN
dashite kudasai
hand in please
'Please hand in your papers by next Friday.'

(5) Tourist guide to a group of people who are going to disperse for shopping (Ohso 1975:126)
rokuji made ni basu ni o-modori kudasai
six hour by GEN bus GEN return
'Please come back to the bus by 6.'

In example (4), the V-*te kudasai* construction is used by a lecturer who is usually considered socially superior than students. As the speaker's authoritative role is a key factor for an utterance to be a command instead of a request (Searle 1969), V-*te kudasai* in this context may function more as a command. The use of *kudasai* in this context, instead of bald imperatives (e.g. V-*te* or V-*ro*), could suggest *kudasai* as a negative politeness strategy. That is, *kudasai* as a marker of "hedges on illocutionary force" (Brown and Levinson 1987:130) or as a marker "to soften the imposition" (Blum-Kulka 1985:219). However, the fact that V-*te kudasai* is said by a lecturer to students does not fulfill the characteristics of negative politeness strategy which also includes "the emphasis of H's relative power" (Brown and Levinson 1987:130).

2.3 *Palapnita* as a performative direct request

In Korean, using a performative verb is one strategy for direct requests; for example, the verb *palata* 'to want, wish, hope' belongs to the performative direct request strategy (Park 2006). In the use of the performative verb *palata*, the different levels of politeness can be observed. As previous studies have noted (Byon 2004; Sohn 1994), the honorifics in Korean is realized in two ways: addressee-honorific and referent-honorific. Different speech level suffix[3] is one way to deliver the addressee-honorifics. For example, using a deferential speech ending *-(n)pnita* shows that the speaker expresses their deference to the listener while using a plain ending *-ta* does not show honorific meaning. With a deferential speech ending suffix *-(n)pnita*, the performative direct request construction *palapnita* follows a noun or a verb plus a nominalizer *ki*. (See Example 6).

(6) imeyil hwakinha-**ki** **pala-pni-ta**
email check-NOMI hope-DEF-DEC
'Hope you check the email.'

In (6), the honorific meaning is conveyed through the addressee-honorific system. In the meantime, the honorific meaning can be enhanced by using the referent-honorific system. Adding the subject honorific marker *(u)si* shows one's respect for a referent. In (7), the performative direct request is realized by using a deferential speech level as in *palapnita* following a verb with the subject honorific marker *si* and the nominalizer *ki*. As the subject honorific marker *(u)si* is used to convey the respect for the subject of the sentence (Yeon and Brown, 2011), the level of politeness in (7) compared to (6) seems higher.

(7) imeyil hwakinha-**si-ki** **pala-pni-ta**
email check-HON-NOMI hope-DEF-DEC
'Hope you check the email.'

The politeness in (7) can be further enhanced by adding an auxiliary verb *-a/e cwu* as in (8). The auxiliary verb *-a/e cwu* has the meaning of benefits for the speaker or someone else (Kim 2019). Also, Yeon and Brown (2011:246) note that "since it implies 'benefit' for the recipient of the action,

[3] Korean is known as having six speech levels: deferential, polite, blunt, familiar, intimate, and plain (Byon 2004; Sohn 1994)

its usage can take on certain politeness functions." Therefore, the level of politeness in (8) seems to be higher than the one in (7).

(8) imeyil hwakinha-**e-cwu-si-ki** **pala-pni-ta**
email check-AUX-HON-NOMI hope-DEF-DEC
'Hope you check the email.'

Therefore, the performative direct request using the performative verb *palata* can be realized at different levels of politeness, resulting in the following constructions: (1) Noun (or Verb-*ki*) *palapnita,* (2) Verb-*si-ki palapnita*, and (3) Verb-*a/e cwu si-ki palapnita*.

3 Data and Method

Twitter has been known as a popular public communication tool during an emergency by the public and official government (Crowe 2012; Sutton et al. 2014). Therefore, municipalities' official twitter accounts for the disaster warning communication were selected for this study.

For Japanese data, Twitter posts from five municipal official Twitter accounts were selected. The list of twitter accounts used in this study are provided in Table 1. Due to the recent change in the emergency warning system in Japan (Japan Meteorological Agency 2013), Twitter posts between 2017 and 2019 were used for this study.

Prefectures/City	Twitter Accounts
▪ Hokkaido, Takikawa	@takikawabousai
▪ Miyagi, Sendai	@sendai_kiki
▪ Tokyo	@tokyo_bousai
▪ Yamanashi, Hokuto	@bousaihokuto
▪ Aichi, Nagoya	@nagoya_bousai

Table 1. Japanese municipal official Twitter accounts

For Korean data, eight municipal official Twitter accounts were used, which is shown in Table 2.

Provinces (*do*) / Cities (*si, gu, gun*)	Twitter Accounts
▪ Gyeonggi-do	@ggdp365
▪ Seoul	@SeoulLifeline
▪ Chungchungnam-do	@ChungNamEMA
▪ Gapyeong-gun	@safegp365
▪ Gangseo-gu	@gangseolifeline
▪ Changwon-si	@cwbangjae
▪ Jeongeup-si	@safe_jeongeup
▪ Namwon-si	@namwon4004

Table 2. Korean municipal official Twitter accounts

Then, Python scripts were run by Redmon (Personal communication, 2019) to search for the keyword 'warning' *keihou* and *kyeongpo* in Japanese and Korean respectively.

As a result, 1029 Japanese tweet postings and fifty-three Korean tweet postings were obtained. Then, we started data cleaning process. First, we eliminated postings where the CTA (call-to-action) statement was not included. Then, we further removed tweets having multiple CTA statement in a single tweet, which was one posting in Korean and four postings in Japanese. As a result, we received 144 Japanese and nineteen Korean tweets. In Japanese, out of the 144, 142 tweets included the target *kudasai* constructions and for Korean, it was sixteen out of nineteen which included the target *palapnita* constructions. Compared to the high token in Japanese data, Korean had a small token, which is one of the limitations in this study. Therefore, we considered the Korean results as preliminary. For the data analysis, we used the open coding method to find emerging themes (Panagiotopoulos et al. 2016).

4 Results

4.1 Japanese Results

Out of the 144 Japanese tweets, the most dominant constructions were the V-*te kudasai* construction (78 tweets) and the *o*-V*stem kudasai* construction (64 tweets). There were two tweets where other request forms were used[4]. Among the 78 tokens of the V-*te kudasai* construction, 77 tokens were found in an independent clause while one token was found in a conjoined clause where the benefactive clause preceded. Out of the 64 tokens of the *o*-

[4] Humble language, *o-negai itashi masu,* was used in one of the tweets, and *kudasai* with a noun was used in another tweet (i.e. *chui* kudasai).

V*stem kudasai* construction, 61 tokens were found in an independent clause while three tokens were found in a conjoined clause. See Table 3.

Types	Target Constructions
(1) Independent imperative direct request	V-*te kudasai* (77 tokens, 53.47%) *o*-V*stem kudasai* (61 tokens, 42.36%)
(2) Benefactive with imperative direct request	V-*te itadaki*[5], *V-te kudasai* (1 token, 0.69 %)
(3) Conclusive form of a verb with imperative direct request	V-*ru* and [6]*o-Vstem kudasai* (2 tokens, 1.39%)
(4) Adverbial form of a verb with imperative direct request	V-*e*[7], *oVstem kudasai* (1 token, 0.69 %)

Table 3. Token frequency of the target constructions in the Japanese data

One of the themes that emerged through the analysis of the constructions was the probability of the event. As shown in Table 4, the *V-te kudasai* constructions included a specific time frame to be watchful. On the other hand, the *o-Vstem kudasai* construction mentioned that the hazard was a probable event. Although this theme did not apply to the whole instances, the usage of each construction with a certain discourse theme was apparent.

Target Constructions	Probability of the hazard	
	Hazard is a probable event	A specific time frame to be watchful
V-*te kudasai* (Total 78 tokens)	3 tokens (2.08 %)	19 tokens (13.19 %)
*o-/go-*V*stem kudasai* (Total 64 tokens)	13 tokens (9.03%)	3 tokens (2.08 %)

Table 4. Probability of the hazard in the Japanese data

A more significant difference was found in the CTA statement as shown in Table 5. There were more instances of V-*te kudasai* when the residents were asked to be watchful for a particular hazard. The *o*-V*stem kudasai* construction, on the other hand, was more likely to be used when the instruction was to watch out for particular information.

[5] *itadaki* is the adverbial form of *itadaku*, which is the humilific form of the verb morau ('give'). Causative+ *-te itadaku* is used as humble expression (Hasegawa 2015, 172).

[6] V-*ru* is the conclusive form of the verb. The tweets used *hikaeru to tomoni* ('along with avoiding').

[7] The tweet used *hikae* ('avoid), which is an adverbial form of the verb *hikaeru*.

Target Constructions	Noun Phrase in CTA (i.e. watch out for NP)			Protective actions (verbs)
	Hazard	Information	Actions	
V-*te kudasai* (78 tokens)	72 tokens (92.31%)	4 tokens (5.13%)	1 token (1.28%)	1 token (1.28%)
*o-/go-*V*stem* kudasai (64 tokens)	6 tokens (9.38%)	58 tokens (90.63%)	0 (0.00%)	0 (0.00%)

Table 5. Types of call-to-action in the Japanese data

Consider the sample tweets of the CTA statement from Tokyo Disaster Prevention (2018) and Takikawa City Crisis Management Office (2017) in Examples (9) and (10).

(9) Tama hokubu/nanbu de wa 2 ka akegata kara
Tama northern/southern in TOP two day dawn from
2 ka asa made ooyuki ni keikai shi-**te kudasai**
two day morning until heavy snow for watch out do please
'In northern and southern Tama area, please watch out for heavy snow from dawn until the morning of February 2nd.'

(10) kongo no kishou jyouhou ni **go**
in the future GEN weather information DAT HON
ryui kudasai
pay attention please
'Please pay attention to the future weather information.'

4.2 Korean Results

In the preliminary results in Korean, among the nineteen tweets with the call-to-action statement, sixteen occurred with the target performative direct requests in three different ways: (1) one independent performative direct request, (2) two conjoined performative direct requests, and (3) a performative conjoined with an imperative. As seen in Table 6, among the target performative direct request constructions, V-*a/e cwu-si-ki palapnita* was the most dominant construction.

Types	Target Constructions
(1) One independent performative direct request (6 tokens, 37.5 %)	N-*palapnita* (2 tokens, 33.33%) V-*si-ki palapnita* (1 token, 16.66 %) V-a/*e cwu-si-ki palapnita* (3 tokens, 50.00%)
(2) Two conjoined performative direct requests (4 tokens, 25%)	V-a/*e cwu-si-ki pala* and V-*a/e cwu-si-ki palapnita* (1 token, 25.00%) V-a/*e cwu-si-ki pala* and V-*si-ki palapnita* (3 tokens, 75.00%)
(3) A performative conjoined with an imperative (6 tokens, 37.5%)	*samkaha-e cwu-si* and V- *a/e cwu-si-ki palapnita* (2 tokens, 33.33%) *samkaha-e cwu-si* and V-*si-ki palapnita* (1 token, 16.66 %) *samkaha-si* and V- *a/e cwu-si-ki palapnita* (3 tokens, 50.00%)

Table 6. Token frequency of the target performatives in the Korean data

When it comes to the six occurrences of the performatives conjoined with an imperative (type 3 in Table 6), the imperatives were also used with the different levels of politeness. Moreover, the co-occurring verb in the imperative was always *samgaha* 'to refrain', which seems to suggest that the restrictive meaning in nature of the verb is likely to occur with imperatives.

Due to the conjoined clauses, the target performative direct request constructions were further examined individually being separated from the conjoined clause. For example, when the two performative direct requests were conjoined with a connective 'and' such as the case (2) in Table 6, each target direct performative construction was counted separately. The same applied to the case (3). As a result, the token frequency of each target performative direct request construction showed as following: two tokens of the N-*palapnita* construction, five tokens of the V-*si-ki palapnita* construction, and thirteen tokens of the V-a/*e cwu-si-ki palapnita* construction. By examining the tokens with performatives, each construction showed a distinctive usage for the CTA statement as in Table 7.

Target Performative Constructions	Pay attention to information	Promotion of Help	
		Self-help	Public help
N-*palapnita* (2 tokens)		2 tokens (100.00%)	
V-*si-ki palapnita* (5 tokens)	3 tokens (60.00%)	2 tokens (40.00%)	
V-*a/e cwu-si-ki palapnita* (13 tokens)		8 tokens (61.53%)	5 tokens (38.46%)

Table 7. Types of call-to-action in the Korean data

Across the three constructions, all performatives in the CTA statement were related to self-help[8], which is the default function in this move. Example (11) shows that the attention to the prevention of the wildfires is requested through the N-*palapnita* construction.

(11) From Changwon Disaster Safety Measures Headquarters (2015)
sanpwul-ul phoham-han kakcong hwacay-yeypang-ey
wildfire-ACC include-REL all kinds fire-prevention-to
kakpyelhi yuuy-**pala-pni-ta**
especially attention-hope-DEC-DEC
'hope (you) especially pay attention to the prevention of fires including wildfires'

However, the V-*si-ki palapnita* construction and the V-*a/e cwu-si-ki palapnita* construction occurred with distinctive meanings. The V-*si-ki palapnita* construction distinctively requested for attention to the information. Example (12) shows that the second performative, V-*si-ki palapnita,* occurs with the request for the attention to the weather information.

[8] The Japanese Cabinet Office (2015) classified the types of help during a natural disaster into the whole society cooperation framework: self-help, mutual-help, and public-help (2015:21). Based on the classification, we defined the self-help as an individual level of help, mutual-help as the community-level of help, and public-help as the assistance from the governmental level.

(12) From Changwon Disaster Safety Measures Headquarters (2012)
siselmwul phihay-ka eps-tolok sacen-taypi-ey
facility damage-NOM not-in order to in advance-prevention-to
mancen-ul kiha-ye **cwu-si-ki** **pala**-mye
a full preparation-ACC make-AUX-HON-NOMI hope-and
aphu-lo palphyo-toy-nun kisang-cengpo-ey
future announce-being-REL weather-information-to
yuuyha-**si-ki** **pala-pni-ta**
pay attention-HON-NOMI hope-DEF-DEC
'.... hope (you) pay attention to the weather forecast information.'

On the other hand, the V-*a/e cwu-si-ki palapnita* construction distinctively asked for mutual help. Example (13) is a tweet in which two V-*a/e cwu-si-ki palapnita* constructions are conjoined with the connective *mye* 'and'. The first occurrence asks for the self-help while the second occurrence of the same construction asks for the mutual help, which is beneficial to the public. Considering the beneficiary feature of the auxiliary *-a/e cwu*, this linguistic feature is reflected in its usage.

(13) From Jeongeup Disaster Safety Measures Deadquarters (2010)
nwun-kil-wuncen, siselmwul ancen-ey
snow-street-driving, facility safety-to
cwuuyha-**ye cwu-si-ki** **pala**-mye,
practice caution AUX-HON-NOMI hope-and,
nay-cip · nay-cempho aph nwun chiwu-ki wuntong-ey
my-home· my-shop front snow clean-NOMI campaign-to
cekku chamyeha-**e cwu-si-ki** **pala-pni-ta**
actively participate-AUX-HON-NOMI hope-DEF-DEC
'Hope (you) practice caution to the facility safety and hope (you) to actively participate in the campaign of cleaning snow in front of my house and shop'

5 Discussion and Conclusion

The findings show polite direct requests are the norm in the call-to-action statements in Japanese and Korean disaster warnings. In Japanese, the polite imperative requests were mostly used in the form of two constructions: V-*te kudasai* and *o*-V*stem kudasai*. In Korean, the polite performative requests were mostly used in the form of three constructions: N-*palapnita,* V-*si-ki palapnita*, and V-*a/e cwu si-ki palapnita*. This frequent use of polite expressions in disaster warnings contradict with the claim by Arai (2013) which the polite expressions should be avoided to convey the sense of emergency. In addition, the results are counter evidence against Brown and Levison's

(1987) claim that the use of imperative direct requests are the norm in urgent situations where the speaker's face threatening acts are not avoided. However, such observation was not found in Japanese and Korean.

Another noteworthy result is that the levels of politeness seem to index different types of instruction. In Japanese, *o*-V*stem kudasai* was mainly used to request for the attention to the information when a hazard is a probable event. Meanwhile, the less polite construction, V*-te kudasai* was largely used for the request for the attention to the hazard with a specific time for being watchful. Thus, the construction with the lower level of politeness was used in contexts where the implied level of intensity is high. In the meantime, the preliminary results in Korean suggest that the three performative direct requests in Korean were used for the request for self-help, which is the main communicative purpose of the CTA statement. However, the different level of politeness in the three constructions seems to suggest the different meaning of each construction. The V*-si-ki palapnita* construction occurred for the request for the information. The politer construction, V*-a/e cwu si-ki palapnita,* was used for the request for mutual-help. Thus, the politer performative direct requests in Korean seemed to occur in situations where the implied level of intensity of the hazard is higher.

These findings indicate that the linguistic realization of CTA statements in disaster warnings is not universal. While Brown and Levinson present FTA strategies as a linguistic phenomenon triggered by universal motives, the current study shows language-specific motives. As the CTAs in Japanese and Korean disaster warnings Twitter posts are produced with directives that denote different degrees of politeness, it seems to indicate different rationales that motivate the Japanese and Korean speakers to use specific directives in disaster warnings. Furthermore, by examining naturally occurring data, we were able to observe not only the different types of directives cross-linguistically but also the different levels of politeness in directives.

However, we acknowledge limitations in this study. The small sample size from Twitter in this study suggests a need for future study with a larger sample using different communication channels. Also, the audience's perception and beliefs about the polite requests in Japanese and Korean disaster warnings should be further examined as the sense of urgency is a subjective concept. Nevertheless, this study adds valuable insights into the use of politeness in the specific social context of disaster warning.

6 References

Arai, K. 2013. How to Transmit Disaster Information Effectively: A Linguistic Perspective on Japan's Tsunami Warnings and Evacuation Instructions. *International Journal of Disaster Risk Science* 4: 150-58.

Austin, J. L. 1962. *How to do things with words*. Edited by J. O. Urmson and Marina Sbisà. Cambridge: Harvard University Press.

Brown, P. and Levinson, S.C. 1987. *Politeness: Some Universals in Language*. (Studies in International Sociolinguistics, 4.) Cambridge: Cambridge University Press.

Blum-Kulka. 1985. Modifiers as Indicating Devices: The Case of Requests. *Theoretical Linguistics* 12(1): 230-30.

Bybee. J. 2006. From Usage to Grammar: The Mind's Response to Repetition. *Language* 82(4):711-33.

Changwon Disaster Safety Measures Headquarters. 2012. [ki-sang-thuk-po] 9wel 8il(tho) 03:00pwulo howukyengpoka palhyo toyesssupnita. Twitter, September 07, 2012.

Changwon Disaster Safety Measures Headquarters. 2015. [kisangcengpo] 2015.3.24.(hwa) 16:00pwulo wuliciyekey kencocwuuypoka kencokyengpolo taychitoyesssupnita. Twitter, March 24, 2015.

Chosun Meida. 2017. Phohangcicin, palppalun caynanmwuncaey simintul 'mancok'. http://www.safekorea.go.kr/idsiSFK/neo/main/main.html

Crowe, A. 2012. *Disasters 2.0: The Application of Social Media Systems for Modern Emergency Management*. Boca Raton: CRC Press. ProQuest Ebook Central.

Farley, J. E. 2007. Call-to-Action Statements in Tornado Warnings: Do They Reflect Recent Developments in Tornado-Safety Research? *International Journal of Mass Emergencies and Disasters* 25: 1-36.

Hasegawa, Y. 2014. *Japanese: A Linguistic Introduction*. Cambridge: Cambridge University Press.

Hokuto City Disaster Preparedness Information. 2018. hokuto shinai ni ooame keiho, boufu keihou, kouzui chuiho, kaminarichuiho ga hatsurei sareteimasu. Twitter, July 28, 2018.

Japan Meteorological Agency. 2013. *Emergency Warning System*.
http://www.jma.go.jp/jma/en/Emergency_Warning/ew_index.html

Jeongeup Disaster Safety Measures Headquarters. 2010. 12.31(kum) cenlapwukto(ceng-up-si)nalssicengpo Twitter, December 30, 2010.

Kawamura, M. 1999. Difference in the Expression of Asking between Japanese and Korean. (In Japanese). *Japanese Language and Culture, Osaka University Departmental Bulletin Paper* 25: 47-62.

Kim, M. 2019. A study on Education Method for '-a/-e juda' and '-ada/eda juda' in Korean Language. (In Korean). Master's thesis, Pusan National University.

Kim-Renaud, Y. 2012. Modern Korean. *The Languages of Japan and Korea*, ed. N. Tranter, 123-67. Oxford, UK: Routledge.

Lindell, M.K., & Perry, R.W. 2004. *Communicating Environmental Risk in Multi-ethnic Communities*. Thousand Oaks, CA: Sage Publications.

Makino, Y. 2008. The Use of Direct forms in Directive Discourse: A Case Study of Natural Discourse in a Residents' Association. (In Japanese). *Japanese Linguistics* 24: 5-29.

Makino, S. & Tsutsui, M. 1986. *A Dictionary of Basic Japanese Grammar*. Tokyo: The Japan Times.

Matsumoto, Y. 1993. Linguistic Politeness and Cultural Style: Observations from Japanese. *Japanese/Korean Linguistics*, eds. P.M. Clancy, 55-67. Stanford, CA: Center for the Study of Language and Information Stanford University.

Narrog, H. 2009. *Modality in Japanese: They Layered Structure of the Clause and Hierarchies of Functional Categories*. Amsterdam: John Bejamins Publishing Company.

Ohso, M. 1983. Invitation, Polite Oder, Personal Request and Begging. *Journal of Japanese Linguistics* 9: 141-150.

Ohso, M. 1974. *On the Illocutionary Force of o-V-stem kudasai Construction in Japanese*. Papers in Japanese Linguistics 3: 123-28.

Park, J. 2006. A Study of Teaching on Request Speech Act for Leaners of Korean. (In Korean). Master's thesis, Sookmyung Women's University.

Panagiotopoulos, P., Barnett, J., Bigdeli, A.Z., and Sams, S. Social Media in Emergency Management: Twitter as a Tool for Communicating Risks to the Public. *Technological Forecasting & Social Change* 111: 86-96.

Searle, J.R. 1969. *Speech Acts: An Essay in the Philosophy of Language*. London, UK: Cambridge University Press.

Searle, J.R. 1976. A Classification of Illocutionary Acts. *Language in Society* 5(1): 1–23.

Sohn, H. (1994). *Korean: Descriptive Grammars*. London and New York: Routledge.

Suh, Y. (2017). A Study about the Request Expression '~ te kudasai' Focusing on Korean Japanese Learners. *Bulletin of Center for Japanese Language and Culture* 15: 1-16.

Sutton, J., Spiro, E.S., Johnson, B., Fitzhugh, S., Gibson, and B., Butts, C.T. 2014. Warning Tweets: Serial Transmission of Messages during the Warning Phase of Disaster Event. *Information, Communication & Society* 17(6): 765-87.

Takikawa City Crisis Management Office. 2017. 9gatsu 18 nichi (getsu) gozen 3ji 26ppun ni boufukeihou narabi ni ooame keihou (shinsuigai) ga happyouni narimashita. Twitter, September 18, 2017.

University of Oklahoma Department of Campus Safety. 2019. 11pm Severe winds will precede the rain and lightning. Stay indoors until these storms pass. A severe thunderstorm warning is in effect. #OUSafe. Twitter, June 15, 2019.

A Systematic, Corpus-Based Methodology for Studying Idiomatic Creativity in Korean and Japanese

YOUNG-MIN OH

1 Introduction

Speakers of every language frequently use many idioms in their daily life. However, idioms have been treated as peripheral because general linguistic knowledge could not explain their semantic interpretation (Chomsky 1980:152). It is not an exaggeration to say that idioms are essential to our linguistic activities. The development of large corpora now allows us to investigate the real use of idioms, including all their rich variation. Despite the importance of idioms and the development of large corpora, little attention has been paid to how language users employ idioms in the real world. This paper will focus on how idioms are manipulated by language users, even though they are learned as fixed expressions in form and meaning.

Japanese/Korean Linguistics 27.
Edited by Michael Barrie.

Here are some examples of idioms.

(1) a. *sono hanashi o kii-te atama ni ki-ta*
that story ACC listen-GER head LOC come-PST [1]
'when listening to the story I got angry'
b. *kwankayk-un paykkop-ul cap-ass-ta*
audience-TOP belly button-ACC hold-PST-DEC
'the audiences rolled with laughter'
c. *Finally, I am afraid, discussion at length and depth will be like "Too many cooks spoil the broth".* [2]

The expressions *atama ni kita* in (1a), and *paykkop-ul cap-ass-ta* in (1b) indicate 'to get angry' (literally to come to one's head) in Japanese and 'to roll with laughter' (literally to hold one's belly button) in Korean, respectively. In (1c) the English idiom describes that when there are too many people involved in trying to do the same thing, the final result will not be good.

What is an idiom? In general, an idiom consists of two or more words, and its overall meaning is not predictable from the sum of its components' meanings - in other words, it is not compositional. Typically, it has a fixed or frozen form (Kunihiro 1985; Miyaji 1986; K. H. Moon 1997; Lim 1998). Idioms are described as fixed expressions by many different researchers (e.g. Fraser 1970; Kim 1971; Kunihiro 1985; Miyazi 1985; Lee 1995; R. Moon 1998; Lim 2003).

At this point one question arises concerning what fixedness or frozenness is. Part of the meaning of fixedness is that speakers cannot substitute one lexical item for another. Observe the following example.

(2) a. *te/ ashi/ kao o arau*
hand feet face ACC wash
'wash hands/ feet/ face'
b. *son/ pal/ elkwul-ul ssis-ta*
hand feet face-ACC wash-DEC
'wash hands/ feet/ face'

---

[1] The interlinear glosses used in language examples are ACC (accusative case), APP (apposition), ATT (attritive), COND (conditional mood), DEC (declarative mood), GEN (genitive case), GER (gerund), INS (instrumental case), IPFV (imperfective), LOC (locative case), NEG (negation), NOM (nominative case), PL (plural), POL (polite register), PPFV (past perfective), PROG (progressive aspect), PRS (present tense), PST (past tense), REL (relative), and TOP (topic).

[2] All real data presented in this paper are extracted from the web corpora koTenTen18, jpTenTen11, and enTenTen15 which are provided by Sketch Engine (Kilgarriff et al. 2014).

In (2a) the Japanese expression *te o arau* means 'to wash one's hands' and the word *te* ('hands') can be replaced by e.g. *ashi* ('feet') or *kao* ('face'). Similarly, in (2b) the words *pal* ('feet') and *elkwul* ('face') can be substituted for the component *son* ('hands') of the Korean expression *son-ul ssis-ta*, which also means 'to wash one's hands.'

However, it is not always possible to replace elements of an expression. Compare the examples (1a-b) and (3a-b).

(3) a. *sono hanashi o kii-te atama/*kao ni ki-ta*
that story ACC listen-GER head /*face LOC come-PST
'when listening to the story I was angry'

b. *kwankayk-un paykkop-ul/ *tali-lul cap-ass-ta*
audience-TOP belly button-ACC/ *leg-ACC hold-PST-DEC
'the audience rolled with laughter'

In this context, with the meaning of 'get angry' the word *atama* ('head') cannot be changed to the word *kao* ('face') in Japanese. Similarly, the term *paykkop* ('belly button') cannot be replaced by the word *tali* ('leg') to indicate the meaning 'to roll with laughter' in Korean.

As for fixedness, R. Moon (1998: 7) refers to it as "lexicogrammatical fixedness–or formal rigidity–" and states that it conveys "some degree of lexicogrammatical defectiveness in units, for example with preferred lexical realizations and often restrictions on aspect, mood, or voice". Senaldi (2015:14) describes the features of fixedness: (a) the component words cannot be replaced or changed, (b) the single constituents are not modifiable and separable, and (c) the components are disposed in a fixed order. [3]

However, speakers use idioms in a flexible manner. Compare (1a-b) to the following examples.

(4) a. *sore o yom-i atama ni <u>kachinto</u> ki-mashi-ta*
that ACC read-when head LOC <u>with a clink</u> come-POL-PST
'when I read that I got quite angry'

b. *sichengca-tul-kkaci paykkop-ul cap-<u>key hay</u>-ss-ta*
viewer-PL-even belly button-ACC hold-<u>make do</u>-PST-DEC
'made even the viewers roll with laughter'

Here, we have the idiom we saw earlier referring to 'getting angry' in Japanese and it is interrupted with the phrase *kachinto* ('with a clink') in (4a),

[3] Senaldi describes four features concerning fixedness. His fourth property is actually not a property of fixedness, but of idioms, and therefore does not belong, so I will only make use of the first three.

and the Korean idiom we saw earlier about 'rolling with laughter', but changed to form a causative structure in (4b). This kind of flexibility in the use of idioms is not only the case in Japanese and Korean, but in most (if not all) languages. (5) shows a flexible use of the English idiom in (1c).

(5) *One developer also cited concerns with the fee structure and wondered whether four agencies proposing one marketing strategy would be like too many cooks preparing the broth*.

In (5) the original English idiom whose form is a sentence is changed to a noun phrase in which the component *spoil* has been replaced with *prepare,* which has been suffixed with the gerundive -ing.

These flexible uses in the examples in (4a-b) and (5) show creativity. How is this possible if idioms are fixed? Why do speakers do this? What limitations and tendencies are there in the ways in which speakers manipulate idioms creatively? By attempting to address these questions, this paper will contribute to the literature on idiomatic creativity.

Creativity is related to all aspects of human culture including language use (see Kaufman and Sternberg 2010). When comparing Casa Mila, which is one of Gaudi's works, to a prototypical office building, we all agree that the former displays a great degree of creativity. The American psychologist Sternberg (1999: 3) defines creativity as "the ability to produce work that is both novel (i.e. original, unexpected) and appropriate (i.e. adaptive concerning task constraints)". Concerning linguistic creativity, the British-American Philosopher Black (1972: 66-67) says:

> Users of language are free to invent new words, to invest old words with new meanings, to modify established syntactical patterns, to use the rhetorical devices of metaphor and irony, and to modify the stereotyped and routine ideas crystallized in the linguistic system. [...] For all its fixity of structure at any given time, a living language has an inherent plasticity and capacity for growth adaptation.

The aims of this paper are to describe a systematic, principled methodology to extract idiomatic variations in Korean and Japanese from a corpus, to identify and document the patterns with which speakers of Korean and Japanese employ idioms creatively, as observed in the data, taking an inductive approach, and to contribute to the creation of a typology of idiomatic creativity and to motivate the typology based on social and cognitive factors.

This paper investigates four idioms each in Korean and Japanese. First, two idioms in each language with the same number of components were chosen, as shown in (6a-b; Korean) and (6c-d; Japanese).

(6) a. *paltung-ey* *pwul-i* *tteleci-ta*
top of the foot-LOC fire-NOM fall-DEC
'fire falls on top of the foot' (to be pressed by urgent business)

b. *ip-ey* *chim-i* *malu-ta*
mouth-LOC spit-NOM dry-DEC
'the spit in one's mouth dries' (nonstop)

c. *me kara uroko ga ochiru*
eye from scale NOM fall
'scales fall from the eye(s)' (to be awakened to the truth)

d. *oya no sune o kaziru*
parents GEN shin ACC gnaw
'to gnaw one's parents' shin(s)' (to depend on one's parents for financial support)

And, additionally, two proverbial idioms from each language with similar meanings were chosen, as seen in (7a-b; Korean) and (7c-d; Japanese).

(7) a. *sakong-i manh-umyen pay-ka san-ulo ka-n-ta*
boatman-NOM many-COND ship-NOM mountain-LOC go-PRS-DEC
'if there are many boatmen, a ship will go to the mountains' (too many cooks spoil the broth)

b. *ttong mwut-un kay-ka kye mwut-un*
shit be smeared with-PPFV dog-NOM chaff be smeared with-PPFV
kay namwula-n-ta
dog scold-PRS-DEC
'the dog smeared with shit scolds the dog smeared with chaff' (one having a major fault blames one who has a minor fault)

c. *sendō ōkushi-te fune yama ni noboru*
captain increase-GER ship mountain LOC climb
'having many captains, a ship will climb a mountain' (too many cooks spoil the broth)

d. *mekuso hanakuso o warau.*
eye boogers (nose) boogers ACC laugh at
'eye boogers laugh at (nose) boogers' (one who does not notice their own fault makes fun of another's fault)

The approach of this paper is to take a cognitive perspective and attempt to motivate the data functionally. It is also to make use of natural examples produced within a real-world context. Unlike the work of R. Moon (1998), Langlotz (2006), and most other idiom researchers, the approach taken is data-driven and inductive.

2 Background

R. Moon (1998) mainly used the Oxford Hector Pilot Corpus (OHPC) which has 18 million words. Obviously, this is extremely small by today's standards. She studied 6,776 fixed expressions and idioms. Because of the limited size of the corpus she had relatively few examples of each. Around 40% of the database of "fixed expression and idioms" (which she calls FEIs) that she observed had lexical variations or some kinds of strongly institutionalized transformations, and around 14% had two or more variants on their canonical forms.

R. Moon's methodology was flawed in that it did not extract variation systematically, but haphazardly, depending on her intuition and the mid-1990s Hector corpus tools. She herself noticed that "finding exploitations and variations of FEIs is the hardest part of corpus-based investigations, and ultimately a matter of serendipity" (ibid.: 51).

Langlotz (2006) used the British National Corpus (BNC), which has 100 million words. In terms of his methodology, for example when searching for *rock the boat* he searched for *rock* within a span of up to 10 words of *boat* i.e. five on the left and five on the right. He found all types of morpho-syntactic and syntactic variation. As for lexical substitution, he said that this can only be approached by intuitive adaptations of the base-form. Furthermore, his results are limited to the creative possibilities that he could anticipate and therefore searched for. This is because he just guessed at possible alternative collocates of the key components of each idiom. He admits that his approach does not lead to systematic extraction of lexically creative uses (ibid.: 228).

K. H. Moon (1997) searched for variations of idiomatic expressions manually from the articles of a Korean daily newspaper for 6 months. He found 1,047 idiomatic expressions including idioms and proverbial idioms, and morphosyntactic variation, lexical substitution, frequency of appearance of the idiomatic expressions and new idiomatic expressions. He pointed out that omission of particles is the most common phenomenon with this being the case in 248 out of 1,047 (23.6%) uses.

Tsuchiya (2013) used the Japanese Web corpus (jpWaC) which has 300 million words and investigated creative uses of 14 idioms and proverbial idioms to find productive patterns of each idiomatic expression. For example, he studied the idiom *gakumon* (learning) *ni* (LOC) *ōdō* (royal road) *nashi* (there is no), which means 'there is no royal road to learning' (i.e. one must learn through hard work). He looked for productive patterns such as "__ *ni* *ōdō* __." All idiomatic expressions he studied show creative uses representing from 13% to 88% of their total uses, and lexical substitution is the most common type of creativity employed.

I would like to discuss the differences between Tsuchiya's methodology and mine. The reason for this is that his is the most similar to mine and close to being systematic and complete. He used eight types of variables to find not only the fixed form but also variants of *gakumon ni ōdō nashi*, and he searched for one or two missing words as shown in Table1. In the left half of Table 1, observe the queries Tsuchiya used to search the corpus. In the right half, compare those I would have employed to study the same idiom.

However, Tsuchiya failed to adequately describe the details of his methodology, so I was forced to guess. Compared to his methods, mine are simpler and more effective in this way: in (i-vi) my searches include not only Tsuchiya's (a-j) but also possible modifiers as well as syntactic alterations that his searches would not return.

Tsuchiya (2013 : 86)	OH			
(a) gakumon ni ōdō X	(i)	gakumon	ni	within a window of -5 to +5 slots
(b) gakumon ni X nashi	(ii)	gakumon	ōdō	
(c) gakumon X ōdō nashi	(iii)	gakumon	nashi	
(d) X ni ōdō nashi	(iv)	ni	ōdō	
(e) gakumon ni X X	(v)	ni	nashi	
(f) gakumon X ōdō X	(vi)	ōdō	nashi	
(g) X ni ōdō X				
(h) gakumon X X nashi		Modifiers		
(i) X ni X nashi				
(j) X X ōdō nashi		Syntactic Alterations		

Table 1. ***Difference in Methods between Tsuchiya (2013) and the Present Study***

In other words, the difference between Tsuchiya's methods and mine relates to modifiers and syntactic alterations of an idiomatic expression. By searching for the relevant terms within a window of -5 to +5 slots from each other I allowed for modifiers and syntactic alterations and my results returned such data.

In addition, even though Tsuchiya used the biggest corpus that I have discussed, yet it is still just 3.6% of the size of the one that I have employed for Japanese (see below).

Unlike the previous studies of idiomatic creativity, I approach the study of idiomatic variation by systematically obtaining all creative uses of the idioms I study in the corpora and by observing a small number of idioms in great detail. In other words, I do not rely on serendipity and intuition to find variation.

3 Methods

I extracted data from two huge web corpora: the koTenTen18 (1.7 bn. words) for Korean and jpTenTen11 (8.4 bn. words) for Japanese. I did this in a principled and systematic way that allowed me to study a wide range of creative uses that are unavailable to intuition. The web corpora are used instead of e.g. the Sejong Corpus (200 mil. eojuls[4]) and the Balanced Corpus of Contemporary Written Japanese (143 mil. words) due to the size of the corpora.

Specifically, I extracted from the entire corpus all uses in which two components in the prototype (fixed/frozen form) were present. That way, I could find creative uses which diverged from the prototype significantly. I manually sorted all data returned, filtering for instances of the idiom. This method allowed me to extract nearly all creative uses from the corpora, apart from uses in which just a single component was employed but which were somehow intended as instantiations of the idiom – it seems likely that there were few of these, if any.

Table 2 shows the corpus query language I used to get the data for uses of two components *me* ('eye') and *uroko* ('scale') together (see (6c) above). This method allowed me to extract all kinds of variations which include not only *me* X *uroko ga ochiru*, *me* X *uroko* X *ochiru*, *me* X *uroko ga* X, *me* X *uroko* X X, *me kara uroko* X *ochiru*, *me kara uroko ga* X, *me kara uroko* X X, but also uses with added modifiers and syntactic alterations. A few examples are as follows: *watashi no me kara ochi-ta uroko* (I GEN eyes from fall-PPFV scale(s), 'the scales that fell from my eyes'), *uroko ga me kara ochiru* (scales NOM eyes from fall, 'scales fall from eyes'), *me kara buatsui uroko o otoshita* (eyes from thick scales ACC drop, '(I) dropped the thick scales from (my) eyes').

Keywords		Corpus Query Lnaguage (CQL)		Range (window)
me	unroko	1st step	[lemma="目"&tag="N.*"]	
		2nd step	positive filtger [lemma="鱗"&tag="N.*"]	-5, +5
		3rd step	filter noise and determine creative uses of the idiom	-5, +5

Table 2. ***CQL to Get the Data for "me uroko"***

[4] An eojul refers to the morphosyntactic combination of one word and particle(s), or one word and its ending(s), or one word alone in Korean.

The first step is to search for the lemma *me* ('eye'). The second step is to apply a positive filter for the lemma *uroko* ('scale'), within a window of -5 to +5 slots. The third step is to manually examine all results and filter out the noise and non-examples, such as literal uses. I determined which uses were literal and idiomatic by examining the context.

As shown in Table 3, there are two ways my methods improve on those of previous researchers. One is that the numbers of words in the corpora I used are far greater.

	corpus	words	language	variations		
				lexical substitution	modifier	syntactic alteration
R. Moon (1998)	OHPC	18 mil.	English	intuition	systematic	systematic
Langlotz (2006)	BNC	100 mil.	English	intuition	systematic	systematic
K.H. Moon (1997)	a Korean daily news paper	articles for 6 months	Korean	manually extracted		
Tsuchiya (2013)	jpWaC	300 mil.	Japanese	systematic	limited	limited
OH	jpTenTen11	8.4 bn.	Japanese	systematic		
	koTenTen18	1.7 bn.	Korean			

Table 3. ***Comparison with the Methods of Previous Studies***

As far as variations, other researchers used intuition or returned limited types of variations, or they rely on manual extraction, whereas my methods systematically extracted all types of possible variation.

4 Results and Analysis

Overall, the results showed four categories of creative uses of idioms. There were examples of contraction in which some of the components are omitted as shown in (8) and (9).

(8) a. *pay-ka* *san-ulo* *ka-n* *kyengwu-ta* (cf. 7a)
[ship-NOM mountain-LOC go-PST.IPFV]ATT case-be.DEC
'it is the case that a ship went to the mountains' (the final result was not good)

b. *paltung-ey* *pwul-i-ta* (cf. 6a)
top of the foot-LOC fire-be-DEC
'It is the fire on top of the foot' (someone is pressed by urgent business)

(9) a. *me kara uroko no hon-da* (cf. 6c)
eye from scale GEN book-be
'it is a book of scales from eyes' (it is an enlightening book)
b. *sune o kajiru* (cf. 6d)
shin ACC gnaw
'to gnaw shin(s)' (to depend on someone's financial support)

The Korean idioms are used without *sakong-i manh-umyen* ('if there are many boatmen') in (8a) and *tteleci-ta* (fall-DEC) in (8b) respectively. Similarly, the Japanese idioms are employed without *ga ochiru* (NOM fall) in (9a) and *oya no* (parents GEN) in (9b).

There were cases of substitution where one or more components are replaced. Some examples are shown in (10) and (11).

(10) a. *paltung-ey pwulttong-i ttele-cyess-ta*
top of the foot-LOC spark-NOM fall-PST-DEC
'the spark fell on top of the foot' (someone was pressed by urgent business)
b. *mwe mwut-un kay-ka*
[sth be smeared with-PST. IPFV] ATT dog-NOM
mwe mwut-un kay namwula-n-ta
[sth be smeared with-PST. IPFV] ATT dog scold-PRS.IPFV-DEC
'the dog smeared with something scolds the dog smeared with something' (one having a fault blames one who has a fault)

Here, *pwul* ('fire') is replaced by *pwulttong* ('spark') in (10a) and in (10b) *ttong* ('shit') and *kye* ('chaff') are replaced with *mwe* ('something').[5]

(11) a. *mimi kara uroko ga ochiru*
ear from scale NOM fall
'scales fall from ears' (when you heard something, you could see the light)
b. *okāsan no sune kajit-teru*
mother GEN shin gnaw-PRS.PROG
'(someone) is gnawing their mother's shin(s)' (someone is depending on their mother for financial support)

---

[5] The substitution of *mwe* (something) for *ttong* (shit) and *kye* (chaff) results in the meaning change of the idiom such that 'the dog smeared with something scolds the dog smeared with something' indicates that someone is criticizing somebody else for a fault that they also have. In this paper, I will not talk about the semantic extension of the idioms resulting from such changes, leaving this issue to future research.

The components *mimi* ('ear') and *okāsan* ('mother') of the Japanese idioms are substituted for the corresponding components from the idiom prototypes *me* ('eye') in (11b) and *oya* ('parents') in (11b).

There were examples of syntactic alteration in which the idiom is used with a modified structure, such as those seen in (12) and (13).

(12) a. *tteleci-n* *paltung-uy* *pwul* *ttaymwuney*
[fall-PST. IPFV] ATT top of the foot-GEN fire due to
'due to the fire having fallen on top of the foot' (due to the urgent business already having happened)

b. *sakong-i* *manh-un* *pay-ka* *san-ulo* *ka-tus*
[boatman-NOM many-ATT] REL ship-NOM mountain-LOC go-as if
'as if the ship with many boatmen goes to the mountains' (as if something goes wrong due to having many people involved)

In (12a) *tteeci-n paltung-uy pwul* ('the fire that fell on top of the foot') is used as a noun phrase based on the original idiom *paltung-ey pwul-i tteleci-ta* ('fire falls on top of the foot'). In (12b), we see that, while the original proverbial idiom consisted of a subordinate clause and a main clause, the subordinate clause has been changed to a relative clause. More examples are presented below in (13).

(13) a. *hanakuso* *o* *warau* *mekuso*
[(nose) booger ACC laugh at] REL eye booger
'eye boogers that laugh at nose boogers' (the one having a fault does not notice their own fault and makes fun of another's fault)

b. *oya* *no* *sune* *wa* *kaji-reru* *uchi*
parents GEN shin TOP gnaw-can during
'during the time when one can gnaw one's parents' shin(s)' (during the time when one can depend on their parents' financial support)

The noun phrase *hanakuso o warau mekuso* ('eye boogers that laugh at nose boogers') in (13a) is a relative clause based on the original idiom *mekuso hanakuso o warau* ('eye boogers laugh at nose boogers'). In (13b), the original *o kaziru* (ACC gnaw) has been changed to the potential form *wa kaji-reru* (TOP gnaw-can) and the whole idiom forms a subordinate clause with *uchi* ('during').

Finally, there were cases of extension, where there is an addition to the prototype form, such as a modifier, as seen in the following examples.

(14) a. *ip-ey* *chim-i* *malu-ko* *talh-tolok* *iyakiha-yss-supni-ta*
mouth-LOC spit-NOM dry-GER run out-until speak-PST-POL-DEC
'(He) spoke until his mouth dried and the spit ran out' (He spoke nonstop)

b. *sakong-i* *nemwu* *manh-umyen*
boatman-NOM too many-COND
'if there are too many boatmen' (if there are too many leaders)

(15) a. *watashi no* *me* *kara* *haraharato* *uroko* *ga* *ochi-ta*
I GEN eye from gently scale NOM fall-PST
'from my eyes the scales fell gently' (I was gradually awakened to the truth)

b. *oya* *no* *sune* *o* *zutto* *kajit-te*
parents GEN shin ACC continuously gnaw-GER
'continuously gnawing one's parents' shin(s)' (continuously depending on one's parents for financial support)

We see that *talh-tolok* ('until running out') in (14a) and *nemwu* ('too') in (14b) are added to the Korean idioms. In the same way, *watashi no* ('my') in (15a) and *haraharato* ('gently') in (15b) are added to the Japanese idioms.

Interestingly, these categories (contraction, extension, syntactic alteration and substitution) are not mutually exclusive. In other words, we find multiple categories of variation that apply to a single use, as shown in (16).

(16) a. *namphyen* *chingchan-ulo* *anay-uy* *ip-i*
husband praise-INS wife-GEN mouth-NOM
malu-ci anh-ass-tan-ta.
dry-NEG-PST-be said-DEC
'It was said that her husband's praise didn't dry the wife's mouth' (it was said that the wife praised her husband nonstop)

b. *me* *kara* *buatsui* *uroko* *ga* *hagare-ta*
eye from thick scale NOM peel off-PST
'thick scales peeled off from my eyes' (I was rudely awakened to the truth)

In (16a), we see both a contraction and an extension. Specifically, the components *chim-i* (spit-NOM) of *ip-ey chim-i malu-ta* are omitted and *anay-uy* (wife-GEN) is added in the Korean idiom. On the other hand, in (16b) the Japanese example includes the addition of a modifier *buatsui* ('thick') and a substitution of *hagareta* ('peeled off') for *ochiru* ('fall').

Idiom variations should be categorized into two groups; one type involves institutionalized uses such as *pay-ga san-ulo kan-ta* ('a ship goes to the mountains') without the first half of the proverbial idiom in Korean and *me kara uroko* ('scales from eyes') without *ga ochiru* (NOM fall) in Japanese. These contracted forms are frequently found in the data. The other type are idioms used in novel or ad-hoc ways such as *tteleci-n paltung-uy pwul* ('the fire having fallen on top of the foot') in Korean and *okāsan no sune kajit-teru* ('someone is gnawing their mother's shin(s)') in Japanese. Such uses may be one-of-a-kind, or occur with low frequency, and reveal a high degree of creativity.

Table 4 represent the total results for the four idioms in each language: this shows the numbers of all uses of the fixed form versus creative uses and what type of variation was observed as a proportion of all observed variation.

Total Uses		**Korean**								**Japanese**							
		paltungey pwuli ttelecita		ipey chimi maluta		sakongi manhumyen payka sanulo kanta		ttong mwutun kayka kye mwutun kaylul namwulanta		me kara uroko ga ochiru		oya no sune o kaziru		send, , kushite fune yama ni noboru		mekuso hanakuso o warau	
Fixed Form (tokens)		901	42%	425	63%	119	21%	141	24%	3,147	14%	1,409	50%	226	44%	463	16%
Creative Uses (tokens)		1,265	58%	251	37%	436	79%	452	76%	18,839	86%	1,428	50%	290	56%	2,365	84%
Total (tokens)		2,166	100%	676	100%	555	100%	593	100%	21,986	100%	2,837	100%	516	100%	2,828	100%
Breakdown of Creative Uses	Contraction	463	27%	225	44%	346	57%	62	11%	17,700	94%	1,142	69%	181	39%	2,265	90%
	Substitution	550	32%	230	45%	76	13%	364	66%	699	4%	360	22%	97	21%	77	3%
	Syntactic alteration	426	25%	1	0%	97	16%	75	14%	36	0%	100	6%	135	29%	42	2%
	Extension	278	16%	50	10%	88	14%	50	9%	461	2%	59	4%	57	12%	142	6%
	Total	1,717	100%	506	100%	607	100%	551	100%	18,896	100%	1,661	100%	470	100%	2,526	100%

Table 4. ***Use of Four Idioms in Korean and Japanese***

Table 4 shows that over fifty percent of the data for seven of the eight idioms involved creative uses. Notice that the type of variation used with highest frequency is substitution for three of the four idioms in Korean and contraction for all four idioms in Japanese, as shown by the grey highlights.

5 Discussion and Conclusion

Having seen the types of variation in the data, we can ask how to motivate this variation, and the creative uses in particular. This requires a discussion of the different types of meaning involved with the processing and use of an idiom. Now I would like to discuss the complex meaning of proverbial and other idioms, describing how this is a motivation for the patterns of fixedness and creativity that we find in the results. Let's look at this example which we saw earlier.

(17) *One developer also cited concerns with the fee structure and wondered whether four agencies proposing one marketing strategy would be like too many cooks preparing the broth*. (=5)

As seen in Figure 1 below, the literal meaning of the idiom *too many cooks spoil the broth* is related to the idiomatic meaning, 'an excessive number of people involved ruin or impair a goal, task, or activity.' However, in actual use, the meaning is different again, such as, in this case *four agencies propose one marketing strategy*. In the left half of the Figure, the square with a dotted line shows the entrenched aspects of idiom use.

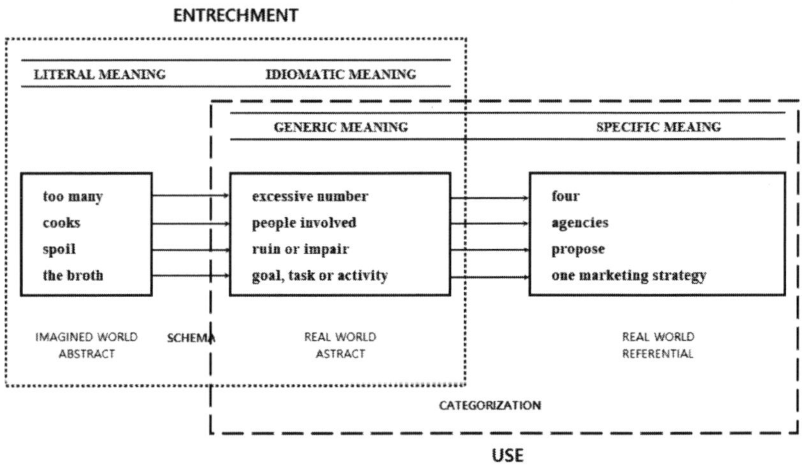

Figure 1. ***Entrenchment vs. Use of Idioms*** [6]

Speakers presumably learn the fixed form, and these associated meanings, first. Without this knowledge, speakers cannot employ idioms. In the right half of the Figure, the rectangle with long dashed lines represents the freer aspects of idiom use and gives rise to their creative potential. Speakers need to have the ability to modify idioms, which have an abstract meaning, in order to make them refer to real-world situations concretely. I refer to this as concretization (semantic function). This appears to be the most important motivation for novel, ad-hoc variation (creative uses). The left and right parts of the main Figure overlap, which motivates the relationship between the fixed form and creative uses. To apply the idiom with its abstract meaning to a concrete, real-world situation, speakers may need to get creative.

[6] It is based loosely on Nabeshima (2016: ch. 9).

Finally, variations of the idiom are either institutionalized or novel. Some examples are shown in Table 5.

I have not gone through my data and categorized all variants as institutionalized or novel, partly because these are greyscale categories and quite difficult to define and differentiate accurately. The most interesting question, for this author at least, is how to motivate the novel variation, as that is what is truly creative on an individual level. It is to address this question that I employ the term "concretization".

INSTITUTIONALIZED USE	NOVEL USE
(a) Too many cooks **(b) Too many cooks <u>in the kitchen</u>** **(c) Too many cooks spoil the <u>soup</u>**	**(i) Too many cooks <u>supposedly</u> spoil the broth.** **(ii) I did not want too many cooks <u>spoiling the broth</u>.**

Table 5. ***Institutionalized Uses vs. Novel Uses***

By "concretization", I refer to the creative use of language in order to ground the abstract (in this case, idiomatic) meaning in the real-world context to which it belongs. In the data, this was achieved through i) extension - the addition of pronouns, plural forms, adverbs, adjectives, etc., ii) syntactic alteration - passivization, causation, the use of relative clauses, etc., and iii) substitution (as well as combinations of these strategies). Of the four types of variation observed, only contraction was not motivated by concretization, but rather by economy.

The phenomenon of a speaker omitting some components of sentences and phrases is ubiquitous in language use. Sapir (1948[1921]:29) states that "all languages have an inherent tendency to economy of expression". This even happens with the use of idioms, despite their relatively fixed forms, as we observed here. From a pragmatic view, Leech (1983: 67) suggests "the economy principle" by which a speaker can shorten an expression, which is achieved by pronominalization or replacement by other pro-forms or ellipsis without changing its meaning, and results in reducing time and effort in communication.

The three competing pressures when a speaker produces an idiom are 1) economy, which is always a pressure in language use, 2) understandability (will the listener know that it's the idiom?), and 3) concreteness (the need to link the abstract meaning of the idiom with the real life situation). We know that all three are important because there is sufficient evidence that speakers shorten idioms, but no evidence that they shorten them too much, such as saying *pal-tung* ('top of the foot') instead of *pal-tung-ey pwul-i tteleci-ta* in Korean, or *me* ('eye') instead of *me kara uroko ga ochiru* in Japanese, because this would not allow listeners to know the speaker is using the idiom. Concretization is the primary phenomenon motivating most types of idiomatic creativity, but some instances of variation are motivated by economy. Using concretization and economy, we can motivate the entire range of examples involving variation.

In this paper, I described a systematic, principled methodology to extract idiomatic variations in Korean and Japanese from a corpus. I identified and documented the patterns with which speakers of Korean and Japanese employ idioms creatively, as observed in the data, taking an inductive approach. I contributed to the creation of a typology of idiomatic creativity and attempted to motivate the typology based on social and cognitive factors.

References

Black, M. 1972. *The Labyrinth of Language*. Harmondsworth: Penguin Books.

Chomsky, N. 1980. *Rules and Representations*. New York: Columbia University Press.

Fraser, B. 1970. Idioms within a Transformational Grammar. *Foundations of Language* 6, 22-42.

Kaufman, J. C. & R. J. Sternberg. 2010. *The Cambridge Handbook of Creativity*. Cambridge University Press.

Kilgarriff, A., V. Baisa, J. Bušta, M. Jakubíček, V. Kovář, J. Michelfeit, P. Rychlý & V. Suchomel. 2014. The Sketch Engine: Ten Years on. *Lexicography* 1, 7-36.

Kim, J. T. 1971. A Study of Idioms. *The Korean Language and Literature* 25: 97-112.

Kunihiro, T. 1985. Kanyōku Ron (Theory of Idioms). *Japanese Linguistics* 1 (4): 4-14. MeijiShoin.

Langlotz, A. 2006. *Idiomatic Creativity*. Amsterdam & Philadelphia: John Benjamins Publishing Company.

Lee, H. J. 1995. A Study of Different Combination of Contemporary Korean Idiomatic Phrase. *Daedong Institute for Korean Studies* 30: 411-44.

Lim, P. Y. 2002. *Ni・Kan ryōkokugo no Kanyōteki Hyōgen no Taishō Kenkyū: Shintaigoi Kanyōku o Chūshin to Shite* (A Contrastive Study of Idiomatic Expressions of Body Part Terms in Japanese and Korean). MeijiShoin.

Miyaji, Y. 1985. Kanyōku no shūhen (Periphery of idioms): Rengo Kotowaza Fukugōgo (Collocation, Proverb, and Compound Words). *Japanese Linguistics* 4 (1): 62-75. Meijishoin.

Moon, K. H. 1999. *Kwuke-uy Kwanyongphyohyen Yenkwu* (A Study of Korean Idiomatic Expressions). Thayhaksa

Moon, R. 1998. *Fixed Expressions and Idioms in English*. A corpus-based approach. Oxford: Clarendon Press.

Nabeshima, KJ. 2016. *Metaphor and Embodiment*. Hitsuji Shobō.

Senaldi, M. S. G. 2015. Casting Light on Idiom Flexibility: A Corpus-based Approach. Doctoral dissertation, Università di Pisa.

Sternberg, R. J. 1999. *Handbook of Creativity*. Cambridge University Press.

Tsuchiya, T. 2013. Teikeihyōgen o Kiban to Shita Gengo no Sōzōsei: Kanyōhyōgen to Kotowaza no Kakuchōyōhō ni Kansuru Shakai/ Ninchiteki Kōsatsu (Language Creativity Based on Formulaic Language: Extensional Usage of Idioms and Proverbs from a Social Cognitive View). Doctoral dissertation, Kyoto University.

Part II

Historical Linguistics

First Person Pronouns in Old Japanese Revisited: Focusing on *a-^{n}ka* and *wa-^{n}ka*

CHIHKAI LIN
Tatung University

1 Introduction

This paper reexamines 1st person pronouns, *a* and *wa*, in Old Japanese from semantic selection. In Old Japanese, there are at least three 1st person pronouns, *a/are*, *wa/ware*, and *marö*. The similar forms *a/are* and *wa/ware* are proposed to be different in their origins. From a diachronic viewpoint, Hamada (1946), Yamada (1954: 55-57), Saeki (1972: 99) and Okazaki (1976) assume that *a* is more archaic than *wa*. Yamada (1954) suggests that pronoun *wa* outnumbers pronoun *a* in Old Japanese (271 tokens vs. 132 tokens). In addition, *a* is used in compounds, whereas *wa* is not (Yamada 1954: 55). Nevertheless, Vovin (2005: 220-222) has questioned Yamada's hypotheses. First, Vovin (2005: 221) has shown that *a* is more frequently used in Late Western Old Japanese than in Early Western Old Japanese, as in Table 1 (from Vovin 2005: 221).

	a-	*wa-*
KK	5	38
NSK	8	28
MYS Vol. 5	7	10
MYS Vol. 15	24	37
MYS Vol. 17	13	13
MYS Vol. 18	3	8
MYS Vol. 20	4	2

Table 1: Different distribution of *a* and *wa* in Old Japanese

Japanese/Korean Linguistics 27.
Edited by Michael Barrie.

Besides, Vovin (2005: 220) points out that it is not a criterion to determine which pronoun is archaic based on whether it appears in a compound. In fact, the two pronouns appear in compounds, such as *wa-N-töri* I-POSS-bird 'my bird' (KK 3) and *a-N-kwo* I-POSS-child 'my children' (NK 8) (Vovin 2005: 220).[1] Thus, Vovin (2005: 222) assumes that *a* and *wa* should have separate origins.[2]

Synchronic distribution also reveals the difference between *a* and *wa*. Vovin (2005: 220) contends that pronouns *a* and *wa* are similar in sociolinguistic and grammatical usage in extant texts, except for the fact that *wa* combines with more case markers than *a*. *Wa* combines with possessive, dative, accusative, and directive case markers (Vovin 2005: 224), whereas *a* combines only with possessive and accusative case markers (Vovin 2005: 238).[3] On the other hand, Kikuzawa (1955: 49) suggests that *a* entails singularity and loneliness, especially personal passion; *wa* expresses plurality and generality. Frellesvig (2010: 138) also points out that *a* is used as an exclusive singular form, excluding second person, while *wa* refers to not only inclusive singular forms but also plural forms, namely, 'I and you'.

Table 2 summarizes the hypotheses of the pronouns *a* and *wa* in Old Japanese.

		a	*wa*	
Same origin	Diachronic	archaic	secondary	Hamada (1946), Yamada (1954), Saeki (1972), Okazaki (1976),
	Synchronic	loneliness	generality	Kikuzawa (1955)
		exclusive singular	inclusive plural	Frellesvig (2010)
Different origins				Vovin (2005)

Table 2: Summary of the differences between *a* and *wa*

Thus far, most previous research has focused on the syntactic differences between *a* and *wa*. Other differences, semantics in particular, are seldom

[1] Vovin (2005: 221) also contends that phonological process does not support Yamada's hypotheses. Suppose that *a* is more archaic than *wa*, it is necessary to postulate a phonological process, ø > w / _a, which is unknown in Old Japanese or even unattested in the history of the Japanese language.

[2] Vovin (2005: 245-247) has discussed the possible origins of *a* and *wa*.

[3] This paper does not include the construction, first person pronoun and accusative case marker, *a-wo* and *wa-wo*, because there are fewer entries for such construction. This issue is left for future research.

discussed. To probe into the semantic difference between the two pronouns, this paper adopts a corpus-based approach to the distribution of the pronouns. The paper is organized as the following. Section 2 introduces the corpus and the data, which focus on nouns after possessive case marker, *-^{n}ka*, *a-^{n}ka* and *wa-^{n}ka* in Old Japanese. Section 3 reports the results in the corpus, and section 4 is concerned with the differences between the nouns after *a-^{n}ka* and *wa-^{n}ka*. Section 5 discusses two issues with regard to the two pronouns, and section 6 concludes this paper.

2 Corpus and Data Selection Criteria

This section introduces the corpus and discusses the data that are analyzed in this paper. As suggested by Vovin (2005: 224), the case markers after the two pronouns are possessive and accusative case markers. To look into a specific construction, this paper explores nouns after possessive case marker, *-^{n}ka*. To account for the differences between *a-^{n}ka* and *wa-^{n}ka*, this paper analyzes poems from seven sources in Old Japanese, as shown in (1).

(1) a. The *Man'yōshū* [Anthology of Myriad Leaves] (万葉集, MYS 759-782 CE),
b. The *Kojiki kayō* [The Songs of the *Kojiki*] (古事記歌謡, KK) from the *Kojiki* [The Records of Ancient Matters] (古事記 712 CE),
c. The *Nihonshoki kayō* [The Songs of the *Nihonshoki*] (日本書紀歌謡, NK) from the *Nihonshoki* [The Annals of Japan] (日本書紀 720 CE),
d. The *Fudoki kayō* [The Songs of *Fudoki*] (風土記歌謡, FK) from the *Fudoki* [Gazetteers] (風土記 713-737 CE),
e. The *Bussoku seki no uta or Bussoku seki ka* [Poems about the stone with footprints of the Buddha] (仏足石歌, BSSK 753 CE),
f. The *Shoku Nihongi kayō* [Poems from the 'Sequence to the Annals of Japan'] (続日本紀歌謡, SNK) from the *Shoku Nihongi* [Sequence to the Annals of Japan] (続日本紀 797 CE),
g. Forms from *Jōgū Shōtoku hōō teisetsu* [A Biography of Prince *Shōtoku*, King of the Law] (上宮聖徳法王帝説, TS).

The poems in the seven sources are scrutinized, and the data in the constructions of *a-^{n}ka* and *wa-^{n}ka* are collected. In the corpus, not every poem is analyzed. In *Man'yōshū* (henceforth MYS), semantograms mix with phonograms in the poems, while poems in the other six sources are exclusively transcribed in phonograms. In the corpus, poems transcribed by semantograms for the first person pronoun, 吾, 我, 余, 己, 朕 and 妾 for example, are excluded, because the semantograms are not of great help determining the real pronunciation.[4]

After data collection, the data are divided into two groups: *a-^{n}ka* and *wa-^{n}ka*. To avoid dialectal variation in MYS, this paper does not discuss Eastern Old Japanese (EOJ) and only focuses on Western Old Japanese (WOJ). In addition, three groups of examples are not analyzed. First, examples with other intervening elements between the pronoun and the possessive case marker are not taken into account. For instance, the corpus excludes tokens like *a-^{n}ka oku-N-tuma* (I-POSS inner-POSS-spouse) 'my most beloved spouse' (MYS XVII: 3978), in which *oku* 'inner' appears between *a-^{n}ka* and the noun, *tuma* 'spouse'. The corpus also excludes examples that derive from nominalization, such as *-aku* in *a-^{n}ka kwopiy-m-aku* (I-POSS long.for-(INF)-TENT-NML) 'my longing' (MYS XV: 3683). Finally, examples without overt possessive case marker *-^{n}ka* like *a-^{n}kwo* 'my beloved' and *a-^{n}kyi* 'my lord' are also excluded. After the corpus data are sorted, the results are reported in section 3.

3 Results

The sorted data are listed in Tables 3 and 4, in which the texts without any example are omitted. For instance, *a-^{n}ka* + noun in Table 3 is only attested in MYS, KK, and NK, and it does not appear in the other three texts, SNK, FK, and BSSK. Table 3 shows nouns that follow *a-^{n}ka*.

	Nouns	Meaning	MYS	KK	NK	Total
1.	miy	'body'	4			4
2.	kwo	'beloved'	2			2
3.	kökörö	'heart'	1		1	2
4.	körömö^{n}te	'sleeve'	1			1
5.	mune	'chest'	1			1
6.	nusi	'master'	1			1
7.	tamey	'sake'	1			1
8.	tökö	'bed'	1			1
9.	se	'male beloved'		1		1
10.	tama	'pearl'			1	1
	Total		12	1	2	15

Table 3: Examples of *a-^{n}ka* + noun

[4] In classical Chinese, 吾, 我 and 余 are first person pronouns. 己 is first person reflexive. 朕 functions not only as first person pronoun but also as a honorific form, often used by the emperor himself. 妾 originally means 'concubine', but it sometimes can be used as a humble form for first person pronoun, especially for women.

Table 3 has ten nouns in three texts, and there are fifteen corpus examples. Twelve examples are attested in MYS and the other three in KK and NK.

Table 4 below lists nouns after *wa-^{n}ka* in six texts. There are twenty two nouns with ninety five examples. Seventy three examples are from MYS, ten from KK and nine from NK. The other three texts have only one example.

	Nouns	Meaning	MYS	KK	NK	SNK	FK	BSSK	Total
1.	se(kwo)	'male beloved'	34		2				36
2.	^{n}k-yimo(kwo) (< ^{n}ka-imo(kwo))	'beloved'	18	1	2		1		22
3.	^{n}k-yipye (< ^{n}ka-ipye)	'house'	4	2	1	1			8
4.	yuwe	'reason'	3						3
5.	pye (< ipye)	'house'	2						2
6.	sönö	'garden'	2						2
7.	inöti	'life'	1		1				2
8.	yö	'world'	1					1	2
9.	kökörö	'heart'		2					2
10.	tatamyi	'rice straw mat'		1	1				2
11.	te	'hand'		1	1				2
12.	tuma	'spouse'		1	1				2
13.	ka^{n}tura	'hair decoration'	1						1
14.	körömö^{n}te	'sleeve'	1						1
15.	mo	'skirt'	1						1
16.	pune	'boat'	1						1
17.	satwo	'village'	1						1
18.	swo^{n}te	'sleeve'	1						1
19.	ta^{n}pyi	'journey'	1						1
20.	ya^{n}two	'dwelling'	1						1
21.	kuni	'land, province'		1					1
22.	na	'name'		1					1
	Total		73	10	9	1	1	1	95

Table 4: Examples of *wa-^{n}ka* + noun

The above two tables are compared in section 4 for the differences between the two pronouns.

4 Differences between nouns after *a-ⁿka* and *wa-ⁿka*

This section discusses the differences between the nouns after *a-^{n}ka* and *wa-^{n}ka*. According to Tables 3 and 4 in section 3, Table 5 below compares *a-^{n}ka* and *wa-^{n}ka* and presents the data by grouping nouns with close meanings. In Table 5 below, there are six groups.

Groups	Nouns	Meaning	*a-^{n}ka*	*wa-^{n}ka*
I.	kwo	'beloved'	2	
	nusi	'master'	1	
	se	'male beloved'	1	36
	imo	'beloved'		22
	tuma	'spouse'		2
II.	miy	'body'	4	
	kökörö	'heart'	2	2
	mune	'chest'	1	
	te	'hand'		2
	inöti	'life'		2
III.	tama	'pearl'	1	
	körömönte	'sleeve'	1	1
	swonte	'sleeve'		1
	mo	'skirt'		1
	kantura	'hair decoration'		1
IV.	tökö	'bed'	1	
	ipye	'house'		10
	tatamyi	'rice straw mat'		2
	sönö	'garden'		2
	yantwo	'dwelling'		1
	satwo	'village'		1
	kuni	'land, province'		1
V.	tamey	'sake'	1	
	yuwe	'reason'		3
	yö	'world'		2
	tanpyi	'journey'		1
	na	'name'		1
VI.	pune	'boat'		1

Table 5: Comparison of *a-^{n}ka* + noun and *wa-^{n}ka* + noun

Group I: This group is concerned with kinship terms, and the key idea is that *wa-^{n}ka* is frequently used to express kinship. Five nouns are attested in this group, *kwo* 'beloved', *nusi* 'master', *se* 'male beloved', *imo* 'beloved' and *tuma* 'spouse'. In this group, the distribution is skewed. The majority goes to *se* 'male beloved' (about 56%, 36/64). *Imo* 'beloved' amounts to 34% of the corpus examples, and the other three nouns to 10%. Overall, 94% (60/64) of the corpus examples follow *wa-^{n}ka*, and only about 6% (4/64) appears after *a-^{n}ka*. This tendency suggests that *a-^{n}ka* and *wa-^{n}ka* are significantly distinct in terms of kinship terms.

Group II: This group is defined as the human body. There are five nouns in this group: *miy* 'body', *kökörö* 'heart', *mune* 'chest', *te* 'hand' and *inöti* 'life'.[5] Despite the fact that *inöti* 'life' does not denote a concrete part of a human body, it is an essential part of human beings, and therefore it is included in this group. With four tokens, *miy* 'body' only appears after *a-^{n}ka*, suggesting that there might be a tendency in Old Japanese for *miy* 'body' to combine with *a-^{n}ka*.[6] On the other hand, *inöti* 'life' only follows *wa-^{n}ka*. This cannot be conclusive because more data are needed to make a significant distinction between *a-^{n}ka* and *wa-^{n}ka* when the following nouns are related to the human body.

Group III: This group is related to clothing or decoration and includes five nouns: *tama* 'pearl', *körömö^{n}te*, 'sleeve', *swo^{n}te* 'sleeve', *mo* 'skirt' and *ka^{n}tura* 'hair decoration'. Although there are five nouns in this group, no conclusion can be drawn from those nouns. This is because there are only six corpus examples for the five nouns. In other words, each noun is only represented by one or two tokens, so there is no reliable conclusion solely based on the six examples.

Group IV: In this group, nouns are related to house or land. This group has seven nouns, *tökö* 'bed', *ipye* 'house', *tatamyi* 'rice straw mat', *sönö* 'garden', *ya^{n}two* 'dwelling', *satwo* 'village' and *kuni* 'land, province'. This group exhibits an interesting distribution. Most of the corpus examples (94%, 17/18) follow *wa-^{n}ka* instead of *a-^{n}ka.* The only noun after *a-^{n}ka* is *tökö* 'bed'. The skewed distribution indicates that *a-^{n}ka* and *wa-^{n}ka* are distinct in terms of the nouns related to house or land.

Group V: This group contains five abstract nouns, and each noun is only attested once in the corpus. The five nouns are *tamey* 'sake', *yuwe* 'reason', *yö* 'world', *ta^{n}pyi* 'journey', and *na* 'name'.[7] There is an interesting

---

[5] *Inöti* 'life' is further analyzed as *i-nö-ti* gall.baladder-genitive-strength, originally meaning the strength of gall bladder.

[6] *A-^{n}ka miy* behaves differently in Middle Japanese. The more prevalent form is *wa-^{n}ka mii*. This distribution confirms Vovin's (2005: preface) proposal that Western Old Japanese and Middle Japanese are different dialects.

[7] *Tamey* and *yuwe* in Old Japanese originally mean 'reason', 'cause' or 'sake' (Vovin 2005: 515), but they usually appear in the construction, *tamey-ni* or *yuwe-ni*, meaning 'for/because of'.

distribution in this group that the five abstract nouns tend to appear after *wa-^{n}ka*. Recall that *inöti* 'life', another abstract noun in group II, also occurs after *wa-^{n}ka*. Thus, probably *wa-^{n}ka* prefers to be associated with abstract nouns.

Group VI: This group includes only one noun, *pune* 'boat', that is difficult to be properly grouped with the previous five groups. In this group, no specific conclusion can be drawn from this single example.

5 Discussion

According to the differences in the nouns between *a-^{n}ka* and *wa-^{n}ka*, it can be temporarily concluded that *a-^{n}ka* and *wa-^{n}ka* in Old Japanese are semantically distinct, but the distinction between *a-^{n}ka* and *wa-^{n}ka* is not always clear-cut, due to the fact that they are interchangeable in many situations. The traditional view concerning the distinction between *a* and *wa* is that *a* is singular and it shows the speaker's loneliness, and *wa* is plural and denotes generality, as suggested by Kikuzawa (1955: 49). However, Kikuzawa's assumption should be re-evaluated. According to the corpus data, there is no clear distinction between singular and plural nouns. Probably the best way to prove that *a* is singular and *wa* is plural is by means of quantity classifier for persons, such as *pyitöri* 'one person' and *putari* 'two people'. In Old Japanese, quantity classifiers for persons in *a-^{n}ka* and *wa-^{n}ka* appear twenty times. *Putari* 'two people' appear twelve times in MYS, one time in KK and one time in NS. *Pyitöri* 'one person' is attested six times in MYS. Among the twenty tokens, only two examples are transcribed phonetically (KK: 20 and NS: 58), and they are in *wa-^{n}ka putari* or *putari wa-^{n}ka*.[8] However, no example like **a-^{n}ka pyitöri* or **pyitöri a-^{n}ka* is found. Thus, there is no quick conclusion that *a-^{n}ka* and *wa-^{n}ka* are distinct in singular and plural nouns.

This paper postulates that collective nouns like kinship nouns and house and land nouns appear after *wa-^{n}ka* because the two groups of nouns are correlated to a group of people or things. The kinship terms after *wa-^{n}ka* are often associated with family members. On the other hand, nouns related to house and land are, such as *ipye* 'house', *sönö* 'garden', *ya^{n}two* 'dwelling', are personal belongings. The results in section 3 also suggest that abstract nouns are associated with *wa-^{n}ka*. Hence, as discussed above, *wa* entails plurality when collective nouns come after *wa-^{n}ka*. This paper treats *wa* as a pronoun, which is traditionally regarded as a general first person pronoun, with more objectivity, in contrast with *a* which is more subjective.

---

[8] The number of poems in KK and NS is based on Takano (1928).

6 Conclusion

Focusing on the unique behavior of possessive marker *a-^{n}ka* and *wa-^{n}ka* in Old Japanese from the semantic selection of the nouns, this paper has adopted a corpus-based approach to the differences between a and *wa* when they are followed by possessive case marker *-^{n}ka*. The results reveal that *a-^{n}ka* and *wa-^{n}ka* are interchangeable in usage, but some distinctions are still made. The corpus data suggest that *a-^{n}ka* and *wa-^{n}ka* are significantly distinct in kinship terms, and nouns related to house or land. The two groups of nouns prefer *wa-^{n}ka* in Old Japanese.

This paper has discussed the possessive case marker *-^{n}ka* in Old Japanese. Accusative case marker *-wo* which also appears after *a* and *wa*, however, is not yet explored. In addition to semantic selection, phonology is another issue that can reveal the difference between *a* and *wa*. For example, Russell (2003) and Vovin (2005) have discussed vowel contraction in Old Japanese, but it demands more investigation to discuss the phonological process in *wa-^{n}k-yimo* 'my beloved'.

References

Frellesvig, B. 2010. *A History of the Japanese Language*. Cambridge: Cambridge University Press.

Hamada, A. 1933. *Kodai Nihongo* [Old Japanese]. Kyoto: Oyashima.

Kikuzawa, S. 1955. Man'yōjidai no Taimeishō [Pronouns in Man'yō Period], in *Man'yōshū Taisei 6 Gengohen* [Studies of Man'yōshū 6: Linguistics], 49-66. Tokyo: Heibonsha.

Okazaki, K. 1976. Jōdai no Itininshō Daimeishi, A-Wa-Are-Wara Hēson no Mondai [First person pronoun in Old Japanese, The problem of doublet a-wa-are-ware], in *Saeki Umetomo Hakase Kijū Kinen Kokugogaku Ronshū* [The Collection of Essays in Honor of Dr. Saeki Umetomo's birthday], 273-302. Tokyo: Hyogensha.

Saeki, U. 1972. *Narajidai no Kokugo* [Japanese in Nara Period]. Tokyo: Sanseitou.

Takano, T. 1928. *Nihon Kayo Shusei* Vol. 1 [A Collection of Japanese Poems Vol.1]. Tokyo: Shunjusha.

Vovin, A. 2005. *A Descriptive and Comparative Grammar of Western Old Japanese*. Vol. 1: *Sources, Script and Phonology, Lexicon, Nominals*. Folkstone, England: Global Oriental.

Yamada, Y. 1954. *Narachō Bunpōshi* [A History of the Nara Period Grammar]. Tokyo: Hōbunkan.

Diachronic Shifts of Korean *Pyello* and Japanese *Amari* from PPI to NPI

YONG-TAEK KIM,

Goergia Institute of Technology,

RUMIKO SHINZATO,

Georgia Institute of Techonology,

SEON-YEOP HWANG

Seoul National University

1 Introduction

This is a corpus-based diachronic analysis of the degree adverbs of Korean *pyello* and Japanese *amari*. The purposes of this study are 1) to delineate the diachronic development of *pyello* and *amari* from positive polarity item (PPI) to negative polarity item (NPI), and 2) to offer an explanatory account as to their polarity shifts, incorporating two concepts: counter-expectation and structural reanalysis of scope.*

The organization of this chapter is as follows. Section 2 explains the corpora used in this study. In section 3, we will show the definition of the PPI and NPI and polarity shifts from PPI to NPI in Korean *pyello* and Japanese *amari*. Sections 4 lays out historical developments of the two adverbs in more detail with explanatory accounts. Section 5 concludes this paper.

---

* We are indebted to the audiences at the 27th Japanese/Korean Linguistics Conference for valuable comments and criticisms. Any mistakes are our responsibility.

Japanese/Korean Linguistics 27.
Edited by Michael Barrie.

2 Corpora

The Korean diachronic corpora used in this study (17th century to 20th century) were processed using a Korean concordance program, "Uniconc."[1] It is mainly from Sejong Historical Corpus, which comprises 15-million word, historical section of the Sejong Corpus, a 200-million word corpus developed as part of the 21st century Sejong Project by the Korean Ministry of Culture and Tourism and the National Institute of Korean Language (1998-2006). The contemporary Korean corpora (21st century) is from Sejong Corpus.

The Japanese corpora (9th century to 20th century) are based on NINJAL's (National Institute for Japanese Language and Linguistics) corpora: The Corpus of Historical Japanese (CHJ) and Balanced Corpus of Contemporary Written Japanese (BCCWJ). For the periods up to Meiji and Taishō, the former corpus is used, while for the periods for Shōwa and Heise, the literary genre of the latter was used. This restricted selection from BCCWJ stems from the attempt to keep the sources homogeneous with the CHJ, whose major genre is literature.

3 Polarity shift from PPI to NPI in *Pyello* & *Amari*

PPI is defined as expressions that cannot felicitously appear in negative contexts, and NPI, as expressions that can only appear felicitously in negative contexts (Wouden 1997: 61).

The primary meaing of Korean *pyello* and Japanese *amari* is '(not) very, (not) much' as NPI in present-day Korean and Japanese as below:

(1K[2])	*na*	*koki*	***pyello***	***an**-mek-e*.
	I	meat	so.much	**NEG**-eat-DECL[3]
(1J)	*watashi*	*niku*	***amari***	*tabe-**nai***.
	I	meat	too.much	eat- **NEG**
	'I do **not** eat meat **much**.'			

However, the original meanings of *pyello* 'especially, distinctly' and *amari* 'excessively, extremely' as PPIs were prevalent through mid-19th century in Korean and 20th century in Japanese (Kawase 2008) as shown below:

[1] UNICONC database was compiled by Professor Jinho Park at Seoul National University.

[2] K and J indicate Korean and Japanese respectively. The transliteration system of each language adopted in this study is an extended Yale system developed by Seongha Rhee (1996) for Korean, and Hepburn system for Japanese.

[3] Abbreviations used in the glass: ACC=accusative AND adnominal CAU=causative COMP=complementizer CONN =connective COP=copula DECL=declarative GEN=genetive HON=honorific NMZL-nominalizer NEG= negative NOM=nominative PST=past Q=question TENT=tentative TOP=topic

(2K) (*YakdAy*) *dAykali-nun* ***pyelno*** *cyek-e* *syang-ul*
(camel) head-TOP **distinctly** small-and face-ACC
po-myen *malsang-i-la.*
see-if horse.face-be-DECL
'(The camel's) head is **distinctly** small, and its face is like a horse.' (*Aakpukacip*, 20th C)

(2J) ***Amari*** *majime* *sugiru* *ningen* *no* *koto wa* *warau.*
extremely serious too people GEN thing TOP laugh
'(He) laughs at the (things belonging to) people who are too **extremely** serious.' (BCCWJ[4], 1990's)

As PPI, *pyello* expresses 'particularly, separately, especially, distinctly' and *amari* denotes 'excessively, extremely.' A shared feature of *distinction* as in the sense of an *outstanding degree, which exceeds the general norm* is used to stress that excessive degree, as in the sense of 'distinctly,' or 'extremely.'

4 Parallel historical changes from PPI to NPI in Korean and Japanese

Through the corpus-based analyses, this paper points out that 1) there is a parallel development between the two-degree adverbs Korean *pyello* and Japanese *amari*, 2) grammaticalization paths of both Korean *pyello* & Japanese *amari* go from PPI to NPI, and 3) similar factors motivated the changes for both paths: counter-expectation and syntactic reanalysis.

4.1 Historical changes from PPI to NPI of Koran *pyello*

4.1.1 Korean *pyello* as PPI through time

Here are some selected examples of *pyello* as PPI from 17th century to 20th century.

(3) *Wuli* ***pyello*** *sal* *hwamwul-ul* *uynonho-toy* *esteha-nyo?*
we particularly buy thing-ACC discuss-CONN how-Q
'How about discussing things to buy **particularly/separately**?' *(Nokeltayenhay,* 1670)

(4) ***Pyelno*** *hAn syunul* *te* *mek-i-ki-lul* *hehA-yasi-ni*
especially one time more eat- CAU-NMZL-ACC allow-PST-CONN
'Since (King Jeongjo) **especially** allowed to eat one more time…' (*Yuhonamyunum*, 1783)

---

4 Balanced Corpus of Contemporary Written Japanese

(5) *Nitochel-un* *ku chyunguy-lul* *phyochyangha-ya*
Lee.Docheol-TOP that loyalty-ACC recognize-CONN
pyelno *pyesol-ul* *cwu-si-lsoy*
especially government.post-ACC give-HON-CONN
'Since Lee Docheol was **specially** given a government post in recognition of his loyalty,...'
(*The Independent,* 1896)

(6) *Ku-nun* *na-myense-pwuthe* *wenkuy-ka*
he-TOP be.born-CONN-from energy-NOM
wangsengha-n *nal-i* ***pyello*** *cek-es-ta.*
high-AND day-NOM distinctively few-PST-DECL
'He has had **very** few energetic days since his birth.'
(*Sayngyuksincen*, 1935)

Pyello most of the time expresses the meanings of 'particularly, separately, especially,' that is the distinction as in the sense of an ***outstanding degree which exceeds the general norm.***

4.1.2 Korean *pyello* as NPI through time

We move onto the NPI usages, as shown below. Negatives are highlighted in bold. Together with negatives, *pyello* here expresses 'not (so) much.'

(7) *Kuykol-i* ***pyelno*** *mwusyew-e* *poy-nun*
appearance-ACC distinctively scary-CONN look-ADN
toy ***ep****.kenal.*
place not.exist-CONN
'Since it is **not** the case that his appearance look **very** scary...'
(Seyuki, 16th C)

(8) *Hwapho* *pilok* *mac-ato*
artillery even.if be.attacked-CONN
pyelno *mwunhecici* ***anih****A-ni.*
distinctively/not.much collapse-CONN NEG-CONN
'Since it is not the case that (the castle) collapsed distinctively/Since (the castle) did **not** collapse **much** despite the enemy's artillery attack' (*Coyachemcay*, 19th C)

(9)

Hakep-un	***pyelno***	*himssu-ci*	***ani**hA-mye.*
studies-TOP	not.much	put.effort-CONN	NEG-CONN

'(The country) does **not** put **much** effort into its studies.' (*Saminphilci*, 1889)

(10)

Ku-paskey-nun	***pyello***	***ep**-sumni-ta.*
that-except.for-TOP	not.much	not.exist-HON-DECL

'There is **not much** else.' (*Sinhakwelpo*, 1907)

4.2 Historical changes from PPI to NPI of Japanese *amari*

4.2.1 Japanese *amari* as PPI through time

Here are some selected examples of *amari* as PPI from 9th century to 20th century.

Heian (9th C ~ 11th C)

(11)

Ito,	***amari***	*fukaku,*	*hito*	*nikukarikeru*	*koto…*
extremely	extremely	strong-minded	person	loathsome	NMZL

'(her) being **extremely** strong-minded, and not lovable…' (*Genji Monogatari, Agemaki,* 1010)

Kamakura (12th C ~ 14th C)

(12)

Amari	*kitanaki*	*nari.*
extremly	dirty	COP

'It is **extremely** dirty.' (*Uji Shuui Monogatari*, 1220)

These are data from Muromachi and Edo.

Muromachi (14th C ~ 17th C)

(13)

Iya	*sore*	*wa*	***amari***	*oogozaru.*
no	that	TOP	extremly	lot

'No, that is **too** much.' (*Toraakira-bon Kyoogen, Hanatorisumoo,* 1642)

Edo (17th C ~ mid 19th C)

(14)

Anmari	*o-samukar-oo*	*to*	*omotte (Fukagawa Shinwa)*
extremely	HON-cold-TENT	COMP	thinking

'Thinking it would be **too** cold…' *(Fukagawa Shinwa,* 1779*)*

Meiji/Taisho (1868~1925)

(15) ***Amari*** *taikutsu itashimashi-ta kara, tada kenbutsu ni…*
extremely bored do-PST since just sightseeing in.order.to
'Since I was too bored [I came out] to do sightseeing, …' (*Tookyoo-byo,* 1901)

Showa (1925~1989 with focus on the 1970's)

(16) ***Anmari*** *sunaona node*
extremely obedient so
'She is **too** obedient, so…' *(Shiki Natsuko,* 1979*)*

Heisei (1989 ~2019, with focus on the 1990's)

(17) *Kojin byooin de wa* ***amari*** *takai kusuri o ataeru to…*
private hospital at TOP extremely expensive drug ACC give COMP
'At a private hospital, if you give **extremely** expensive drugs, (it may get taken away at the insurance audit).' (*Dokutoru Manboo Ikyokuki*, 1993)

Japanese *amari* started as PPI, expressing the meanings of 'extremely' and 'too much.' Noteworthy is the fact that *amari* noticeably cooccurs with another adverb of extremity, *ito*. (10%)

4.2.2 Japanese *amari* as NPI through time

Now we move onto NPI examples. As noted in Hirosaka (1996: 59), there are no clear, uncontroversial examples of NPI through Heian. In our investigation of the next period, Kamakura, there appeared no clear examples of NPI. Thus, we started showing NPI examples from the Muromachi period.

Muromachi (14th C ~ 17th C)

(18) *Iroiro uso o tsuite-mooshita tokorode,*
various lies ACC tell even.though
amari *hara-mo-otachyara* ***nu****.*
so.much get.mad NEG
'Even though I told various lies, he did **not** get mad **so much**.'[5] (*Toraakira-bon kyoogen, Buaku,* 1642)

---

[5] It seems that this period is still transitional from PPI to NPI, with very few examples showing the co-occurrence of *amari* with a negative. According to Kawase (2008), this particular example could be interpreted as the negation of *amari* as PPI.

Edo (17th C ~ mid 19th C)

(19) ***Amari*** *urami* *mo* *iimase* ***nu***.
so.much complaint even say NEG
'She does **not** even complain ***so much***.' (*Shimabara Yasamonogatari,* 1764)

Meiji/Taisho (1868~1925)

(20) …***amari*** *yuujin* *to* *iu* *mono* *mo* *tazunete* *ko*-***na***-*katta*.
so.much friend COMP call people even visit come-NEG-PST
'(For that reason,) people called friends did **not** come visit him **much**.' (*Naze Haha o Yobu*, 1917)

Showa (1925~1989 with focus on the 1970's)

(21) *Boo.on* *o* *hairyo-shita* *mono* *rashii* *ga,*
soundproog ACC consider-PST thing hear but
amari *kooka* *wa* ***na***-*sa* *sooda*.
so.much effect TOP NEG look.like
'I heard that this was meant to be soundproof, but it looks like it is **not so** effective.' (*Mikkai,* 1977)

Heisei (1989 ~2019, with focus on the 1990's)

(22) …*iiwake* *wa* *tabun* ***amari*** *shi*-***nai*** *to* *omou*.
excue TOP probably not.much make- NEG COMP think
'(Although he brags about himself with insignificant things, but) I think he probably does **not** make excuses **so much**' (*Supootoniku no Koibito,* 1999)

As NPI, together with negatives, *amari* expresses the meaning of 'not so much.'

4.3 An explanatory account

This section aims to provide an explanatory account of the diachronic developments delineated above. To this end, two notions from the grammaticalization framework are considered as possible factors, namely "counter-expectation" and "syntactic reanalysis."

4.3.1 Counter-expectation factor as a trigger

A counter-expectation refers to the speaker's point of view in opposition to normative viewpoints held by the general public (Traugott and Dasher 2002). It has been noted that the rhetoric of counter-expectation plays a role in grammaticalization especially in the case of adverbs. For instance, (23a) is an example of *in fact* as a verbal adverb where "fact" is in contrast with "feeling," while in (23b) the same adverb functions as a sentence adverb and implicates the sense of counter-expectation.

(23) a. *Humanity, comfortably engaged elsewhere in the business of living, is absent* ***in fact****, but everywhere in feeling.*
(United Airlines Magazine, May 1997, cited in Traugott 1999: 182)

b. *It's almost as if he were avoiding the evening's moment of truth. The moment is,* ***in fact****, about 45 minutes, the main body of the play, during which Mr.Quinton…holds the stage and acts up a primeval cataclysm all by himself.*
(New York Times, July 29, 1996, review of Phaedra, cited in Traugott 1999: 183)

In the current case, the counter-expectation factor seems to have worked in the bridging context from PPI *pyello* and *amari* to NPI *pyello* and *amari*. We believe that bridge contexts played an important role where *pyello* is ambiguous between PPI and NPI interpretations. Here's an example. As PPI, (24) can be understood as (24a), whereas as NPI, as (24b). Due to high frequency, *pyello*+ negative came to be established as a collocational unit, or prefab, the meaning of *pyello* as in the sense of 'distinctly' has bleached out and it has a new meaning of 'so much' as NPI in a negative sentence.

(24) *Syangso* *mal-ul* *syangkohA-mye* *syangkothi-ani-m-i*
appeal words- ACC review-and review-NEG- NOMZ- NOM
pyello *kwankin-thi* ***ani****hA-ni*
distinctly/so.much important- **NEG**-since
[*Coyakimwun*, 19th C (collection of *The Academy of Korean Studies*)]

(24a) **PPI:** 'As for the words of appeal, since it is **not** the case that it is **distinctly** important to review it' (**counter to general expectation**)

(24b) **NPI:** 'As for the words of appeal, since it is **not so** important to review it, (so don't worry…).' (**on a scale of importance**)

Similarly, we believe that bridge contexts played a crucial role in which *amari* is ambiguous between PPI and NPI interpretations. Hirosaka (1996: 49) offers Example (25), which may serve as a bridging context from PPI to NPI. She states that Example (25) inherently has two interpretations. One meaning is 'Cakes are usually *very* sweet but counter to that/my expectation, it is *not* the case that the cakes at this store are *extremely* sweet,' thus, it is the negation of the generally approved expectation. The same sentence can also mean, 'the degree of sweetness is not high.' The former is close to a PPI reading, while the latter is an NPI interpretation (Shinzato 2018: 68).

(25) *Kono mise no keeki wa* ***amari*** *amaku-**nai**.*
this bakery GEN cake TOP **extremely/so.much** sweet-**NEG**
(Hirosaka 1996: 49 with our glosses)

(25a) **PPI:** 'It is **not** the case that cakes at this bakery are **extremely** sweet (**counter to general/my expectation**).' Or 'Cakes at this bakery are not extremely sweet (**against general expectation/counter to my expectation**)

(25b) **NPI:** 'Cakes at this bakery are not so sweet (**on a scale of sweetness**).'

In addition, Example (18) in 4.2.2 could allow the PPI reading with the shade of counter expectation:

(18a) PPI: 'Since I told various lies it is expected he will get **extremely** mad, but (counter to my expectation), that was not the case.'

It is generally said that high degree words cannot be negated as in **unmuch* or **unmany* (Hoekstra 2011: 35). When counter-expectation comes into play, high degree words could become negated as in the sense of *not **too** distinct, not **too** extreme,* contrary to one's expectation. When the counter-expectation fades out, what is left is a simple negation of the degree as *so much*.

4.3.2 Syntactic reanalysis of scope

The bridge context facilitated the following syntactic reanalysis of *pyello*, as shown in (26):

(26) [[***pyello*** *kwankinhA*]S-*ci* ***ani****hA*] (**PPI**)
↓
[[***pyello*** *kwankinhA*]S-*ci* ***ani****hA*] (**PPI**)/
[[***pyello***] *kwankin* [-*thi* ***ani****hA*]]$_S$ (**NPI**)
↓
[[***pyello***] *kwankin* [-*thi* ***ani****hA*]]$_S$ (**NPI**)

In the first stage, *pyello* has scope over a positive predicate. The intermediate stage is transitional allowing both PPI-like and NPI-like interpretations. In NPI-like reading, *pyello* is modifying the negative *ani*. In the last stage, *pyello* is in agreement within the same sentence and thus categorized as NPI.

Likewise, the bridge context facilitated the following syntactic reanalysis of *amari*:

(27) [[***amari****(ni) amaku*]$_S$-***nai***]] (**PPI**)

↓

[[***amari****(ni) amaku*]$_S$-***nai***]] (**PPI**)/[[***amari***] *amaku*-[***nai***]]$_S$ (**NPI**)

↓

[[***amari***] *amaku*-[***nai***]]$_S$ (**NPI**)

In the first stage, ***amari*** has scope over a positive predicate. The intermediate stage is transitional allowing both **PPI**-like and **NPI**-like interpretations. In the last stage, ***amari*** agrees within the same sentence and thus categorized as NPI.

4.4 Summarizing the two grammaticalization paths

Putting Korean and Japanese data together, the following reanalysis can be formulated:

It is NOT the case that the distinct/extreme feature exists (**PPI**)

↓

NOT the distinct/extreme feature exists (**PPI**)/

NOT TOO MUCH distinct/extreme feature exists (**NPI**)

↓

The selected feature does NOT exist SO MUCH (**NPI**)

4.5 Historical quantitative analysis of *pyello* and *amari*: From PPI to NPI

Historical change of *pyello* from PPI to NPI between 17th century and early 21st century is shown in Table 1:

	PPI	NPI
17C	100.0	0.0
18C	100.0	0.0
~mid 19C	75.8	24.2
1889-1899	73.5	26.5
early 20C	32.0	**68.0**
early 21C	0.0	100.0

Table 1: Changes of the *pyello* usage through time

The graphic representation of polarity shift of *pyello* is illustrated in Figure 1:

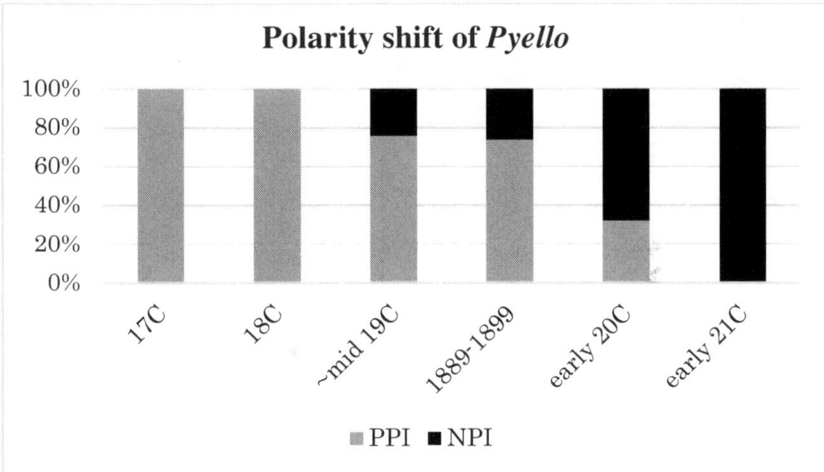

Figure 1 Polarity shift of *pyello*

The dominance of NPI over PPI occurred around the early 20th century. *Pyello* as PPI ceased to be used in present-day South Korean.[6]

Historical change of *amari* from PPI to NPI between the 8th century and early 21st century is shown in Table 2:

	PPI (%)	NPI (%)
Heian (794-1192)	100.0	0.0
Kamakura (1192-1336)	100.0	0.0
Muromachi (1336-1573)	75.8	24.2
Edo (1603-1868)	73.5	26.5
Meiji/Taisho (1868-1926)	32.0	**68.0**
Showa 1970	16.4	83.6
Heisei1990	12.4	87.6

Table 2 Changes of *amari* through time

[6] Interestingly, pyello as PPI is still used in present-day North Korean.

The graphic representation of polarity shift of *amari* is illustrated in Figure 2:

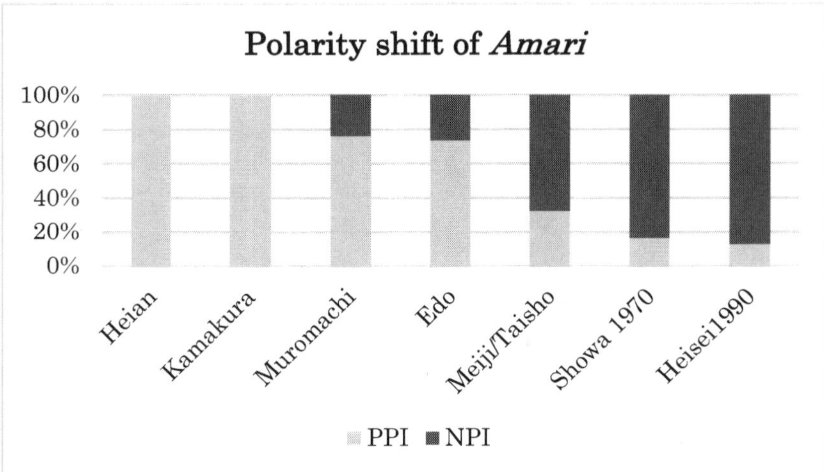

Figure 2. Polarity shift of *amari*

It is apparent the dominance of NPI over PPI occurred around the Meiji/Taisho period.

5. Conclusion

This study traced the developmental paths of the two degree adverbs, Korean *pyello* and Japanese *amari* and noted their parallel development from PPI to NPI. It also pointed out that two factors, "counter-expectation" and "syntactic reanalysis" are equally operative in both languages to motivate such a change. Polarity studies have mainly focused on synchronic semantic studies and have seldom been discussed in diachronic contexts. It is hoped that this study will fill in such a gap.

References

Hirosaka, Naoko. 1996. "'*Amari*' ni tsuite no ichi koosatsu [A thought concerning '*amari*']." *Nihongo, Nihon Bungaku* 8: 48–66.

Hoekstra, Eric. 2011. Negative polarity in morphology: The case of Frisian FOLLE 'much many' as compared to Dutch VEEL. *Linguistics in the Netherlands*: 25–38.

Horn, Laurence. 1989. *A History of Negation*. Chicago: University of Chicago Press.

Kawase, Tadasu. 2008. "Jaku-hitei to kado o arawasu fukushi no shi-teki koosatsu." Paper presented at the 9th Nihongo Bunpoo Gakkai.

Rhee, Seongha, 1996. *Semantic of Verbs and Grammaticalization: The Development in Korean from a Cross-Linguistic Perspective*. Hankuk publisher, Seoul.

Shinzato, Rumiko. 2018. Amari/anmari/anma and totemo/tottemo in history and discourse, in Mutsuko Edo Hudson, Yoshiko Matsumoto, and Junko Mori (eds.), *Pragmatics of Japanese: Perspectives on Grammar, Interaction, and Culture*, 49-73. Amsterdam: John Benjamins.

van der Wouden, Ton. 1997. *Negative Contexts: Collocation, Polarity and Multiple Negation*. London & New York: Routledge.

Part III

Acquisition

Three Modes of Applying Phonemic Merge and Acquisition of Syllable Types*

KEI FURUKAWA

The University of Tokyo

1 Introduction

The paper proposes a mechanism for creating hierarchical structures within a syllable and elucidates how the basic order of acquisition of syllable types is determined by such a mechanism. Simultaneously, parallelism is retained with the process by which human infants acquire hierarchical structures, such as combining cups. In the past decades, acquisition of syllable types in the first language has been widely studied. Descriptive studies found that acquisition of syllables starts from CV followed by CVC and, finally, syllables that contain consonant clusters, such as CCV/CVCC (Levelt et al., 2000; Demuth & Fee, 1995). Children create isolated CV and CVC words at approximately one year of age, whereas CCV/VCC words are acquired by approximately 2 years old (McLeod, Doorn, & Reed, 2001). In several languages without consonant clusters, such as Japanese and Korean, CV is acquired before CVC (Kim et al., 2016; Tsuji et al., 2014).

* I would like to thank the audience at JK 27 for the helpful comments and suggestions. This work is supported by Grant-in-Aid for JSPS Fellows (19J14493).

Japanese/Korean Linguistics 27.
Edited by Michael Barrie.

In theoretical studies, such as those within the framework of Optimality Theory (Prince & Smolensky, 1993), the acquisition of syllable types is explained by changing the ranking of faithfulness and markedness constraints, such as ONSET, NO-CODA, and *COMPLEX (Levelt & Vijver, 2004). This explanation by the ranking of constraints is useful when describing phonological patterns. However, it cannot explain the mechanism of the occurrence of hierarchical structures in a syllable. Thus, an explanation should be provided regarding how hierarchical structures are created and how the acquisition order of the hierarchical structures is determined.

Regarding the process by which human infants acquire hierarchical structures, Greenfield (1991) proposed a distinction between three strategies of object combination (Figure 1).

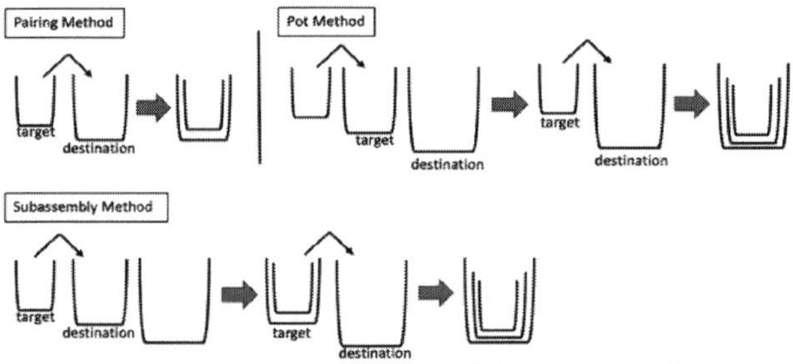

Figure 1. Pairing, Pot, and Subassembly Methods (Adapted from Greenfield, 1991).

In the development of strategies for combining objects, Greenfield (1991) reported that the pairing method preceded the pot method, which preceded the subassembly method. The pot method posits that a simple object is targeted and combined with other objects. By contrast, a previously formed subunit is targeted and combined with a new object in the subassembly method, which was unobserved in nonhuman primates (Conway & Christiansen, 2001). Notably, Greenfield pointed out the analogy between the developmental stages in the hierarchical organization of combining objects and phoneme combination in a syllable. Moreover, Fujita (2017) defined three modes of applying Merge on syntax based on the three strategies of Greenfield (Figure 2).

Building on Fujita (2017), Tanaka (2017) proposed three modes of applying Merges and described syllable typology by referring to three subtypes of Merge. However, the three subtypes of Merge in Tanaka (2017) is incompatible with those of Fujita (2017) because the merge in Tanaka (2017) has the problem that segments can be merged to a place that is not a node (Figure 3).

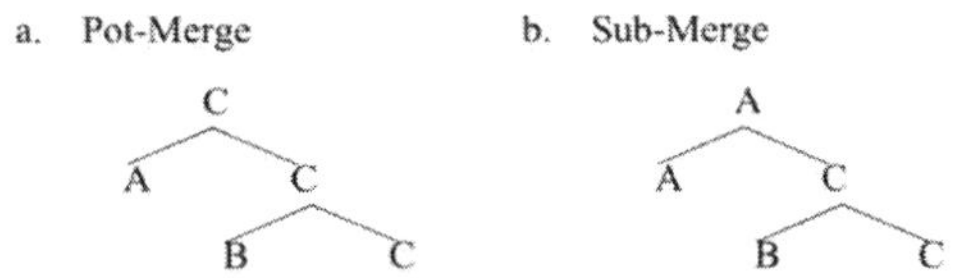

Figure 2. Pot-merge and Sub-merge (Fujita, 2017)

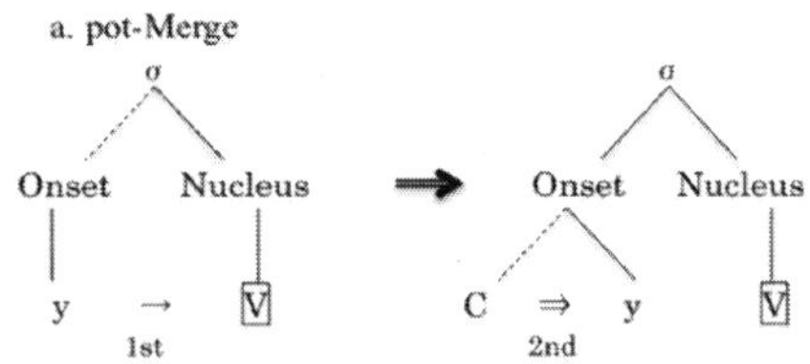

Figure 3. pot-Merge (Tanaka, 2017)

If Pot-Merge as defined in Fujita (2017) is applied to the already merged y and V, then the allowable pattern is (a) or (b), as shown in Figure 4. Both differ from the structure in Tanaka (2017).

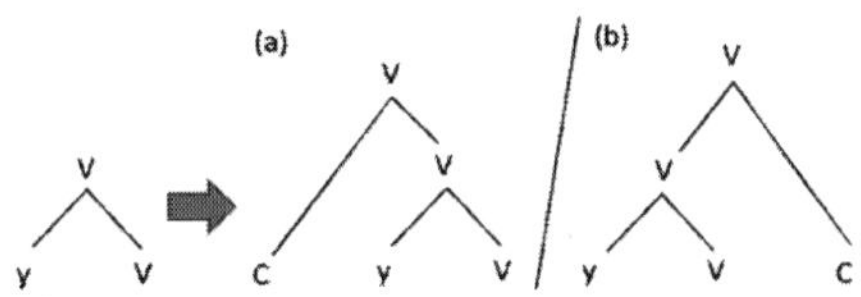

Figure 4. Pot-Merged Structure Predicted from Fujita (2017)

2 Definition of Phonemic Merge

To explain the acquisition of syllable types without the aforementioned problem, the present study proposes three modes of applying Phonemic Merge that apply three means of applying Merge corresponding to those of Greenfield (1991) and Fujita (2017). Unlike syntactic Merge in Fujita (2017), the proposed Phonemic Merge is characterized by (a) asymmetricality and (b) sonority-headedness.

2.1 Asymmetricality

The first property of Phonemic Merge is asymmetricality, which indicates that one of two merged objects is the target of an operation, whereas the other is the destination of the operation (i.e., head). In other words, the output of the Phonemic Merge of α and β is not merely a set formation, such as $\{\alpha, \beta\}$, but a functionalized pair, such as $\beta(\alpha)$.

Notably, asymmetricality differs from having linear order. Asymmetricality mentioned here does not contain any information on linear ordering, such as head-initial or head-final. Therefore, if one of the objects is the destination of the operation and the other is the target of an operation of Phonemic Merge, then the head-initial and head-final are acceptable with regard to asymmetricality.

For example, Figure 5(a) indicates that the target of the operation is A and B because the operation is symmetric. However, this scenario does not meet the requirement of asymmetricality because one of the two elements should be the destination (head). Conversely, Figure 5(b) and (c) show that one component is the target of an operation and the other is the destination, thus satisfying the asymmetricality requirement. The difference between (b) and (c) points to linear order, and they are equal in terms of asymmetricality.

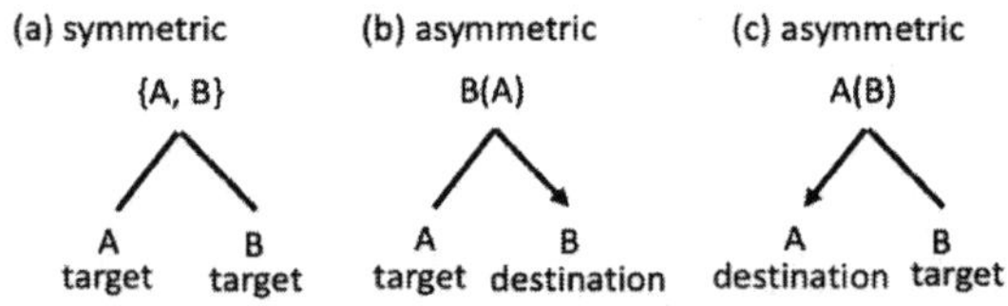

Figure 5. Examples of symmetric and asymmetric relationship. The destination of an arrow represents the head.

Asymmetricality in Phonemic Merge is assumed for two reasons. First, the pot and subassembly methods cannot be distinguished without assuming asymmetricality in terms the target of the operation. Second, it emphasizes parallelism between the development of three strategies for combining objects, such as combining cups, and for combining phonemes.

If Phonemic Merge is a symmetric operation, then both elements to be merged are targets of the operation. In this sense, the target must be the output of the previous operation not only in the subassembly method but also in the pot method. However, the pot method should be distinguished from the subassembly method because the latter, which pertains to the ability to make the product of one operation the target of another operation, is unique to human beings (Conway & Christiansen, 2001). Therefore, to distinguish the pot method from the subassembly method in terms of the target of an operation, asymmetricality should be assumed in Phonemic Merge.

Agreeably, as mentioned in Fujita (2017), one can also assume that the operation is symmetric during merging and becomes asymmetric during labeling. However, when a child combines objects, such as cups, one of the two objects is the target and the other is the destination. Assuming that Phonemic Merge is asymmetric, then the parallelism between combining the cups and combining phonemes can be retained. For these reasons, asymmetricality was assumed as characteristic of Phonemic Merge.

2.2 Sonority-headedness

The second property assumed for Phonemic Merge is sonority-headedness, which denotes that the target of the Phonemic Merge must have lower sonority than the destination. In other words, the head of two merged objects must have higher sonority. If one of the two merged components is a previously merged node as in $\beta(\alpha)$, then sonority-headedness refers to the sonority of the head of a combined pair (i.e., β in $\beta(\alpha)$).

For example, when combining two phonemes of /t/ and /a/ with Phonemic Merge, putting /t/ into /a/ is allowed because /a/ is higher in sonority than /t/, as shown in in Figure 6(a). In contrast, putting /a/ into /t/ is impossible because doing so violates the requirement of sonority-headedness, as shown in Figure 6(b). Figure 6(a), which is head-final, and (b), which is head-initial, satisfy the requirement of sonority-headedness because this characteristic is independent of linear order. Conversely, the destination of the Phonemic Merge between Figure 6(c) and (d) has lower sonority than the target and thus leads to a violation in sonority-headedness.

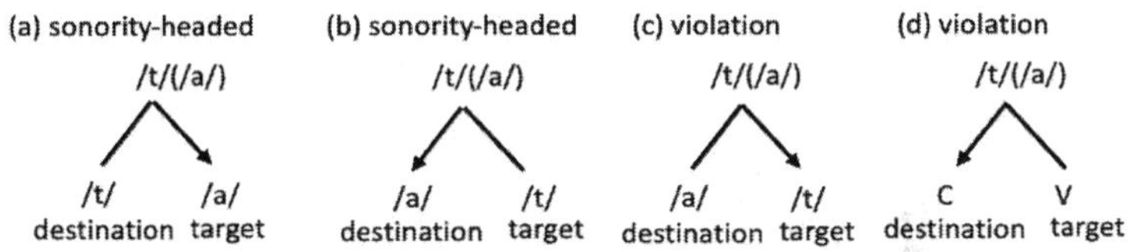

Figure 6. Examples of satisfaction or violation of sonority-headedness. The destination of an arrow represents the head.

Sonority-headedness as a property of Phonemic Merge is assumed for two reasons. The first is to satisfy the requirement of the sonority-sequencing principle. That is, the nuclei of a syllable constitute a peak of sonority, and sonority value decreases gradually toward both ends of the syllable. By assuming that the element with a higher sonority has the property of becoming the head, the candidates in which the element with lower sonority becomes the head, as shown in Figure 6(c) and (d), can be excluded.

Second, by assuming sonority-headedness, confirming the similarity between the constraint applied on combining cups and that applied on combining phonemes is possible. In terms of combining cups, if the operation entails putting one cup into the other, then the target of the operation should be smaller in size than the destination. In other words, the heads of two merged objects must be larger in size. Thus, sonority can be analogous to the size of the cup, and combining objects and phonemes can be regarded in the same manner.

2.3 Motivation for Assuming Phonemic Merge

Phonemic Merge should be hypothesized for the human species for two reasons. The first is to answer the question of why humans can create binary branching structures in syllables. The approach using Optimality Theory does not explain the reason why various branching structures can become candidates of an input. This point is interesting due to the structural differences between the speech sounds of human beings and melodies of songbirds. Human beings and songbirds are said to be the only species capable of vocal learning (Doupe & Kuhl, 1999). This trait is common to both species due to hierarchies in their sounds. That is, hierarchy in human speech sounds are regarded as phoneme, syllable, foot, and so on, whereas that in songbirds pertains to note, syllable, and motif. In contrast, humans differ from songbirds in that humans are the only species that can construct binary branching structures. To the best of my knowledge, clear evidence does not exist to show that songbirds have a binary branching structure for their songs. For example, songbirds can chunk three components into one, that is, they can make three syllables out of a, b, and c into one motif and iterate them as (abc), (abc), (abc). However, whether songbirds can create binary branching structures, such as {(ab) c} or {a (bc)}, for a motif when it consists of more than two elements remains unclear.

On the other hand, the internal structure of syllable in human speech is considered binary branching rather than chunking. For example, the same CVC sequence can be analyzed as having a right branch in English and a left branch in Japanese (Kubozono, 1990), thus creating binary branching structures, such as {(ab) c} and {a (bc)}, for a syllable that consists of more than two elements. If human being is the only species that can create a binary branching structure for speech, then a mechanism for creating such structure should be assumed for syllable acquisition.

The second reason for assuming Phonemic Merge is to ensure parallelism between the order of development for the combination of objects and that for the combination of phonemes, as pointed out by Greenfield (1991). To enable parallelism between the three modes of combining objects and the manner of combining phonemes, Phonemic Merge should possess the abovementioned properties.

3 Three Modes of Applying Phonemic Merge

This section defines the three modes of applying Phonemic Merge, namely, Pair-, Pot-, and Sub-Merge and reinterprets the pair, pot, and subassembly methods, respectively, as introduced by Greenfield (1991). This study echoes the view of the three modes of applying Merge in Fujita (2017), that is, Pair-Merge, Pot-Merge, and Sub-Merge are not sub-types of Phonemic

Merge. The study proposes that Phonemic Merge is a single operation, and the manner of applying such a unitary operation can be classified into three. By assuming the differences in cost between the three modes of applying Phonemic Merge, the order of acquisition of syllable structures and its parallelism with the combination of objects can be explained.

3.1 Pair-Merge

Greenfield (1991) stated that the pair method is a single step operation, whereas the pot and subassembly methods require multiple steps. However, the present study redefines the pair, pot, and subassembly methods, focuses on whether the target and destination of the operation are simple or complex, and ignores the number of steps. The pair method is defined as an operation where the operation target and destination are simple. Figure 7(a) illustrates a scenario where two cups are combined using the pair method.

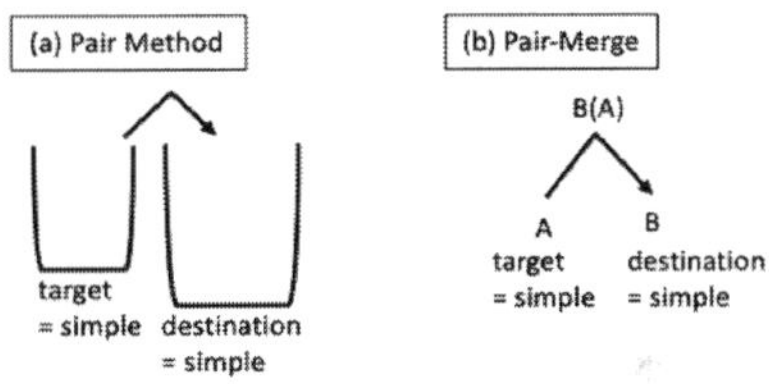

Figure 7. Definition of Pair Method and Pair-Merge (solid lines). The destination of an arrow represents the head.

At this time, A and B are the target and destination, respectively (Figure 7(a), which corresponds to asymmetricality. In addition, element B as the destination is expected to be larger than A due to the restrictions on the size of the cups.

If the target and destination of the Phonemic Merge are simple, then the mode of applying Phonemic Merge is defined as Pair-Merge. In Figure 7(b), phonemes A and B are combined by Pair-Merge. At this point, phonemes A and B are the target and destination, respectively, which corresponds to asymmetricality. In addition, phoneme B as the destination is expected to be higher in sonority than A due to sonority-headedness. Thus, as a result of Phonemic Merge, node B(A) is created.

3.2 Pot-Merge

The pot method is an operation where the target and destination of the operation are simple and complex, respectively. Figure 8(a) demonstrates a scenario where cups are combined by the pot method. The target is simple because it is a single cup, whereas the destination is complex because it consists of more than one cup.

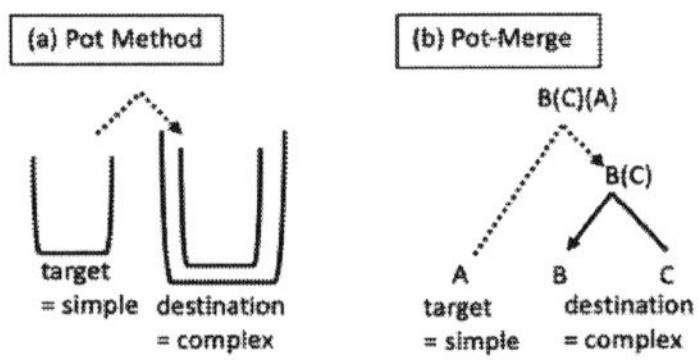

Figure 8. Definition of Pot Method and Pot-Merge. Solid and dotted lines represent Pair- and Pot-Merges, respectively. The destination of an arrow represents the head.

If the target and destination of the Phonemic Merge are simple and a previously merged branching node, respectively, then the mode of the Phonemic Merge is defined as Pot-Merge. Figure 8(b) shows that phoneme A and a branching node B(C) is combined by Pot-merge. The derivation of the structure in Figure 8(b) is as follows. The first Phonemic Merge is performed with B and C as the destination and target, respectively, and classified as Pair-Merge because the target and destination are simple. Node B(C) is the output of the first Phonemic Merge. Next, a second Phonemic Merge is performed with A as the target (simple) and B(C) as the destination (complex). This mode is classified as Pot-Merge. In addition, due to sonority-headedness, element B, which is the head of B(C), is expected to have a higher sonority than A. As a result of this Pot-Merge, node B(C)(A) is constructed.

3.3 Sub-Merge

The subassembly method is redefined as an operation in which the target of the operation is complex and the destination of the operation is simple or complex. Figure 9(a) indicates that the cups are combined by the subassembly method. The target is complex because it is made of two cups, whereas the destination is simple.

If the target of the Phonemic Merge is a previously merged branching node, then the mode of the Phonemic Merge is defined as Sub-merge. Figure 9(b) shows that branching node B(A) and phoneme C are combined by Sub-merge. The derivation of the structure of Figure 9(b) is as follows. First, the first Phonemic Merge is performed with B and A as the destination and

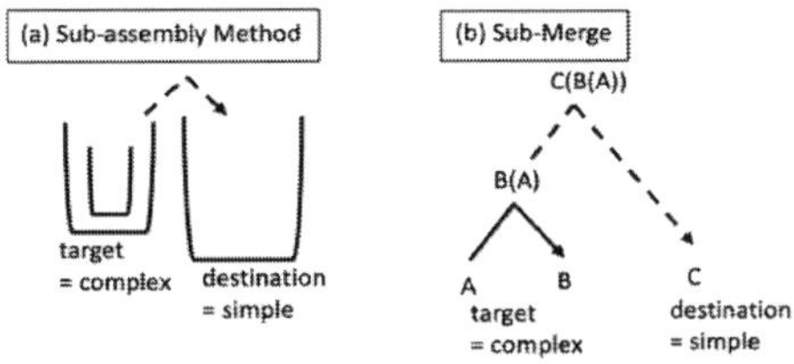

Figure 9. Definition of Subassembly Method and Sub-Merge. Solid and dashed lines represent Pair-Merge and Sub-Merges, respectively. The destination of an arrow represents the head.

target, respectively and classified as Pair-merge because the target and destination are simple. The output of Phonemic Merge becomes B(A) by asymmetricality, which states that one of two components should be the head. Next, a second Phonemic Merge is performed with B(A) and C as the target and destination, respectively, and categorized as Sub-Merge because the destination and target are simple and branching/complex, respectively. In addition, C is expected to have a higher sonority than B, which is the head of B(A), due to sonority-headedness. As a result of this Sub-merge, node C(B(A)) is created by asymmetricality. An important point of the subassembly method and Sub-Merge is that recursiveness is observed because the target is the output of the previous operation.

4 Acquisition of Intermediate Structures

This section demonstrates the order of syllable acquisition reflecting the acquisitional order of the three modes of applying Phonemic Merge. The assumption is that Pair-, Pot-, and Sub-Merges are acquired in this order, which is parallel to the development of strategies for combining objects. I will explain the syllable structures that can be assembled at each acquisition stage. By comparing data introduced in Greenfield (1991), parallelism between the acquisition order of Pair-, Pot-, and Sub-merges and acquisition order of the pair, pot, and subassembly method are shown. In addition, the study argues the inclusion relationship between each Phonemic Merge system.

4.1 No-Merge Period

As a first step, the study considers the period before acquiring Phonemic Merge where no modes of applying Phonemic Merge have been obtained. Phonemes produced in the No-Merge Period does not construct any structure of syllables because constructing a syllable as a node requires at least

Pair-Merge. As expected, unmarked phonemes that are easy to articulate, such as vowels or nasals, will be produced.

4.2 Pair-Merge Period

As a second step, the study assumes that a Phonemic Merge is acquired because it is the most unmarked application methods of Phonemic Merge. At this period, among the structures that can be created by Pair-Merge, CV as a syllable is fixed to grammar, taking into account the interaction with other factors, such as articulatory constraints. Figure 10 shows the merging between C and V by Pair-Merge.

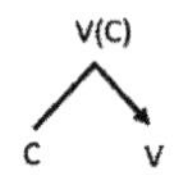

Figure 10. Derivation of CV. Solid lines represent Pair-Merge. The destination of an arrow represents the head.

Figure 10 shows that the target and destination are C and V, respectively, and classified as a Pair-Merge because both are single phonemes. As a result of Phonemic Merge, the output becomes node V(C). Thus, the syllable V(C) is fixed to the grammar. In contrast, the CVC syllable cannot be constructed in the Pair-Merge period because Pot-Merge is required to create the CVC structure, which will be explained in the next section.

In addition, by assuming the order of acquiring the three modes of applying Phonemic Merge, providing one reason why the markedness constraints of *COMPLEX and NO-CODA are dominant in the initial state is possible. According to Levelt et al. (2000), the constraints of *COMPLEX and NO-CODA are higher than FAITH in the initial state of grammar when the CVC and CCVCC syllables have not been produced. In the Pair-Merge period, the constraints of *COMPLEX and NO-CODA are higher than FAITH in ranking because onset, rhyme, and coda as branching nodes have not been acquired.

Another evidence to support parallelism between syllable acquisition and combining objects is that the periods where a child produces CV syllables and combines objects by the pair method are largely coincident. Greenfield (1991) mentioned that an infant pronounces *na* when saying 'no', or *ma* when saying 'milk' at approximately 12 months of age. The pair method for combining objects is observed within the same period.

Notably, however, the idea of the three modes of applying Phonemic Merge is insufficient to exclude other possible candidates. For example, Phonemic Merge ignores linear order, such that Pair-Merge can create the

VC syllable. However, in actual syllable acquisition data, the VC syllable is acquired much later. Therefore, VC is considered not fixed in the Pair-Merge period because the candidate of VC is excluded by other articulatory constraints, such as 'a syllable must have an onset'.

4.3 Pot-Merge Period

In the third period, the study assumes that a Pot-Merge has been acquired. The CVC syllable, which is most unmarked in the structure that can be created by Pot-Merge, is fixed to grammar, taking into account the interaction with other factors. Figure 11 shows how the CVC syllable is derived by Pot-merge.

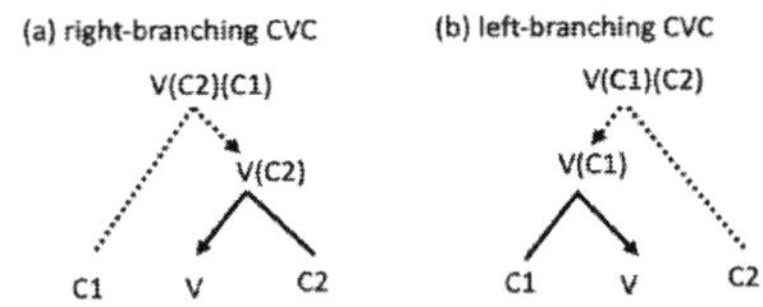

Figure 11. Derivation of right- and left-branching CVC. Solid and dotted lines represent Pair- and Pot-merges, respectively. The destination of an arrow represents the head.

The structure of CVC, for example, is derived from the Pair-Merge of V and C followed by the Pot-Merge of C and Rhyme (Figure 11). First, Pair-Merge is executed with C2 and V as the target and destination, respectively, and classified as a Pair-Merge because both are single phonemes. As a result of asymmetricality and sonority-headedness, the output becomes node V(C2). Next, Phonemic Merge using C1 and V(C2) as the target and destination, respectively, is executed and classified as Pot-Merge because the destination is a branching node. As a result, the CVC syllable and rhyme V(C) are fixed to grammar.

In addition, constructing a left-branched structure for CVC is possible because the asymmetricality of Phonemic Merge in the study lacks linear order, as shown in Figure 11. Kubozono (1990) proposed that syllables in English are left-branching, whereas Japanese syllables are right-branching based on data of blending. In the present study, Phonemic Merge is contrasted with government phonology (Kaye, Lowenstamm, & Vergnaud, 1990), that is, the right- and left-branching CVC can be constructed by Pot-merge.

According to Levelt and Vijver (2004), *COMPLEX dominates FAITH, whereas FAITH dominates NO-CODA when CVC syllables are produced. In the Pot-Merge period, the constraint of NO-CODA becomes inactive by acquiring Pot-Merge because rhyme as a branching node is fixed to grammar.

In arguing for the parallelism between syllable acquisition and object combination method acquisition, the periods of both acquisitions do not necessarily coincide. Thus, that the order of acquisition is parallel is important. Interestingly, the periods where the syllable structure using Pot-Merge is produced and where the object is combined by the pot method in fact nearly coincide. Importantly, the classification of methods of combining phonemes in Greenfield (1991) differs from the present study. CVC is regarded as the structure using the subassembly method in Greenfield (1991), whereas CVC is constructed by Pot-Merge in this study. As a result, a difference exists between the timing of acquisition of the combination of objects and that of the combination of phonemes. Greenfield (1991) stated that the pot method becomes dominant for a combination of objects approximately 16 months after birth, whereas the subassembly method is observed approximately 22 months after birth. Reportedly, the utterance of the word *ball* was observed at 15 months of age. Greenfield (1991) classified the syllable structure of *ball* as left-branching and as a structure constructed via the subassembly method. If *ball* is classified as a subassembly method, then a large difference is noted between the timing when the subassembly method is observed in the combination of objects and that when the utterance of ball is observed. However, using the proposed Phonemic Merge, the syllable structure of *ball* is CVC, which can be constructed with Pot-merge. As a result, the study infers that the acquisition timing of the pot method and Pot-Merge are nearly the same.

4.4 Sub-Merge Period

In the fourth step, the study assumes that Sub-Merge has been acquired. Figure 12 shows how Pair- and Sub-merges derive the syllable CCV/CVCC. The derivation of CCV is described as follows. First, Pair-Merge is executed with C1 and C2 as the target and destination, respectively, and classified as Pair-Merge because both are single phonemes. The sonority of C2 is expected to be higher than C1. As a result, the output becomes node C2(C1). A Phonemic Merge using C2(C1) and V as the target and destination, respectively, is then executed and classified as Sub-Merge because the target is a branching node. As a result, the syllable of V(C2(C1)) is projected. Thereby, a (Complex) onset as a branching node is fixed to grammar. Complex coda can also be derived by Sub-Merge, as shown in Figure 12. Thereby, a (Complex) coda as a branching node is fixed to grammar.

Moreover, according to Levelt and Vijver (2004), the FAITH constraint dominates NO-CODA and *COMPLEX when syllables that contain consonant clusters are produced. In the Sub-Merge period, onset/coda as a branching node is fixed to grammar. In other words, the constraint of *COMPLEX becomes inactive by acquiring Sub-Merge.

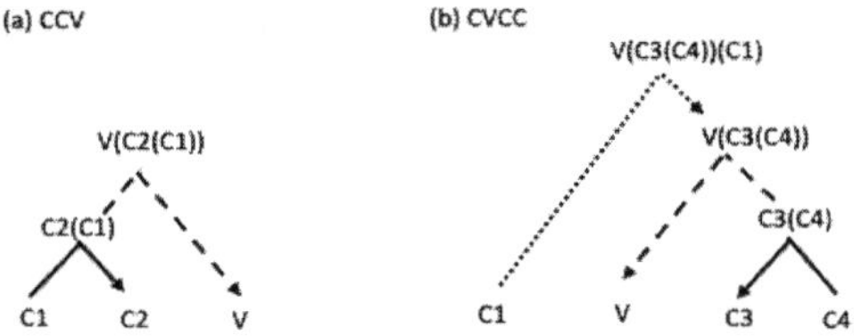

Figure 12. Derivation of CCV and CVCC. Solid and dashed lines represent Pair- and Sub-merges, respectively. The destination of an arrow represents the head.

4.5 Implications Regarding Syllable Acquisition and Syllable Typology

This section examines the implications of syllable acquisition, which is inferred from the order of acquisition of Pair-, Pot-, and Sub-Merges, taking into account interaction with other constraints. Furthermore, the study assumes that syllables are obtained in the following order: Pair-Merge > Pot-Merge > and Sub-Merge systems. In the same manner, the combination of objects is obtained in the following order: pair > pot > subassembly methods. The reason for such sequences is that the cost can be assumed to be lowest when the target and destination of the operation are simple, second lowest when only the destination is complex, and highest when the target is the output from the previous operation. Assuming that Pair-, Pot-, and Sub-merges are acquired in this order, the study predicts that the syllable structure will be acquired from the center of Figure 13 outward.[1]

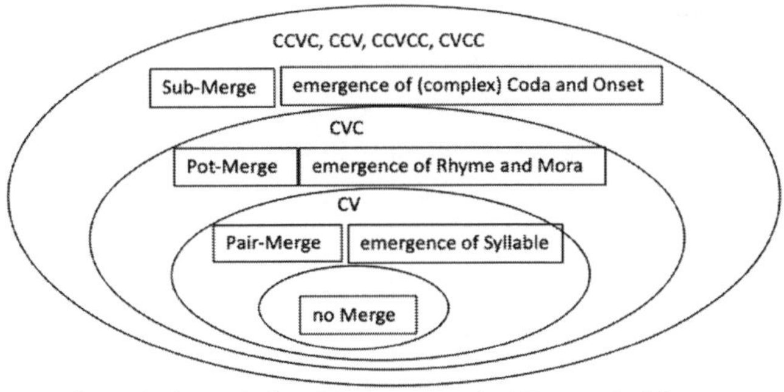

Figure 13. Inclusive relationship between the Phonemic Merge systems

In other words, Figure 13 indicates several implications in syllable acquisition. For example, if a child has acquired a complex onset, then the child

[1] It should be noted that the inclusion relationship in Figure 13 is predicted by disregarding ONSET, assuming that ONSET is involved independent of the order of difficulty of the three types of applying Phonemic Merge.

has acquired Sub-Merge. In addition, the child has acquired the syllable structure created by Pot-Merge because the Sub-Merge system indicates the Pot-Merge system. Therefore, the implication that the child who acquired the complex onset always acquires CVC is derived. This implication is pointed out by Kaye and Lowenstamm (1981) in the context of typology. That is, if one language has a complex onset, then such language always has a coda. The study proposes that the implications in typology stem from the Pair-, Pot-, and Sub-Merge systems in syllable acquisition. In other words, the implications in syllable acquisition are derived from the three modes of applying Phonemic Merge, where implications in language typology emerge as a result. That is, even if the typological implication states that a language that has a CCV syllable must have a CVC syllable, whether or not CCV or CVC is acquired first in the language is not guaranteed. However, from the viewpoint of acquisition, if CVC is acquired before CCV in a certain language, then the typological perspective guarantees that if a language has CCV, then it must have CVC.

Notably, even within the same language, the order of complex coda acquisition and complex onset acquisition varies dependent on the child (Levelt, 2000). Another interpretation for the observation is that if CCV and CVCC are taken as a single category, then no fluctuation exists in the basic order of acquisition of (i) CV, (ii) CVC, and (iii) CCV/VCC, which reflects the developmental order of the (i) pair, (ii) pot, and (iii) subassembly systems.

5 Conclusion

The study defined Phonemic Merge and the three modes of applying it to determine how the branching structures in syllables are constructed and to rationalize the order of syllable acquisition: (i) CV, (ii) CVC, and (iii) CCV/CVCC. In summary, the basic order of syllable acquisition is a reflection of the acquisition of (i) Pair-, (ii) Pot-, and (iii) Sub-Merges in this order. At the same time, the reason for why the constraints of *COMPLEX and NO-CODA are high in the initial state within the framework of Optimality Theory can be explained. The difficulty of obtaining Pair-, Pot-, and Sub-merges can be reflected in *COMPLEX and NO-CODA within the same framework. Notably, the order of syllable acquisition is determined not only by the difficulty of Pair-, Pot-, and Sub-Merges, but also by interaction among the three types of applying Phonemic Merge and other factors.

The study has certain limitations. The theory proposed in the study is a theory-internal analysis. Even if the theory can equate the development of combining objects with the acquisition of syllable structure, the study lacks independent evidence regarding whether they are really derived from the same mechanism.

References

Conway, C. M., & Christiansen, M. H. 2001. Sequential learning in non-human primates. *Trends in cognitive sciences*, *5*(12), 539-546.

Demuth, K., & Fee, E. J. 1995. Minimal prosodic words in early phonological development. *Ms, Brown University and Dalhousie University*.

Doupe, A. J., & Kuhl, P. K. 1999. Birdsong and human speech: common themes and mechanisms. *Annual review of neuroscience*, *22*(1), 567-631.

Greenfield, P. M. 1991. Language, tools and brain: The ontogeny and phylogeny of hierarchically organized sequential behavior. *Behavioral and brain sciences*, *14*(4), 531-551.

Fujita, K. 2017. On the parallel evolution of syntax and lexicon: A Merge-only view. *Journal of neurolinguistics*, *43*, 178-192.

McLeod, S., Van Doorn, J., & Reed, V. A. 2001. Normal acquisition of consonant clusters. *American journal of speech-language pathology* *10*(2), 99-110.

Kaye, J., & Lowenstamm, J. 1981. Syllable structure and markedness theory. *Theory of markedness in generative grammar*, 287-315.

Kaye, J., Lowenstamm, J., & Vergnaud, J. R. 1990. Constituent structure and government in phonology. *Phonology*, *7*(1), 193-231.

Kim, M., Kim, S. J., & Stoel-Gammon, C. 2017. Phonological acquisition of Korean consonants in conversational speech produced by young Korean children. *Journal of child language*, *44*(4), 1010-1023.

Kubozono, H. 1990. Phonological constraints on blending in English as a case for phonology-morphology interface. *Yearbook of morphology*, *3*, 1-20.

Levelt, C. C., Schiller, N. O., & Levelt, W. J. 2000. The acquisition of syllable types. *Language acquisition*, *8*(3), 237-264.

Levelt, C. C., & Van de Vijver, R. 2004. Syllable types in cross-linguistic and developmental grammars. *Constraints in phonological acquisition*, *204*, 218.

Smolensky, P., & Prince, A. 1993. Optimality Theory: Constraint interaction in generative grammar. *Optimality Theory in phonology*, 3.

Tanaka, S. 2017. The shape and function of phonology in evolutionary linguistics: Why we can explore language origins from extant languages, and how. *Journal of the phonetic society of Japan*, *21*(1), 88-104.

Tsuji, S., Nishikawa, K., & Mazuka, R. 2014. Segmental distributions and consonant-vowel association patterns in Japanese infant-and adult-directed speech. *Journal of child language*, *41*(6), 1276-1304.

Part IV

Syntax/Semantics

Un-Blackboxing Aboutness: A New Perspective from Japanese Gapless Clausal Modifiers*

KAZUHIKO FUKUSHIMA

Relatives—or more accurately noun modifying clauses (NMCs)—in Japanese, Korean, and Chinese have been controversial since a mixture of gapped and gapless NMCs, e.g. (1-2) below are found throughout (Yoon 1995, Matsumoto 1997, Murasugi 2000, Tsai 2008, Zhang 2002, Kubota & Lee 2015, Lee & Lee 2012, Ishii 2018, Fukushima 2019 etc.—relatively recent ones).

There are two major issues surrounding these NMCs: (i) A long-standing dispute over a proper syntactic/structural approach to NMCs, which is reflected in contentious debates between the proponents of uniform treatments vs. the supporters of disjoint ones, and (ii) the exact semantic mechanisms for NMC-head noun combinations, in particular regarding ABOUTNESS in the context of gapless NMCs.

Issue (i) centers around whether syntax (especially movement) has any role to play or not. As far as issue (ii) goes, despite the fact that the concept

---

* Comments obtained from the following people are highly appreciated: Koyo Akuzawa, Kaoru Horie, Jim Huang, Ikumi Imani, Toru Ishii, Koji Kawahara, Kwang-sup Kim, Jaklin Kornfilt, Yusuke Kubota, Keiko Murasugi, David Oshima, Osamu Sawada, Satoshi Tomioka, and Kei Yoshimoto. The work reported here is part of the NINJAL collaborative research project 'Cross-linguistic Studies of Japanese Prosody and Grammar'. *Kansai Gaidai University* (kaz.zisin@gmail.com)

Japanese/Korean Linguistics 27.
Edited by Michael Barrie.

of aboutness has been taken for granted by virtually all researchers and some sporadic plausible informal but case-by-case observations are available, there has been *no* explicit/formal characterization of it. As far as I can tell, aboutness is a black box.[1] With the former issue taking a back seat, the latter issue is what this paper addresses head-on drawing mostly on Japanese data, though the general approach offered here is highly relevant to other languages as well. (For issue (i), see Fukushima (2019) upholding a syntactically disjoint approach. More on this point below.)

1 Gapped and Gapless NMCs in Japanese, Korean, and Chinese

In (1) are gapped NMCs (regular relatives) in Japanese with gaps corresponding to obligatory arguments or an optional element. (Corresponding examples in Korean and Chinese are not included here since they would be straightforward and transparent as the Japanese ones here.) Subject, direct object, and indirect object gaps of intransitive, transitive, and ditransitive verbs are observed in (1a-d), respectively. It is possible and conventional (but superficially necessary) to suppose a gap corresponding to an optional adverbial element ('the method') in examples like (1e).

(1) Gapped NMCs:

a. [NP[NMC *gap*$_i$ sin-da (-toyuu)] sakka$_i$]
die-PAST -COMP novelist
'the novelist that died' (intransitive verb)

b. [NP[NMC *gap*$_i$ hon-o kai-ta (-toyuu)] sakka$_i$]
book-ACC write-PAST -COMP novelist
'the novelist that wrote the book' (transitive)

c. [NP[NMC sakka-ga *gap*$_i$ kai-ta] hon$_i$]
novelist-NOM write-PAST book
'the book that the novelist wrote' (transitive)

d. [NP[NMC sakka-ga genkoo-o *gap*$_i$ okut-ta] syuppansya$_i$]
novelist-NOM manuscript-ACC send-PAST publisher
'the publisher that the novelist sent the manuscript to' (ditransitive)

e. [NP[NMC sakka-ga hon-o (*gap*$_i$) kai-ta] hoohoo$_i$]
novelist-NOM book-ACC write-PAST method
'the method that the novelist wrote the book with'

[1] Philosophers, on the other hand, have dealt explicitly/rigorously with the notion of (possibly distinct) aboutness in a more broader context. One recent example is Yablo (2014) employing, as in this paper, the conception of a proposition being a set of worlds and partitions of these worlds. As we see from Yablo's considering 'subtraction', 'metaphor', 'regular presuppositions', 'free pragmatic presuppositions' and 'unstated premises' in terms of aboutness (see Morton 2014), he considers the notion to be much more general and wide-ranging than in this paper. Aboutness dealt with here is more restricted, focusing on an NMC-head noun relationship.

Semantically, all these gaps can be substituted by the head nouns, eliminating them to complete a proposition. Thus the semantics for gapped NMCs is straightforward in these cases vis-à-vis gapless ones.[2] It is noted that the complementizer *-toyuu* 'hearsay' is optional in the examples to follow. Being optional, they are not always included below and when not present, it is assumed to be simply left unpronounced.[3]

In contrast to (1), gapless NMCs (the so-called aboutness relatives) in Japanese, Korean, and Chinese are exemplified in (2a-f). These are gapless since the head noun is combined with a sentence that is a semantically complete proposition—no gap is called for. Due to this fact, a proper (aboutness) relationship between these NMCs and their head nouns has to be established via a semantic/pragmatic inference that takes into account the denotations of the head nouns vis-à-vis those of the NMCs. For example, the head noun *hon* 'book' in (2a) can plausibly be construed to be a factor of some sort that brings about the situation (i.e., the content of the NMC) where its reader becomes smart.

(2) Gapless NMCs:

a. [$_{NP}$[$_{NMC}$ atama-ga yokunar-u (-toyuu)] hon] (Japanese)
head-NOM become.good-PRES -COMP book
'(Lit.) the book that the head becomes good'
pragmatic inference: 'the book whose reader becomes smart'

b. [$_{NP}$[$_{NMC}$ sakan-ga yakiagar-u] nioi] (Japanese)
fish-NOM roast.up-PRES smell
'(Lit.) the smell that a fish is roasted up'
pragmatic inference: 'the smell that fish emits when roasted up'

c. [$_{NP}$[$_{NMC}$ meli-ka cohaci-nun] chayk] (Korean)
head-NOM become.good-REL book
'a book that one becomes smart by reading' (Kubota & Lee 2015)

d. [$_{NP}$[$_{NMC}$ sayngsen-i tha-nun-ru] naymsay] (Korean)
fish-NOM roast-PRES smell
'the smell that comes from fish burning' (Lee & Lee 2012)

---

[2] However, matters are actually more complicated than this as also shown below regarding coordination examples. For one thing, as in (1e), there is no *structural* connectivity between a gap and the head noun unlike what we find in English (witnessed with pied-piping), e.g., *the tools* *(***with***) ***which***$_i$ *they squeezed the grapes* ***gap***$_i$. In contrast, in an example like [$_{NP}$[$_{NMC}$ *Taroo-ga kita*] *mati*] 'the town **from** which/**to** which Taroo came' (Matsumoto 1997), there is no way to tell what the exact shape/type of a supposed gap might be, if there is any for that matter. This observation is one piece of evidence for the claim below letting gapless NMCs (or more generally appositives) to subsume those with supposedly optional adverbial gaps (see below).

[3] The COMP *-tokorono* 'such that (formal/authoritative)' is also possible but left out due to its rather stilted 'translational' ring.

e. [NP[NMC Lulu tan gangqin] de shengyin] (Chinese)
Lulu play piano DE sound
'the sound which (is produced by) Lulu's playing piano' (Zhang 2002)

f. [NP[NMC qiche zhengzai xingshi] de sudu] (Chinese)
car PROG run DE speed
'the current speed of the car's running' (Zhang 2008)

g. Appositive construction in Japanese:
[NP[NMC atama-ga yokunar-u] (-toyuu) zizitu/uwasa]
head-NOM become.good-PRES COMP fact/rumor
'the fact/rumor that (, I hear,) the head becomes good, i.e., that someone becomes smart'

An example of the appositive construction is included in (2g) for the sake of comparison. There is a striking similarity between this and gapless NMCs above in that in each case, the head noun is combined with a *complete* proposition. There has to be an aboutness relation between the head nouns (call them 'fact-nouns' for the ease of identification) and their NMC in (2g) as well. The NMC is an instance/content of a fact or rumor, respectively.

Given the data above, a new syntactic/structural approach to NMCs is proposed by Fukushima (2019) that groups together (i) gapped NMCs on one hand and (ii) gapless NMCs on the other hand—another disjoint approach (see Whitman 2019 and Huang 2003 for recent support for a dual approach). Though Fukushima's neo-dual approach clearly separates the two kinds of NMCs, unlike by predecessors, the boundary is drawn based on PROPOSITIONAL COMPLETENESS, focusing not merely on the presence/absence of a gap per se but rather on how *obligatory* such a gap is. OBLIGATORINESS here is based on the notion of argument saturation. NMCs without an obligatory gap (inclusive the cases with a supposedly optional gap) are taken to be an appositive structure on a par with (2g), while the ones with an obligatory gap are true relatives. Only the former involves aboutness as seen below.

Though I yield more detailed empirical exposition to Fukushima (2019) regarding the syntactic distinctions and discussion, I briefly touch upon the central motivation for the neo-dual approach. Hitherto unnoticed/unexplored empirical evidence for the approach comes from coordination of modified head nouns as in (3).

(3) a. [NP[NMC sakka-ga *gap*$_i$ kai-ta (-toyuu)] [hon-to kizi]$_i$]
novelist-NOM write-PAST COMP book-and article
'the book and article [that the novelist wrote]' (DO & DO: possible)

b. [NP[NMC sakka-ga *gap*$_i$ kai-ta] [hon-to zizitu]$_i$]
novelist-NOM write-PAST book-and fact
≠ 'the book [that the novelist wrote] and the fact [that the novelist wrote the book]' (DO & FACT-NOUN: impossible)
= 'the book and fact [that the novelist wrote]' (DO & DO: possible)

c. [NP[NMC seizika-ga wairo-o (*gap*) uketot-ta] [basyo-to zizitu]]
politician-NOM bribe-ACC accept-PAST place-and fact
'the place [where the politician accepted the bribe] and the fact [that the politician accepted the bribe]' (with an optional gap; ADV & FACT-NOUN: possible)

d. [NP[NMC atama-ga yokunar-u] [hon-to zizitu]] (gapless)
head-NOM become.good-PRES book-and fact
'the book [the head (i.e. reader) becomes good (i.e. smart)] and the fact that (someone) becomes smart
' (with no gap; GAPLESS HEAD & FACT-NOUN: possible)

e. [NP[NMC seizika-ga wairo-o uketot-ta] [uwasa-ka zizitu]]
politician-NOM bribe-ACC accept-PAST rumor-or fact
'the rumor [that the politician accepted the bribe] or the fact [that the politician accepted the bribe]' (gap irrelevant; FACT-NOUN & FACT-NOUN: possible)

The generalization is that when there is an obligatory gap, the entire coordinated head nouns are forced to fill the gap as in (3a). It is notable that while a double DO reading is possible for (3b), there is no 'fact-noun' reading available for it.

In contrast, when a modifying clause is propositionally complete, head nouns corresponding to an adverbial and a fact-noun can be coordinated as in (3c). Given this, it is rather awkward to suppose an optional gap for the head noun *basyo* 'place' in (3c), which will have to be a postpositional phrase with *-de* 'at' (like *basyo-de*). However, there is *no* formal match between the head noun and the gap (see note 2 above where a contrast between Japanese and English is given regarding the lack/presence of formal connectivity).[4]

Moreover, if there were such an optional gap, then one of the coordinated head nouns, namely, *zizitu* 'fact' would be a serious semantic misfit for the gap. On the other hand, if it is the case that only one of the conjoined head nouns is affected by gap-filling mechanism, that would violate the Coordination Structure Constraint (construed at least as a constraint on representation).

Possible coordination is also observed for the combination of a gapless

[4] The same connectivity problem does not arise for case-markers *-ga* (nominative), *-o* (accusative), or *-ni* (dative) since they are a reflection of purely formal/structural (case) requirements and semantically vacant.

head noun (*hon* 'book') and a fact-noun (*zizitu* 'fact') seen in (3d). Also, it is no surprise that two coordinated fact-nouns (*uwasa* 'rumor' and *zizitu*) can share an NMC as in (3e). Thus the presence of an obligatory gap demarcates the boundary between true relatives vs. appositives.[5]

2 Semantics of NMCs

For the most part, this section outlines the semantic interpretation of NMCs reflecting the differences introduced above. Ways to interpret both types are illustrated but it is gapless NMCs requiring aboutness that receive most attention. Though the syntactic aspects of NMCs are not central to this paper as stated already, simple syntactic analyses are provided to furnish the bases for semantic composition, which is TYPE-DRIVEN TRANSLATION (Klein & Sag 1985). Here and below, the cases involving coordination like (3) are ignored.

Syntactically, gapped NMCs (true relatives) instantiate a filler-gap structure, while any gapless NMCs are appositives. Recall that a gap is relevant for obligatory arguments *exclusively*. Semantically, NMCs with a gap are given regular garden variety intersective semantics but those without a gap employ the function Contextual-Relevance (C-REL) defined below to accommodate aboutness between a head noun and its clausal modifier.

2.1 The key lexical items

Both types of NMCs are clausal nominal modifiers and the CONSTRAINT-BASED SYNTACTIC THEORY (Sag et. al. 2003) designates them as a selector of a modified noun.[6] This is reflected in the lexical definitions in (4).

---

[5] A note of caution is due here regarding how to interpret the coordination data. Apparently similar data given in (i) ought not to be confused with (3b-d). Coordination in (i) is between two *independent* NPs, only the first of which contains an NMC and the second of which comes with the demonstrative *sono* 'such/that'. The second independent NP can refer to the state of affairs expressed by a proposition constructed combining the NMC and the head noun *hoohoo* meaning: 'such a fact, i.e., the author wrote the book with a certain method'. In contrast, the interpretation of (3b) is: 'the method the author wrote the book with and the fact that the author wrote the book' where the NMC distributes over the conjuncts. We should note that in the second conjunct of this latter reading, the method is not part of the proposition modifying *zizitu*. The coordination data in (3b-d) involve conjoined head nouns both of which are modified by a single clause.

(i) a. [$_{\text{NP}_1}$ [$_{\text{NMC}}$ sakka-ga hon-o (*gap*$_i$) kai-ta] hoohoo$_i$]-to [$_{\text{NP}_2}$ sono zizitu]
novelist-NOM book-ACC write-PAST method-and such fact
'[the method [that the novelist employed writing the book]] and [such a fact (i.e., the novelist wrote the book with the method)]'

b. [$_{\text{NP}_1}$ [$_{\text{NMC}}$ sakka-ga *gap*$_i$ kai-ta] hon$_i$]-to [$_{\text{NP}_2}$ sono zizitu]
novelist-NOM write-PAST book-and such fact
'[the book [that the novelist wrote]] and [such a fact (i.e., the novelist wrote the book)]'

Also, as we can see from the contrast between (ib) and (3b), an impossible DO & FACT-NOUN reading can be salvaged by adding the same demonstrative. This, however, renders the second conjunct in (ib) an independent NP irrelevant of direct modification by the NMC.

[6] The attributes HEAD, SPR, COMPS, MOD are head features. In addition to other syntactic rules, the ARGUMENT REALIZATION PRINCIPLE (for gap introduction), GAP PRINCIPLE (for gap per-

(4) a. Lexical entry of the relativizer *-toyuu* (for gapped NMCs):
$\{$HEAD *reltvzr*; SPR $<>$; COMPS $<$ S[GAP$\{\boxed{1}$NP$_{\boxed{2}}\}$] $>$; MOD N$'_{\boxed{2}}$; STOPGAP$\{\boxed{1}$NP$\}$; SEM...$\}$
b. Lexical entry of the appositivizer *-toyuu* (for gapless NMCs):
$\{$HEAD *appstvzr*; SPR $<>$; COMPS $<$ S[GAP $\{\ \}$] $>$; MOD N$'$; SEM...$\}$

In (4a) is the relativizer *-toyuu* which subcategories for and combines with a sentence with a gap (see the non-empty set value for the GAP attribute) and yields a gapped NMC. At the same time, it terminates the chain of gaps. Due to the MOD specification inherited from the relativizer head, the NMC acts as a modifier for an N$'$.[7]

The values of the SEM attribute is left out here (i.e., 'SEM ...') but will be made explicit in the next subsection.

A notation like '$\boxed{1}$N$'$' indicates token identity and another like 'NP$_{\boxed{2}}$' indexical (referential/semantic) identity. Though not shown in (4a) the referential identity between the head noun and the gap is reflected in the semantic translation of the relativizer given below in the form of variable sharing between the translation of the head noun and that of the NMC.

The appositivizer *-toyuu* (4b) is different from the relativizer in that it selects a sentence without a gap, i.e., S[GAP $\{\ \}$]. It also acts as a modifier of an N$'$, however.

In (5a) is a vastly simplified structure of our example NP with a gapped NMC in (1b) above where a gap is introduced and transmitted within the NMC, and terminated by the relativizer. There is a direct semantic connection in terms of indexing between the head noun and the gap mediated by *reltvzr* and this helps to identify the semantic role of the head noun vis-à-vis the NMC.

(5) a. [$_{\text{NP}}$ [$_{\text{NMC}}$ *gap*$_{\boxed{1}}$ hon-o kai-ta]-toyuu$_{reltvzr}$ sakka$_{\boxed{1}}$]
'the novelist [that wrote the book]'
b. [$_{\text{NP}}$ [$_{\text{NMC}}$ atama-ga yokunar-u]-toyuu$_{appstvzr}$ hon]
'the book [whose reader becomes smart]'

---

colation) and HEAD FILLER RULE (for gap cancellation) of Sag et. al. build syntactic structures.

[7] Following Fukui (1995), it is assumed that simply the top most N$'$ is an NP in Japanese. The latter can be a GENERALIZED QUANTIFIER (GQ of $<< e,t >,t >$, Barwise & Copper 1988) accompanied by a semantic determiner like *subete-no* 'all-GEN' or a mechanism like existential closure. The elements or factors turning a bare common noun (CN of $< e,t >$) into a GQ is not frequently reflected/apparent in Japanese syntactic structure per se. As Fukushima (1991, 1993, 2003) demonstrates, NPs do not always have to be a GQ since an NP external (aka 'floating') numeral classifier like *san-nin* 'three-CL(person)', as a semantic determiner, mediates the quantificational relation between two sets of individuals, namely CN and VP meanings included in the sentence as seen in [[$_{\text{CN}}$ *Gakusei-ga*] *kinoo* ***san-nin*** [$_{\text{VP}}$ *ki-ta*]] 'Three students came yesterday'.

On the other hand, the combination of a gapless NMC and its head noun in (2a) above is simply analyzed with the appositivizer as in (5b) where *appstvzr* simply combines with a gapless sentence to form an NMC to modify the head noun. Crucially, unlike in (5a) where the gap and head noun share indexing, there is no direct semantic link between the NMC and the head noun in (5b) other than a syntactic modification relation, making it necessary for an extra mechanism to render the combination of the two semantically plausible.

Provided with respective (albeit simplified) syntactic structures of gapped and gapless NMCs as the bases for semantic composition, the exact mechanism for semantic interpretation of each type is explicated in the next two subsections. Corresponding to the syntactic division, semantic analyses for the two also comes in two different flavors. In particular, due to the additional task of accommodating aboutness, gapless NMCs conceptually require far more apparatus than gapped ones as shown below.

2.2 Semantics of gapped NMCs

Gapped NMCs like (1b)/(5a) are rather straightforward since, as shown above, they instantiate a filler-gap structure for which a regular intersective semantics can readily be furnished as in (6). Necessary lexical items and their translations are given in (6a-b). Semantically, *reltvzr* (6a) mediates an intersective relation between two sets of individuals: a set of authors (the head noun) in (6b) and a set of individuals who wrote the book (the gapped NMC) in (6c). (A semantic derivation for the NMC is not given here since that is peripheral to the workings of *reltvzr*.) *Reltvzr -toyuu* is attached to the translation of the NMC as in (6d). Then, after combining with the head noun *sakka*, it reduces to (6e). (Here and below, '*book*' in the formulas stand for a (possibly plural) individual. Also tense is ignored.)

(6) *hon-o kai-ta-toyuu sakka* 'the author that wrote the book' (=(1b))
a. *toyuu* (*reltvzr*): $\lambda P \lambda Q \lambda x.P(x)\ \&\ Q(x)$
b. *sakka* 'novelist': $\lambda y.\mathbf{novelist}'(y)$
c. *gap hon-o kai-ta*: $\lambda z.\mathbf{write}'(book, z)$
d. *gap hon-o kai-ta-toyuu*:
$\lambda P \lambda Q \lambda x.P(x)\ \&\ Q(x)(\lambda z.\mathbf{write}'(book, z))$
reduction: $\lambda Q \lambda x.\mathbf{write}'(book, x)\ \&\ Q(x)$
e. *gap hon-o kai-ta-toyuu sakka*:
$\lambda Q \lambda x.\mathbf{write}'(book, x)\ \&\ Q(x)(\lambda y.\mathbf{novelist}'(y))$
reduction: $\lambda x.\mathbf{write}'(book, x)\ \&\ \mathbf{novelist}'(x)$

The final line says that it is a set of individuals that are both a writer of a book and a novelist. It is noted that since this is equivalent to a CN, it could serve as an argument of a semantic determiner (Barwise & Cooper 1981) to build a GQ.

2.3 Semantics of gapless NMCs: Aboutness un-blackboxed

Next, let us move on to gapless NMCs an example of which is (2a)/(5b). Though there is no need to worry about the existence of a gap, the conceptual setup needed here is more complex since we need to accommodate aboutness. First, after Potts (2002), I assume that an appositive clause is a nominalized proposition as in (7a). As the illustration demonstrates, the function '$^{\cap p}$' converts a proposition p into its nominalized counterpart. (A nominalized proposition is indicated with SMALL CAPS as HEAD-BECOME-GOOD.) Additionally, a set, PFR in (7b), of potentially familiar relations (PFRs) is adapted from Yoon (1995) but, unlike in Yoon, a PFR is a two place predicate with individual arguments. PFRs are not mere thematic roles but originate from more general cognitive conception based, for example, on semantic, pragmatic, and/or even encyclopedic knowledge.

(7) Semantic assumptions:
a. an appositive clause as a nominalized proposition, $^{\cap p}(p)$:
$p \in D_{<s,t>} \Rightarrow {}^{\cap p}(p) \in D_{<e>}$ (where $^{\cap p}(p) = [\iota x : \forall w \in p, w \leq x]$), e.g.:
a proposition: $\lambda w.\textbf{become.good}'(w)(head) = \{w_1, w_2, w_3\}$
a nominalized proposition:
$^{\cap p}(\lambda w.\textbf{become.good}'(w)(head)) = [w_1 \bigoplus w_2 \bigoplus w_3]$
b. PFR: {AGENT, THEME, LOCATION, SOURCE, GOAL, TIME, INSTRUMENT, REASON, CAUSE, BENEFICIARY, RESULT, SIGN, METHOD, TOPIC, INSTANCE ... }

Building on these, the core of the current semantic account of aboutness is given in (8).

(8) Capturing aboutness:
a. Cand-PFR$_{book}$: $\mathcal{R} \in$ PFR : $\lambda \mathcal{R} \exists x \exists y.(\mathcal{R}(x,y) \cap \textbf{book}'(x) \neq \emptyset)$
b. Contextual-Relevance (C-REL) function (aka aboutness):
$\mathcal{R}, \mathcal{S} \in$ Cand-PFR$_{book}$: $\lambda q \lambda y \iota \mathcal{R} \forall \mathcal{S}.(\| \mathcal{S}(y, {}^{\cap p}(q)) \cap \textbf{book}'(y) \| \leq \| \mathcal{R}(y, {}^{\cap p}(q)) \cap \textbf{book}'(y) \|)$
c. *-toyuu* (*appstvzr*): $\lambda p \lambda P \lambda x.(P(x) \,\&\, (\text{C-Rel}(x,p))(x, {}^{\cap p}(p))$

First, as part of the contextual/background (encompassing encyclopedic) information evoked by the concept of 'book', a set of PFRs, Cand-PFR$_{book}$ (candidate PFRs) is constructed as in (8a) above. This collects PFRs that are relevant (compatible) in conjunction with book-individuals in the domain of the model. For example, this set may include PFRs like THEME (e.g. being an object to be published), INSTRUMENT (e.g. being a tool to accomplish a goal), and CAUSE (e.g. being an instigator of controversies), for example, as in (9b-e) modulo the model setup.

(9) a. Cand-PFR$_{book}$ = {THEME, INSTRUMENT, CAUSE}
b. $\exists x.\textbf{book}'(x) = \{w_1, w_2, w_3, w_4, w_5, w_6, w_7, w_8, w_9, w_{10}\}$
c. $\exists x.\text{THEME}(book, x) = \{w_1, w_2, w_3, w_4, w_5, w_6, w_7\}$
d. $\exists x.\text{INSTRUMENT}(book, x) = \{w_1, w_3, w_5, w_7\}$
e. $\exists x.\text{CAUSE}(book, x) = \{w_1, w_{10}\}$

Second, the function Contextual-Relevance (C-REL) in (8b) above picks out the most widely applicable PFR from Cand-PFR$_{book}$. In addition, with a help of $^{\cap p}$, the function nominalizes its argument proposition serving as one of the arguments of a PFR. The PFR chosen this way is the most contextually relevant one. In the present rendition, this means that in the largest number of worlds, the conjunction of propositions based on the PFR and the one based on the CN $\lambda x.\textbf{book}'(x)$ turns out to be true. Continuing with (2a)/(5b) as our example with $^{\cap p}$(*the-head-becomes-good*) = HEAD-BECOME-GOOD, INSTRUMENT can be designated as the most relevant PFR (modulo the model) as in (10).

(10) a. $\mathcal{R}$ = INSTRUMENT given:
b. $\exists x.\text{THEME}(x, \text{HEAD-BECOME-GOOD}) \cap \textbf{book}'(x) = \emptyset$
c. $\exists x.(\text{INSTRUMENT}(x, \text{HEAD-BECOME-GOOD}) \cap \textbf{book}'(x) = \{w_1, w_3, w_5\}$
d. $\exists x.(\text{CAUSE}(x, \text{HEAD-BECOME-GOOD}) \cap \textbf{book}'(x) = \{w_{10}\}$

Third, *appstvzr -toyuu* in (8c) internalizes C-REL and mediates the semantic relation between a proposition (NMC, to be nominalized) and the head noun as in (11). (11a) reflects proposition nominalization. Then, along with the supposition that the PFR INSTRUMENT is favored by the model, the head noun *hon* is tied in to generate (11b). The final line indicates that it is a set of individuals (equivalent to a CN) the members of which are (i) a book and (ii) in an INSTRUMENT-relationship with a (nominalized) proposition HEAD-BECOME-GOOD.

(11) *atama-ga yokunar-u-toyuu hon* 'the book that the head becomes good' (=(2a))
a. *atama-ga yokunar-u-toyuu*:
$\lambda p \lambda P \lambda x.(P(x)\,\&\,(\text{C-REL}(x,p))(x,{}^{\cap p}(p)))(\textit{the-head-becomes-good})$
reduction 1:
$\lambda P \lambda x.(P(x)\,\&\,(\text{C-REL}(x,\textit{the-head-becomes-good}))$
$(x,{}^{\cap p}(\textit{the-head-becomes-good})))$
reduction 2:
$\lambda P \lambda x.(P(x)\,\&\,(\text{C-REL}(x,\textit{the-head-becomes-good}))$
$(x,\text{HEAD-BECOME-GOOD}))$
reduction 3:
$\lambda P \lambda x.(P(x)\,\&\,\text{INSTRUMENT}(x,\text{HEAD-BECOME-GOOD}))$
b. *atama-ga yokunar-u-toyuu hon*:
$\lambda P \lambda x.(P(x)\,\&\,\text{INSTRUMENT}(x,\text{HEAD-BECOME-GOOD}))$
$(\lambda y.\mathbf{book}'(y))$
reduction:
$\lambda x.(\mathbf{book}'(x)\,\&\,\text{INSTRUMENT}(x,\text{HEAD-BECOME-GOOD}))$

With regard to more 'traditional' appositive cases like (2g) above (repeated in (12a)), the aboutness relationship between an NMC and its head noun (e.g., *zizitu*) is determined in a similar way (again, modulo the model setup). (This remark applies to instances with superficial adverbial gaps as well, though no demonstration is offered here.)

(12) a. [NP [NMC atama-ga yokunar-u] (-toyuu) zizitu/uwasa]
head-NOM become.good-PRES COMP fact/rumor
'the fact/rumor that (, I hear,) the head becomes good, i.e., that someone becomes smart'
b. $\lambda x.(\mathbf{fact}'(x)\,\&\,\text{INSTANCE}(x,\text{HEAD-BECOME-GOOD}))$

This indicates a set of individuals that are facts and instantiated by a (nominalized) proposition HEAD-BECOME-GOOD.

3 Concluding remarks

Here are the main results of this paper:

• Gapped NMCs are treated as a filler-gap construction where a gap is filled/discharged obligatorily, while gapless NMCs are appositives where a gap is irrelevant. For the former, the relativiser mediates between the gap and its filler enabling simple intersective semantics. The appositivizer, on the other hand, handles an aboutness relationship for the latter.

• More specifically, for appositives, C-REL above formally captures the concept of aboutness. The most widely applicable PFR with respect to a specific head noun is designated as the relevant aboutness relation provided with a model setup.

• This paper initiates a debate regarding a proper formal semantic characterization of NMCs, in particular, those involving aboutness, which has long been left untouched—a step forward.

Admittedly, the exposition in this paper is preliminary and not exhaustive. For example, a typological question regarding to what extent aboutness can be accommodated cross-linguistically needs to be addressed. Keiko Murasugi (p.c.) draws attention to the fact that cross-linguistic ranges are quite different regarding how far languages allow aboutness to penetrate when dealing with NMCs. For example, English goes only as far as 'traditional' appositives (the fact-noun construction) tolerating the concept for a limited selection of PFRs like INSTANCE, while Japanese, Korean, and Chinese extend its coverage quite far. According to the current system, since all gapless NMCs (optionally but superficially gapped relatives, aboutness relatives, or traditional appositives) are all appositives calling for aboutness, we would expect relatively the same range of coverage cross-linguistically.

I have no definite or informative answer to the question above. I can only point out that languages are different in leniency and dynamism—perhaps due to (mostly diachronic) sociocultural influences/factors—concerning how much access/accommodation they allow in terms of pragmatic, contextual, social, and/or encyclopedic information in conjunction with a certain context-sensitive construction like NMCs, the 'major subject' construction, or 'topicalization'. For example, though utterly anecdotal, the Japanese (along with Korean and Chinese) culture with a strong Confucian undercurrent is supposed to be an example where voluntarily considering or even imagining the intentions, backgrounds, and/or feelings of others is highly valued and promoted. The stronger such a tendency is, the higher the level of aboutness might be.

In this connection, it is quite interesting to discover that there is a micro-variation between Japanese and Korean (both being aboutness-heavy languages) regarding how deeply aboutness-inclined they can be. From the contrast in (13) (adapted from Lee & Horie 2019), we see that aboutness alone is sufficient to establish a direct modificational relation between the NMC and its head noun *mukai* 'opposite side' in Japanese (13a), while such an attempt is impossible for Korean (13b), necessitating a mediating expression *kos* 'place' between the two. It appears that in Korean, not all potential gapless NMC-head noun combinations can be accommodated to the extent that they can be in Japanese more easily. In the former, *macunphyen* 'opposite side' alone seems unable to be construed as a modifyee of a gapless NMC, even with the help of contextual information. To render the PFR LOCATION as the best aboutness candidate, a specific lexical item *kos* 'place' is ostensively added.

(13) a. [$_{NP}$[$_{NMC}$ watasitati-ga sum-u] mukai] (Japanese)
we-NOM live-PRES opposite.side
'the opposite side [we live], i.e., the opposite side from where we live'
b. [$_{NP}$[$_{NMC}$ wulitul-i sa-nun] *(kos) macunphyen (Korean)
we-NOM live-PRES:ATTR place opposite.side
'the opposite side of the location [where we live]'

Even between typologically and culturally very close languages such as Japanese and Korean, we find minute differences regarding how aboutness is employed for NMCs. We can, then, imagine that the discrepancies between Japanese and English in terms of factors determining aboutness-strength is far greater than those between Japanese and Korean or Chinese.

In spite of some loose ends to be tied up (additionally, for example, the treatment of coordination examples seen in (3) above), it is hoped that its neo-dual classification of NMCs and its rare attempt of formalizing aboutness can be appreciated.

References

Barwise, Jon and Robin Cooper. 1981. Generalized quantifiers and natural languages. *Linguistics and Philosophy* 4:159–219.

Fukui, Naoki. 1995. *Theory of projection in syntax*. Stanford: CSLI.

Fukushima, Kazuhiko. 1991. Phrase structure grammar, montague semantics, and floating quantifiers in japanese. *Linguistics and Philosophy* 14:581–628.

Fukushima, Kazuhiko. 1993. Model theoretic semantics for japanese floating quantifiers and their scope properties. *Journal of East Asian Linguistics* 2:213–228.

Fukushima, Kazuhiko. 2003. Verb-raising and numeral classifiers in japanese: Incompatible bedfellows. *Journal of East Asian Linguistics* 12:313–347.

Fukushima, Kazuhiko. 2019. East asian relatives revisited: On the disunity between gapped & gappless relatives. In *Proceedings of the 14th Workshop on Altaic Formal Linguistics*, vol. 14, pages 65–76.

Huang, James C.-T. 2003. The syntax and semantics of prenominals: Construction or composition? *Language and Linguistics* 17:431–475.

Lee, Jaehyun and Kaoru Horie. 2019. Relational noun modifying constructions in japanese and korean: The differential divisions of labor between pragmatics and grammar. Poster presented at Japanese and Korean Linguistics 27.

Ishii, Toru. 2018. On so-called "gapless" constructions in japanese. *Journal of Japanese Linguistics* 33:137–194.

Lee, Jeong-Shik and Lee Chungmin Lee. 2012. Gap in "gapless" relative clauses in korean and other asian languages. In *Proceedings of the 26th Pacific Asia Conference on Language and Computation*, vol. 26, pages 640–645.

Kubota, Yusuke and Jungmee Lee. 2015. The coordinate structure constraint as a discourse-oriented principle: Further evidence from japanese and korean. *Language* 91:642–675.

Matsumoto, Yoshiko. 1997. *Noun-modifying construction in Japanese*. Amsterdam: John Benjamins.

Morton, Adam. 2014. *Review of Aboutness* (Yablo 2014). Notre Dame Philosophical Reviews. https://ndpr.nd.edu/news/aboutness/.

Murasugi, Keiko. 2000. An antisymmetry analysis of japanese relative clauses. In Artemis Alexiadou et al., ed., *The Syntax of Relative Clauses*, pages 231–263. Amsterdam: John Benjamins.

Potts, Christopher. 2002. The lexical semantics of parenthetical-as and appositive-which. *Syntax* 5:55–88.

Sag, Ivan A., Thomas Wasow, and Emily Bender. 2003. *Syntactic theory: A formal introduction*. Stanford: CSLI, 2nd edn.

Tsai, Hui-Chin Joice. 2008. On gapless relative clauses in chinese. Nanzan Linguistics: Special Issue 5.

Whitman, John. 2019. The prehead relative clause problem. In *Proceedings of the 8th Workshop on Altaic Formal Linguistics*, vol. 8, pages 361–380.

Yablo, Stephen. 2014. *Aboutness*. Princeton: Princeton University Press.

Yoon, Jae-Hak. 1995. The semantics of relative clauses in korean. In N. Akatsuka, ed., *Japanese/Korean Linguistics*, vol. 4, pages 413–428. Stanford: CSLI.

Zhang, Niina. 2002. Gapless relative clauses as clausal licensors of relational nouns. *Language and Linguistics* 9:1005–1028.

Personal Pronouns as Markers of Spatial Deictic Anchors: the Case of the Demonstrative System in Kikai Ryukyuan

RIHITO SHIRATA
Shigakukan University

1 Introduction

In several dialects of Kikai Ryukyuan (henceforth KR), proximal demonstratives can form compounds with personal genitive pronouns (Shirata 2018). In Shito'oke dialect, for example, objects close to the addressee can be referred to by *daa-uri*, which consists of the second person genitive *daa* and the proximal demonstrative *uri*. Though personal genitive pronouns generally mark possessors (e.g. *daa* t^hii 'your hand(s)'), *daa-uri* is used regardless of the possessor of its referent (see (1)).

(1) ***Daa-uree*** *waa* *mun=doo*.
2SG.GEN-this.TOP 1SG.GEN thing=ASRT
'That (in your hand) is mine.' (Shirata 2018: 41)

Japanese/Korean Linguistics 27.
Edited by Michael Barrie.

In the literature on demonstratives, Imai (2003, 2018) introduced the notion of 'anchor': the basis on which parameters (such as proximity) of spatial deixis are calculated. By adopting his terminology, *daa* in *daa-uri* can be considered as a marker of the addressee anchor which indicates that proximity denoted by *uri* would be calculated on the basis of the addressee. However, it has not been clear whether such an analysis is generally applicable to personal pronouns incorporated in demonstratives in KR.

The incorporation of second person pronouns into demonstratives has also been reported in Siwi (a Berber language), where the demonstratives with incorporated second person markers show 'allocutivity' or addressee agreement, i.e. the incorporated person markers inflect according to gender/number of the addressee (e.g. *wok* 'that(M.SG) (near you(M.SG))', *wom* 'that(M.SG) (near you(F.SG))', *werwən* 'that(M.SG) (near you(PL))', see Souag 2014). In KR too, second person pronouns incorporated into demonstratives can function as allocutive markers, because the pronouns inflect for number and honorification (e.g. *dannaa* 'you(PL)', *naami* 'you(HON)').

This paper examines personal pronouns incorporated into demonstratives in KR, with a focus on number and honorific/non-honorific distinctions to see whether the personal pronouns mark spatial deictic anchors and whether the demonstratives with second person markers show allocutivity.

2 Kikai Ryukyuan

KR is an endangered Ryukyuan language spoken on Kikai island (Kikai-chō, Ōshima-gun, Kagoshima prefecture, Japan, see Figure 1), which is located at the northeastern edge of the Ryukyuan-speaking area. Fluent speakers of KR are mostly in their late fifties or older; younger generations generally have only a passive knowledge or limited lexical knowledge of the language.

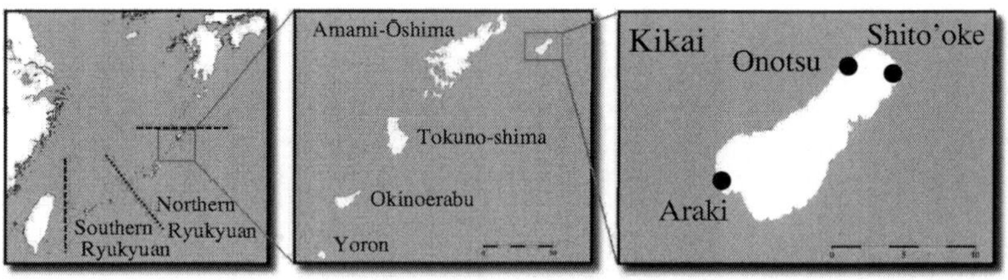

Figure1: Ryukyuan islands / Amami islands / Kikai island[1]

[1] We thank Thomas Pellard (CRLAO-CNRS) for offering us the maps shown here. We rearranged them and added the place names.

The examples presented in this paper are elicited data obtained during fieldwork conducted by the author from 2017 to 2019 with the help of 6 consultants in their 70s or 80s from Shito'oke, Araki and Onotsu villages (two consultants from each village). The KR data shown in this paper are those from the Shito'oke dialect (henceforth SKR), unless otherwise indicated. Similar phenomena have also been observed in the Onotsu and Araki dialects (henceforth OKR and AKR).

3 Background

3.1 Overview of demonstratives in KR

According to the previous studies (Iwakura 1941 and Uchima 1978), demonstratives in KR had a three-way formal deictic distinction: *hu-* (proximal), *u-* (medial) and *a-* (distal) series. Some dialects have lost either the *hu-* or *u-* series and transitioned to a two-way distinction system (Shirata 2018). For example, SKR and AKR lost the *hu-* series and transitioned to a system consisting of the *u-* (proximal) and *a-* (distal) series, while OKR lost the *u-* series and transitioned to a system consisting of the *hu-* (proximal) and *a-* (distal) series. In SKR, AKR and OKR, personal genitive pronouns can form compounds with proximal demonstratives as exemplified in (2).

(2) SKR/AKR *Daa-uri* *miširi!*
OKR *Daa-(hu)ri*[2] *miširi!*
2SG.GEN-this show.IMP
'Show me that (in your hand)!'

3.2 'Anchor' in analysis of spatial deixis

Imai (2003, 2018) analyzed spatial deixis in languages using the notion of 'anchor',[3] which is defined as 'the basis on which parameters of spatial deixis are calculated' (Imai 2018: 516). For example, Korean demonstrative stem *ku-* can be classified as an addressee-anchored proximal marker, because demonstratives with *ku-* refer to something in the addressee's territory. On the other hand, Japanese *so-* can be considered to have two functions: to mark addressee-anchored proximity and to mark speaker-anchored medial distality, because demonstratives with *so-* refer not only to something in the

---

[2] In OKR, the compound of the second person marker *daa* and proximal demonstrative stem *hu-* can be contracted to be *daa-* (e.g. *daari* < *daa-huri* 'that (near you)', *daan* < *daa-hun* 'that(ADN) (near you)', *daama* < *daa-huma* 'there (around you)', see Shirata 2018).

[3] Imai (2003) avoided using the term 'reference point', because the base of deixis is not restricted to a point and the punctual point of the location of a person (such as the speaker and adderssee) is hard to determine.

addressee's territory, but also to something somewhat far from the speaker and the addressee (see Imai 2018 and the summary of the above analysis on *ku-* and *so-* shown in Table 1).

	Korean *ku-*	Japanese *so-*
Addressee-Anchored Proximity	✓	✓
Speaker-Anchored Medial Distality	X	✓

Table 1: Functions of Korean *ku-* and Japanese *so-* (based on Imai 2018)

3.3 'Allocutivity' and demonstratives

The notion of allocutivity was originally introduced for the description of Basque by Bonaparte (1862). According to Antonov (2015: 56), in Basque, 'the addressee is systematically encoded in all declarative finite verb forms even when s/he is not an argument of the verb' in certain pragmatic circumstances as exemplified in (3). In (3), allocutive markers *-k* and *-n* are used for male and female addressees, respectively, despite that the addressees do not come up in the utterance.

(3) Allocutive markers *-k* and *-n* in Basque (Antonov 2015: 57)
 a. *Bilbo-ra* *n-oa-**k***
 Bilbao-ALL 1SG-go-ALLOC:M
 'I am going to Bilbao.' (male addressee)
 b. *Bilbo-ra* *n-oa-**n***
 Bilbao-ALL 1SG-go-ALLOC:F
 'I am going to Bilbao.' (female addressee)

Antonov (2015) classifies addressee honorific markers such as Japanese -*(i)mas(i)-* as allocutive markers too (see (4)).

(4) Allocutive marker *-(i)mas(i)-* in Japanese (Antonov 2015: 59)
 a. *itta*
 go-PRF
 'I/(S)He went.'
 (neutral verb, no allocutive ending; non-addressee-honorific)
 b. *ik-**imasi**-ta*
 go-ALLOC-PRF
 'I/(S)He went.'
 (neutral verb, allocutive ending; addresee-honorific)

Souag (2014) argues that allocutivity is observed in demonstratives too. He describes allocutivity as follows.

> Allocutivity may be defined as the indexation of features of the addressee (or more broadly of the addressee's relationship to the speaker) where the addressee is not an argument. ... The term ... has mainly been used in reference to verbal systems. (Souag 2014: 554)

According to Souag (2014), medial (or addressee-anchored) demonstratives in Siwi (a nothern Berber language spoken in Egypt) are descended from sequences of a proximal demonstrative, the locative marker *ɣuṛ* and a second person pronoun with gender/number declension. The medial demonstratives synchronically show allocutivity, i.e. they inflect according to the number/gender of the addressee. For example, demonstrative masculine singular pronouns *wo-k* (< *wa ɣuṛ-ək* (this.M.SG at-2SG.M)), *wo-m* (< *wa ɣuṛ-əm* (this.M.SG at-2SG.F)) and *we-rwən* (< *wa ɣuṛ-wən* (this.M.SG at-2PL)) are used respectively for a male addressee, a female addressee and multiple addressees as in (5).

(5) Allocutivity in Siwi demonstratives (Souag 2014: 539)

a. *yə-ṃṃ-as:* *a* *wəldi...*
3SG.M-say-3SG.DAT oh my son
wo-k *xer* *a-ẓuwwar*
DEM.M.SG-ADD:M.SG good M.SG-great
'He told him: O my son... that is a great good.'

b. *yə-ṃṃ-as* *i* *talt-ənnəs:*
3SG.M-say-3SG.DAT to woman-3SG.GEN
wo-m *ge-yə-nfu-yanax*
DEM.M.SG-ADD:F.SG IRR-3SG.M-benefit-1PL.DAT
'He told his wife: this one will benefit us.'

c. *yə-ṃṃ-asən:* ***we-rwən*** $agg^{w}id$ *n* *ṛəḅḅi*
3SG.M-say-3PL.DAT DEM.M.SG-ADD:PL. man GEN God
'He told them: this is a man of God.'

4 Incorporated person markers in demonstratives in KR

4.1 Basic demonstratives and personal genitive pronouns

Basic demonstratives (without incorporated person markers) in SKR are shown in Table 2. There are two demonstrative stems: proximal *u-* and distal *a-*, and three suffixal endings *-ri*, *-ma*, and *-n*, which derive general nominals, locational nominals and adnominals, respectively. General nominals *uri* and *ari* can function as third person pronouns[4] too.

[4] There are plural forms *u(ri)nnaa* and *a(ri)nnaa* which refer to multiple people.

		Proximal	Distal
Nominal	Thing / Human	*uri*	*ari*
	Place	*uma*	*ama*
Adnominal		*un*	*an*

Table 2: Basic demonstratives in SKR

Personal genitive pronouns in SKR are shown in Table 3. Personal pronouns show inflection according to number. Second person honorific forms are used for addressees senior to the speaker. As for the genitive case, the first person and non-honorific second person have a form without a case particle, whereas the second person honorific takes the genitive case particle *=nu*.

		SG	PL
1		*waa*	*wannaa*
2		*daa*	*dannaa*
	HON	*naami=nu*	*naača=nu*

Table 3: Personal genitive pronouns in SKR[5]

4.2 Overview of the incorporation of person markers

When the second person singular non-honorific genitive *daa* and the proximal stem *u-* form compounds, they denote proximity to the addressee (see (6)). *Daa* is mandatory if the referent of the demonstrative expression is close to the addressee but not to the speaker. If the referent is also close to the speaker, the proximal demonstrative alone can be used instead.

(6) a. ***Daa-uree*** *waa* *mun=doo.* (=(1))
2SG.GEN-this.TOP 1SG.GEN thing=ASRT
'That (in your hand) is mine.'

b. ***Daa-un*** *hasaa* *waa* *mun=doo.*
2SG.GEN-this.ADN umbrella.TOP 1SG.GEN thing=ASRT
'That umbrella (in your hand) is mine.'

c. ***Daa-uma****=kai* *kʰyun=kara* *maččuuri!*
2SG.GEN-here=to come.NPST=CSL wait.PROG.IMP
'I will come to you. So wait for me!'

5 Personal pronouns also have dual forms: *wattai* (1DU), *dattai* (2DU) and *nattatooru* (2DU.HON). Strictly speaking, *wannaa* and *wattai* are exclusive forms distinguished from inclusive counterparts: *waača* and *ariwattai*. We have not investigated whether dual/inclusive forms can be incorporated into demonstratives.

When the referent of a proximal demonstrative is close to the speaker but not to the addressee, the first person singular genitive *waa* can optionally be incorporated, especially in a contrastive context (see (7)).

(7) a. ***(Waa-)uree*** *daa* *mun=doo.*
(1SG.GEN-)this.TOP 2SG.GEN thing=ASRT
'This (in my hand) is yours.'
b. ***(Waa-)un*** *hasaa* *daa* *mun=doo.*
(1SG.GEN-)this.ADN umbrella.TOP 2SG.GEN thing=ASRT
'This umbrella (in my hand) is yours.'
c. ***(Waa-)uma****=kai* *k*^{h}*uu!*
(1SG.GEN-)here=to come.IMP
'Come here!'

Based on these facts, in the compounds consisting of the personal pronoun *daa/waa* and proximal demonstratives, spatial deictic anchors and proximity are separately marked by *daa/waa* and *u-*, respectively. On the other hand, in most other languages including Japanese and Korean, anchors and proximity are marked by single morphemes (see 3.1).

4.3 Additive plurality in incorporated person markers

When the speaker is addressing multiple people, the second person plural form *dannaa* is required to be used in compound deictic expressions to refer to objects close to the addressees (see (8a/b)). In cases where the speaker uses some other expression to clarify that s/he is talking to more than one person, however, the singular form *daa* turns out to be felicitous even with multiple addressees (see (8c/d)).

(8) [Some people are helping S move. S finds that they are about to move S's belongings to the wrong location.]
a. ***Dannaa-uree*** *ǰaa=kai* *mučči*
2PL.GEN-this.TOP where=to have.SEQ
ikyun=či=yo?
go.NPST=QUOT=WHQ
'Where are you going to bring those?'
b. ***Dannaa-un*** *p*^{h}*akoo* *ǰaa=kai*
2PL.GEN-this.ADN box.TOP where=to
mučči *ikyun=či=yo?*
have.SEQ go.NPST=QUOT=WHQ
'Where are you going to bring those boxes?'

c. *Danna=ya* **daa-uri**=*ba* *ǰaa=kai*
2PL.GEN-this=TOP 2SG.GEN-this= ACC where=to
mučči *ikyun=či=yo?*
have.SEQ go.NPST=QUOT=WHQ
'Where are you going to bring those?'

d. *Danna=ya* **daa-un** *p*^{h}*aku=ba* *ǰaa=kai*
2PL.GEN-this=TOP 2SG.GEN box= ACC where=to
mučči *ikyun=či=yo?*
have.SEQ go.NPST=QUOT=WHQ
'Where are you going to bring those boxes?'

Judging from these facts, not only the plural form *dannaa* but also the singular form *daa* can mark the addressee anchor in demonstratives in the utterance to multiple addressees. Therefore, it is not the case that the grammatical number of the incorporated second person marker is in agreement with the number of addressees. We argue that the plural form is selected (in (8a/b)) to fulfill the pragmatic requirement that the speaker has to clarify whom s/he is speaking to.

4.4 Associative plurality in incorporated person markers

Personal genitive plural pronouns incorporated into demonstratives can also refer to the group of people represented by the speaker or addressee. In the locational demonstratives in (9), for example, plural forms of the person markers appear despite that there are only a single speaker and a single addressee in the situation. The compound *dannaa-uma*, which consists of the second person plural marker *dannaa* and the proximal locational demonstrative *uma,* is used to refer to the place where the addressee lives (i.e. the mainland), while the first person plural maker *wannaa* is optionally added to the locational demonstrative *uma* to refer to the place where the speaker lives (i.e. the island). According to our consultants, the demonstratives with the singular person markers *waa-uma* and *daa-uma* tend to refer to limited places around the speaker and the addressee respectively, while those with the plural markers *wannaa-uma* and *dannaa-uma* refer to broader places (with more people). We argue that, in (9), plural forms *wannaa* and *dannaa* mark associative plurality, i.e. they denote that the demonstratives are anchored to the group of people living around where the speaker/addressee lives.

(9) [S is talking on the phone with a person living on the mainland.]

Wannaa-umaa	*ačusan=ŋa*
1PL.GEN-here.TOP	hot.NPST=but
dannaa-umaa	*k^hyaashi=yo?*
2PL.GEN-here.TOP	how=WHQ

'It is hot here (on the island). How about your place (on the mainland)?'

4.5 Honorification in incorporated person markers

When the addressee is senior to the speaker, the use of non-honorific second person markers is avoided even in compound demonstrative expressions, and honorific markers are used instead. In (10), for example, the honorific second person singular *naami*, with the genitive case marker *=nu*, is incorporated into demonstratives to denote that they are anchored to the senior addressee. By comparing (10) with (6), it can be said that the incorporated second person markers (at least apparently) show allocutivity in terms of honorific/non-honorific distinction.

(10) a.

Naami=nu-uree	*waa*	*mun*	*den=ŋa.*
2SG.HON=GEN-this.TOP	1SG.GEN	thing	COP.HON=ASRT

'That (in your hand) is mine.' (senior addressee)

b.

Naami=nu-un	*hasaa*
2SG.HON=GEN-this.ADN	umbrella.TOP

waa	*mun*	*den=ŋa.*
1SG.GEN	thing	COP.HON=ASRT

'That umbrella (in your hand) is mine.' (senior addressee)

5 Conclusion

We examined demonstratives with incorporated personal pronouns in KR and found that not only singular and non-honorific forms but also plural and honorific forms of personal markers can appear in demonstratives. The incorporated second person markers (at least apparently) are in agreement with addressee(s) in some occasions (as in (8a/b) and (10)). However, based on the fact that first person pronouns can also be incorporated into demonstratives (as in (7)), and given that there are cases where second person singular/plural forms are used irrespective of the number of the addressee(s) (as in (8c/d) and (9)), the data shown above cannot be accounted for by referring only to the possibility of allocutivity, or addressee agreement. Alternatively, we argue that the incorporated personal pronouns mark spatial deictic anchors, so that the demonstratives refer to objects close to the person(s) denoted by the pronouns. It is notable that, in our analysis, anchors and proximity are separately marked by personal pronouns and the proximal demonstrative stem, respectively.[6]

A remaining issue is concerning the difference between proximal demonstratives alone and those with the incorporated first person singular marker *waa*, both of which can refer to objects close to the speaker. All we know about the difference between them, is that the first person marker cannot be incorporated into demonstratives in cases where not only the speaker but also the addressee is touching the referent of the demonstrative (see (11)).

(11) [S and A are bringing someone else's belongings together.]

(#Waa-)uree	*t^haa*	*mun=ka?*
(1SG.GEN-)this.TOP	who.GEN	thing=Q

'Whose is this?'

The example (11) leads us to speculate that overt person markers in demonstratives can be used only when the denoted person is closer to the referent than anyone else, making that person the most suitable as the anchor for the demonstrative. On the other hand, proximal pronouns alone can refer to objects close to the speaker regardless of the distance from the referent to other people. More detailed research is needed to prove or disprove our hypothesis on incorporated person markers.

Abbreviations

1DU: first person dual, 1PL: first person plural, 1SG: first person singular, 2DU: second person dual, 2PL: second person plural, 2SG: second person singular, 3PL: third person plural, 3SG: third person singular, ACC: accusative, ADD: addressee, ADN: adnominal, ALL: allative, ALLOC: allocutive, ASRT: assertive, COP: copula, DAT: dative, DEM: demonstrative, F: feminine, GEN: genitive, IRR: irrealis, HON: honorific, M: masculine, NOM: nominative, NPST: non-past, PRF: perfect(ive), PROG: progressive, Q: question, QUOT: quotative, SEQ: sequential, SG: singular, TOP: topic, WHQ: wh-question.

Acknowledgements

This work was supported by JSPS KAKENHI Grant Numbers 16K21248 and 19K00646, and the NINJAL collaborative research project 'Endangered Languages and Dialects in Japan' (PI: Nobuko Kibe). We would like to express our gratitude to our consultants.

---

[6] This characterization does not apply to the contracted forms observed in OKR (see Footnote 2).

References

Antonov, A. 2015. Verbal allocutivity in a crosslinguistic perspective. *Linguistic Typology* 19(1): 55-85.

Bonaparte, L-L. 1862. *Langue basque et langues finnoises*. London: Strangeways & Walden.

Imai, S. 2003. *Spatial Deixis*. A dissertation submitted to the Faculty of the Graduate School of the State University of New York at Buffalo.

Imai, S. 2018. Japanese spatial deixis in crosslinguistic perspective. *Handbook of Japanese Contrastive Linguistics*, eds. Pardeshi, P. and T. Kageyama, 507-532. Berlin: De Gruyter Mouton.

Iwakura, I. 1941. *Kikaijima hōgenshū* [Glossary of Kikai dialects]. Tokyo: Chūō kōron sha.

Shirata, R. 2018. Kikaijima hokubuhōgen no shijishi no chokuji yōhō ni tsuite [On the deictic use of demonstratives in Northern Kikai dialects]. *Nantō Bunka* [Ryukyuan culture] 40: 41-53.

Souag, L. 2014. The development of addressee agreement on demonstratives. *Diachronica* 31(4): 535-563.

Uchima, C. 1978. Kikaijima shito'okehōgen no bumpō [Grammar of the Shito'oke-Kikai dialect]. *Ryūkyū no hōgen* [Ryukyuan dialects] 4: 65-126.

Intervention Effects and (Bare) Indeterminates*

KIMIKO NAKANISHI

KEN HIRAIWA

1 Intervention Effects of Indeterminates

In Japanese, indeterminates like *dare* 'who' give rise to various interpretations depending on a particle that they appear with, as exemplified in question in (1a) and universal quantification in (1b) (Kuroda 1965, among others).[1]

(1) a. [Dare-ga ki-ta *(**ka**)] wakara-na-i.
who-Nom come-Past KA know-Neg-Pres
'I don't know who came.'

b. [[Dare-ga yon-da] kyaku]*(-**mo**) ki-ta.
who-Nom invite-Past guest-MO come-Past
'For every person x, the guest(s) that x invited came.'

---

* We would like to thank Chris Davis, Tomohiro Fujii, Sabine Iatridou, Ikumi Imani, Yusuke Kubota, Shigeru Miyagawa, Osamu Sawada, Satoshi Tomioka, and the audience of the 27th Japanese/Korean Linguistics for their valuable comments and suggestions. This research has been funded by the JSPS Grant-in-Aid for Scientific Research (C) (No. 16K02645), to which the second author is grateful.

[1] In addition to (1), indeterminates may be interpreted as an existential quantifier in (i), a negative polarity item in (ii), and a free choice item in (iii).

(i) Dare*(-**ka**)-ga ki-ta.
who-KA-Nom come-Past
'Someone came.'

(ii) Dare*(-**mo**) ko-nakat-ta.
who-MO come-Neg-Past
'No one came.'

(iii) Dare*(-**demo**) kite-ii.
who-DEMO come-may
'Anyone can come.'

Japanese/Korean Linguistics 27.
Edited by Michael Barrie.

Shimoyama (2001, 2006) and Kratzer & Shimoyama (2002) present a Hamblin analysis, while Takahashi (2002) proposes a determiner-raising analysis, of indeterminates. In their Hamblin analysis, indeterminates introduce sets of alternatives that keep expanding until they meet an operator that selects them. In Takahashi's analysis, an indeterminate and a particle (*ka* or *mo*) are base-generated as a unit, and the latter undergoes movement to a surface position.

In both analyses, two important predictions follow: It is expected that indeterminates occur in the scope of *ka* or *mo*, and that they associate with the closest *ka* or *mo*.[2] The latter is viewed as an intervention effect in (2), where the indeterminate is unable to associate with *ka* or *mo* at a distance due to the presence of an intervening *ka* or *mo*.

(2) *[... [... [... indeterminate ...] *ka/mo* ...] *ka/mo* ...]

Example (3) shows that an indeterminate must be c-commanded by *ka* or *mo*, as Harada (1972) originally observed for a *wh*-question (see Takahashi 2002). Example (3) is ungrammatical because the particle *mo* attached to the object *Taro* is unable to associate with the indeterminate within the subject.

(3) *[[Dare-ga yon-da] kyaku]-ga Taro-**mo** home-ta.
who-Nom invite-Past guest-Nom Taro-MO praise-Past
'For every person x, the guest(s) that x invited praised Taro.'

The following example from Nishigauchi (1990: 164) shows that an indeterminate obeys locality: (4) lacks the reading in (4a) where *dare* associates with the universal *mo* due to the intervening particle *ka*. The only reading available in (4) is where the indeterminate *dare* associates with *ka*, and *mo* is interpreted as an additive particle.[3]

[2] We say that an indeterminate "associates" with a particle when its interpretation is determined by the particle.

[3] The additive particle *mo* does not require the presence of indeterminates, as in (i).

(i) [[Taro-ga yon-da] kyaku]-**mo** ki-ta.
Taro-Nom invite-Past guest-MO come-Past
'(lit.) Also the guest(s) that Taro invited came.'

(4) Intervention in the universal quantification
[[[[Dare-ga kai-ta **ka**] Mary-ga siritagattei-ru]
who-Nom wrote-Past KA Mary-Nom know.want-Pres
tegami]-ni]-**mo** John-ga henzi-o kai-ta.
letter-Dat-MO John-Nom reply-Acc write-Past
a. *'For every person y, and for every letter x, such that Mary wants to know whether y wrote x, John wrote a reply to x.'[4]
b. 'Also to the letter such that Mary wants to know who wrote it, John wrote a reply.'

We now turn our attention to so-called unconditionals (or concessive conditionals), such as (5). When an indeterminate appears in the unconditional clause, as in (5a), we obtain a universal-like interpretation (cf. Haspelmath & König 1998). In contrast, when there is no indeterminate present, as in (5b), the reading available is analogous to an alternative unconditional in English of the form *whether or not ...*[5]

(5) a. [Dare-ga ki-te-**mo**] Jiro-wa ki-ni si-na-i.
who-Nom come-Cond-MO Jiro-Top matter-Dat do-Neg-Pres
'Whoever comes, Jiro wouldn't care.'
b. [Taro-ga ki-te-**mo**] Jiro-wa ki-ni si-na-i.
Taro-Nom come-Cond-MO Jiro-Top matter-Dat do-Neg-Pres
'Whether or not Taro comes, Jiro wouldn't care.'

On the surface, the configuration in (6) is like the one in (4); the indeterminate is in an embedded question within the unconditional clause, and *mo* appears at a distance.

(6) Intervention in the unconditional
[Taro-ga [dare-ga kuru **ka**] kii-te-**mo**]
Taro-Nom who-Nom come KA ask-Cond-MO
Jiro-wa ki-ni si-na-i.
Jiro-Top matter-Dat do-Neg-Pres
a. *'Whoever the person x is such that Taro asks whether x comes, Jiro wouldn't care.'
b. 'Whether or not Taro asks who comes, Jiro wouldn't care.'

---

[4]The paraphrase in (4a) is taken from Shimoyama (2006: fn. 9).
[5](5b) also has the reading that corresponds to *even if* conditional (*even if Taro comes, ...*).

(6) lacks the universal-like reading in (6a); rather, it is interpreted as an alternative unconditional, as in (6b). In particular, the indeterminate associates with *ka*, and the unconditional clause is interpreted as if there is no indeterminate, just like in (5b). We might as well conclude then that in both (4) and (6), the association of the indeterminate with *mo* is intervened by *ka*.

However, in our earlier work (Nakanishi & Hiraiwa 2019, and Hiraiwa & Nakanishi 2020), we argued that *mo* in unconditionals like (4) does not associate with an indeterminate, unlike *mo* in universal quantification, but rather with a covert Q-operator (see section 2). Thus, the intervention effects in (4) and (6) are not completely parallel. However, in both cases, the intervention effect is caused by the same intervening element. We explore both semantic and syntactic approaches to intervention (Shimoyama 2001, 2006, Rawlins 2008, 2013, and Takahashi 2002), and show along the way that they all suffer from some empirical problems. We propose an alternative syntactic analysis, demonstrating that it is capable of explaining various examples of intervention, including novel examples with unconditionals. Crucially, we show that intervention effects can be found even when there is no overt intervening operator such as *ka* or *mo* (contra Shimoyama 2001, 2006) or intervening Q-verb (contra Rawlins 2008, 2013).

2 Semantics of Bare Indeterminates in Unconditionals

It has been generally assumed that indeterminates must co-occur with *ka* or *(de)mo*. However, in Nakanishi & Hiraiwa (2019) and Hiraiwa & Nakanishi (2020), we showed that indeterminates can appear "bare" without *ka* or *(de)mo* in unconditional clauses. Besides the form with *mo* exemplified in (5) and (6) above, there are other forms of unconditionals, where the overt presence of *ka* or *(de)mo* leads to ungrammaticality, as in (7).

(7) [Dare-ga {ko-yooga/ki-tatte/kuru-nisitatte/kuru-nisiro/
who-Nom come-Subj/come-Cond/come-Cond/come-Subj/
kuru-niseyo/kuru-nodeare}(-*(**de)mo**/***ka**)], Taro-wa yorokob-u.[6]
come-Subj/come-Subj-(DE)MO/KA Taro-Top please-Pres
'Whoever comes, T will be pleased.' (Hiraiwa & Nakanishi 2020)

[6]The verbs in (7) are glossed either as subjunctive or conditional. However, we do not have a strong commitment to the distinction between the two as the task is not straightforward. We simply point out here that a subjunctive form is also used in unconditionals in English.

(i) a. Rain or shine, we're having our party outside today. = Whether it rains or shines, ...
b. Come what may, we will go ahead with our plan. = Whatever may happen, ...
(Quirk et al. 1985: 156, 1101–2)

Examples of this kind are also noted by Shimoyama (2006: fn. 27), but they are simply presented as an exception without any explanation.

In Nakanishi & Hiraiwa (2019) and Hiraiwa & Nakanishi (2020), we presented a Hamblin analysis of Japanese unconditionals based on Rawlins's (2008, 2013) analysis of English unconditionals such as (8).

(8) Whatever Al has, he should stay home. (Rawlins 2013: 146)

In essence, under Rawlins's analysis, both unconditional clauses and *if*-clauses are conditionals that provide domain restrictions in a pointwise manner to an operator in the main clause such as a modal (cf. Kratzer 1981, 1986). While *if*-conditional clauses provide a single restriction, unconditional clauses provide a set of restrictions. This is so because an unconditional clause is syntactically interrogative, which means that semantically it denotes a set of propositions (Rawlins 2013: section 3.1).

In a Hamblin semantics, *wh*-items introduce alternative sets of individuals, as in (9a) (Hamblin 1973). Abstracting away from the details, the denotation of the unconditional clause in (8) is a set of propositions of the form 'Al has a cold', 'Al has the flu', etc., as in (9b). In Rawlins's analysis, the unconditional clause is interrogative, hence the Q-operator is syntactically present within the unconditional clause, as in (9c). Rawlins assumes that the Q-operator only lets alternatives through, as in (10).[7] We will discuss in section 3 whether (10) is an appropriate denotation for the Q-operator.

(9) a. $[\![\textbf{what}]\!]^{w,g} = [\![\textbf{whatever}]\!]^{w,g} = \{x \in D_e\text{: non-human}(x)(w)\}$[8]

b. $[\![\textbf{whatever Al has}]\!]^{w,g}$
$= \{p\text{: } \exists x[\text{non-human}(x)(w) \;\&\; p = \lambda w'.\text{ Al has x in w}']\}$

c. $[\![Q]\!]^{w,g}$ $([\![\textbf{whatever Al has}]\!]^{w,g})$ = (10b)

(10) $[\![Q\alpha]\!]^{w,g} = [\![\alpha]\!]^{w,g}$ (Kratzer & Shimoyama 2002: section 3)

Rawlins further argues that each alternative in (9c) provides a domain restriction to the modal in the main clause. Putting the details aside, the denotation of the entire unconditional construction is provided in (11), where each alternative has a conditional paraphrase.

---

[7]Rawlins (2013: section 2.4) later modifies the semantics of Q-operator, and claims that the Q-operator introduces two presuppositions (namely, exhaustivity and mutual exclusivity). We put aside these presuppositions as they are not crucial to the main argument of the paper.

[8]Rawlins initially presents the compositional analysis of unconditionals without considering the contribution of *-ever*. See Rawlins (2013: section 4.3) for the meaning of *-ever*, where he claims that it introduces an ignorance presupposition.

(11) { in all the closest worlds where Al has a cold, he stays home,
in all the closest worlds where Al has the flu, he stays home, ... }

(11) cannot be the final denotation of (8), however, because in Hamblin's system, a declarative sentence must denote a singleton set. Rawlins suggests that a default universal operator in (12) is inserted in the LF of an unconditional, as in (13) (see also Menéndez-Benito 2006). As a result, (8) denotes a singleton whose sole member is the conjunction of the propositions in (11).

(12) $[\![\forall\alpha]\!]^{w,g} = \{\lambda w'. \forall p[p \in [\![\alpha]\!]^{w,g} \rightarrow p(w')=1]\}$

(13) [∀ [[Q [... *wh-* ...]] [main clause]]]

In Nakanishi & Hiraiwa (2019) and Hiraiwa & Nakanishi (2020), we also showed that an unconditional clause in Japanese is syntactically an interrogative.[9] Then it is easy to see how Rawlins's analysis extends to Japanese. Following Shimoyama's (2001, 2006) Hamblin analysis, we assume that indeterminates denote sets of individuals, as in (14a) (see also Hagstrom 1998). In a Hamblin semantics, most of other lexical items denote singleton sets; for instance, the verb *kuru* 'come' (or its subjunctive form *ko-yooga*; cf. footnote 6) denotes a singleton set 'x comes', as in (14b). The two are combined by applying functional application in a pointwise manner. As a result, we obtain a set of propositions of the form 'a comes', 'b comes', etc., as in (14c). Since the unconditional clause is a question, the covert Q-operator takes scope over the clause, as in (14d). Assuming that the denotation of the Q-operator is (10), the denotation of the unconditional clause is the same as (14c).

(14) a. $[\![\textbf{dare}]\!]^{w,g} = \{x \in D_e: \text{human}(x)(w)\}$
b. $[\![\textbf{ko-yooga}]\!]^{w,g} = \{\lambda x \lambda w'. \text{come}(x)(w')\}$
c. $[\![\textbf{dare-ga ko-yooga}]\!]^{w,g}$
$= \{p: \exists x[\text{human}(x)(w) \;\&\; p=\lambda w'. \text{come}(x)(w')]\}$
d. $[\![Q]\!]^{w,g}([\![\textbf{dare-ga ko-yooga}]\!]^{w,g}) = (14c)$

Each proposition in (14d) provides a domain restriction to the main clause modal operator. The entire sentence combines with the universal operator in (12), yielding a singleton that contains the conjunction of the alternatives.

---

[9]We provided two pieces of evidence for the interrogative view. First, the indeterminate *naze* 'why', which is only licensed in a question and under an existential construal, is also licit in unconditionals (see Hiraiwa and Nakanishi 2020 for actual examples). Second, the sentential disjunctive connective *soretomo* 'or', which can disjoin questions but not declaratives, can disjoin unconditional clauses (see again Hiraiwa and Nakanishi 2020).

In sum, our previous work showed that the overt presence of *ka* or *(de)mo* is neither a necessary nor a sufficient condition for the use of indeterminates. Furthermore, we argued that indeterminates may associate with a covert operator, hence the existence of "bare" indeterminates.

3 Intervention Effects and Unconditionals

Having introduced our analysis of bare indeterminates in unconditionals, we now turn our attention to intervention effects. In section 3.1, we review Shimoyama's (2001, 2006) semantic analysis of intervention. Then in section 3.2, we show that Rawlins's (2008, 2013) analysis of unconditionals requires a departure from Shimoyama's analysis. In section 3.3, we extend Rawlins's analysis to novel examples of intervention in unconditionals. Section 3.4 examines Takahashi's (2002) syntactic analysis of intervention. Throughout this section, we show that each analysis has some shortcomings.

3.1 Shimoyama's Analysis of Intervention in Universal Quantification

Let us summarize Shimoyama's (2001, 2006) analysis of intervention in the universal quantification in (4), repeated as (15). The LF is provided in (16).

(15) [[[[Dare-ga kai-ta **ka**] Mary-ga siritagattei-ru]
who-Nom wrote-Past KA Mary-Nom know.want-Pres
tegami]-ni]-**mo** John-ga henzi-o kai-ta.
letter-Dat-MO John-Nom reply-Acc write-Past
*'For every person y, and for every letter x, such that Mary wants to know whether y wrote x, John wrote a reply to x.' (= (4))

(16) *[... [... [... indeterminate ...] *ka* ...] *mo* ...]

On a Hamblin analysis, intervention effects naturally follow from how the system works. The alternatives introduced by the indeterminate keep expanding until they meet the first relevant operator. Shimoyama (2006) entertains the idea that *ka* and *mo* are the only lexical items that select Hamblin alternatives and return singletons, which predicts that an indeterminate must appear in the scope of *ka* or *mo* and that it must associates with the closest *ka* or *mo*. Her claim is motivated by the long-standing observation that indeterminates must co-occur with *ka* or *mo*.

To this end, among the two denotations of the Q-operator presented in (17), Shimoyama leans towards (17a), where *ka* returns a singleton set whose sole member is a question denotation (Groenendijk & Stokhof 1984).

(17) a. $[\![Q\alpha]\!]^{w,g} = \{\lambda w'. \forall p[p\in[\![\alpha]\!]^{w,g} \rightarrow [p(w)=1 \leftrightarrow p(w')=1]]\}$
b. $[\![Q\alpha]\!]^{w,g} = [\![\alpha]\!]^{w,g}$ (= (10)) (Kratzer & Shimoyama 2002)

Assuming the denotation in (17a), *ka* in (15) combines with the Hamblin alternatives and returns a singleton. Then there are no alternatives left for *mo* to combine with, hence the lack of the universal reading.[10]

However, there are problems with Shimoyama's analysis. For one thing, as clear from the examples of unconditionals, indeterminates can be used without *ka* or *mo*, which shows that the dependency between indeterminates and these particles is not mandatory. For another, as Shimoyama herself points out (2006: fn. 29), it is not empirically true that *ka* and *mo* always require the presence of indeterminates in its scope.

3.2 Rawlins's Analysis of Intervention in Universal Quantification

As shown in section 2, in Rawlins's (2008, 2013) analysis of unconditionals, the denotation of the Q-operator must be the alternative-passing function in (17b). However, under this view, we wrongly predict that in (15), the alternatives introduced by the indeterminate expand until they meet *mo*.

As a possible way out, Rawlins takes up on a possibility that Shimoyama (2006) mentions (fn. 24) and quickly dismisses (fn. 28): It is a question-embedding verb (Q-verb), rather than *ka*, that returns a singleton set. In the configuration in (18), which is like (16) except that the Q-verb is added, it is the Q-verb, not *ka*, that blocks the association with *mo*.

(18) *[... [... [... [... indeterminate ...] *ka*] Q-verb ...] *mo* ...]

Ka, whose denotation is (17b), lets through the alternatives introduce by the indeterminate, but the alternatives are caught by the Q-verb, leaving no alternatives for the universal *mo* to combine with (and thus *mo* is interpreted as the additive particle). In this way, the intervention effect can be explained even if the denotation of the Q-operator is a trivial one in (17b).

[10] Shimoyama (2006: fn. 10, 29) suggests that the universal *mo* is lexically distinct from the additive *mo*. While the former is a Hamblin alternative-selecting function, the latter is not.

3.3 A Hamblin Analysis of Intervention in Unconditionals

We are now ready to revisit the intervention in the unconditional in (6), repeated in (19). The LF of the unconditional clause is given in (20).

(19)

Taro-ga	[dare-ga	kur-u	**ka**] {kii-te-**mo** /
Taro-Nom	who-Nom	come-Pres	KA ask-Cond-MO /
ki-kooga}	Jiro-wa	ki-ni	si-na-i.
ask-Subj	Jiro-Top	matter-Dat	do-Neg-Pres

*'Whoever the person x is such that Taro asks whether x comes, Jiro wouldn't care.' (= (6))

(20) *[... [... [... [... indeterminate ...] *ka*] Q-verb ...] Q][11]

Rawlins's semantic analysis is capable of explaining the intervention effect here. Since the unconditional clause is an interrogative, a Q-operator is present at the position that scopes over the entire clause. The association between the indeterminate and this Q-operator is intervened by the Q-verb, not by *ka*. Assuming that *ka* is a trivial function in (17b), it lets through the alternatives introduced by the indeterminate, but the alternatives are caught by the Q-verb, which returns a singleton set.

Because of this intervention effect, the unconditional clause in (19) does not denote a set of alternatives introduced by the indeterminate. Rather, it denotes a set consisting of two propositions, positive and negative propositions (see also Karttunen 1977, Groenendijk & Stokhof 1984). More specifically, the unconditional clause in (19) denotes a set that contains the propositions 'Taro asks who comes' and 'Taro doesn't ask who comes'. Following the same step as the one discussed in section 2, the truth conditions of (20) are that Jiro wouldn't mind if Taro asks who comes and Jiro wouldn't mind if Taro doesn't ask who comes. This is exactly what (19) expresses (see (6b)).

The current analysis predicts that there should be no intervention effects when a Q-verb is absent. This prediction is borne out: When the Q-verb *kiku* 'ask' in (19) is replaced with a regular embedding verb such as *iu* 'say', as in (21), we obtain the reading that is unavailable in (19). This is expected under the present analysis; since there is no intervener, the alternatives introduced by the indeterminate associates with the Q-operator, which lets through the

[11] Following Rawlins (2013), we assume that the Q-operator is syntactically a head, and thus the schematic structure here reflects the head parameter.

alternatives, and each alternative provides a domain restriction to the main clause modal operator.

(21) [Taro-ga [dare-ga kur-u to] {it-te-**mo** /
Taro-Nom who-Nom come-Pres Comp {say-Cond-MO /
i-ooga}] Jiro-wa ki-ni si-na-i.
say-Subj} Jiro-Top matter-Dat do-Neg-Pres
'Whoever the person x is such that Taro says that x comes, Jiro wouldn't care.'

However, the current analysis faces a serious challenge when confronted with examples such as (22), where the same intervention effect as (19) is observed without any Q-verb.

(22) [[Dare-ga saisyoni ik-u **ka** toiu] mondai-o Taro-ga
who-Nom first go-Pres KA C question-Acc Taro-Nom
ronzi-yooga], watasi-ni-wa kankee na-i.
discuss-Subj 1Sg-Dat-Top matter Neg-Pres
a. * 'Whoever the person x is such that Taro discusses a question of whether x will go first, I don't care.'
b. 'Whether or not Taro discusses a question of who will go first, I don't care.'

Assuming that *ka* in (22) is an alternative-passing function given in (17b), the alternatives introduced by the indeterminate should expand until they meet the Q-operator that scopes over the unconditional clause. This wrongly predicts that (22) has the interpretation in (22a). Rather, the only reading available is (22b), the reading that obtains if *ka* is taken as an intervener.

Example (22) is contrasted with (23), where *ka* as well as a Q-verb is absent. As expected, in (23) the indeterminate associates with the covert Q-operator of the unconditional clause.

(23) [[Dare-ga saisyoni ik-u toiu] kanoosei-o Taro-ga
who-Nom first go-Pres C possibility-Acc Taro-Nom
ronzi-yooga], watasi-ni-wa kankee na-i.
discuss-Subj 1Sg-Dat-Top matter Neg-Pres
'Whoever the person x is such that Taro discusses a possibility that x will go first, I don't care.'

The contrast here suggests that *ka* is an intervener after all.

Taking stock, in section 3.1, we introduced Shimoyama's idea that *ka* denotes a function in (17a) that returns singletons, and pointed out some problems of this view. Since Shimoyama does not provide any independent argument for (17a), there is no strong reason to believe that the denotation of the Q-operator must be (17a). If Rawlins's analysis of unconditionals is on the right track, it serves as a piece of evidence for choosing the alternative-passing function in (17b) over (17a). Moreover, our analysis of unconditionals in Japanese provides supporting evidence for (17b). As shown in sections 3.2 and 3.3, if the denotation of the Q-operator is (17b), we need to assume that in examples such as (15) and (19), the true intervener is a Q-verb, not *ka*. However, this analysis is unable to account for example (22), where the intervention effect is observed in the absence of a Q-verb.

In order to keep the Hamblin analysis of unconditionals intact, we maintain Rawlins's assumption that the Q-operator is alternative-passing, as in (17b). As a way of explaining problematic examples of intervention such as (22), we explore a syntactic analysis of intervention, to which we turn next.

3.4 Takahashi's Analysis of Intervention in Universal Quantification

Takahashi (2002) claims that a determiner is base-generated in the position where it selects an indeterminates and that it moves to a surface position, namely, to D. The derivation of example (24) is illustrated in (25).

(24) [[Dare-ga yon-da] kyaku]*(-**mo**) ki-ta.
who-Nom invite-Past guest-MO come-Past
'For every person x, the guest(s) that x invited came.' (= (1b))

(25) $[_{DP}$ ... $[_{NP}$ ... $[_{CP}$ ... indeterminate t_{mo}...] NP] D *mo* ...]

Under this determiner-raising analysis, (26) is ungrammatical because the association of the indeterminate in RC_1 with *mo* is intervened by *ka*. The configuration in (27) violates relativized minimality (Rizzi 1990) / Minimal Link Condition (Chomsky 1995).

(26) *[[$_{RC2}$[[$_{RC1}$ Dare-o hihan-si-ta] dare-**ka**]-o taiho-si-ta]
who-Acc criticism-do-Past who-KA-Acc arrest-do-Past
keikan]-**mo** basse-rare-ta.
police.man-MO punish-Pass-Past
'(Lit.) Every policeman that arrested someone that criticized a person was punished.' (Takahashi 2002: 591)

(27) *[... [... [$_{CP}$ ... indet t_{mo}...] indet-D *ka*] ... D *mo* ...]
[F] [F] [F]

We argue, however, that the ungrammaticality of (26) is not due to intervention, but due to some syntactic reason. If, as Takahashi assumes, the particle *ka* is in a position that c-commands the indeterminate *dare*, we would expect (26) to be grammatical under the reading where the particle *mo* is interpreted as additive. Contrary to this prediction, (26) is outright ungrammatical.

Example (28) serves as a piece of supporting evidence for our claim. This example is ungrammatical even though there is no intervention involved, which demonstrates that a particle directly attached to a certain indeterminate cannot associate with another indeterminate.

(28) *[[$_{RC2}$[[$_{RC1}$ Dare-o hihan-si-ta] dare-**mo**]-o taiho-si-ta]
who-Acc criticism-do-Past who-MO-Acc arrest-do-Past
keikan]-ga basse-rare-ta.
police.man-Nom punish-Pass-Past
'(Lit.) Every policeman that arrested everyone that criticized a person was punished.'

Thus, we conclude that the ungrammaticality of (26) has nothing to do with intervention effects.

Before ending this section, we mention some additional questions raised by the determiner-raising analysis. First, it is not entirely clear whether the particles *ka* and *mo* are determiners to begin with (see Watanabe 2006, Hiraiwa 2017). Second, as Takahashi himself admits, determiner-raising violates the head movement constraint in the sense that the head movement of *mo* in (25) crosses intermediate heads as well as the CP relative clause boundary, and it is also immune to islands, which is unexpected if D moves.

4 Toward a Proper Understanding of Intervention Effects

We have seen so far that both semantic and syntactic accounts of intervention effects have some problems. In this section, we propose an alternative syntactic account of intervention. Intervention effects in (4)/(15) and (6)/(19) are schematically represented as (29a) and (29b), respectively.

(29) a. *[... [... [$_{CP}$ ... indeterminate] ... *ka* ...] ... *mo* ...]
b. *[... [... [$_{CP}$ ... indeterminate] ... *ka* ...] ... Q ...]

We assume that the particles *mo*, *ka*, and its covert counterpart Q share some feature [F], as illustrated in (30).

(30) *... indeterminate[F] ... X_1[F] ... X_2[F] (X = *ka*, *mo*, Q)

It follows that X_2 cannot associate with the indeterminate in the presence of the intervening X_1, which may be *ka*, *mo*, or Q. This in turn predicts that there are nine logically possible patterns of intervention effects; besides the two in (29), the seven patterns in (31) should be attested. In the following, we show that this prediction is borne out.

(31) a. *[... [... [$_{CP}$ ... indeterminate] ... *ka* ...] ... *ka* ...]
b. *[... [... [$_{CP}$ ... indeterminate] ... *mo* ...] ... *mo* ...]
c. *[... [... [$_{CP}$ ... indeterminate] ... *mo* ...] ... *ka* ...]
d. *[... [... [$_{CP}$ ... indeterminate] ... *mo* ...] ... Q ...]
e. *[... [... [$_{CP}$ ... indeterminate] ... Q ...] ... *ka* ...]
f. *[... [... [$_{CP}$ ... indeterminate] ... Q ...] ... *mo* ...]
g. *[... [... [$_{CP}$ ... indeterminate] ... Q ...] ... Q ...]

The pattern in (31a) has been widely reported in the literature (Nishigauchi 1990: 30, Watanabe 1992: 263, and Saito 2017: 2, among others).

(32) ??John-wa [Mary-ga nani-o kat-ta **ka** dooka]
John-Top Mary-Nom what-Acc buy-Past KA how.KA
Tom-ni tazune-ta no (desu **ka**)?
Tom-Dat ask-Past C Cop KA
'What did John ask Tom whether he bought?'
(Watanabe 1992: 263, slightly modified)

The patterns in (31b) and (31c) are also found in the literature, as in (33) and (34), respectively (Shimoyama 2006: 146–147, for instance).

(33) [[Dare-ga yon-da kyaku]-**mo** tabe-ta ryoori]-**mo** oisikat-ta.
who-Nom invite-Past guest-MO eat-Past food-MO tasty-Past

a. *the reading where the indeterminate associates with the lower *mo* as well as with the upper *mo* (unparaphrasable)

b. 'The food that, for every person x, the guest(s) that x had invited ate was also good.'

(34) [Dare-ga yon-da kyaku]-**mo** ki-masita **ka**?
who-Nom invite-Past guest-MO come-Past KA

a. *the reading where the indeterminate associates with *mo* as well as with *ka* (unparaphrasable)

b. 'Did for every person x, the guest(s) that x invited come?'

The pattern in (33d) is a case where an indeterminate and *-mo* appear in an unconditional clause, as in (35).

(35) [[Dare-ga yon-da kyaku]-**mo** ko-yooga] kankee na-i.
who-Nom invite-Past guest-MO come-Subj matter Neg-Pres

a. *the reading where the indeterminate associates with *mo* as well as with the covert Q-operator (unparaphrasable)

b. 'Whether or not for every person x, the guest(s) that x invited comes, I don't care.'

The patterns in (31e)–(31g) are the cases where an indeterminate is in an unconditional clause, and another operator appears in a position that c-commands the unconditional clause, as in (36)–(38).

(36) [Dare-ga ko-yooga] Taro-ni kankee arimas-u **ka**?
who-Nom come-Subj Taro-Dat matter be-Pres KA

a. *'Who is the person x such that whether or not x comes matter to Taro?'

b. 'Whoever comes, does it matter to Taro?'

(37) [[Dare-ga ko-yooga] ki-ni si-na-i] otoko]-**mo** kaet-ta.
who-Nom come-Subj matter-Dat do-Neg-Pres man-MO leave-Past

a. *'For every person y, and for every man x, such that x doesn't care whether y comes, x left.'

b. 'Also the man who doesn't care whoever comes left.'

(38) [[Dare-ga ko-yooga] Taro-ga okor-ooga]
who-Nom come-Subj Taro-Nom get angry-Subj
watasi-ni-wa kankee na-i.
1Sg-Dat-Top matter Neg-Pres

a. *'Whoever the person x is such that Taro gets angry whether or not x comes, I don't care.'

b. 'Whether or not Taro gets angry whoever comes, I don't care.'

All of these data show that indeterminates are subject to intervention effects and they can be explained by our feature-based minimality.

5 Conclusions

In this paper, we compared semantic and syntactic accounts of intervention effects, primarily basing ourselves on examples with bare indeterminates in unconditionals. We showed that existing semantic and syntactic accounts are not without problems, and proposed an alternative syntactic account. Another contribution here is to establish that intervention effects arise even when there is no overt particle *ka* or *mo*. It follows that the dependency between indeterminates and an overt operator is not compulsory, therefore corroborating our claim in Hiraiwa & Nakanishi (2019) and Nakanishi & Hiraiwa (2020) that the long-standing generalization that indeterminates require the presence of *ka* or *(de)mo* is unwarranted.

References

Chomsky, N. 1995. *The Minimalist Program*. Cambridge, MA: MIT Press.

Groenendijk, J., & M. Stokhof. 1984. Studies on the Semantics of Questions and the Pragmatics of Answers. Doctoral dissertation, University of Amsterdam.

Hagstrom, Paul. 1998. Decomposing Questions. Doctoral dissertation, MIT.

Hamblin, Charles. 1973. Questions in Montague English. *Foundations of Language* 10: 41–53.

Haspelmath, M., and E. König. 1998. Concessive Conditionals in the Languages of Europe. *Adverbial Constructions in the Languages of Europe*, ed. J. van der Auwera, 563–640. Berlin: Mouton de Gruyter.

Harada, K. I. 1972. Constraints on WH-Q Binding. *Descriptive & Applied Linguistics* 5: 180–206.

Hiraiwa, K. 2017. Labeling Roots: Indeterminates and Particles. *Proceedings of NELS 47*, ed. A. Lamont & K. Tetzloff, 79–88. Amherst, MA: GLSA.

Hiraiwa, K., & K. Nakanishi. 2020. Bare Indeterminates in Unconditionals. *Proceedings of the 94th Annual Meeting of the Linguistic Society of America.*

Karttunen, L. 1977. Syntax and Semantics of Questions. *Linguistics and Philosophy* 1: 3–44.

Kratzer, A. 1981. The Notional Category of Modality. *Words, Worlds, and Contexts: New Approaches in World Semantics*, ed. H.-J. Eikmeyer & H. Rieser, 38–74. Berlin: Walter de Gruyter.

Kratzer, A. 1986. Conditionals. *Proceedings of Chicago Linguistics Society 22*, ed. A. M. Farley, P. Farley & K. McCollough, 1–15. Chicago, IL: CLS.

Kratzer, A., & J. Shimoyama. 2002. Indeterminate Pronouns: The View from Japanese. *Proceedings of the 3rd Tokyo Conference on Psycholinguistics*, 1–25.

Kuroda, S.-Y. 1965. Generative Grammatical Studies in the Japanese Language. Doctoral dissertation, MIT.

Menéndez-Benito, P. 2006. The Grammar of Choice. Doctoral dissertation, University of Massachusetts at Amherst.

Nakanishi, K., & K. Hiraiwa. 2019. Nihongo no Hadaka Huteego: Zyoohozyookensetu ni okeru Ninka Mekanizumu o toosite [Bare Indeterminates in Japanese: A View from a Licensing Mechanism in Unconditionals]. *Hiteehyoogen no Koozoo, Imi, Kinoo [The Structure, Meaning, and Function of Negative Expressions]*, ed. O. Sawada, H. Kishimoto, and I. Imani, 154–179. Tokyo: Kaitakusya.

Nishigauchi, Taisuke. 1990. *Quantification in the Theory of Grammar*. Dordrecht: Kluwer Academic Publishers.

Quirk, R., S. Greenbaum, G. Leech, & J. Svartvik. 1985. *A Comprehensive Grammar of the English Language*. London, UK: Longman.

Rawlins, K. 2008. (Un)conditionals: An Investigation in the Syntax and Semantics of Conditional Structures. Doctoral dissertation, UCSC.

Rawlins, K. 2013. (Un)conditionals. *Natural Language Semantics* 40: 111–178.

Rizzi, L. 1990. *Relativized Minimality*. Cambridge, MA: MIT Press.

Saito, M. 2017. Japanese *Wh*-phrases as Operators with Unspecified Quantificational Force. *Language and Linguistics* 18: 1–25.

Shimoyama, J. 2001. WH-constructions in Japanese. Doctoral dissertation, University of Massachusetts at Amherst.

Shimoyama, J. 2006. Indeterminate Phrase Quantification in Japanese. *Natural Language Semantics* 14: 139–73.

Takahashi, D. 2002. Determiner Raising and Scope Shift. *Linguistic Inquiry* 33: 575–615.

Watanabe, A. 1992. Subjacency and S-structure Movement of *Wh*-in-situ. *Journal of East Asian Linguistics* 1: 255–291.

Watanabe, A. 2006. Functional Projections of Nominals in Japanese: Syntax of Classifiers. *Natural Language and Linguistic Theory* 24: 241–306.

A Semantic Analysis of Embedded Tense in Finite Control in Japanese*

YUSUKE KUBOTA
National Institute for Japanese Language and Linguistics

KOYO AKUZAWA
Kyoto University

1 Introduction

Obligatory control is standardly observed in non-finite clauses, not in finite clauses. See, for example, the contrast in (1) in English:

(1) a. John planned [PRO to run for the election].
b. *John planned [that PRO would run for the election].
(cf. John planned that he would run for the election.)

The finite/non-finite distinction plays an important role in exploring the properties of control, since PRO is standardly taken to be licensed in a non-finite clause, not in a finite clause in which the predicate inflects for tense and agreement.

Japanese verbs lack inflections triggered by grammatical agreement with the subject; instead, they are accompanied by various suffixal endings such

* This work was supported by JSPS KAKENHI 15K16732, 19K13165 and the NINJAL collaborative research project 'Cross-linguistic Studies of Japanese Prosody and Grammar'; we'd like to thank the audiences at JK2019 and the Semantics Workshop in Nagoya for feedback.

Japanese/Korean Linguistics 27.
Edited by Michael Barrie.

as tense, aspect and modality. It is controversial how the notion of finiteness in such a language can be defined,[1] but it has been widely noted by various authors that embedded clauses without the tense morpheme show largely parallel behaviors to infinitival clauses in English (see especially Kageyama, 1993). Consider, for example, the contrast in (2): in (2a) the embedded verb does not carry tense, whereas in (2b) the embedded verb has an overt past tense morpheme attached to it, and the former indices control but the latter doesn't.[2]

(2) a. John$_i$-wa [ϕ_i tegami-o dasi]-wasure-ta.
J.-TOP letter-ACC post-forget-PST
'John forgot to post the letter.'

b. John$_i$-wa [$\phi_{i/j}$ tegami-o dasi-ta] koto-o wasure-ta.
J.-TOP letter-ACC post-PST NC-ACC forget-PST
'John forgot posting the letter.'

But Japanese exhibits control in certain tensed clauses such as *koto*-marked complements in (3). In (3a,b), the missing subject obligatorily refers to the matrix subject John, whereas in (3c) it can refer to someone else as well.

(3) a. John$_i$-wa [ϕ_i hako-o ake-ru] koto-o ketuisi-ta.
J.-TOP box-ACC open-NPST NC-ACC decide PST
'John decided to open the box.'

b. John$_i$-wa [ϕ_i hako-o ake-ta] koto-o kookaisi-ta.
J.-TOP box-ACC open-PST NC-ACC regret-PST
'John regretted having open the box.'

c. John$_i$-wa [$\phi_{i/j}$ hako-o ake-ru] koto-o soozoosi-ta.
J.-TOP box-ACC open-NPST NC-ACC imagine-PST
'John imagined that he would open the box.'

Note that, despite the different properties in terms of control, the embedded clause carries an overt tense morpheme in all these sentences. Since Japanese is a pro-drop language, the status of the missing subject in (3a,b) has been controversial in the literature (Fujii 2006, 2012; Hasegawa 1984/85; Uchibori, 2000, among others): PRO should not be able to appear in tensed clauses, but

[1] See Takezawa (2016) for a recent overview and discussion of the inflection of Japanese verbs, and Tagawa (2019) for a recent morpho-syntactic discussion on the notion of finiteness in Japanese.

[2] We use the following abbreviations: TOP (topic), NOM (nominative), ACC (accusative), DAT (dative), PST (past), NPST (non-past), ASP (aspect), NC (nominal complementizer).

if the missing subject is pro, its obligatorily bound status remains a mystery. Following this line of research, we call control in tensed clauses 'finite control' in this paper.[3]

In the literature, syntactic approaches have been dominant as an explanation for why control is observed in tensed clauses (see, for example, Fujii, 2006 and Uchibori, 2000). Details vary, but most previous studies share the idea that PRO is licensed in certain tensed clause in which the tense is, in some sense, 'defective'. Akuzawa and Kubota (2019) have recently argued against the defective tense approach and claimed that the complement clauses in (3a,b) are fully tensed clauses and that the missing subject in (3a,b) is pro, rather than PRO. In Akuzawa and Kubota's (2019) account, finite control is induced semantically, that is, by the lexical meanings of the embedding verbs. Several pieces of evidence favor Akuzawa and Kubota's (2019) semantic analysis of finite control in Japanese over syntactic approaches, but they do not provide an explicit analysis of the embedded tense, which has been a central issue in the literature.

The present paper addresses this important remaining issue in the semantic analysis of finite control in Japanese, focusing on *koto*-taking control verbs. Specifically, we show that once we make explicit the lexical semantic properties of control verbs pertaining to the temporal relations between the matrix and embedded events, the observations which have (sometimes) been taken to support the defectiveness of embedded tense fall out straightforwardly as a consequence of the inherent semantic properties of the control verbs.

2 Two observations about embedded tense in control clauses

This section introduces two empirical observations about the temporal interpretations of control clauses: tense alternation possibilities and the restrictions on the distributions of temporal adverbials.

Before moving on to the specific phenomena, we introduce here a semantic classification of typical control verbs on the basis of their lexical meanings. For the purpose of the present paper, we focus on the following four classes: attitudinal, factive, attemptive and implicative. A non-exhaustive list of verbs from each category is given below:

[3] Finite control is not a phenomenon peculiar to Japanese; it has been noted in various languages including Balkan languages (Zec, 1987; Landau, 2004, 2006), Korean (Gamerschlag, 2007; Lee, 2009) and Chinese (Wang, 2011).

(4) a. **Attitudinal:** *ketui-suru* ('decide'), *siburu* ('hesitate'), *kuwadateru* ('plan')
 b. **Factive:** *kookai-suru* ('regret'), *hansei-suru* ('reflect on'), *zihu-suru* ('take pride in')
 c. **Attemptive:** *kokoromiru* ('try'), *kokoro-gakeru* ('keep in mind'), *torikumu* ('set about')
 d. **Implicative:** *sippai-suru* ('fail'), *seikoo-suru* ('succeed'), *zityoo-suru* ('refrain from')

Let us now turn to the first observation, pertaining to the alternation of embedded tense. It is well known that control verbs impose certain restrictions on the embedded tense (Fujii, 2006, 2016; Nakau, 1973; Sakaguchi, 1990; Uchibori, 2000). Here, we take up Fujii's (2006, 2016) observation, according to which control verbs do not allow tense alternation in the embedded clause. In (5), control verbs listed above in (4) exhibit a pattern in which they are compatible with either the nonpast or the past tense only. By contrast, non-control verbs typically do not impose any such restriction on the tense form of the embedded clause; note that the non-control verb *soozoo-suru* ('imagine') in (6) is compatible with both nonpast and past complements.

(5) a. John-wa [hako-o ake-ru/*ta] koto-o ketuisi-ta.
 J.-TOP box-ACC open-NPST/PST NC-ACC decide-PST
 b. John-wa [hako-o ake-*ru/ta] koto-o kookaisi-ta.
 J.-TOP box-ACC open-NPST/PST NC-ACC regret-PST
 c. John-wa [hako-o ake-ru/*ta] koto-o kokoromi-ta.
 J.-TOP box-ACC open-NPST/PST NC-ACC try-PST
 d. John-wa [hako-o ake-ru/*ta] koto-ni seikoosi-ta.
 J.-TOP box-ACC open-NPST/PST NC-DAT succeed-PST

(6) John-wa [hako-o ake-ru/ta] koto-o soozoosi-ta.
 J.-TOP box-ACC open-NPST/PST NC-ACC imagine-PST

Based on this observation, Fujii (2006, 2016) claims that control verbs do not allow tense alternation in the embedded clause.

The other important observation about the embedded tense is that different types of control verbs behave differently as to whether they allow for separate temporal adverbials in the matrix and embedded clauses (Nakau, 1973; Uchibori, 2000; Fujii, 2012). Unlike attitudinal verbs and factive verbs, attemptive verbs and implicative verbs do not allow for separate temporal adverbials:

(7) a. John-wa [rainen senkyo-ni de-ru] koto-o kotosi
J.-TOP next.year election-DAT run-NPST NC-ACC this.year
ketuisi-ta.
decide-PST

b. John-wa [kyonen senkyo-ni de-ta] koto-o kotosi
J.-TOP last.year election-DAT run-PST NC-ACC this.year
kookaisi-ta.
regret-PST

c. *John-wa [rainen senkyo-ni de-ru] koto-o kotosi
J.-TOP next.year election-DAT run-NPST NC-ACC this.year
kokoromi-ta.
try-PST

d. *John-wa [rainen senkyo-ni de-ru] koto-ni kotosi
J.-TOP next.year election-DAT run-NPST NC-DAT this.year
seikoosi-ta.
succeed-PST

Some of the facts noted above have been taken by previous authors to support particular types of analyses of finite control in Japanese. Due to space limitations, we cannot provide a review of these previous proposals in this paper, but we acknowledge here that, regardless of theoretical assumptions, the facts themselves need to be accounted for. Our own account, presented in section 4, differs from major accounts in the previous literature in offering a semantic explanation for these observations.

3 Is embedded tense defective?

Most previous studies attribute the observations in the previous section to the defectiveness of embedded tense. For example, Fujii (2006) suggests the following syntactic generalization dubbed 'Tense Alternation Generalization (TAG)', and assumes that the embedded tense of control verbs is defective.

(8) **Tense Alternation Generalization:** Tensed subordinate clauses in Japanese act like infinitives if and only if their predicate doesn't alternate between nonpast and past tense forms.

Similarly, Uchibori (2000) claims that some control verbs do not allow separate temporal adverbials since their embedded tenses are syntactically so defective that they cannot have independent temporal domain.

The notion of defective tense thus plays an important role in both Fujii's and Uchibori's syntactic accounts, and with respect to two related (but distinct) sets of empirical patterns, but it remains unclear what exactly is meant by this notion. In particular, it is unclear how 'defective tense' fits in the overall tense system of Japanese, which overwhelmingly exhibits relative tense in embedded contexts (Teramura, 1984; Ogihara, 1996; Kusumoto, 1999). Moreover, Uchibori's account suggests that defectiveness is a graded notion, but then, the correlation between this notion and the property of control is unclear. That is, how defective does a predicate have to be in order to license control?

In addition to the conceptual problems noted above, the 'defectiveness' approach has at least two major empirical problems. First, some control verbs such as *kookai-suru* ('regret') permit tense alternation with stative predicates as discussed in Akuzawa (2018) and Akuzawa and Kubota (2019).[4]

(9) John-wa [Tokyo-ni i-ru/ta] koto-o kookaisi-ta.
J.-TOP Tokyo-in be-NPST/PST NC-ACC regret-PST
'John regretted being/having been in Tokyo.'

Second, the missing subject can sometimes appear overtly. This is problematic because nominative case is standardly taken to be licensed by finite T(ense) (Takezawa, 1987).

(10) John$_i$-wa [ϕ_i/kare$_i$/zibun$_i$-ga hako-o ake-ru] koto-o
J.-TOP he/himself-NOM box-ACC open-NPST NC-ACC
ketuisi-ta.
decide-PST
'John decided to open the box himself.'

In view of the difficulties of the 'defectiveness' approach, we take the embedded tense of *koto*-complement clauses to be non-defective. In the next section, we show that a semantic approach adequately captures the observations about tense and temporal interpretation of control verbs from section 2, which are updated and summarized in (11).

(11) Tense property of embedded clause in finite control

	tense form	separate temporal adverbials
attitudinal	*-ru/*-ta*	yes
factive	*-ru/-ta*	yes
attemptive	*-ru/*-ta*	no
implicative	*-ru/*-ta*	no

[4] The fact that *kookai-suru* allows tense alternation is originally noted by Uchibori (2000, 204), but she does not consider this verb as a control verb.

4 A non-defective analysis of embedded tense in control clauses

In this section, we show that both the tense alternation generalization (including its exceptions) and the restrictions on the distribution of temporal adverbials follow from the semantic analysis of finite control proposed by Akuzawa and Kubota (2019), once we spell out the meanings of control verbs in detail. Since our analysis crucially involves temporal interpretation, we start by laying out some assumptions about tense interpretation (in particular, in embedded contexts) and then move on to the analysis of control verbs.

4.1 Embedded tense in Japanese

As discussed by many authors (Teramura, 1984; Ogihara, 1996; Kusumoto, 1999), Japanese has a relative tense system. This means that tense in embedded contexts are interpreted with respect to the event time of the matrix clause rather than the speech time (as in languages with the absolute tense system such as English). This can be seen most clearly with temporal adverbial clauses such as *ato-de* ('after') and *mae-ni* ('before') clauses (see, e.g., Ogihara, 1996). In Japanese, the past tense is obligatory in 'after' clauses and the nonpast tense is obligatory in 'before' clauses:

(12) a. John-wa yuuhan-o tabe-ru/*ta-mae-ni te-o arat-ta.
J.-TOP dinner-ACC eat-NPST/PST-before hand-ACC wash-PAST
'John washed his hands before having dinner.'

b. John-wa yuuhan-o tabe-*ru/ta-ato-de sanpo-ni ik-u.
J.-TOP dinner-ACC eat-NPST/PST-after walk-DAT go-NPST
'John will take a walk after having dinner.'

The 'before' clause locates the matrix event before the embedded event, so, the embedded event is in the future with respect to the matrix event time. Thus, the nonpast tense is obligatory, regardless of whether the embedded event is in the past or future relative to the speech time. Similarly, the past tense marking is obligatory in 'after' clauses.

There are several different ways to implement relative tense in a formal compositional system. Here, we loosely follow the approach proposed by Kubota et al. (2012), which recognizes the notion of 'evaluation time' as a key primitive concept. The idea in a nutshell is that tense locates the event time with respect to the evaluation time, and that the evaluation time is set to different times depending on the syntactic context in which the tense morpheme appears. Roughly, the evaluation time is set to the speech time in matrix clauses and to the matrix event time in embedded clauses.

On this assumption, the meanings of the nonpast and past tenses can be formulated as follows, where t_{eval} designates the evaluation time:[5]

(13) a. $[\![\text{ -}ru\ ]\!] = \lambda P \lambda x \lambda t \lambda w.P(x)(t)(w) \wedge t \geq t_{eval}$

b. $[\![\text{ -}ta\ ]\!] = \lambda P \lambda x \lambda t \lambda w.P(x)(t)(w) \wedge t < t_{eval}$

4.2 Lexical meanings of control verbs

We now move on to the analysis of the lexical meanings of the specific control verbs. In what follows, we focus on the four types of control verbs introduced in section 2, specifically, attitudinal, factive, attemptive and implicative verbs. These four classes of verbs constitute the major types of *koto*-taking control verbs.[6] Attitudinal and attemptive verbs are future-oriented due to their lexical meanings, whereas factive and implicative verbs are non-future-oriented, again, due to their lexical meanings.

Among the four types of verbs, attitudinal and factive verbs allow for separate temporal adverbials in the embedded and matrix clauses, as noted in section 2. These verbs have meanings whose temporal components are easier to identify, so we deal with them first, starting with attitudinal verbs.

Intuitively, attitudinal verbs are incomparable with the past tense since the embedded clause needs to have future reference with respect to the matrix event time. To be more concrete, building on Akuzawa and Kubota's (2019) modal analysis of control verbs, the attitudinal verb *ketui-suru* ('decide') can be analyzed as follows (here and in what follows, the presuppositional component is underlined; $Alt^{volit}_{x,t,w}$ designates the set of volitional alternative worlds for x at t in w):

(14) $$\lambda P \lambda x \lambda t \lambda w.\underline{\forall w' \in Alt^{epst}_{x,t,w} : \exists t' > t.\exists Q.\mathbf{discret}(Q)(x)(t)(w') \wedge [P(x)(t')(w') \rightarrow Q(x)(t)(w')]}; \forall w'' \in Alt^{volit}_{x,t,w}.Q(x)(t)(w'')$$

That is, *ketui-suru* presupposes that the controller x recognizes that engaging in some activity Q that is at his/her discretion at t (i.e. the matrix time) is a necessary condition for the realization of P (i.e. the content of the embedded clause) at a future time t', and asserts that x has a volitional commitment to Q. (We leave unanalyzed the primitive predicate **discret**, where

---

[5] For the sake of expository ease, we treat the evaluation time as a free variable. Making the analysis fully compositional involves treating this variable as a λ-bound parameter that is explicitly passed from the embedded clause to the higher clause. Since nothing crucially hinges on this detail, we stick to the simplifying assumption in what follows.

[6] But it should be kept in mind that they are by no means exhaustive. In particular, we do not deal with *koto*-taking aspectual verbs inducing control such as *hazimeru* ('begin'), *tuzukeru* ('continue') and *oeru* ('finish'). Extending the present approach to these verbs is a task for future research.

$\mathbf{discret}(P)(x)(t)(w)$ iff P is at x's discretion at t in w.) Crucially, the verb shifts the time of P to future ($t' > t$) due to its lexical meaning.

Assuming that the temporal variable is existentially closed in matrix clauses, the denotations for (5a) with nonpast and past tenses come out as in (15) and (16), respectively (where t_{now} is the speech time).

(15) $\exists t < t_{now}.\underline{\forall w' \in Alt^{epst}_{\mathbf{j},t,w} : \exists t' > t.\exists Q.\mathbf{discret}(Q)(\mathbf{j})(t)(w')}$
$\underline{\wedge[[\mathbf{open\text{-}the\text{-}box}(\mathbf{j})(t')(w') \wedge t' \geq t] \rightarrow Q(\mathbf{j})(t)(w')]}$;
$\forall w'' \in Alt^{volit}_{\mathbf{j},t,w}.Q(\mathbf{j})(t)(w'')$

(16) $\exists t < t_{now}.\underline{\forall w' \in Alt^{epst}_{\mathbf{j},t,w} : \exists t' > t.\exists Q.\mathbf{discret}(Q)(\mathbf{j})(t)(w')}$
$\underline{\wedge[[\mathbf{open\text{-}the\text{-}box}(\mathbf{j})(t')(w') \wedge t' < t\,] \rightarrow Q(\mathbf{j})(t)(w')]}$;
$\forall w'' \in Alt^{volit}_{\mathbf{j},t,w}.Q(\mathbf{j})(t)(w'')$

(15) is a contradiction (with $t' > t$, $t' < t$), so it follows that *ketui-suru* is incompatible with the past tense.

In contrast to the future-oriented verbs, factive verbs such as *kookai-suru* ('regret') are past-oriented (or, more precisely, non-future-oriented), given the nature of the semantic relations they express. The key idea here is that one can only regret things whose consequences are relevant at the time of regretting. This means that, for eventive predicates, the relevant event needs to have already happened (note that nonpast tense of eventive predicates in Japanese is future-oriented, thus excluding the simultaneous interpretation).[7] For stative predicates, since the nonpast tense is compatible with the simultaneous interpretation, both the past and nonpast tenses are predicted to be acceptable. Thus, an apparent exception to TAG receives a natural explanation in our semantic account.

The lexical meaning for *kookai-suru* ('regret') can be specified as follows:

(17) $\lambda P \lambda x \lambda t \lambda w.\quad \exists t', t''.t' \leq t \wedge t'' < t' \wedge P(x)(t')(w) \wedge \underline{\forall w' \in Alt^{epst}_{x,t,w}.}$
$\underline{\exists Q.\mathbf{discret}(Q)(x)(t'')(w') \wedge [Q(x)(t'')(w') \rightarrow \neg P(x)(t')(w')]}$;
$\forall w'' \in Alt^{desider}_{x,t,w}.Q(x)(t'')(w'')$

---

[7] Things are actually a bit more complex here since there are certain examples in which the nonpast tense is acceptable with eventive predicates, such as the following:

(i)	John-wa	kagyoo-o	tug-u	koto-o	imasara	kookaisi-tei-ru.
	J.-TOP	family.business-ACC	take.over-NPST	NC-ACC	at.this.stage	regret-PROG-NPST

'John regrets having decided to take over his family business at this late stage.'

Examples such as (i) sound much better than examples such as (5b) (with the nonpast tense). It is currently unclear what the relevant factors are that improve the acceptability of factive control verbs with embedded nonpast tense. We leave this issue for future study.

(17) introduces two conditions in its presupposition: (i) P (i.e. the embedded event) obtains at t', which is either simultaneous with or preceding the matrix time t (the factive component), and (ii) there was some action Q, which was at x's discretion at a time t' preceding t'' and which could have prevented P. On the basis of this presupposition, the sentence asserts that at the matrix time t, x wishes (or, finds it desirable) to have actually done Q at t''.

The event time t' of P is constrained to either be simultaneous with or precede the matrix event time. On the standard assumption that the nonpast tense of eventive predicates has (relative) future reference, it is correctly predicted that *kookai-suru* is compatible with past tense only when the embedded verb is eventive. By contrast, with stative predicates, which allow for the simultaneous/present interpretation for the nonpast tense, the nonpast tense is predicted to be acceptable. This is indeed the case (Uchibori, 2000, 204), and, as noted by Akuzawa (2018) and Akuzawa and Kubota (2019), this fact constitutes important counterevidence to Fujii's TAG (which by assumption is a purely syntactic condition).

We now turn to the other two classes of verbs, namely, attemptive and implicative verbs. As compared to attitudinal verbs, for which the relevant goal-oriented attitude is strictly inside the mind of the attitude holder (i.e. the controller), attemptive verbs have a stronger entailment with respect to how the attitude holder behaves in the actual world at the event time. Roughly, in the case of *kokoromiru* ('try'), the attitude holder has to be engaged in some activity which is a precondition for the realization of the event denoted by the embedded clause (at least in the most typical cases). Thus, the meaning of *kokoromiru* can be characterized as follows:

(18) $$\lambda P \lambda x \lambda t \lambda w.\, \underline{\forall w' \in Alt^{epst}_{x,t,w}.\exists t' \supseteq t.P(x)(t')(w') \rightarrow \mathbf{prep}(P)(x)(t)(w')}; \mathbf{prep}(P)(x)(t)(w)$$

Here, $\mathbf{prep}(P)(x)(t)(w)$ is true iff x engages in some activity at t in w that counts as a preparatory stage for P. (18) presupposes that x realizes that engaging in the preparatory activity of P is a necessary condition for the realization of P, and asserts that x does actually engage in such an activity. Assuming an interval-based semantics, the temporal interval at which $\mathbf{prep}(P)$ holds has to be a subinterval of the interval at which P holds (i.e. $t' \supseteq t$). This effectively imposes a simultaneity condition on the matrix and embedded event times, predicting the obligatoriness of the embedded nonpast tense (see below) and the impossibility of separate temporal adverbial modification (which we discuss in the next section).

Given the lexical entry for *kokoromiru* in (18), the denotation for (5c) with the past tense comes out as follows:

(19) $\exists t < t_{now}.\ \underline{\forall w' \in Alt^{epst}_{\mathbf{j},t,w}.\exists t' \supset t.[\mathbf{open\text{-}the\text{-}box}(\mathbf{j})(t')(w') \wedge t' < t] \rightarrow}$
$\underline{\mathbf{prep}(\lambda x \lambda t_0 \lambda w.\mathbf{open\text{-}the\text{-}box}(x)(t_0)(w) \wedge t_0 < t)(\mathbf{j})(t)(w')}$;
$\mathbf{prep}(\lambda x \lambda t_0 \lambda w.\mathbf{open\text{-}the\text{-}box}(x)(t_0)(w) \wedge t_0 < t)(\mathbf{j})(t)(w)$

Here, the embedded tense locates the event time t' of opening the box in the past relative to the matrix event time t. But this contradicts with the lexical meaning of the attemptive verb *kokoromiru* ('try'), which requires the runtime t of the preparatory stage to be a proper subinterval of the runtime t' of the whole event. Thus, the unacceptability of the past tense in (5c) is correctly predicted.

Finally, for implicative verbs, we build on Akuzawa and Kubota's (2019) idea that verbs such as *seikoo-suru* ('succeed') and *sippai-suru* ('fail') have as their presuppositions the meanings of attemptive verbs. Specifically, we assume the following meaning for *seikoo-suru*, which roughly says that 'succeed P (at t)' presupposes that at some subinterval t' of t, 'try P' is true and asserts that P actually obtains at t.

(20) $\lambda P \lambda x \lambda t \lambda w.\underline{\exists t' \subseteq t.\mathbf{try}(P)(x)(t')(w)}; P(x)(t)(w)$

The predicate **try** is by assumption identical to the meaning of *kokoromiru* in (18).

Then, in (5d) with the past tense, given the lexical meaning of the implicative verb *seikoo-suru* ('succeed') in (20) which effectively evaluates the whole embedded event as a matrix event, the assertion of the sentence has the following form:

(21) $\exists t < t_{now}.\mathbf{open\text{-}the\text{-}box}(x)(t)(w) \wedge t < t_{eval}$

Here, $t < t_{eval}$ is the semantic contribution of the embedded past tense, and by assumption t_{eval} gets identified with the matrix event time t. But that leads to the contradiction $t < t$. Thus, implicative verbs are incomparable with embedded past tense.

In this section, we have shown that the tense restrictions that different types of control verbs in Japanese exhibit receive semantic explanations. In particular, it should now be clear that Fujii's TAG is not only redundant in most cases, but also is less plausible than the semantic analysis in certain cases (specifically, with factive verbs, which the TAG-based analysis would need to analyze as an exception without any principled reason). Our analysis finds motivation from independently motivated lexical semantic properties of the relevant verbs and the independently motivated assumption that embedded tense in Japanese is relative tense rather than absolute tense.

4.3 Temporal adverbials

The analysis of temporal adverbials is essentially parallel to the analysis of tense morpheme restrictions. Temporal adverbials introduce restrictions on the temporal locations of the events they modify, and, depending on the lexical meanings of control verbs, such restrictions may or may not lead to contradictions.

Following authors such as Dowty (1979) and Stump (1985), we assume that temporal adverbials are modifiers of temporal abstracts, formally of type $\langle\langle i, st\rangle, \langle i, st\rangle\rangle$ (where i is a variable over temporal intervals and s is a variable over worlds). For example, the denotation of *kinoo* ('yesterday') can be written as in (22), which adds the condition that the runtime of the event is temporally located within the time frame corresponding to yesterday:

(22) $\lambda P_{\langle i,st\rangle} \lambda t \lambda w. P(t)(w) \wedge t \subseteq \mathbf{yesterday}$

(7a), which has the attitudinal verb *ketui-suru* ('decide') as its main verb, receives the following translation:

(23) $\exists t < t_{now}. \underline{\forall w' \in Alt^{epst}_{\mathbf{j},t,w} : \exists t' > t. \exists Q. \mathbf{discret}(Q)(\mathbf{j})(t)(w')}$
$\underline{\wedge[[\mathbf{run\text{-}for\text{-}el}(\mathbf{j})(t')(w') \wedge t' \subseteq \mathbf{next\text{-}yr}] \rightarrow Q(\mathbf{j})(t)(w')]};$
$\forall w'' \in Alt^{volit}_{\mathbf{j},t,w}. Q(\mathbf{j})(t)(w'') \wedge t \subseteq \mathbf{this\text{-}yr}$

Here, as already discussed in the previous section, the lexical meaning of the verb locates the embedded event in the future relative to the matrix event time, so the events are temporally disjoint with one another. The additional temporal restrictions introduced by the embedded and matrix temporal adverbials are consistent with this lexical meaning of the verb, so, the sentence is correctly predicted to be acceptable. The case of factive verbs can be explained similarly. Since the account is completely parallel, except that the temporal order of the matrix and embedded events is reversed, we omit the details.

Things are different in the case of the other two classes of verbs, which involve more complex relations between the matrix and embedded event times. Simply put, these verbs impose overlap conditions on the embedded event time and its evaluation time (which corresponds to the matrix event time in the case of attemptive verbs), and this conflicts with the temporal disjointness condition introduced by the temporal adverbials in the matrix and embedded clauses in (7c,d).

For example, (7c) receives the following translation:

(24) $$\begin{array}{l} \exists t < t_{now}. \\ \forall w' \in Alt^{epst}_{\mathbf{j},t,w} : \exists t' \supseteq t.[\mathbf{run\text{-}for\text{-}el}(\mathbf{j})(t')(w) \wedge t' \subseteq \mathbf{next\text{-}yr}] \\ \rightarrow \mathbf{prep}(\lambda x \lambda t \lambda w.\mathbf{run\text{-}for\text{-}el}(x)(t)(w) \wedge t \subseteq \mathbf{next\text{-}yr})(\mathbf{j})(t)(w'); \\ \mathbf{prep}(\lambda x \lambda t \lambda w.\mathbf{run\text{-}for\text{-}el}(x)(t)(w) \wedge t \subseteq \mathbf{next\text{-}yr}) \wedge t \subseteq \mathbf{this\text{-}yr} \end{array}$$

The meaning of *kokoromiru* requires the matrix event time t (i.e. the time of the preparatory stage of the embedded event) to be a proper subinterval of the embedded event time t', given the nature of preparatory stage. However, the temporal adverbials *kotosi* ('this year') and *rainen* ('next year') do not overlap with one another, so, if t and t' are subintervals of these temporal intervals, then, t and t' will have to be completely disjoint, and the former cannot be a subinterval of the latter. Thus, (24) necessarily leads to a contradiction.

The case of implicative verbs such as *seikoo-suru* ('succeed') is slightly more complicated, but the ill-formedness of disjoint temporal modification follows from essentially the same reason. The translation for (7d) is given in (25).

(25) $$\begin{array}{l} \exists t < t_{now}. \\ \exists t' \subseteq t.\mathbf{try}(\lambda x \lambda t \lambda w.\mathbf{run\text{-}for\text{-}el}(x)(t)(w) \wedge t \subseteq \mathbf{next\text{-}yr})(\mathbf{j})(t')(w); \\ [\mathbf{run\text{-}for\text{-}el}(\mathbf{j})(t)(w) \wedge t \subseteq \mathbf{next\text{-}yr}] \wedge t \subseteq \mathbf{this\text{-}yr} \end{array}$$

Note crucially here that given the lexical meaning in (20), an implicative verb evaluates the embedded event P at the matrix event time t. This has the consequence that the two temporal adverbials *kotosi* ('this year') and *rainen* ('next year') from the embedded and matrix clauses both target the same event time t. But then, the disjointness of the temporal extensions of *kotosi* and *rainen* directly leads to a contradiction.

In this section, we have shown that the two empirical phenomena discussed in the literature pertaining to the temporal interpretations of control verbs in Japanese receive independently motivated explanations by formalizing the lexical semantics of control verbs explicitly within the standard temporal/modal semantics. Note in particular that, on the proposed account, the distributional patterns that different control verbs exhibit with respect to these phenomena all fall out as natural consequences of the semantic analyses.

5 Conclusion

In this paper, we have proposed an analysis of temporal interpretation of finite control in Japanese with *koto*-taking verbs. We started with two empirical observations in the literature pertaining to the temporal interpretation of these control verbs: the 'Tense Alternation Generalization' (TAG) by Fujii (2006) and the distributional restrictions on temporal adverbial modifiers with certain control verbs. While these empirical phenomena have sometimes been used by previous authors to motivate particular syntactic assumptions about the status of the tense morpheme in the embedded clauses in *koto*-taking control verbs, we have shown in this paper that all the relevant empirical facts pertaining to these generalizations receive independently motivated semantic accounts. To demonstrate this point, we have formulated explicit analyses of selected classes of control verbs building on formal semantic approaches to modal and temporal expressions.

The results of the present paper have important implications for the wider cross-linguistic literature on finite control and defective tense (cf. Stiebels, 2007; Gamerschlag, 2007; Spyropoulos, 2008; Smirnova, 2009) in that it shows that a semantic approach offers a better explanation for TAG than a syntactic approach both empirically and conceptually. Empirically, it has a wider coverage in extending naturally to apparent exceptions with factive verbs. Conceptually, it is more explanatory in that it derives the relevant patterns from independently motivated semantic properties, rather than stipulating TAG as a separate principle.

References

Akuzawa, K. 2018. *Kontorooru Genshoo-no Toogo-teki Imi-teki Bunseki: Shubun-Dooshi-to Hobun-keishiki-no Taioo-Kankei (Syntactic and Semantic Analysis of Control Phenomena: Correspondence between Matrix Verb and Complement Clause Structure).* Doctoral Dissertation, University of Tsukuba.

Akuzawa, K. and Y. Kubota 2019. A semantic analysis of finite control in Japanese. In *Proceedings of Japanese/Korean Linguistics*, Volume 26, pp.

Dowty, D. 1979. *Word Meaning and Montague Grammar.* Dordrecht, Holland: D. Reidel.

Fujii, T. 2006. *Some Theoretical Issues in Japanese Control.* Doctoral Dissertation, University of Maryland.

Fujii, T. 2012. On the calculus of control and lack of overt agreement morphology. In *Nanzan Linguistics*, Volume 8, pp. 1–16.

Fujii, T. 2016. Fukubun-no koozoo-to umekomi hobun-no bunrui (Structures of bi-clausal sentences and classification of embedded clauses). In K. Murasugi, M. Saito, Y. Miyamoto, and K. Takita (Eds.), *Nihongo Bunpoo Handobukku: Gengo Riron-to Gengo Kakutoku-no Kanten-kara (Handbook of Japanese Grammar: Linguistic Theory and Language Acquisition)*, pp. 2–37. Tokyo: Kaitakusha.

Gamerschlag, T. 2007. Semantic and structural aspects of complement control in Korean. In *ZAS Papers in Linguistics*, Volume 47, pp. 81–123.

Hasegawa, N. 1984–1985. On the so-called "zero pronouns" in Japanese. *The Linguistic Review 4*, 289–341.

Kageyama, T. 1993. *Bunpoo to Go-Keisei (Grammar and Word Formation).* Tokyo: Hituzi Syobo.

Kubota, Y., J. Lee, A. Smirnova, and J. Tonhauser 2012. Cross-linguistic variation in temporal adjunct clauses. In *Cahier Chronos*, Volume 25, pp. 141–161. Amsterdam/Atlanta: Rodopi.

Kusumoto, K. 1999. *Tense in Embedded Contexts.* Doctoral Dissertation, University of Massachusetts at Amherst.

Landau, I. 2004. The scale of finiteness and the calculus of control. *Natural Language and Linguistic Theory 22*, 811–877.

Landau, I. 2006. Severing the distribution of pro from case. *Syntax 9*, 43–60.

Lee, K. Y. 2009. *Finite Control in Korean.* Doctoral Dissertation, University of Iowa.

Nakau, M. 1973. *Sentential complementation in Japanese.* Tokyo: Kaitakusha.

Ogihara, T. 1996. *Tense, Attitudes, and Scope.* Dordrecht: Kluwer Academic Publishers.

Sakaguchi, M. 1990. Control structures in Japanese. In *Japanese/Korean Linguistics*, Volume 1, pp. 303–317.

Smirnova, A. 2009. A case against 'defective' tense in the Bulgarian subjunctive. In *Formal Approaches to Slavic Linguistics 17*, pp. 200–215. Michigan Slavic Publications.

Spyropoulos, V. 2008. Finiteness and control in Greek. In W. Davies and S. Dubinsky (Eds.), *New Horizons in the Analysis of Control and Raising*, pp. 159–183. Dordrecht: Springer.

Stiebels, B. 2007. Towards a typology of complement control. In *ZAS Papers in Linguistics*, Volume 47, pp. 1–80.

Stump, G. T. 1985. *The Semantic Variability of Absolute Constructions.* Dordrecht: D. Reidel.

Tagawa, T. 2019. Futei(kei)-toshite-no *-ru*-kei to *ka* sengen tooisetsu (*-ru* as an infinitival form and disjunctive coordination with *ka*). In I. Iori and T. Tagawa (Eds.), *Nihongo-no Tensu Asupekuto Kenkyuu-o Toinaosu:* Suru*-no Sekai (Reconsidering Tense and Aspect in Japanese: The World of* suru*)*, Volume 1, pp. 1–23. Tokyo: Hituzi Syoboo.

Takezawa, K. 1987. *A Configurational Approach to Case-marking in Japanese.* Doctoral Dissertation, University of Washington.

Takezawa, K. 2016. Inflection. In T. Kageyama and H. Kishimoto (Eds.), *Handbook of Japanese Lexicon and Word Formation*, pp. 459–487. Boston/Berlin: Walter de Gruyter.

Teramura, H. 1984. *Nihongo-no Shintakusu-to Imi (Syntax and Semantics of Japanese) II.* Tokyo: Kurosio.

Uchibori, A. 2000. *The Syntax of Subjunctive Complements: Evidence from Japanese.* Doctoral Dissertation, University of Connecticut.

Wang, D. 2011. *Pro-Datsuraku Gengo-niokeru Zero-Yooso-no Toogo-teki Bunseki: Nihongo-to Chuugoku-go-o Chuushin-ni (Syntactic analysis of Zero Elements in Pro-drop Languages: Focusing on Japanese and Chinese).* Doctoral Dissertation, University of Tsukuba.

Zec, D. 1987. On obligatory control in clausal complements. In M. Iida, S. Wechsler, and D. Zec (Eds.), *Working Papers in Grammatical Theory and Discourse Structure*, Number 11 in CSLI Lecture Notes, pp. 139–168. Stanford: CSLI Publications.

How to Eat Your Cake and Have it Too in Japanese: Causal Pluralism and the Role of Agentivity[1]

YOSUKE SATO

1 Introduction

It is widely acknowledged in the Japanese literature (Ikegami 1980/1981, 1981; Kageyama 1996; Tsujimura 2003) that causative accomplishment verbs in Japanese do not necessarily entail the resulting change of state named by the verbs, yielding a non-culminating, zero change-of-state (CoS) interpretation. Example (1) illustrates this point.

(1) Megumi-ga kinoo tikaraippai doa-o
Megumi-NOM yesterday with.all.one's strength door-ACC
sime-ta-kedo, zenzen simara-naka-tta-nda-yo.
close-PST-but at.all close-NEG-PST-COP-PRT

'Megumi closed the door yesterday with all her strength, but it didn't close at all.'

[1] I thank Duk-Ho An, Rahul Balusu, Mike Barrie, Tanmoy Bhattacharya, Lauren Clemens, Mitcho Erlewine, Nobu Goto, Shin Kitada, Seunhung Lee, Beth Levin, Keiko Murasugi, Mamoru Saito, Yutaka Sato, Makiko Tawa, Shaio Wei Tham, Elisabeth Verhoeven, Phillip Wolff, Tomo Yoshida, Dwi Hesti Yuliani, the audience members at the workshops at ICU (May 2019) and NUS (May 2019) and at JKL 27 held at Sogang University (October 2019) and my students at Seisen University for helpful comments. Special thanks to Heidi Harley and Fabienne Martin for invaluable discussions on non-culminating accomplishments. This research is supported by the Japan Society for the Promotion of Science, Grant-in-Aid for Scientific Research (C) (Project #JP19K00560, April 2019–March 2023).

Japanese/Korean Linguistics 27.
Edited by Michael Barrie.

As first noted by Tsujimura (2003), however, when the agent subject in (1) is replaced with a non-volitional causer subject, the non-culminating, zero CoS construal can no longer be obtained, as shown in (2).

(2) Kyuna kaze-ga kinoo doa-o sime-ta-kedo,
sudden wind-NOM yesterday door-ACC close-PST-but
#zenzen simara-naka-tta-nda-yo.
at.all close-NEG-PST-COP-PRT
'A sudden wind closed the door yesterday, but it didn't close at all.'

Tsujimura (2003: 398) summarizes the puzzle illustrated by the contrast between (1) and (2) as follows:

> … what seems to be common in all languages that exhibit the event cancellation phenomenon is intentionality … In Japanese, if the agent of the action denoted by the verb does not have the intention to carry out the event but the event instead takes place by accident, cancellation of the event is not possible. … Thus, a remaining challenge is determining whether or how such intentionality should be represented in the lexical representation of verbs.

This paper addresses Tsujimura's puzzle, which remains unexplored in the Japanese literature, and outlines a plausible solution to the puzzle within Martin's (2015, 2019) event-tokenization theory of causation types. Of crucial import for my present purposes is the Causal Pluralism Hypothesis from Martin's theory that two causation types must be conceptualized differently depending on the intentionality of the external argument in subject position. More specifically, agentive causation is tokenized by the agent's action as well as the theme's CoS sub-event tokens whereas non-agentive causation is tokenized by the theme's CoS token alone. I show that this hypothesis interacts with the maximality requirement of the partitive perfective operator PFV_M (Koenig and Muansuwan 2000; Altshuler 2014, 2016; Martin 2019; Martin and Gyarmathy, forthcoming) to yield the intentionality-sensitive distribution of the non-culminating, zero CoS construal of causative accomplishment verbs in Japanese.

2 The Data: Non-Culminating Accomplishments and the Role of Intentionality in Japanese

What is crucial for the non-culminating, zero CoS construal of causative accomplishment verbs to hold in Japanese is the intentionality of an agentive argument in subject position: see also Lee (2015) and Beavers and Lee (in press) for the same observation in Korean causative accomplishments. This observation is illustrated below in (3–4).

(3) Megumi-ga kinoo ukkari/matigatte doa-o
Megumi-NOM yesterday accidentally/by.mistake door-ACC
sime-ta-kedo, #zenzen simara-naka-tta-nda-yo. (accidental agent)
close-PST-but at.all close-NEG-PST-COP-PRT
'Megumi closed the door accidentally/by mistake yesterday, but it didn't close at all.'

(4) Doa-ga kinoo hoanzyoo-no riyuu-de sime-rare-ta-kedo,
door-NOM yesterday security-GEN reason-for close-PASS-PST-but
#zenzen simara-naka-tta-nda-yo. (implied agent)
at.all close-NEG-PST-COP-PRT
'The door was closed for a security reason yesterday, but it didn't close at all.'

The example in (3) shows that the accidental agent in subject position cannot license the non-culminating, zero CoS construal with the causative accomplishment verb *simeru* 'to close'. The example in (4) contains the direct passive construction in its first clause. Our world knowledge tells us that there has to be an intentional agent involved for the door to be closed for a security reason. The impossibility of the non-culminating, zero CoS reading in this example, then, indicates that the mere presence of an implied agent inferred from our world knowledge is not sufficient to license the relevant reading.

The examples in (5–8) further illustrate the generalization above regarding the strong correlation between the non-culminating, zero CoS construal of accomplishment verbs and the intentional agent in subject position.

(5) Hikari-ga kinoo otiba-o moyasi-ta-kedo, simetteite
Hikari-NOM yesterday fallen.leave-ACC burn-PST-but were.wet
zenzen moe-nak-atta-yo. (volitional agent)
at.all burn-NEG-PST-PRT
'Hikari burned the fallen leaves yesterday, but they didn't burn at all since they were wet.'

(6) Yamakazi-ga kinoo koya-o moyasi-ta-kedo, #unyoku zenzen
wild.fire-NOM yesterday hut-ACC burn-PST-but luckily at.all
moe-nak-atta-yo. (non-volitional causer)
burn-NEG-PST-PRT
'A wild fire burned the hut, but luckily it didn't burn at all.'

(7) Madoka-ga kinoo ukkari netabako-de
Madoka-NOM yesterday accidentally smoking.in.bed-due to
koya-o moyasi-ta-kedo, #unyoku zenzen moe-nak-atta-yo.
hut-ACC burn-PST-but luckily at.all burn-NEG-PST-PRT
(accidental agent)
'Madoka accidentally burned the hut due to her smoking in bed, but luckily it didn't burn at all.'

(8) Kono ie-no koya-ga kinoo hooka-de moyas-are-ta-kedo,
this house-GEN hut-NOM yesterday arson-by burn-PASS-PST-but
#unyoku zenzen moe-nak-atta-yo. (implied agent)
luckily at.all burn-NEG-PST-PRT
'The hut of this house was burned in an arson attack yesterday, but luckily it didn't burn at all.'

The example in (5) with the intentional agent in subject position allows for the non-culmination, zero CoS construal with the verb *moyasu* 'to burn'. The example in (6) blocks this construal due to the causer subject *yamakazi-ga* 'wild fire-NOM'. The examples in (7) and (8) show that neither the accidental agent nor the implied agent suffices to yield the construal under investigation.

We have seen thus far that the possibility of the non-culminating, zero CoS interpretation of causative accomplishment verbs such as *simeru* 'to close' and *moyasu* 'to burn' is controlled by the presence of an intentional agentive external argument in subject position. There are, then, two research questions that will need to be answered by this phase of the research. One is why the non-culminating, zero CoS reading correlates with the intentionality of the subject referent in Japanese. The other is how the event/conceptual structure of accomplishment verbs adequately captures this correlation. I address these two questions in the rest of this paper.

3 Causal Pluralism, Event-Tokenization, and PFV$_M$

In this section, I will introduce two analytical tools to answer the research questions raised at the end of the previous section: Martin's (2015, 2019) event-tokenization theory of causation types (section 3.1) and Altshuler's (2014, 2016) theory of partitive perfective operators (section 3.2). I will then show how these two theories interact to explain the robust link between subject's intentionality and the non-culminating, zero CoS reading.

3.1 Martin's (2015, 2019) Event-Tokenization Theory of Causation Types

Martin's (2015, 2019) event-tokenization theory of causation types hypothesizes that two types of causation must be distinguished depending on the agentivity of lexical causative statements: agentive causation and non-agentive causation. The theory in question is further supplemented with two assumptions depicted in Figure 1.

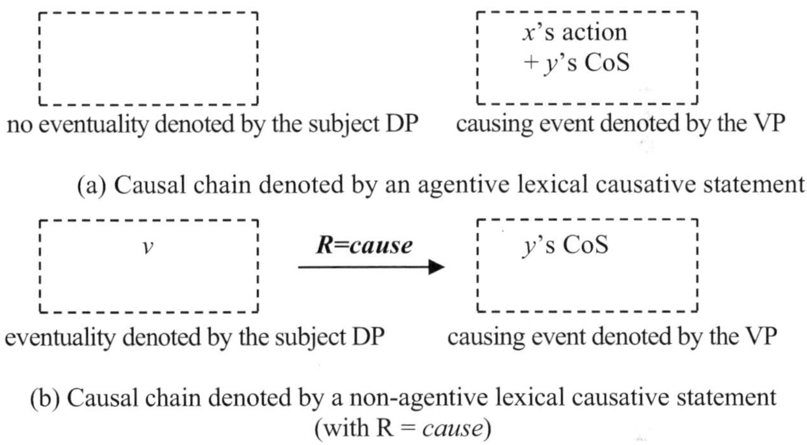

Figure 1 Causal chains denoted by lexical causative statements (from Martin 2019:20)

One assumption is that the two types of causation differ in terms of whether a subject DP introduces an eventuality, an assumption that plays no crucial role in this paper. The other assumption is that the causing events denoted by the VP in the two causation types are fleshed out in two different ways. More specifically, the causative VP in the agentive causation type is tokenized by two sub-event tokens—the agent's action and the theme's CoS tokens—whereas the causative VP in the non-agentive causation type is tokenized by the theme's CoS sub-event token alone. Hereafter, I dub this second assumption within Martin's event-tokenization theory the Causal Pluralism Hypothesis.

3.2 Altshuler's (2014, 2016) Partitive Perfective Operator/PFV$_M$

The perfective operator PFV is standardly defined as denoting that the event *e* it is existentially quantified over is complete with respect to a particular predicate *P*, as shown in (10).

(9) $[\![\mathrm{PFV}_C]\!] = \lambda P \exists e\, (P(e))$ (standard perfective) (Martin 2019:8)

However, Koenig and Muansuwan (2000), Altshuler (2014, 2016), Martin (2019, forthcoming), Martin and Gyarmathy (forthcoming), and Martin et al. (2018) propose that (South) East Asian languages such as Thai, Hindi, and Mandarin Chinese have a perfective operator whose denotation is different from this standard definition shown in (9). More concretely, perfective operators in these languages form a partitive operator in the sense of Altshuler (2014, 2016) in that they denote not event completion, but event maximality, as shown in (10). A simplified version of Altshuler's (2014, 2016) original modalized definition of event maximality is given in (11).

(10) $[\![\mathrm{PFV}_M]\!] = \lambda P \exists e\, (\mathrm{MAX}\ (e, \mathrm{P}))$ (weak perfective) (Martin 2019:9)

(11) MAX (e, P) :=
   a. *e* is a part of a possible P-event and
   b. *e* is not a proper part of any actual event that is part of a possible P-event.
(Martin 2019:9)

The definition in (11) is designed to capture Altshuler's (2014:761) notion of *Maximal Stage Requirement*, which he developed to capture the semantics of the simple form of perfective in Hindi. This requirement is satisfied either when an event culminates or ceases to develop any further toward a VP-denoted event. The crucial component of this definition of event maximality for my present purposes is that the PFV$_M$, as defined in (11), only requires that there must be some part of a VP-denoted event materialized in the real world. Martin (2019) points to the contrast in acceptability between (12a) and (12b) in Mandarin Chinese to show that the perfective marker *–le* in this language instantiates PFV$_M$.

(12)a. # Lùlu kāi-le nèi-shàn mén, érqiě hái zài kai.
   Lulu open-PFV that-CLF door and still PROG open
   'Intended: Lulu opened that door, and she is still opening it.'
  b. Lùlu kāi-le nèi-shàn mén, dànshì mén gēnběn méi kāi.
   Lulu open-PFV that-CLF door but door at.all NEG.PFV open
   'Lulu opened that door, and it didn't open at all.'
(Mandarin Chinese: Martin 2019:9)

The example in (12a) sounds anomalous because it does not meet the maximality requirement defined as in (11); that is, the door-opening event still continues toward a VP-denoted event at the utterance time, and hence it is not the case that the event ceases to develop any further. By contrast, the same requirement is satisfied in the example in (12b) because the door-opening event is understood as ceasing to develop any further toward the VP-denoted event, even though the event itself does not reach the intended resultant CoS in this particular case.

3.3 Explaining the Link between Intentionality and Non-Culmination

Having reviewed Martin's (2015, 2019) event-tokenization theory of causation types and Altshuler's (2014, 2016) partitive theory of perfectives, we are now ready to tackle the central issue of this paper, namely, how we can establish the link between the agentivity of the external argument in subject position and the non-culminating, zero CoS construal of a particular causative accomplishment verb, as witnessed by the contrast between (13a) and (13b).

(13) a. Megumi-ga doa-o ake-ta-kedo, zenzen aka-nak-atta-yo.
Megumi-NOM door-ACC open-PST-but at.all open-NEG-PAST-PRT
'Megumi opened the door, but it didn't open.'
b. Kaze-ga doa-o ake-ta-kedo, #zenzen aka-nak-atta-yo.
wind-NOM door-ACC open-PST-but at.all open-NEG-PAST-PRT
'A wind opened the door, but it didn't open at all.'

To start off, let us note that Japanese is endowed with the PFV_M, just as in Mandarin Chinese. This is evidenced by the semantic incongruence of the example in (14): the door-opening event initiated by Megumi fails to cease to develop further toward the VP-denoted event but is still ongoing at the utterance time, in violation of the maximality stage requirement imposed by the PFV_M.

(14) # Megumi-ga doa-o ake-ta-kedo, mada akete-iru-yo.
Megumi-NOM door-ACC open-PST-but still open-PROG-PRT
'Megumi opened the door, and she is still opening it.'

As for the syntax of agentive causation and non-agentive causation, I propose that these two types of causation are associated with two distinct syntactic structures schematically depicted in (15) and (16), respectively. This proposal follows in the footsteps of the recent hypothesis (Folli and Harley 2004; Schäfer 2008; Harley 2013; Martin 2019) that the agent vs. causer argument is introduced in the syntax through different flavors of *v* heads.

(15) Syntax of Agentive Causation

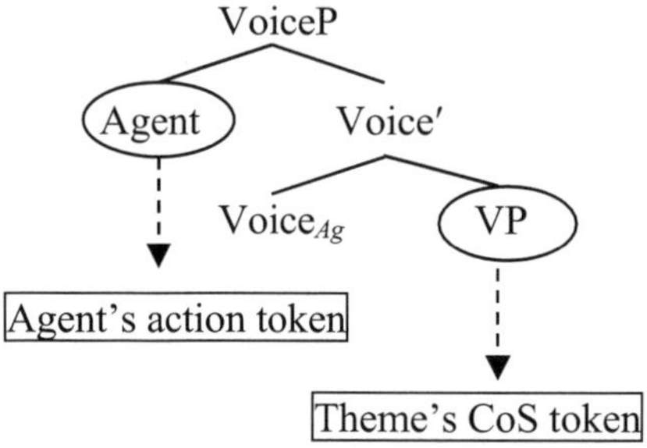

(16) Syntax of Non-Agentive Causation

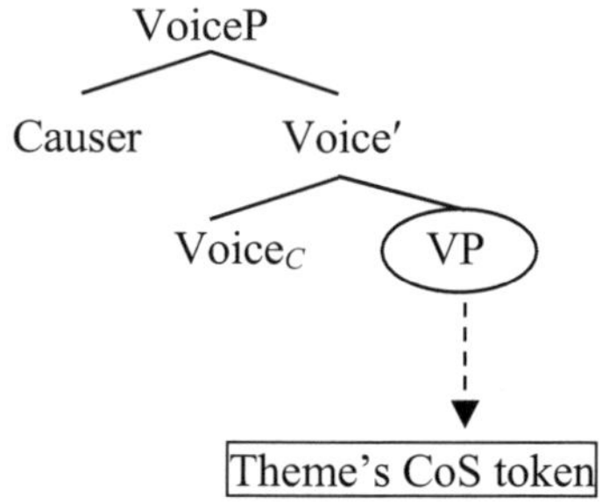

I further propose that the VoiceP layer projected by the Voice$_{Ag}$ introduces the agent's action sub-event token whereas the VP layer uniformly introduces the theme's CoS sub-event token. This proposal is intended to capture in purely syntactic terms Martin's central hypothesis that agentive causation is tokenized by the agent's action and the theme's CoS whereas non-agentive causation is tokenized only by the theme's CoS alone.

Let us now return to the crux of the matter: the contrast between (13a) and (13b). The example in (13a) instantiates agentive causation. By hypothesis, then, this example is syntactically associated with the structure shown in (15), which, in turn, yields two sub-event tokens – the agent's action and the theme's CoS – to incarnate the relevant causation type. Recall from section 3.2 that the maximality requirement of PFV$_{M}$ can be satisfied as long as there is some part of the whole VP-event instantiated in the actual world. Given this, the relevant requirement can be met even by any causally inefficacious part of the agent's preparatory/initiating action(s) without also necessarily bringing about the intended resultant CoS of the theme argument. This explains why the non-culminating, zero CoS construal is available with the causative accomplishment verb *akeru* 'to open$_{tr}$' in the presence of the agentive subject.

By contrast, the example in (13b) instantiates non-agentive causation. This means that the example is syntactically associated with the derivation shown in (16), which, in turn, produces the theme's CoS (introduced by the VP) as the sole sub-event token to flesh out the relevant causation type. It is crucial to note, then, that, unlike in (13a), the maximality requirement of the PFV$_{M}$ can only be satisfied by returning some amount of change on the part of the theme argument in (13b) due to the lack of the agent's action sub-event token. This requirement imposed on the theme's CoS, thus, inevitably clashes with the negative follow-up statement in the second clause in (13b), which asserts that the door did not undergo any CoS at all as the result of the wind (blowing, for example).

As Martin (2019) points out, this analysis effectively states that non-agentive causative VPs are conceptualized in the same way as inchoative VPs in that both types of VPs have the theme's CoS as their sole sub-event token in their event structure. In other words, the example in (13b) is semantically contradictory for the same reason that the inchoative statement shown in (17) or the passive statement shown in (18) is.

(17) Doa-ga ai-ta-kedo, #zenzen aka-nak-atta-yo.
door-NOM open-PST-but at.all open-NEG-PAST-PRT
'The door opened, but it didn't open.'

(18) Doa-ga ake-rare-ta-kedo, #zenzen aka-nak-atta-yo.
door-NOM open-PASS-PST-but at.all open-NEG-PAST-PRT
'The door was opened, but it didn't open at all.'

What about the sensitivity of the non-culminating, zero CoS reading to the agentivity of the external argument in subject position? Recall from (4) and (8) that the mere presence of an implied agent in a passive construction is not sufficient to license the reading in question. I maintain that this syntactic restriction also follows from the base position of the agentive argument in (15). More concretely, such an argument can only be introduced in the specifier of Voice_{Ag}. This flavor of *v*, in turn, yields the agent's action token to instantiate the agentive causation type. These two observations combine together, then, to ensure that an agentive argument in subject position, and only such an argument, may license the non-culminating, zero CoS interpretation through the aid of the Voice_{Ag} layer.

4 Two Arguments for the Causal Pluralism Hypothesis

I have shown in the previous section how the Causal Pluralism Hypothesis adopted from Martin's (2015, 2019) event-tokenization theory of causation interacts with the maximality requirement of the PFV_M in Altshuler's (2014, 2016) theory of partitive perfective operators to account for the distribution of the non-culminating, zero CoS construal of causative accomplishment verbs governed by the agentivity of the external argument in subject position. In this section, I present two independent arguments in favor of the differences with respect to the nature and number of sub-event tokens involved in the identification of agentive vs. non-agentive causation events in Japanese. One argument is concerned with different onset times as measured by time-frame adverbials; the other argument is based on different interpretations imposed on the theme's CoS in the two types of causative constructions embedded under aspectual verbs. Both arguments are modeled on Martin's (2015,

2019) diagnostics for the identification of sub-event tokens developed in English and French.

4.1 Different Onset Times as Measured by Time-Frame Adverbials

Time-frame adverbials such as *gohun-de* 'in five minutes' are known to measure the time span between the onset and result state/end point of a complete eventuality denoted by a verb. Keeping this general observation in mind, consider the examples in (19–20).

(19) Megumi-ga kinoo *gohun-de* kono omoi doa-o
Megumi-NOM yesterday five.minutes-in this heavy door-ACC
nantoka sime-ta-kedo, doa-zitai-wa *honno zyuubyoo-kurai-de*
somehow close-PST-but door-itself-TOP only ten.seconds-about-in
sima-tta-yo.
close-PST-PRT
'It took Megumi five minutes to manage to close this heavy door yesterday, but actually the door itself closed in just about ten seconds.'

(20) Tuyoi kaze-ga kinoo *gohun-de* kono omoi doa-o
strong wind-NOM yesterday five.minutes-in this heavy door-ACC
sime-ta-kedo, #doa-zitai-wa *honno zyuubyoo-kurai-de*
close-PST-but door-itself-TOP only ten.seconds-about-in
sima-tta-yo.
close-PST-PRT
'It took Megumi five minutes to manage to close this heavy door yesterday, but actually the door itself closed in just about ten seconds.'

The examples in (19) and (20) instantiate the agentive and non-agentive causation types, respectively, as indicated by the choice of the external argument in subject position (i.e., *Megumi-ga* 'Megumi-NOM' in (19) vs. *tuyoi kaze-ga* 'strong wind-NOM' in (20)). The example in (19) is semantically coherent despite the fact that two temporally conflicting time-frame adverbials – *gohun-de* 'in five minutes' and *honno zyuubyoo-kurai-d*e 'in just about ten seconds' – occur in the same sentence. This pattern, however, is not acceptable in the example in (20). The contrast here is exactly what we predict under the Causal Pluralism Hypothesis introduced in section 3.1. Recall that the event described in (19) is a case of the agentive causation type, and hence is tokenized by the agent's action and the theme's CoS sub-event tokens. Therefore, the time span of the latter sub-event may well be construed as shorter ('in just about ten seconds') than the time span of the whole causing event ('in five minutes') which also contains the former sub-event.

This 'different onset' construal is impossible with the event denoted in (20), however. As a case of the non-agentive causation type, the event is tokenized in terms of the theme's CoS sub-event token alone. Accordingly, the entire causing event there would be construed as completed in both five minutes and in just about ten seconds, thereby giving rise to contradiction. To put it differently, the example in (20) is rendered semantically gibberish for the same reason that the inchoative counterpart of (20), shown in (21), is.

(21) Kono omoi doa-ga kinoo tuyoi kaze-de *gohun-de*
this heavy door-NOM yesterday strong wind-by five.minutes-in
sima-tta-kedo, #doa-zitai-wa *honno zyuubyoo-kurai-de*
close-PST-but door-itself-TOP only ten.seconds-about-in
sima-tta-yo.
close-PST-PRT
'This heavy door closed in five minutes due to a strong wind yesterday, but the door itself closed in just about 10 seconds.'

4.2 Different Interpretations on Theme's CoS under Aspectual Verbs

The agentive and non-agentive causative types also yield different interpretations regarding the theme's CoS when embedded as syntactic complements of aspectual verbs such as *hazimeru* 'to begin'. To illustrate this point, consider the examples in (22–23). Just as in (19–20), these examples instantiate the agentive and non-agentive causation types, respectively.

(22) Megumi-ga doa-o sime-hazime-ta-yo.
Megumi-NOM door-ACC close-begin-PST-PRT
'Megumi began closing the door.'

(23) Tuyoi kaze-ga doa-o sime-hazime-ta-yo.
strong wind-NOM door-ACC close-begin-PST-PRT
'A strong wind began closing the door.'

For (22) to be truthfully uttered, some preparatory action(s) on the part of the agentive subject *Megumi* must have started at the utterance time; for example, she approached the door, lay her right hand on the door knob to turn it. Crucially, however, no change developing toward the intended result state of the theme has to happen yet on the part of the door. The availability of this zero CoS reading is straightforwardly derived if the agentive causation type involves the agent's action as well as the theme's CoS sub-tokens, as per the Causal Pluralism Hypothesis; the aspectual verb *hazimeru* 'to begin' may well modify only the agent's action component of the whole VP-causing event. On the other hand, for (23) to be truthfully uttered, it must be the case that the door has already begun undergoing some initial changes ultimately leading toward the intended result state at the utterance time; for example, the door started closing a bit with its hinges squeaking or with the air being pushed out as it began to seal. Again, the necessity of some CoS on the theme in (23) follows if we assume that the aspectual verb can only modify the theme's CoS component in the non-agentive causation type, of which (23) is an archetypical example.

5 Conclusion

In this article, I have investigated the agentivity-sensitive distribution of the non-culminating, zero CoS interpretation of causative accomplishment verbs in Japanese, an empirical puzzle explicitly noted for the first time by Tsujimura (2003). My proposed analysis of the robust link between the subject's agentivity/intentionality and the non-culminating construal draws on Martin's (2015, 2019) event-tokenization theory of agentive vs. non-agentive causation and the maximality requirement of the partitive perfective operator/PFV_M in the sense of Altshuler (2014). I have also presented two independent arguments in favor of the crucial assumption behind my proposed analysis, namely, that agentive causation is tokenized in terms of the agent's action and the theme's CoS whereas non-agentive causation is tokenized in terms of the theme's CoS alone.

The results obtained in this paper have important typological as well as theoretical implications. Typologically, the data reported here and the description thereof convincingly show that Japanese behaves on a par with many other areally unrelated languages, including Malagasy (Travis 2000), Tagalog (Dell 1983), Salish (Bar-el 2005; Gerdts 2008; Kiyota 2008; Jacobs 2011), Mandarin Chinese (Tai 1984), Korean (Lee 2015; Beavers and Lee, in press), English (Oehrle 1976), Indonesian (Sato 2019) and many other languages documented in Demirdache and Martin's (2015) pioneering work, all reported to exhibit the non-culminating zero CoS reading of causative accomplishment verbs only when their surface subject is associated with agentivity/intentionality. A sample of some representative data from several of the typologically diverse range of languages mentioned above is given in (24–28).

(24) English (Martin and Schäfer 2015:87)
a. Ivan taught me Russian, but I did not learn anything.
b. Lipson's textbook taught me Russian, #but I didn't learn anything.

(25) French (Martin 2015:248)

a. Dr Li m'a soigné, mais je n'ai pas guéri du tout.
Dr Li me=has treated but I NEG=has NEG cured at all
'Dr. Li treated me, but I didn't recover at all.'

b. Ce séjour chez ma soeur m'a soigné, #mais je n'ai pas guéri du tout.
this stay at my sister me=has treated but I NEG=has NEG cured at all
'This stay at my sister's treated me, but I didn't recover at al.'

(26) Salish (Halkomelem/Saanich) (Gerdts 2008; Kiyota 2008; Jacobs 2011)

a. niʔ cən q̓a:y-t tᶿə spəʔəθ ʔiʔ ʔəwə niʔ -əs q̓a:y.
AUX 1.SBJ die-CTR DET bear and NEG AUX-3SG.SBJ die
'I killed the bear, but it didn't die.'

b. ləʔəqsən kʷəʔ qʷəy-nəxʷ tə spéʔəs, #ʔiʔʔawa s-qʷəy.
AUX 1.SG INF die-NCTR DET bear ACC NEG NOM-die
'I (accidentally) killed the bear, but it didn't die.'
((26a) from Gerdts 2008, as cited in Jacobs 2011:25; (26b) from Kiyota 2008:59)

(27) Korean (Lee 2015:60, 108)

a. ku-ka changmwun-ul kkay-ss-ta. kulena changmwun-i kkay-ci-ci anh-ass-ta.
he-NOM window-ACC break-PST-DEC but window-NOM break-PASS-COMP NEG-PST-DEC
'He broke the window. But the window was not broken.'

b. chentwung-i changmwun-ul kkay-ss-ta. #haciman, changmwun-i kkay-ci-ci anh-ass-ta.
thunder-NOM window-ACC break-PST-DEC but window-NOM break-PASS-COMP NEG-PST-DEC
'The thunder broke the window. But the window was not broken.'

(28) Indonesian (Sato 2019: 2)

a. Budi membunuh Ali, tapi dia tidak mati.
Budi kill Ali but he NEG die
'Budi killed Ali, but he didn't die.'

b. Gempa bumi membunuh Ali, # tapidia tidak mati.
quake earth kill Ali but he NEG die
'The earthquake killed Ali, but he didn't die.'

In other words, the Japanese data introduced here lend further credence to Demirdache and Martin's (2015) Agent Control Hypothesis defined in (29). Of special note in this context is striking parallel between the Agent Control Hypothesis and Tsujimura's (2003) generalization quoted in section 1.

(29) The availability of non-culminating construals for accomplishments correlates with the control of the agent over the described event: whenever an accomplishment … admits a non-culminating construal, this is the case only if we can ascribe agenthood to the subject. If the subject of the very same verb is a (pure) causer, culmination cannot be cancelled. (Demirdache and Martin 2015:187)

The analytic details of my approach to non-culminating interpretations of causative verbs also have some theoretical imports. As stated in the introduction, it has been one of the perennial issues in the lexical semantics/event structure literature whether the apparently extra-linguistic notion of agentivity is linguistically represented, and if so, how. The results of this paper show that the answer is resounding yes. Agentivity must be represented at the syntax-semantics interface due to its clear repercussions on the result implication of causative accomplishment verbs. I have argued for the particular view that an agentive argument is base-generated in the specifier of the functional Voice_{Ag} head, which, in turn, introduces the agent's action sub-event token in the mapping to the event/conceptual structure. The presence vs. absence of agentivity formalized in this fashion, I have further argued, interacts with the maximality requirement of PFV_M to yield agentivity-sensitive non-culminating, zero CoS construals of causative accomplishment verbs in Japanese.

References

Altschuler, D. 2014. A typology of partitive aspectual operators. *Natural Language & Linguistic Theory* 32:735–775.

Altschuler, D. 2016. *Events, states and times: An essay on narrative discourse in English*. Berlin: De Gruyter.

Bar-el, L. 2005. Aspectual distinctions in Skwxwu7mesh. Doctoral dissertation, University of British Columbia.

Beavers, J., and J. Lee. In press. Non-culmination in Korean caused change-of-state predicates. *Linguistics* (special issue).

Dell, F. 1983. An aspectual distinction in Tagalog. *Oceanic Linguistics* 22/23:175–206.

Demirdache, H., and F. Martin. 2015. Agent control over non-culminating events. *Verb classes and aspect*, ed. E. B. López, J. L. Honrubia, and S. R. Rosique, 185–217. Amsterdam/Philadelphia: John Benjamins.

Folli, R., and H. Harley. 2004. Flavors of *v*: Consuming results in Italian and English. *Aspectual inquiries*, ed. R. Slabakova and P. Kempchinsky, 95–120. Dordrecht: Kluwer.

Gerdts, D. 2008. Halkomelem limited control constructions. A paper presented at Spring 2008 Colloquium Series, Department of Linguistics, University of British Columbia, Vancouver.

Harley, H. 2013. External arguments and the mirror principle: On the distinctness of voice and *v*. *Lingua* 125:34–57.

Ikegami, Y. 1980-1981. 'Activity' – 'Accomplishment' – 'Achievement' – doosi imi koozoo no ruikei. *The Rising Generation* 1980.12–1981.3. Tokyo: Kenkyusha.

Ikegami, Y. 1981. *"Suru" to "naru" no gengogaku: Kotoba to bunka no taiporozii e no siron*. Tokyo: Taisyuukan.

Jacobs, P. 2011. Control in Sḵwx̱wú7mesh. Doctoral dissertation, University of British Columbia.

Kageyama, T. 1993, *Bunpoo to gokeisei*. Tokyo: Hituzi Syobo.

Kageyama, T. 1996. *Doosi imiron: Gengo to ninti no setten*. Tokyo: Kurosio Publishers.

Kiyota, M. 2008. Situation aspect and viewpoint aspect: From Salish to Japanese. Doctoral dissertation, University of British Columbia.

Koenig, J-P, and N. Muansuwan. 2000. How to end without ever finishing: Thai semi-perfectivity. *Journal of Semantics* 17:147–182.

Lee, J. 2015. An intention-based account of accomplishments in Korean. Doctoral dissertation, University of Texas, Austin.

Martin, F. 2015. Explaining the link between agentivity and non-culminating causation. *Proceedings of the 25th Semantics and Linguistic Theory Conference*, ed. S. D'Antonio, M. Moroney and C. Little, 246–266. Linguistic Society of America and Cornell Linguistics Circle.

Martin, F. 2019. Aspectual differences between agentive vs. non-agentive uses of causative predicates. Ms., Humboldt-Universität zu Berlin.

Martin, F. Forthcoming. Non-culminating accomplishments. *Language and Linguistics Compass*.

Martin, F., and Z. Gyarmathy. Forthcoming. A more fine-grained typology of perfective operators. *Empirical issues in syntax and semantics,* vol. 12, ed. C. Piñón. Paris: CSSP-CNRS.

Martin, F., and F. Schäfer. 2015. Sublexical modality in defeasible causative verbs. *Modality across syntactic categories*, ed. A. María L. Rivero, and A. Salanova, 87–108. Oxford: Oxford University Press.

Martin, F., H., Sun, H. Demirdache, and J. Liu. 2018. Monomorphemic verbs in mandarin Chinese: Lexical aspect, event structure and non-culminating construals. Ms., Université de Nantes and Humboldt-Universität zu Berlin.

Oehrle, R. 1976. The grammatical status of the English dative alternation. Doctoral dissertation, MIT.

Sato, Y. 2019. How can one kill someone twice in Indonesian? Ms., Seisen University.

Schäfer, F. 2008. *The syntax of (anti-) causatives: External arguments in change-of-state contexts*. Amsterdam: John Benjamins.

Tai, J. H.-Y. 1984. Verbs and times in Chinese: Vendler's four categories. *Papers from the parasession on lexical semantics*, ed. D. Testen, V. Mishra, and J. Drogo, 289–296. Chicago, IL: Chicago Linguistic Society.

Travis, L. 2000. Event structure in syntax. *Events as grammatical objects: The converging perspectives of lexical semantics and syntax*, ed. C. Tenny and J. Pustejovsky 145–185. Palo Alto, CA: CSLI.

Tsujimura, N. 2003. Event cancellation and telicity. *Japanese/Korean Linguistics 12*, ed. W. McClure, 388–399. Stanford, CA: CSLI Publications.

A Source of Defeasibility: Evidence from Japanese Object Experiencer Predicates*

YUSUKE YAGI
Waseda University

1 Introduction

Since Dowty (1979), causative verbs are often analyzed into a decomposed event structure as (1a), where x and y are participants of the event. For instance, the English verb *break* is decomposed into (1b)[1].

(1) a. [[x ACT] CAUSE [$_{Result}$ y ...]]
b. *break* = [[x ACT] CAUSE [$_{Result}$ y BECOME <break>]]

The analysis assumes that the eventuality denoted in *Result* in (1a) happens in the actual world. However, more recent studies point out that this is not always the case. Martin and Schäfer (2017) investigates the class of verbs which they call *defeasible causative verbs*. A defeasible causative verb entails *Result* only when they are used with an agentive subject. Consider sentences (2). In (2a), *taught me Russian* entails *I learn Russian*, and negating this result leads to contradiction. On the other hand, the contradic-

* This study is a part of my Master's thesis submitted to Waseda University, Japan. I thank Masakazu Kuno, Christopher Tancredi, Ayaka Sugawara for insightful suggestions and criticism. All remaining errors are my own.

[1] Notation of decomposed structures is based on Rappaport Hovav and Levin (2010).

Japanese/Korean Linguistics 27.
Edited by Michael Barrie.

tion is not observed in (2b), meaning that *taught me Russian* there does not entail *I learn Russian*. That is, *taught me Russian* is *defeasible* in (2b).

(2) a. Lipson's textbook taught me Russian, #but I did not learn anything.
b. Ivan taught me Russian, but I did not learn anything.
(Martin and Schäfer 2017: 87)

Defeasibility of causative predicates is observed across languages. (3) is from German and (4) is from Japanese. The predicates in (b)-sentences are defeasible and negating an existence of the caused eventuality does not induce contradiction.[2]

(3) a. Dieses Detail schmeichelte Maria,
This detail flattered Marie,
#aber sie fühlte sich überhaupt nicht geschmeichelt.
but she felt REFL absolutely NEG flattered.
'This detail flattered Mary, but she felt absolutely not flattered.'
b. Hans schmeichelte Maria, aber sie fühlte
Hans flattered Marie, but she felt
sich überhaupt nicht geschmeichelt.
REFL absolutely NEG flattered.
'John flattered Mary, but she felt absolutely not flattered.'
(Martin and Schäfer, 2017: 88)

(4) a. Uta-ga Mary-o nagusameta kedo,
song-Nom Mary-Acc comforted but,
#kanojo-wa nanimo kanji naka-tta
she-Top anything feel Neg-Past
'A song comforted Mary, but she felt nothing.'
b. John-ga Mary-o nagusameta kedo,
John-Nom Mary-Acc comforted but,
kanojo-wa nanimo kanji naka-tta
she-Top anything feel Neg-Past
'John comforted Mary, but she felt nothing.'

Martin (2015) and Martin and Schäfer (2017) argue that defeasibility of causative predicates is contingent on agentivity of the subject. As in the (a)-sentences in (2)-(4), a causative predicate entails *Result* when the predicate

[2] Abbreviations used in this study are followings: Acc = Accusative; Nom = Nominative; Top = Topic; Neg = Negation, REFL = reflexive.

takes an inanimate subject. When the subject is agentive as in the (b)-sentences, the predicate is defeasible.

They formalize the argument with *sublexical modality* – a modal component embedded within a word. In the case of (2), *teach* has a sublexical modal component. This is schematized as (5), where the square operator represents the modal component.

(5) *teach* = [[*x* ACT] □ CAUSE [$_{Result}$ *y* LEARN *z*]]]

However, notice that the combination of an agentive subject and a causative predicate does not always induce defeasibility. For instance, lexical causative verbs[3] like *break*, *fly*, *open*, *close*, etc. always require the caused event to happen, regardless of agentivity of the subject.

(6) a. John opened the window, #but it didn't open.
b. The wind opened the window, #but it didn't open.

In order to account for the difference between (2)-(4) and (6), Martin and Schäfer (2017) has to stipulate that only a certain subset of causative predicates contains the modal component.

If we accept their conclusion, then we have to clarify what defines the defeasible causative class. Is there any criterion that determines what verbs will have the modality? Without such a criterion, we have no choice but to admit that the class is defined by mere idiosyncrasy.

In this study, I will investigate defeasible causative verbs in Japanese and argue the appeal to idiosyncrasy is not necessary: There is a criterion to determine what verbs are defeasible. Moreover, I will argue that defeasibility is not depending on agentivity of the subject, but on a manner specification of the verb. Thus, this study aims at making the theory about the causative predicates more explanatory.

For the purpose of this study, I follow Rappaport Hovav and Levin's (2010) analysis of verbs.They classify verbs into two types: *manner verbs* and *result verbs*. The former specifies how the event is performed while the latter defines a result of the event. The classification is formalized with the decompositional structure of verbs mentioned in (1). Idiosyncratic information, or *verbal roots*, of manner verbs modify the abstract predicate ACT as in (7a). A verbal root of result verbs becomes an argument of the abstract predicate BECOME as in (7b).

[3] The terminology *lexical causative verbs* is adopted from Pylkkänen (2008).

(7) a. *run* = [*x* ACT$_{\langle\text{run}\rangle}$]
b. *break* = [[*x* ACT] CAUSE [*y* BECOME <break>]]

In what follows, I will argue that the notion *manner* is crucial in determining absence or presence of defeasibility. The rest of this study is organized as follows. In section 2, I will make important observations on which the proposal of this study is based. In section 3, I propose a generalization over defeasible causative predicates. The generalization is formalized in section 4. A consequence of the proposal is discussed in section 5. Section 6 concludes the study.

2 Key Observations

2.1 Analytic v.s. Synthetic Causative Verbs

As we saw in (4), the Japanese verb *nagusameru* ('comfort') shows defeasibility with an agentive subject. In fact, defeasibility is generally observed with object experiencer psych-verbs[4]. Interestingly, however, defeasibility is not observed in similar psych predicates that are built syntactically with the periphrastic causative verb/morpheme *–(s)ase*. Compare (8) and (9):

(8) a. John-ga Mary-o nagusameta/hagemasita kedo,
John-Nom Mary-Acc comforted/encouraged but,
kanojo-wa nanimo kanji-nak-atta.
she-Top anything feel-Neg-Past
'John comforted/encouraged Mary, but she felt nothing.'
b. Uta-ga Mary-o nagusameta/hagemasita kedo,
Song-Nom Mary-Acc comforted/encouraged but,
#kanojo-wa nanimo kanji-nak-atta.
she-Top anything feel-Neg-Past
'A song comforted/encouraged Mary, #but she felt nothing.'

[4] Previous literature (notably Tsujimura (2003)) claims that Japanese exhibits defeasibility even with lexical causative predicates. In fact, native speakers of Japanese I consulted disagree about the judgement of (i).

(i) John-ga otiba-o moyasita kedo, zenzen moe-nak-atta.
John-Nom fallen.leaf-Acc burned but, at-all burn-Neg-Past
'John burned fallen leaves, but they didn't burn at all.'

The judgement varies from completely acceptable to completely bad. Also, some native speakers of Japanese note that it may depend on verbs employed: *Kowasu* ('break') is less acceptable but *moyasu* ('burn') is much better. I have no explanation on why such wide speaker variations are observed.

(9) a. John-ga Mary-o yorokob-ase-ta /kandou-sase-ta
John-Nom Mary-Acc be.pleased-Cause-Past/be.touched-Cause-Past
kedo, #kanojo-wa nanimo kanji-nak-atta.
but, she-Top anything feel-Neg-Past
'John caused Mary to be pleased/touched, #but Mary felt nothing.'

b. Uta-ga Mary-o yorokob-ase-ta /kandou-sase-ta
Song-Nom Mary-Acc be.pleased-Cause-Past/be.touched-Cause-Past
#kanojo-wa nanimo kanji-nak-atta.
she-Top anything feel-Neg-Past
'A song caused Mary to be pleased/touched, #but Mary felt nothing.'

The verbs *nagusameru* ('comfort') and *hagemasu* ('encourage') exhibit defeasibility when used with an agentive subject: the resultant change-of-feeling can be negated without inducing contradiction in (8a). Notice that these verbs are morphologically simplex, meaning that they are lexically causative. On the other hand, the predicates in (9) entail the resultant change-of-feeling regardless of agentivity of the subjects. Negating the results leads to contradiction both in (9a) and (9b).

2.2 Durativity

The predicates in (8) and the ones in (9) also contrast in durativity of the causing events. In order to see this, consider the sentences in (10).

(10) a. John-ga 5-fun-kan Mary-o nagusameta/hagemasita
John-Nom 5-min-for Mary-Acc comforted/encouraged
(kedo, Mary-wa nanimo kanji-nak-atta.)
(but, Mary-Top anything feel-Neg-Past)
'John comforted/encouraged Mary for five minutes, (but she didn't feel anything)'

b. Uta-ga 5-fun-kan Mary-o hagemasita.
Song-Nom 5-min-for Mary-Acc encouraged
'The song caused Mary to feel encouraged for five minutes'

c. John-ga/Uta-ga 5-fun-kan Mary-o yorokob-ase-ta.
John-Nom/Song-Nom 5-minute-for Mary-Acc be.pleased-Cause-Past
'John/The song caused Mary to be pleased for five minutes'

In (10a), the adverbial *5-fun-kan* 'for five minutes' primarily measures the duration of John's action. Thus, the sentence can describe a situation where, for example, John tried encouraging Mary for five minutes, and Mary was encouraged for 2 minutes or was not encouraged at all. This interpretation is unavailable in (10b) and (10c). Rather, *5-fun-kan* in these sentences measures the length of Mary's (improved) feeling. This fact indicates that the causing events of *nagusameru*/*hagemasu* can be durative when they are used with an agentive subject as in (10a), but the causing events are punctual when they are used with a non-agentive subjects. Moreover, (10c) shows that the causing events of syntactically-built causative predicates are punctual regardless of agentivity of the subject.

3 Proposal

3.1 Interpreting the Observation

Beavers and Koontz-Garboden (2012) claims that durativity stands as a diagnostic for 'manner verbs' in Rappaport Hovav and Levin's (2010) sense. The diagnostic is based on Rappaport Hovav and Levin's (2010) suggestion that 'the vast majority' of manners are complex, and Dowty's (1979) claim that complex manners require intervals consisting of more than two moments to evaluate (i.e., durativity).

Beavers and Koontz-Garboden adopt for their durativity test *take*/*spend five minutes*. *Take five minutes* has only an *after five minutes* reading (i.e. describing 'the interval to elapse before the event' (Kearns, 2000)) when it embeds punctual telic predicates, but either an *after five minutes reading* or a *during five minutes* reading with telic durative predicates. Durative atelic predicates are generally anomalous with *take five minutes* with a *during* reading, but they can be used with *spend five minutes* for the reading. They gave the following examples.

(10) a. John spent five minutes exercising/jogging/playing/running. (*during*)

b. It took Jim five minutes to break the window. (*after*)

c. It took Jim five minutes to clean the table. (*after*/*during*)

(Beavers and Koontz-Garboden 2012: 348)

In (10a), the uncontroversial manner verbs exhibit durativity, meaning that they encode a manner. The lack for durativity in (10b) shows that the typical result verb *break* does not specify any manner. Beavers and Koontz-Garboden argue that the presence of durativity in (10c) is not due to manner, but to complexity of the change the verb specifies. Since *clean* encodes a change along multi point scales, it results in a durative predicate.

What does the discussion imply for the observation in 2.2? We saw there that the morphologically simplex verbs *nagusameru*/*hagemasu* exhibit durativity when used with an agentive subject. Recall also that the durative reading is compatible with the phrase that denies the change-of-feeling (i.e. *kedo, Mary-wa nanimo kanji-nak-atta* 'but Mary didn't feel anything'), meaning that the verbs are atelic. Thus, I argue that the observation in 2.2 tells us that the verbs *naguasmeru*/*hagemasu* in (9a) specify a manner when they select an agentive subject. On the contrary, the lack of durativity of the morphologically complex predicates *yorokobaseru* in (9c) and *nagusameru*/*hagemasu* used with an inanimate subject in (9b) indicates that these predicates do not specify a manner.

3.2 Generalization

The argument I made in the above section is summarized in (11). Interestingly, (11) is completely parallel with the fact on defeasibility observed in 2.1, summarized in (12).

(11) a. *nagusameru/hagemasu*
=> manner is specified when used with animate subjects, unspecified with inanimate subjects
b. *yorokobaseru/kandousaseru*
=> manner is always unspecified

(12) a. *nagusameru/hagemasu*
=> defeasible when used with animate subjects, non-defeasible with inanimate subjects
b. *yorokobaseru/kandousaseru*
=> always non-defeasible

Combining these observations, I propose the following generalization.

(13) When a causative verb specifies a manner of causation, then the result is not entailed (i.e. defeasible). If not, then the result is entailed.

I will describe how the generalization works for the Japanese object experiencer predicates.

First of all, notice that it is not surprising at all that *yorokob-ase-ru* and *kandous-ase-ru* lack manner specification. As the morphological complexity shows, these predicates are built from the intransitive roots *yorokobu* or *kandou-suru* and the general causative morpheme *–(s)ase*. It seems to be quite safe to conclude that such a general morpheme lacks any specification other than its grammatical function (i.e. causativization). The predicate *yorokob-ase-ru* can be roughly decomposed into (14a), which can be translated into Rappaport Hovav ad Levin's (2010) notation in (14b).

(14) a. *yorokob* + -(*s*)*ase*
be.pleased + CAUSE
b. [[*x* ACT] CAUSE [*y* BECOME <pleased>]]

Since syntactically complex causative predicates formed with –(*s*)*ase* always lack a manner specification, the predicates entail the result.

On the other hand, *nagusameru* and *hagemasu* are inherently causative in that they do not have inchoative counterparts. I argue that these verbs by themselves introduce the meaning of change-of-feeling and causation. Since causation is also a part of the lexical meaning, it can get idiosyncratic specification in terms of manner. Though the specified manner is quite vague and is hard to explicate, I believe it is something like *act soothingly*. This is schematically represented in (15a), which is translated into (15b).

(15) a. *nagusameru*
CAUSE (with manner) be.comforted
b. [[*x* ACT$_{\langle\text{soothing}\rangle}$] CAUSE [*y* BECOME <comforted>]]

The generalization in (13) claims that since *nagusameru* contains a manner specification, the result is not entailed.

Why, then, is the result entailed when the verbs are used with inanimate subjects? I argue that the manner specified by the verbs are cancelled when the verbs select an inanimate subject. This argument is based on the intuition of Martin (2015), namely:

> [W]e do not differentiate the wind that may blow out a fire from the wind that may close a door through distinctive features: All these winds are undifferentiated for us. (p. 257)

Following Martin, I argue that inanimate entities cannot manifest a manner. Thus, when the verbs *nagusameru*/*hagemasu* take an inanimate subject, there is a contradiction: The verbs require that the subject manifest the manners they specify, but the inanimate subject cannot do so. In order to resolve this, the specified manners are cancelled as a last resort. Then the verbs result in manner-less predicates and entail the result, as generalization (13) suggests.

3.3 Constraint on Manner Cancellation

Beavers and Koontz-Garboden (2012) observes that manner verbs are generally incompatible with inanimate subjects. For instance, ballistic motion verbs, which they argue to be manner-specified, do not select inanimate subjects.

(16) a. John flipped/threew/tossed Sandy the ball with his new glove.
b. #The new glove flipped/threw/tossed Sandy the ball.
c. #The wind flipped/threw/tossed Sandy the ball.

If manner cancellation were applicable to (16b) and (16c), the sentence would be acceptable, just as the manner-specified verbs *nagusameru* can take an inanimate subject. How and why is manner cancellation allowed for predicates *nagusameru*/*hagemasu* and not for the ones in (16)?

I argue this is for a pragmatic reason. In order to see this, compare the decomposed structures of *hagemasu*/*nagusameru* and the ballistic motions verbs in (17). (I take it for granted that double object verbs like *throw* have an underlying causal structure. See Harley and Jung (2015) and Beck and Johnson (2004) for justification.)

(17) a. *nagusameru* = [[*x* ACT<soothing>] CAUSE [*y* BECOME <comforted>]]
b. *hagemasu* = [[*x* ACT< soothing >] CAUSE [*y* BECOME <encouraged>]]
c. *flip* = [[*x* ACT<flip>] CAUSE [*y* HAVE *z*]]
d. *throw* = [[*x* ACT<throw>] CAUSE [*y* HAVE *z*]]

Now consider the manner-less counterparts of (17a)-(17d):

(18) a. *nagusameru* = [[*x* ACT] CAUSE [*y* BECOME <comforted>]]
b. *hagemasu* = [[*x* ACT] CAUSE [*y* BECOME <encouraged>]]
c. *flip* = [[*x* ACT] CAUSE [*y* HAVE *z*]]
d. *throw* = [[*x* ACT] CAUSE [*y* HAVE *z*]]

Notice that the decomposed structures in (18c) and (18d) are no longer indistinguishable, since what makes *flip* and *throw* distinct from each other in (17) is their manner specifications. On the other hand, (18a) and (18b) are still distinguishable from each other, because the distinctive parts of the verbal meanings (being comforted/encouraged) are still intact. In short, cancellation does not work for the ballistic motion verbs because the integral, distinctive part of the verbal meaning cannot be cancelled.

4 Formalization

In this section I formalize the generalization proposed in (13) with modal semantics. I adopt Neo-Davidsonian event semantics (Parsons 1990), and follow Hacquard (2006, 2010) in that the modal base and the ordering source take an event-type argument instead of a world-type one. The general denotation I propose for the causative predicates discussed so far is followings.

(19) Let φ be a causative predicate with a resultant event (or state[5]) ψ. Then,

$$[[\varphi]]^{w@} = \lambda x.\lambda y.\lambda e.\ \textbf{subject}(e, y, w@)$$
$$\& \ \forall w' \in max_{g(e)}(\cap f(e))\ [\exists e'\ \textbf{cause}(e, e', w')\ \&\ \psi(e', x, w')],$$

where

a. f is a circumstantial modal base: $f(e) = \{p \mid p$ is a proposition denoting the laws of nature and other relevant facts of $w@\}$

b. g is an ordering source: $g(e) = \{q \mid q$ is a proposition denoting the norms inherently associated with $e\}$

c. $max_{g(e)}$ selects the most ideal world(s) from $\cap f(e)$, given the ordering source $g(e)$[6].

Crucially, notice that $\cap f(e)$ always contains the evaluation world $w@$, since for all the propositions p in $f(e)$, $w@ \in [[p]]$. Following Kratzer (2015), I argue that the ordering source anchors to the norm specified by each predicate. I further stipulate that norms are designated by a manner the predicate has. Thus, if a predicate does not have any manner specification, the norm of that predicate is null. Below, I will demonstrate how the denotation in (19) derives the fact observed so far.

First, consider the morphologically simplex verb *nagusameru* taking an agentive subject.

(20) a. John-ga Mary-o nagusameta kedo,
John-Nom Mary-Acc comforted but,
kanojo-wa nanimo kanji-nak-atta.
she-Top anything feel-Neg-Past
'John comforted Mary, but she felt nothing.'

b. [[John ACT<soothingly>] CAUSE [Mary BECOME <comforted>]]

c. $\lambda e.\ \textbf{subject}(e, \text{John}, w@)\ \textbf{soothing}(e)$
$\& \ \forall w' \in max_{g(e)}(\cap f(e))\ [\exists e'\ \textbf{cause}(e, e', w')\ \&\ \textbf{be.comforted}(e', \text{Mary}, w')]$

5 In this study, I ignore the difference between an event and a state and state both as *e*.

6 See Hacquard (2011) and reference therein for the validity of the *max* operator.

Since the verb has a manner specification, the ordering source orders the worlds in $\bigcap f(e)$ based on the propositions contained in $g(e)$, say, *John's intention of acting soothingly is realized*, etc. The *max* operator selects the best world(s) from $\bigcap f(e)$ based on $g(e)$. This best world(s) may or may not contain the actual world, hence defeasibility.

If the manner is cancelled (i.e. If *nagusameru* takes an inanimate subject), the norm to which the ordering source anchors becomes null, leading the ordering source to be vacuous. The worlds in $\bigcap f(e)$ are thus ordered vacuously, and the proposition embedded under the modality becomes true every world in $\bigcap f(e)$. Since $\bigcap f(e)$ necessarily contains the evaluation world $w_{@}$, the causation is not defeasible in $w_{@}$, as predicted. The same reasoning goes for the analytic causative predicates (*yorokobaseru*/*hagemasu*).

Summarizing so far, I have argued that defeasibility of causative predicates is closely connected with a manner specification. If a predicate specifies a manner of causation, then the resultant eventuality is defeasible. If not, then the result is entailed. As long as the present analysis is valid, defeasibility is no longer an unpredictable property: Presence or absence of defeasibility is predicted based on whether a predicate specifies a manner of causation.

5 Consequence on Manner/Result Complementarity

The present analysis has an interesting consequence. Actually, manner sensitivity is observed in a wide range of causative predicates.

(21) John broke the window, #but it didn't break.

(22) a. John gave Mary the book, #but she didn't get it.
b. John threw Mary the ball, but she didn't get it.
c. John sent/wrote Mary the letter, but she didn't get it.

(23) a. John made Mary leave, #but she didn't leave.
b. John caused Mary to leave, #but she didn't leave.
c. John urged/goaded/pressured Mary to leave, but she didn't leave.

The verbs *break*, *give*, *make*, and *cause* seem not to specify a manner, and they do entail the existence of the caused eventuality. On the other hand, the verbs in (22b, c) and (23c) seem to specify a manner, and the result can be negated.

The above observation suggests a hypothesis that the manner sensitivity is true for every causative verb. If this hypothesis turns out to be valid, we can derive Manner/Result Complementarity (Rappaport Hovav and Levin, 2010).

Manner/Result Complementarity bans verbs from specifying both manner and result. That is, it rules out decomposed structure (24).

(24) *[[*x* ACT$_{\langle \text{manner} \rangle}$] CAUSE [*y* BECOME <result>]]

I argue that Manner/Result Complementarity is an illusion caused by the modal component and manner sensitivity of causative predicates discussed above. Imagine that there is a verb which specifies both manner and result. Since this root is necessarily associated with causative event structure ('result' cannot be defined without it), it interacts with the modal base and the ordering source proposed in this study. The manner specification makes the result defeasible by the reasoning described in section 4, so no specific result is entailed. Thus, even if the verb specifies a result as well as a manner, that cannot be observed in the entailment pattern and the verb comes across looking like it specifies only a manner.

6 Conclusion

As mentioned in Introduction, the aim of this study is to build a more explanatory theory on causative predicates. I have argued that defeasibility is not an idiosyncratic or unpredictable fact. Rather, defeasibility is a side effect of a manner specification. The present study also can derive Manner/Result Complementarity, the constraint no one else has an explanation for. I believe this study shows that the lexical property of causative predicates are better-organized than previously thought, and that for at least defeasibility we do not need to appeal to idiosyncrasies.

References

Beavers, J. T., & A. Koontz-Garboden. 2012. Manner and result in the roots of verbal meaning. *Linguistic Inquiry* 43(3): 331-369.

Beck, S., & K, Johnson. 2004. Double objects again. *Linguistic Inquiry* 35(1): 97-123.

Dowty, D. R. 1979. *Word meaning and montague grammar: The semantics*. Dordrecht; Boston: D. Reidel.

Hacquard, V. 2006. Aspects of modality. Doctoral dissertation, MIT.

Hacquard, V. 2010. On the event relativity of modal auxiliaries. *Natural Language Semantics* 18(1): 79-114.

Hacquard, V. 2011. Modality. In C. Maienborn, K. von Heusinger & P. Portner (Eds.), *Semantics: An international handbook of natural language meaning*: 1484-1515. Berlin: Mouton de Gruyter.

Harley, H., & H, Jung. 2015. In support of the P HAVE analysis of the double object construction. *Linguistic Inquiry* 46: 703-730.

Kearns, Kate. 2000. *Semantics*. New York: St. Martin's Press.

Kratzer, A. 2015. *Creating a family: Transfer of possession*. Talk presented at the Workshop on Modality Across Categories. Barcelona (Universitat Pompeu Fabra), November 5.

Martin, F. 2015. Explaining the link between agentivity and non-culminating causation. *Proceedings of SALT* 25: 246-266.

Martin, F., & Schäfer, F. 2017. Sublexical modality in defeasible causative verbs. In Arregui, A., Rivero, M. L., & Salanova, A. (Eds.), *Modality across syntactic categories*: 87-108. Oxford: Oxford University Press.

Parsons, T. 1990. *Events in the semantics of English: A study in subatomic semantics*. Cambridge, Mass.: MIT Press.

Pylkkänen, M. 2009. Introducing arguments. Cambridge, Mass.: MIT Press.

Rappaport Hovav, M., & B, Levin. 2010. Reflections on Manner/Result complementarity. In Doron, E., Sichel, I., & Hovav, M. R. (Eds.), *Syntax, Lexical Semantics, and Event Structure*: 21-38

Tsujimura, N. 2003. Event cancellation and telicity. *Japanese/Korean Linguistics* 12: 388-399.

Prosody and *wh*-scope in Osaka Japanese

HITOMI MINAMIDA
Cornell University

1 Introduction

It has been claimed that (Tokyo) Japanese is sensitive to *wh*-islands if the appropriate prosody is assigned (Deguchi and Kitagawa 2002, Ishihara 2003, *a.o.*). In (1), for example, the *wh*-word *dare* 'who' is normally bound by the embedded Q-marker *ka*, yielding a matrix yes/no question **(embedded scope (ES) reading)**. Under the right prosodic conditions, however, the association between the *wh*-word and the matrix Q-marker *ka* is claimed to be possible, which gives us a matrix *wh*-question **(matrix scope (MS) reading)**. The two associations are schematized in (2).

(1) *Tokyo Japanese*
Jiro-wa [Marina-ga *dare* -o yonda**-ka**] itta(**-ka**)?
Jiro-TOP Marina-NOM who-ACC called/invited-Q said-Q
ES reading: 'Did Jiro say [who$_i$ Marina called/invited t_i]?'
MS reading: 'Who$_i$ did Jiro say [whether Marina called/invited t_i]?'

(2) [... [... *wh* ... +Q] ... +Q]?

Japanese/Korean Linguistics 27.
Edited by Michael Barrie.

Deguchi and Kitagawa's and Ishihara's claim is that there is a one-to-one mapping between prosody and interpretation in Tokyo Japanese. However, these researchers did not conduct any perception experiments to support this claim, as pointed out by Hirotani (2005). Hirotani (2005) did conduct a series of perception experiments on the construction in (2) in Tokyo Japanese. Her experiments were a forced-choice task; participants listened to each recorded question with ES or MS prosody in Tokyo Japanese and they chose either the yes/no answer or the *wh*-answer shown on the screen. Hirotani (2005) found the following things. First, with ES prosody, yes/no answers are preferred. This is expected because ES prosody is the prosody for yes/no questions. Second, with MS prosody, there is no preference between the two types of answers. This is surprising because MS prosody is the prosody for *wh*-questions. As a consequence, Hirotani (2005) concluded that (2) is unambiguous with ES prosody, while it is ambiguous with MS prosody.

In Tokyo Japanese, *wh*-scope is marked by the range of F0 pitch compression (Deguchi and Kitagawa 2002, Ishihara 2003, *a.o.*).[1] The F0 peaks of *wh*-words are boosted because they are semantically focused words (*P(rosodic)-focalization* in Ishihara's (2003) terminology). P-focalization reduces the F0 peaks of the words in the *wh*-scope domain (*Post-FOCUS reduction* in Ishihara's (2003) terminology).

Disambiguation of (2) by prosody has been reported to be observed in Fukuoka Japanese and Korean. However, these languages use different strategies for *wh*-scope marking from Tokyo Japanese. Fukuoka Japanese and Busan Korean[2] use "an exceptional high flat F0 contour" (Hwang 2015: 37; see also Hwang (2006), *a.o.* for these varieties). Hwang (2009) also reports Seoul Korean data; she claims that boundary tones are the cues to disambiguate (2).

In this paper, I present new findings from my two pilot experiments on the interaction of *wh*-scope and prosody in Osaka Japanese, a variety hitherto unstudied for this phenomenon. Section 2 discusses the differences between Tokyo and Osaka Japanese in terms of how *wh*-interrogatives are pronounced. Section 3 shows that Osaka Japanese uses F0 pitch compression to mark *wh*-scope with my data from a mini production experiment. Section 4 presents my pilot survey data, which show results similar to Hirotani's (2005) experiments. I claim that (2) is unambiguous, but allows what I call "pragmatic" answers. Section 5 compares my Osaka Japanese data with Hwang's (2015) Tokyo Japanese, Fukuoka Japanese, and Busan Korean data and sug-

---

[1] The range of F0 pitch compression can be understood in terms of prosodic phrasing (see Hirotani 2005). See the results of my production experiment in Section 3. See also the discussion in Kitagawa and Hirose (2012).

[2] Hwang (2015) calls this variety "South Kyŏngsang Korean", but I will call it "Busan Korean" in this paper for convenience.

gests a possible explanation for the difference in acceptability of (2) with MS prosody across these languages. Section 6 concludes the paper.

2 *Wh*-interrogatives in Tokyo and Osaka Japanese

In Tokyo Japanese, when *wh*-words are used as interrogative words, they are all accented (Kitagawa 2005, Shimoyama 2006). This pitch accent along with semantic focus are considered to cause F0 pitch compression (Kitagawa 2005). (3) shows the tone patterns of some *wh*-interrogatives in Tokyo Japanese. In (3), apostrophes represent pitch accent, which is indicated by a sharp F0 fall (H*+L), following McCawley's (1968) notation. Thus, the words in (3) are all realized as HL.

(3) Wh-*interrogatives in Tokyo Japanese*[3]
da're 'who', *na'ni* 'what', *do'ko* 'where', *i'tu* 'when', etc.

In Osaka Japanese, in contrast, *wh*-interrogatives are all unaccented.[4] There are two big differences between Osaka and Tokyo Japanese (McCawley 1968, Haraguchi 1977, Kori 1987, Pierrehumbert and Beckman 1988). First, unlike in Tokyo Japanese, where all words begin in L unless the first mora is accented, words begin either in H or L in Osaka Japanese. Second, in low-beginning unaccented words, the final mora is realized as H when the words are pronounced in isolation or occur before another low-beginning word; when the words appear before a high-beginning word, all the moras in the low-beginning words are realized as L.[5]

(4) shows how *wh*-interrogatives are pronounced in Osaka Japanese. Following McCawley's (1968) notation, an apostrophe in front of the word indicates that the word is low-beginning, but that does not mean that low-beginning words are "preaccented" in McCawley's sense. The high-beginning *wh*-interrogatives in (4a) are realized as HH, while the low-beginning *wh*-interrogatives in (4b) are realized as LH when they are pronounced in isolation or when they occur before a low-beginning word.

---

[3] The data here are from Shimoyama's (2006) (5).

[4] In this paper, "Osaka Japanese" refers to the varieties spoken in the Osaka metropolitan area or *Kei-Han-Shin* (Kyoto-Osaka-Kobe). Osaka Japanese data in this section are from the author's observations as a native speaker.

[5] In Tokyo Japanese unaccented words, on the other hand, only the first mora is realized as L (McCawley 1968, Haraguchi 1977, Pierrehumbert and Beckman 1988, *a.o.*).

(4) Wh-*interrogatives in Osaka Japanese*

a. *High-beginning words*
dare 'who', *doko* 'where', etc.

b. *Low-beginning words*
'nani 'what', *'itu* 'when', etc.

3 *Wh*-scope marking in Osaka Japanese

I ran a mini production experiment to verify how *wh*-scope is marked in Osaka Japanese. The data show that Osaka Japanese uses the same strategy as Tokyo Japanese: it uses F0 pitch compression (or prosodic phrasing).

3.1 Procedure

In this experiment, I tested how the structure in (5) is disambiguated by prosody in Osaka Japanese. I used the complementizer *-te*[6] (*-tte* in Tokyo Japanese) as the embedded complementizer. Since *-te* is the so-called quotative complementizer, it is [±Q], depending on the prosody. It is [+Q] when ES prosody is assigned, while it is [−Q] when MS prosody is assigned. I will call the structure in (5) the ***te*-construction**. I did not test the structure in (2) because whether it allows the MS reading is controversial. I will call the structure in (2) the ***ka*-construction** because the embedded complementizer is *-ka*, which is always [+Q].

(5) [... [... *wh* ... ±Q] ... +Q]?

The experiment took place in March 2019 in the Phonetics Lab at Cornell University. I had one female native speaker of Osaka Japanese as a participant. She lived in Ithaca, New York, United States at the time of the recording. She is a non-linguist and was naïve about the purpose of this experiment.

The stimuli are the two sentences in (6) and (7). They include *dare* 'who' and *'nani* 'what' to compare how high-beginning and low-beginning *wh*-interrogatives mark *wh*-scope. Following the similar experiments by researchers such as Hirotani (2005) and Hwang (2015), the words in the stimuli except for the *wh*-words are all accented to see F0 pitch compression clearly. The procedure is almost the same as the procedure of Hwang (2015). I told the participant that (6) and (7) can have two interpretations and be uttered with two prosodic patterns. I showed her the two contexts and two model answers for each sentence at the same time in written text in Osaka Japanese, given in

[6] This *-te* is different from the one that occurs in gerundive forms, which are called *te*-forms in L2 grammar.

(6) and (7). I gave her time to think and practice. After that, I asked her to repeat each sentence eleven times. I discarded the first recording and analyzed the rest of the ten recordings, following Kubozono (2007). Apostrophes in (6) and (7) show the location of pitch accent and high/low-beginningness.

(6) *High-beginning* dare

Ji'ro-wa [Ma'rina-ga *dare* (-o) 'Mino'h-ni yo'nda**-te**] (
Jiro-TOP Marina-NOM who-ACC Minoh-to invited-C/Q
Go'ro-ni) yu'uta(**-ka**)?
Go'ro-to said-Q

ES reading: 'Did Jiro say (to Goro) [who$_i$ Marina invited t_i to Minoh]?'
MS reading: 'Who$_i$ did Jiro say (to Goro) [that Marina invited t_i to Minoh]?'

a. *ES reading*
Answer: うん、言うたで。 ('Yes, (Jiro) said.')
Context: まりなは昨日誰かを箕面に呼んで、次郎はそのことを五郎に言うたやんな？
('Marina invited someone to Minoh yesterday, and Jiro told Goro about it, right?')

b. *MS reading*
Answer: 太郎。 ('Taro.')
Context: まりなは昨日誰かを箕面に呼んで、次郎はそのことを五郎に言うたけど、私、まりなが誰（を）呼んだか知らんねん。（だから、聞くで。）
('Marina invited someone to Minoh yesterday, and Jiro told Goro about it, but I do not know who Marina invited. (So I will ask you.)')

(7) *Low-beginning* nani

Ji'ro-wa [Ma'rina-ga *'nani* (-o) 'Naga'o-ni mo'rota**-te**] (
Jiro-TOP Marina-NOM what-ACC Nagao-from received-C/Q
Go'ro-ni) yu'uta(**-ka**)?
Go'ro-to said-Q

ES reading: 'Did Jiro say (to Goro) [what$_i$ Marina received t_i from Nagao]?'
MS reading: 'What$_i$ did Jiro say (to Goro) [that Marina received t_i from Nagao]?'

a. *ES reading*
Answer: うん、言うたで。 ('Yes, (Jiro) said.')
Context: まりなは昨日何かを長尾に貰うて、次郎はそのことを五郎に言うたやんな？
('Marina received something from Nagao yesterday, and Jiro told Goro about it, right?')

b. *MS reading*
Answer: 本。 ('A book/books.')
Context: まりなは昨日何かを長尾に貰うて、次郎はそのことを五郎に言うたけど、私、まりなが何（を）貰うたか知らんねん。（だから、聞くで。）
('Marina received something from Nagao yesterday, and Jiro told Goro about it, but I do not know what Marina received. (So I will ask you.)')

3.2 Results

I analyzed the data with Praat (Boersma and Weenink 2018). Figures 1 and 2 present the pitch tracks of (6), which involve the high-beginning *wh*-interrogative *dare* 'who' with ES and MS prosody, respectively. *Go'ro-ni* 'Goro-to' was not recorded because the participant could not figure out how to utter the sentence with it.[7] The figures show that the F0 peak of the *wh*-word is boosted and that the F0 peaks of the words in *wh*-scope are lowered, which indicates that Osaka Japanese uses the same strategy as Tokyo Japanese to mark *wh*-scope. Recall that *wh*-interrogatives in Osaka Japanese are all unaccented, unlike their Tokyo Japanese counterparts. The data show that even unaccented words can cause F0 pitch compression.

I measured the F0 peaks of the *wh*-word and the matrix verb in each prosodic pattern. The results of the two sample t-test are in Table 1, which shows that the mean F0 peaks of the matrix verb and the *wh*-word are significantly different between the two prosodic patterns at the 0.05 significance level.

	ES (Hz)	**MS (Hz)**	**p-value**
***Wh*-word**	266.42	301.81	$p < 0.0001$ $(t = 7.56, df = 13.74)$
Matrix verb	283.13	151.41	$p < 0.0001$ $(t = -13.7, df = 11.86)$

TABLE 1 Results of the two sample t-test on (6)

[7] However, this does not mean that (6) with *Go'ro-ni* 'Goro-to' is ungrammatical because another Osaka Japanese speaker (my consultant) was able to include it in her speech.

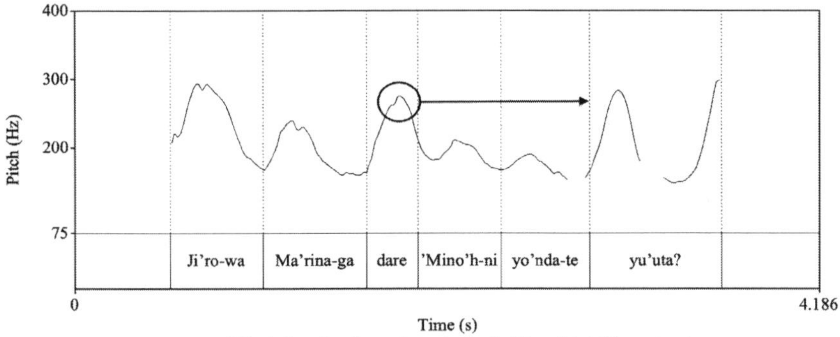

FIGURE 1 High-beginning *dare* 'who' (6) with ES prosody

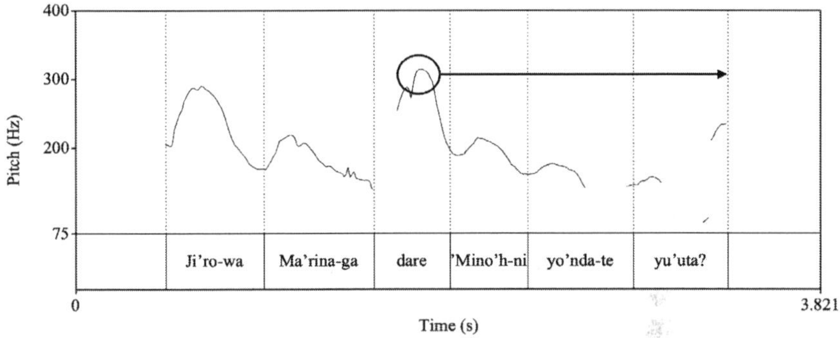

FIGURE 2 High-beginning *dare* 'who' (6) with MS prosody

Figures 3 and 4 are the pitch tracks of (7), where the *wh*-word is the low-beginning *'nani* 'what'. Again, *Go'ro-ni* 'Goro-to' was not recorded for the same reason mentioned above. The figures tell us that low-beginning *wh*-words also cause F0 pitch compression. This fact is interesting. Recall that *'nani* is low-beginning unaccented, which is realized as LH. The data show that the H tone on the second mora of *'nani* 'what' is raised due to the semantic focus of the word and reduces the F0 peaks of the words in the domain. However, the F0 pitch compression effect is small in Figure 3 because there are some bumps in the *wh*-domain.

As I did for the high-beginning *dare* 'who', I measured the F0 peaks of the *wh*-word and the matrix verb in both prosodic patterns. I applied the two sample t-test to the data and Table 2 shows the results. The data show that the mean F0 peaks of the matrix verb and the *wh*-word are significantly different between the two prosodic patterns at the 0.05 significance level.

	ES (Hz)	MS (Hz)	p-value
***Wh*-word**	278.95	295.02	$p = 0.0005$ ($t = 4.28, df = 17.41$)
Matrix verb	349.36	165.64	$p < 0.0001$ ($t = -17.16, df = 13.74$)

TABLE 2 Results of the two sample t-test on (7)

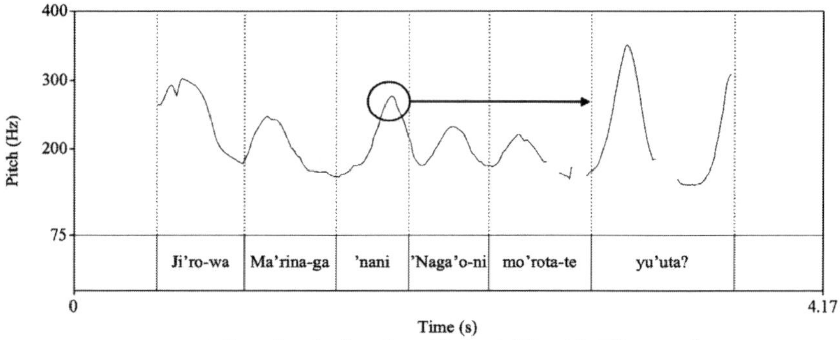

FIGURE 3 Low-beginning *'nani* 'what' (7) with ES prosody

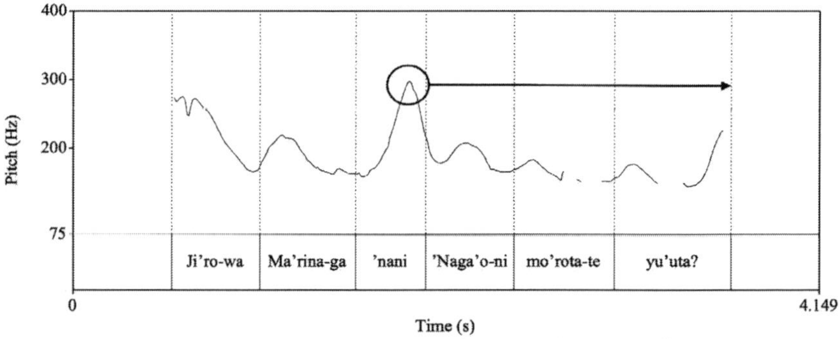

FIGURE 4 Low-beginning *'nani* 'what' (7) with MS prosody

3.3 Discussion

I showed that Osaka Japanese uses F0 pitch compression in *wh*-scope marking. Recall that *wh*-interrogatives in Osaka Japanese are all unaccented, unlike their Tokyo Japanese counterparts and that the pitch accent in *wh*-interrogatives causes F0 pitch compression in Tokyo Japanese (Kitagawa 2005). My data support Pierrehumbert and Beckman's (1988) claim that any H+L sequence can work as pitch accent in Osaka Japanese.[8] However, the effect of F0 pitch compression was smaller in Figure 3. It is possible that prosodic phrasing rather than F0 pitch compression is what is operative for

[8] In my stimuli, the *wh*-words are followed by L (*'Mino'h* and *'Naga'o*: LHL).

disambiguation (Hirotani 2005). The data also showed that the F0 peak of the *wh*-word is higher in the MS reading than in the ES reading in both (6) and (7), replicating the results in Kitagawa and Hirose (2012) for Tokyo Japanese.

4 Perception study

This section presents the data from my pilot perception experiment. My data show similar results as Hirotani's (2005) data for Tokyo Japanese. I argue that the structure in (2) is in fact unambiguous and that it looks ambiguous because it allows pragmatic answers.

4.1 Procedure

I conducted an online survey, using PsyToolkit (Stoet 2010, 2017). Ten Osaka Japanese speakers participated in the survey.[9] As a control, I compared the *ka*-construction in (2) and the *te*-construction in (5). As I mentioned in Section 3, the difference between the two constructions is the embedded complementizer. In the *ka*-construction, it is *-ka*, which is [+Q], while in the *te*-construction, it is *-te*, which is [−Q]. The example sentences are in (8) and (9). Apostrophes indicate the location of pitch accent.

(8) Ka-*construction in Osaka Japanese*
Ji'ro-wa [Ma'rina-ga *dare* yo'nda-**ka**] yu'uta(**-ka**)?
Jiro-TOP Marina-NOM who.ACC called/invited-Q said-Q
ES reading: 'Did Jiro say [who$_i$ Marina called/invited t_i]?'
MS reading: 'Who$_i$ did Jiro say [whether Marina called/invited t_i]?'

(9) Te-*construction in Osaka Japanese*
Ji'ro-wa [Ma'rina-ga *dare* yo'nda-**te**] yu'uta(**-ka**)?
Jiro-TOP Marina-NOM who.ACC called/invited-C/Q said-Q
ES reading: 'Did Jiro say [who$_i$ Marina called/invited t_i]?'
MS reading: 'Who$_i$ did Jiro say [that Marina called/invited t_i]?'

I made four sentences each for the two constructions (4 × 2). Words were all accented except for the *wh*-words *dare* 'who' and *'nani* 'what'. I used the verbs *yo'nda* 'called/invited' and *mo'rota* 'received' for the embedded verb and the verbs *yu'uta* 'said' and *ki'ita* 'heard/asked' for the matrix verb. The *wh*-words were in direct object position. The eight sentences were assigned either ES or MS prosody in Osaka Japanese (8 × 2). The sixteen sentences

[9] Most participants were undergraduate students at Ritsumeikan University in Kyoto, Japan. I had eleven participants, but excluded the data from one participant because s/he stopped answering the questions in the middle of the survey and did the whole survey again.

were paired with either a yes/no answer or a *wh*-answer as in (10) (16 × 2).[10] I added sixty-four filler items to the thirty-two experimental items.

(10) *Two answer types*

a. *Yes/No answer*
うん、言うたで。 ('Yes, (Jiro) said.')

b. Wh-*answer*
太郎。 ('Taro.')

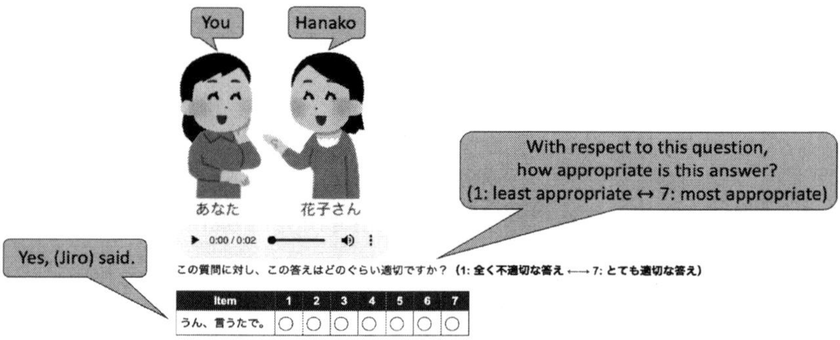

FIGURE 5 Survey screen

I asked my participants to listen to each question recorded by the author. They rated the appropriateness of the recorded question with respect to the yes/no answer or the *wh*-answer on the screen. I used a 7-point Likert scale, where 1 is the least appropriate and 7 is the most appropriate. This is a crucial difference with Hirotani's (2005) experiments, as hers were a forced-choice task, where participants were forced to choose either a yes/no answer or a *wh*-answer after listening to each question. Unlike her experiments, my survey tested how appropriate each combination is. I did not provide any context, except for the picture[11] in Figure 5, where "you" and Hanako are having a conversation and Hanako is asking you a question.

We have the following prediction. If Deguchi and Kitagawa's (2002) and Ishihara's (2003) analysis is correct, both the *ka*-construction and the *te*-construction would behave in the same way with both ES and MS prosody.

---

[10] The stimuli included "hybrid answers", which involve both a yes/no answer and a *wh*-answer (e.g. "Yes, Taro."). However, I decided not to use them as experimental items and treated them as filler items because I did not find anything interesting.

[11] I used a picture from *Irasutoya* (`https://www.irasutoya.com/`), following the terms and conditions. It is copyrighted by Mr. Takashi Mifune.

4.2 Results

I transformed the ratings into z-scores to eliminate scale bias and averaged them, but I did not test for statistical significance due to the small number of participants ($n = 10$). Figure 6 and Table 3 show that yes/no answers were strongly preferred in both constructions with ES prosody, which means that the two constructions behave similarly with ES prosody. Surprisingly, Figure 7 and Table 4 show that the two constructions behave differently with MS prosody; *wh*-answers were strongly preferred in the *te*-construction, whereas there was no strong preference in the *ka*-construction, as Hirotani (2005) found for Tokyo Japanese. Note that the error bars in the figures show standard deviation.

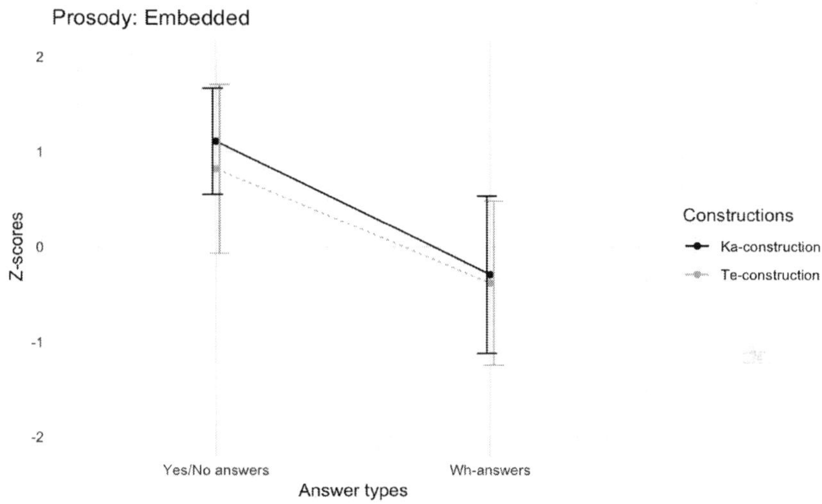

FIGURE 6 ES prosody

	Yes/No answers	*Wh*-answers
***Ka*-construction**	1.11 (0.56)	−0.29 (0.83)
***Te*-construction**	0.82 (0.89)	−0.38 (0.86)

TABLE 3 ES prosody: Average z-scores (SD)

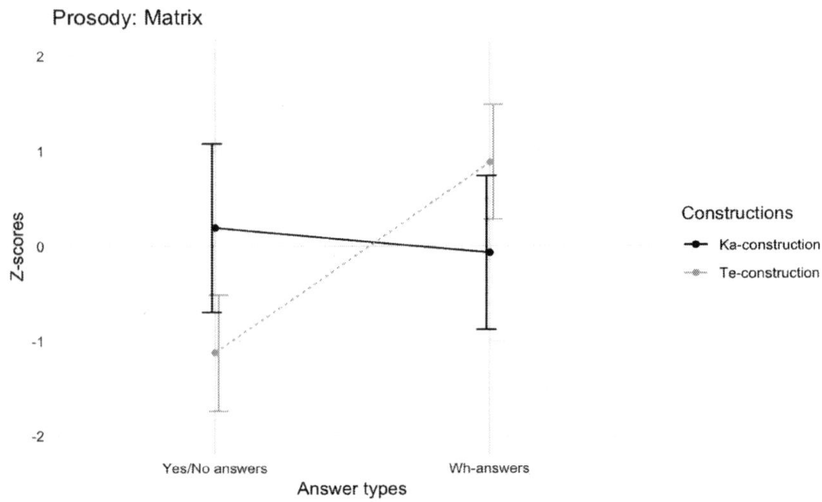

FIGURE 7 MS prosody

	Yes/No answers	***Wh*-answers**
***Ka*-construction**	0.19 (0.89)	−0.07 (0.81)
***Te*-construction**	−1.13 (0.61)	0.88 (0.61)

TABLE 4 MS prosody: Average z-scores (SD)

4.3 Pragmatics

I conducted a mini survey after the main survey to see if every combination between construction and prosody is well-formed. In this mini survey, the same ten participants listened to two sentences each for the three combinations (*-ka* + ES, *-te* + ES, and *-te* + MS) and four sentences for *-ka* + MS from the main survey. I asked them to rate the naturalness of the prosody, using a 7-point Likert scale (1: not natural at all and 7: very natural). The mean ratings were 6.75 for *-ka* + ES, 2.38 for *-ka* + MS, 5.4 for *-te* + ES, and 5.95 for *-te* + MS; *-ka* + MS was rated substantially lower than the other combinations.

This fact can explain why there was no preference between the two answer types in this condition. Since I did not tell my participants beforehand that some stimuli might sound unnatural or ill-formed, they may have made an effort to interpret the ill-formed questions, using the two strategies in (11). It is possible that the same explanation holds for Hirotani's (2005) Tokyo Japanese data.

(11) *Two strategies*

a. **Strategy I**: Ignore MS prosody and interpret the questions with the embedded Q-marker *-ka* (= yes/no questions)

b. **Strategy II**: Ignore the embedded Q-marker *-ka* and interpret the questions with MS prosody (= *wh*-questions)

Also notice in Figures 6 and 7 and Tables 3 and 4 that although *wh*-answers are dispreferred with ES prosody, the ratings are slightly better than yes/no answers in the *te*-construction with MS prosody. I claim that this is what the previous studies have interpreted as ambiguity in the *ka*-construction in (2). Some speakers try to provide a "super-informative" answer to matrix yes/no questions. In English, for example, a speaker may answer a question like "Did Mary say who bought the book?" with "Yes, Bill.", providing a value for the variable associated with the embedded *wh*-word.

To sum up, the *ka*-construction in (2) is not ambiguous, but looks ambiguous because of pragmatics. Deguchi and Kitagawa (2002) and Ishihara (2003) claim that there is a one-to-one correspondence between prosody and interpretation and Hirotani (2005) argues against this claim. In fact, these two claims are partially correct; there is a one-to-one correspondence between prosody and interpretation, but the *ka*-construction in (2) with MS prosody is ill-formed.

5 Comparison with Tokyo Japanese, Fukuoka Japanese, and Busan Korean

Hwang (2015) conducted perception experiments on Tokyo Japanese, Fukuoka Japanese, and Busan Korean. Her experiments used a forced-choice task, like Hirotani's (2005): participants chose a yes/no answer or a *wh*-answer after listening to each question with ES or MS prosody in each variety. The embedded complementizer was *-ka* in Tokyo and Fukuoka Japanese and *-ci* in Busan Korean. She did not provide any context. (12) shows one of the stimuli in Busan Korean.

(12) *Busan Korean*

Kyengchal-un	[kunal	Yumi-ka	[*nwukwu*]-lul	mannassnun-**ci**]
police-TOP	that.day	Yumi-NOM	who-ACC	met-Q

mwuless-eyo**?**
asked-ending

ES reading: 'Did police ask [who$_i$ Yumi met t_i on that day]?'
MS reading: 'Who$_i$ did the police ask [whether Yumi met t_i on that day]?' (Hwang 2015: (6))

Hwang (2015) concluded that all three languages can overcome *wh*-islands with MS prosody. She found that all Busan Korean participants almost always chose *wh*-answers in this condition, which tells us that Busan Korean can override *wh*-islands with MS prosody.[12]

However, she reports that there was between-speaker variability as to how acceptable *wh*-answers were in the *ka*-construction with MS prosody in Tokyo and Fukuoka Japanese. In Tokyo Japanese, the acceptance rate ranged from 0% to 100%, which means that one speaker never allowed *wh*-answers, while another speaker always allowed *wh*-answers. I claim that the speaker with 0% acceptability consistently used Strategy I in (11a), while the speaker with 100% acceptability consistently used Strategy II in (11b). In Fukuoka Japanese, in contrast, the range was from 17.7% to 100%, which means that there were no Fukuoka Japanese participants who never allowed *wh*-answers in this condition. Why were there no Fukuoka Japanese participants who consistently used Strategy I? In other words, why do Fukuoka Japanese speakers tend to use prosody?

Recall that Fukuoka Japanese and Busan Korean use a high F0 plateau prosody to mark *wh*-scope (Hwang 2006, *a.o.*). As pointed out by Hwang (2015) herself, F0 pitch compression, which is used in Tokyo and Osaka Japanese, can be used to mark focus, but the high plateau prosody is exclusively used for *wh*-scope marking. I claim that the availability of the high plateau prosody prompts Fukuoka Japanese speakers to use prosody in *wh*-island violation contexts.

6 Conclusion

In this paper, I showed that Osaka Japanese marks *wh*-scope by F0 pitch compression and that the structure in (2) is unambiguous. (2) appears to be ambiguous because it yields a "super-informative" yes/no answer.

Acknowledgments

I would like to thank Mats Rooth, John Whitman, and Draga Zec for helpful comments. I would also like to thank the participants of this study. Finally, thank you to Kayoko Minamida for discussion about Osaka Japanese prosody and interpretations. Of course, all errors are my own.

[12] Probably, Seoul Korean can also overcome *wh*-islands with MS prosody (see Hwang 2009).

References

Boersma, P. and Weenink, D. (2018). *Praat: Doing phonetics by computer [Computer program]*. Version 6.0.43.

Deguchi, M. and Kitagawa, Y. (2002). Prosody and *wh*-questions. In *Proceedings of NELS 32*, pages 73–92.

Haraguchi, S. (1977). *The tone pattern of Japanese: An autosegmental theory of tonology*. Tokyo: Kaitakusha.

Hirotani, M. (2005). *Prosody and LF interpretation: Processing Japanese wh-questions*. PhD thesis, University of Massachusetts Amherst.

Hwang, H. (2009). *Wh*-phrase questions and prosody in Korean. In *Japanese/Korean Linguistics*, volume 17, pages 295–309. Stanford, CA: CSLI Publications.

Hwang, H. K. (2006). Intonation patterns of *wh*-interrogatives in South Kyungsang Korean and Fukuoka Japanese. *Eoneohak, Journal of the Linguistic Society of Korea*, 45:39–59.

Hwang, H. K. (2015). Overriding syntactic islands with prosodically marked *wh*-scope in South Kyŏngsang Korean and two dialects of Japanese. In *Korean Linguistics*, pages 17:1, 33–77. Amsterdam: John Benjamins.

Ishihara, S. (2003). *Intonation and interface conditions*. PhD thesis, Massachusetts Institute of Technology.

Kitagawa, Y. (2005). Prosody, syntax and pragmatics of *wh*-questions in Japanese. *English Linguistics*, 22:2:302–346.

Kitagawa, Y. and Hirose, Y. (2012). Appeals to prosody in Japanese *wh*-interrogatives – Speakers' versus listeners' strategies. *Lingua*, 122:608–641.

Kori, S. (1987). The tonal behavior of Osaka Japanese: An interim report. In *Ohio State University Working Papers in Linguistics*, volume 36, pages 31–61.

Kubozono, H. (2007). Focus and intonation in Japanese: Does focus trigger pitch reset? In *Proceedings of the 2nd Workshop on Prosody, Syntax, and Information Structure*, pages 1–27.

McCawley, J. (1968). *The phonological component of a grammar of Japanese*. The Hague: Mouton.

Pierrehumbert, J. and Beckman, M. (1988). *Japanese tone structure*. Cambridge, MA: MIT Press.

Shimoyama, J. (2006). Indeterminate phrase quantification in Japanese. *Natural Language Semantics*, 14:139–173.

Stoet, G. (2010). PsyToolkit – A software package for programming psychological experiments using Linux. *Behavior Research Methods*, 42(4):1096–1104.

Stoet, G. (2017). PsyToolkit: A novel web-based method for running online questionnaires and reaction-time experiments. *Teaching of Psychology*, 44(1):24–31.

Korean vs. Chinese on Anaphoric Definites With(out) a Determiner

MYUNG-KWAN PARK

ARUM KANG

1 Introduction

The goal of this paper is to investigate bare nouns in donkey constructions and their anaphoric definite forms in Korean and Chinese. Specifically, we compare them with their counterparts in Mandarin Chinese (MC) by adding to the recent cross-linguistic studies of their distribution (Chierchia 1998; Izumi 2011). Our puzzle starts from the distinct behavior of bare nouns in donkey sentences. As illustrated from (1) to (2), unlike in English, in Korean the donkey anaphora can occur in distinct forms such as a (definite) demonstrative-preceded one and a bare NP. In (1), the donkey anaphora occurs in object position. Both the DP *ku tangnakwi* in (1a) and the bare NP *tangnakwi* in (1b) as donkey anaphora in this position give rise to a definite interpretation in the sense that they are construed as having a referentially bound reading, specifically having a co-varying of bound variables (e.g. 'Kim owns a donkey x and beats x, Lee owns a donkey y and beats y, etc.'), as in (1ai) and (1bi).

Japanese/Korean Linguistics 27
Edited by Michael Barrie.

(1) a. [Tangnakwi$_1$-lul] kwiwu-nun nongpwu-nun motwu
donkey-Acc raise-Rel farmer-Top all
(kocip-ul phiwu-myen) [**ku tangnakwi**$_1$-lul]
stubbornness-Acc exhibit-if the/that donkey-Acc
ttayli-nta.
beat-Dcl
'Every farmer who owns a donkey beats the donkey.'
i) **universal** (discourse old): 'Kim owns x and beats x, Lee owns y and beats y, etc.'

b. [Tangnakwi$_1$-lul] kwiwu-nun nongpwu-nun motwu
donkey-Acc raise-Rel farmer-Top all
(kocip-ul phiwu-myen) [**tangnakwi**$_1$-lul] ttayli-nta.
stubbornness-Acc exhibit-if donkey-Acc beat-Dcl
'Every farmer who owns a donkey beats the donkey.'
i) **universal** (discourse old): 'Kim owns x and beats x, Lee owns y and beats y, etc.'

In Korean, bare anaphora in donkey sentences does not show subject-object asymmetry. When the donkey anaphora occurs in subject position, both the definite anaphora *ku tangnakwi* and the bare anaphora *tangnakwi* also convey a referentially bound reading regardless of being marked with a Nominative or topic particle, as in (2a) and (2b):

(2) a. [Tangnakwi$_1$-lul] kwiwu-nun nongpwu-nun motwu
donkey-Acc raise-Rel farmer-Top all
[**ku tangnakwi**$_1$-ka] kocipsulep-tako sayngkakha-nta.
the/that donkey-Nom stubborn-Dcl think-Dcl
'Every farmer who owns a donkey thinks that the donkey is stubborn.'
i) **universal** (discourse old): 'Kim owns x and thinks x is stubborn, Lee owns y and thinks y is stubborn, etc.'

b. [Tangnakwi$_1$-lul] kwiwu-nun nongpwu-nun motwu
donkey-Acc raise-Rel farmer-Top all
[**tangnakwi**$_1$-ka] kocipsulep-tako sayngkakha-nta.
donkey-Nom stubborn-Dcl think-Dcl
'Every farmer who owns a donkey thinks that the donkey is stubborn.'
i) **universal** (discourse old): 'Kim owns x and thinks x is stubborn, Lee owns y and thinks y is stubborn, etc.'

In contrast, MC is in sharp contrast with Korean in the distribution of bare nouns in donkey constructions in the sense that they show subject-object asymmetry. In the MC donkey sentence of (3a), the demonstrative DP *na-tou luzi* in matrix object position co-varies with the RC-internal bare NP antecedent, the sentence being construed as 'each farmer beating his own donkey' as in (3i). But the corresponding bare NP *luzi* in (3b), unlike its Korean counterpart, does not convey a referentially bound reading, rather only receiving a generic reading (Jenks 2015; Bi and Jenks 2018):

(3) a. Mei-ge you [luzi$_1$] de nonfu dou
every-Clf have donkey DE farmer all
hui da **na-tou** **luzi$_1$**
will beat that.Dem-Clf donkey
'Every farmer who owns a donkey beats the/that donkey.'
i) **universal** (discourse old): 'Kim owns x and beats x, Lee owns y and beats y, etc.'

b. Mei-ge you [luzi$_1$] de nonfu dou hui
every-Clf have donkey DE farmer all will
da **luzi$_2$**
beat donkey
'Every farmer who owns a donkey beats that donkey.'
i) **generic:** 'Every farmer who owns a donkey beats donkeys in general.'[1]

However, when the donkey anaphora occurs in subject position, both the definite anaphora *na-tou luzi* and the bare anaphora *luzi* can give rise to a referentially bound reading, specifically a co-varying of bound variables.

(4) a. Mei-ge you [luzi$_1$] de nonfu dou
every-Clf have donkey DE farmer all
hui renwei **na-tou** **luzi$_1$** hen jue
will think that.Dem-Clf donkey very stubborn
'Every farmer who owns a donkey thinks that the/that donkey is very stubborn.'

b. Mei-ge you [luzi$_1$] de nonfu dou
every-Clf have donkey DE farmer all
hui renwei **luzi$_1$** hen jue
will think donkey very stubborn
'Every farmer who owns a donkey thinks that the donkey is very stubborn.'

[1] Note that there tend to be dialect variations on the generic vs. bound reading depending on the regions.

It might lead us to predict that subject bare NPs in Korean and MC donkey sentences necessarily gives rise to a referentially bound reading, which is not true. For example, when Korean and MC bare NPs in (5) are realized together with numeral classifiers, they stop serving any longer as a co-varying anaphor:

(5) a. [tangnakwi sey mali$_1$-lul] khiwu-nun nongpwu-nun motwu
donkey three Clf-Acc raise-Rel farmer-Top all
tangnakwi sey mali$_1$-ka kocipsulep-tako sayngkakha-nta.
donkey three Clf-Nom stubborn-Dcl think-Dcl
'Every farmer who owns three donkeys thinks that three donkeys are stubborn.'

b. Mei-ge you [san-ge luzi$_1$] de nonfu dou
every-Clf have three-Clf donkey DE farmer all
hui renwei **san-ge** **luzi$_1$** hen jue.
will think three-Clf donkey very stubborn
'Every farmer who owns three donkeys will think that three donkeys are very stubborn.'

The above observations bring us to the main questions of the present work, with special attention given to the syntactic-o-semantic function of bare nouns. Specifically, we address the following questions: first, in investigating the structure and construal of the donkey anaphora or anaphoric definiteness in Korean and MC, we tackle the issue of subject-object (a)symmetry in the use of bare nouns and their empty counterparts as an anaphoric definite. Unlike Korean, why does MC exhibit subject-object asymmetry in this regard? Second, how can we account for the reason why Korean and MC bare NPs quantified by numeral and classifiers stop serving a referentially bound or co-varying interpretation? Third, can we widen our view of cross-linguistic variations to the cases in other languages where like in Korean, the donkey anaphora is served by bare nouns?

Relevantly to the issues to be investigated in this paper, building on the concepts of German 'weak' and 'strong' definite articles proposed in Schwarz (2009), Jenks (2015) demonstrates a distinction between the definite expressing uniqueness and the one expressing familiarity in MC. Specifically, the former is realized with a bare noun, while the latter with a demonstrative (except in subject position). Based on this distinction, Jenks goes on to argue that in numeral classifier (NC) languages like MC, the donkey anaphora calls for anaphoric definites and can only be realized as indexical expressions, whose indices are dynamically assigned (e.g., along the line of dynamic semantics in Groenendijk & Stokhof 1991, Chierchia 1995, among others).

Just like MC, Korean employs two distinct paradigms of strong D (i.e., anaphoric definites) with the overt marking *ku* 'the/that' and weak D (i.e., uniqueness-denoting definites) as a bare noun (Kang 2012 et seq.). If in Korean, strong D and apparently weak D both give rise to a co-varying reading, it would be surprising because it challenges the prior assumption that strong D's require a salient antecedent, while weak D's do not. To overcome this challenge, we suggest that Korean employs two mechanisms giving rise to co-variation in donkey sentences: first, directly through (dynamic) binding, and second, indirectly through type shifting. The first is achieved by the overt demonstrative marked strong D, and the second, by the covert demonstrative marked but type-shifted strong D. To put it differently, in the latter case of the co-varying interpretation available to donkey sentences, Korean opts to use the strategy operative as in the *product-producer* relation of bridging contexts where the strong D is generally deployed. As will be detailed later, the major motivation of the split mechanism comes from the cross-linguistic consideration of anaphoric definites (or strong D) (Moroney (2019)). Furthermore, the current empirical data leads us to the thesis that unlike in MC, the same effects arise in Korean bare noun anaphora because such anaphora can be served by not only overt but also covert demonstrative marked strong D.

The remainder of this paper is as follows: Section 2 we explore the empirical dimensions of bare nouns and show the distinct use of bare noun anaphora between Korean and MC. Section 2 deals with theoretical issues on definiteness including the cross-linguistic system of definiteness. Section 3 examines the Korean definiteness system. It will be investigated how the Korean bare nouns split into the dichotomy of overt and covert demonstrative-marked strong D. I conclude in Section 4 with some suggestions for further implications and the remaining questions of this study.

2 Previous literature on definiteness

2.1 Two types of definiteness: Strong vs. weak D

Starting from the well-known facts on English *the*, which encodes both uniqueness and familiarity, there has been a wide variety of cross-linguistic study on typologically distinct ways of encoding definiteness. Based on the Fering and German language from (22) to (23), Schwarz (2009) claims that the types of definite determiners should be analyzed in terms of the distinct paradigm of strong and weak definites, as follows.

Table 2. The definite article paradigm in Ferin (From Ebert 1971) and German:

	Fering				German
Article Type	**m.Sg.**	**f.Sg**	**n.Sg.**	**PL**	Preposition +Def
weak (Elbert's A-form) strong (Elbert's D-from)	a di	at det (jÜ)	at det	a dön (dö)	vom von dem

(6) a. Ik skal deel tu **a/*di** kuupmaan
I must down to $\text{the}_{\text{weak}}/\text{the}_{\text{strong}}$ grocer
'I have to go down to the grocer.'
b. Oki hee on hingst keeft. ***A/Di**
Oki has a horse bought $\text{the}_{\text{weak}}/\text{the}_{\text{strong}}$
hingst haaltet.
horse limps
'Oki has bought a horse. The horse limps' (Ebert, 1971, p.161)

(7) a. Hans ging zu **dem** Haus
Hans went to $\text{the}_{\text{strong}}$ house
b. Hans ging **zum** Haus
Hans went to the_{weak} house
'Hans went to the house.' 'Hans went to the house.'
(Schwarz, 2009)

Based on the anaphoric-only semantics indexed with a familiar discourse referent (Heim 1982, Kamp and Reyle 1993), as illustrated below, Schwarz's formal implementation of definites are essentially situational where the strong D (i.e. anaphoric definites) involves an explicitly expressed relation with an antecedent (i.e. as an unpronounced indexical argument), whereas the weak D does not bear such an index.

(8) a. $[\![\iota]\!]$: $\lambda s_r\, \lambda P{:}\exists!x[P(x)(s_r)].\ \iota x P(x)(s_r)$
b. $[\![\iota^x]\!]$: $\lambda s_r\, \lambda P \lambda y{:}\exists!x[P(x)(s_r) \cap x=y].\ \iota x[P(x)(s_r) \cap x=y]$

Since Schwarz, it has been noted that languages differ in the pattern of D they mark. The following table shows the pattern of definiteness marking across languages (adapted from Jenks 2018, Kang to appear):

Table 3. Different types of definiteness marking across languages

	Bipartite	Marked anaphoric	Generally marked	Null marked	Marked unique
unique	Def_{weak}	∅	Def	∅	Def_{weak}
anaphoric	Def_{strong}	Def_{strong}	Def	∅	∅
Language	German, Lakhota	Korean, MC, Akan, Wu, Tai, Czech	Cantonese, English	Shan, Hindi	unattested

As mentioned before, MC does not have a weak article, and the weak D is realized using bare nouns. The strong article is lexicalized by the demonstrative, as shown below (Jenks 2018: (10a):

(9) a. **Yueliang** sheng shang lai le.
Moon rise up come LE
'The moon has risen.'
b. Jin-zhujiao ling xuesheng jin-le yanjiushi.
Kim-TA bring student in-Perf office
Keshi Piao-jiaoshou henhende piping-le
but Piao-professor severely scold-Perf
*(**na-ge**) **xuesheng**
that CLF student
'TA Kim brought a student to the office. But Prof. Park scolded the student severely.'

Furthermore, Schwarz notes that the weak D and the strong D induce distinct semantic effects in different types of bridging use (Clark 1975, Hawkins 1978, Prince 1981). The weak article is used in *part-whole* bridging contexts, whereas the strong article is used in *product-producer* bridging contexts. There is an evident cross-linguistic tendency for the split use of definite articles in the two different bridging contexts. Below are German in (10) and MC in (11) examples illustrating the two different types (Schwarz 2013: (15), Jenks 2018: (14)):

(10) a. *Part-whole* relation

Der	Kühlschrank	war	so	groß,	dass	der
The	fridge	was	so	big	that	the
Kürbis	Problem los			**im/#in dem**		
pumpkin	Without a problem			in-the$_{weak}$/in the$_{strong}$		
Gemüsefach	Untergebracht	warden		konnte.		
crisper	stowed	be		could		

'The fridge was so big that the pumpkin could easily be stowed in the crisper.'

b. *Producer-product* relation

Das	Theaterstück		missfiel	dem	Kritiker	so	sehr,
The	play		displeased	the	critic	so	much
dass	er	in seiner	Besprechung		kein	gutes	Haar
that	he	in his	review		no	good	hair
#am / an dem			Autor	ließ.			
on-the$_{weak}$/on the$_{strong}$			author	left			

'The play displeased the critic so much that he tore the author to pieces in this review.'

(11) a. *Part-whole* relation

Chezi	bei	jingcha	lanjie	le	yinwei	mei
car	PASS	police	intercept	LE	because	NEG
you	tiezhi	zai	**paizhao**		shang.	
have	sticker	at	license.plate		on	

'The car was intercepted by the police because there wasn't a sticker on the license plate.'

b. *Producer-product* relation

Paul	renwei	na shou shi	hen youmei,	jishi	ta
Paul	think	that CLF poem	very beautiful	although	he
bu	renshi	#(**na wei**)	**shiren**.		
NEG	know	that CLF	poet		

'Paul thinks that poem is very beautiful although he doesn't know of the poet.'

The difference in terms of the situational relationship between the two individuals involved is fairly straightforward: when considering wholes and their parts, it is clear that there is a containment relationship between the two (i.e. *fridge – crisper*; *car – license plate*), which in turn ensures that whenever we are looking at a situation that contains the whole, it will also contain the part in (10a) and (11a). This is not the case for the relationship between products and their producers (i.e. *play - author*; *poem – poet*). A situation containing a product does not generally contain a producer in (10b) and (11b).

What is interesting is that the weak D in *part-whole* bridging relation can yield a co-varying interpretation. Initially observed in Schwarz (2009), as shown below, the steering wheel in German and the roof in MC receive a co-varying interpretation (Schwarz 2009: (252), Jenks 2018: (30)):

(12)

Wenn	ein Auto	in	diesem	Staat	registriert	ist,
When	a car	in	this	state	registered	is
muss	es	eine Hupe		**am**	**Lenkrad haben**.	
Must	it	a horn		on-the$_{weak}$	steering wheel	

'If a car is registered in this state, it must have a horn on the steer ing wheel.'

(13)

Mei	ge	mai le	fangzi	de	ren	dou
every	CLF	buy LE	house	DE	people	all
xuyao	xiuli	(#**na ge**)		**wuding**		
need	fix	that CLF		roof		

'Everyone that bought a house needed to fix the roof.'

Although there is no explicit antecedent that the weak D could depend on, the co-varying reading is available because the weak D could relate to the prior antecedent in an indirect way (i.e., *car-steering wheel*, *house-roof*). Furthermore, the weak D refers to the unique referent that is part of any related event (i.e. a unique steering wheel is part of the horn-existing event, a unique roof is part of the home-buying event).

3 The definiteness system in Korean

It has been argued that Korean employs a distinct system of definiteness-encoding articles such as the covert D operator as in (14) and the overt *ku* 'the/that' as in (15) (Kang 2012, 2015, Ahn 2017, Cho 2017, Kang to appear, a.o.):

(14) Weak D in Korean

(*ku)	tal-i	palk-ta.
KU	moon-Nom	bright-Decl

'The moon is bright.'

(15) Strong D in Korean

Kim cokyo-ka	ecey	haksayng-ul		yenkwusil-ey
Kim TA-Nom	yesterday	student-Acc		office-at
teylikotulewa-ss-ta.				
bring-Past-Dcl				
kulentey	pak kyoswu-ka		**(ku)**	**haksayng-ul**
but	Park-professor-Nom		the/that	student
simhakey	kkwucic-ess-ta.			
severely	scold-Past-Dcl			

'TA Kim brought a student to the office but Prof. Park severely scolded the student.'

Although Korean bare nouns in default form express (in)definiteness and number, the effect of definiteness is achieved even when definites are replaced by bare nouns. As shown below, Korean does not require the definite determiner *ku* 'the/that' to encode anaphoric definites, as attested in question-answers in (16), narrative sequences in (17), the consequent clause of conditionals in (18), and that of conditionals with symmetric interpretation in (19):

(16) A: Cheli-ka chayk-ul sa w-ass-ni?
Cheli-Nom book-Acc buy.come-Pst-Q
B: chayk-i yeki iss-ney-yo.
book-Nom here be-Exl-Hear.Hon
'Did Cheli buy and bring a book? The book is here.'

(17)

Cheli-ka	ecey	chayk-lul sassta.
Cheli-Nom	yesterday	book-Acc bought
(Ku) chayk-i	cikum	chayksang-wuey iss-ta.
that book-Nom	now on-Loc	desk be-Dcl

'Cheli bought a book yesterday. That book is now on the desk.'

(18)

Cheli-ka	chayk-ul sa-myen,	(ku) chayk-ul
Cheli-Nom	book-Acc buy-if	(that) book-Acc
ta	ilk-e peli-nta.	
all	read.finish-Dcl	

'If Cheli buys a book, he finishes reading the whole book.'

(19) Yehaksayng-i namhaksayng-ul cinachi-l ttay myen,
girl.student-Nom boy.student-Acc pass.by-if
(ku) yehaksayng-i (ku) namhaksayng-ul
(that)girl.student-Nom (that) boy.student
nolyepo-ass-ta.
glare-Pst-Dcl
'If a girl student passes by a boy student, she glared at him.'

Accordingly, it may be assumed that the occurrence of *ku* is optional for an anaphoric interpretation.

Just as empirically evidenced across languages, the complementary distribution of strong and weak D is recognized in Korean bridging contexts. Resisting the strong article *ku* 'the/that' altogether, *part-whole* bridging only uses the weak D (i.e. bare nouns), whereas *product-producer* bridging can use the strong D (i.e. *ku*-preceded NP) (Kang to appear: (37)):

(20) a. *Part-whole* relation
kyelhonsik-ey ka-ss-ta.
wedding-to go-Pst-Decl
(*ku) sinpu-ka phalansayk-ul ip-ess-ta.
KU bride-Nom blue-Acc wear-Pst-Decl
'I went to a wedding. The bride/#that bride wore blue.'
b. *Producer-product* relation
nay-ka onul sosel-ul han-kwen sa-ss-nuntay,
I-Nom today novel-Acc one-CL buy-Pst-Con
(ku/*i/*ce) ceca-nun phulangsuin-i-ta.
KU/this/that author-Top French-be-Decl
'I bought a novel today. The author is French.'

Additionally, Korean displays the same patterns as German and MC in the sense that it is quite natural to expect that KU receives a co-varying reading. On the other hand, as shown in (22) if there is no environment for proper indexing, the use of KU is infelicitous (Kang to appear: (34)-(35)):

(21)

Mina-nun	ecey	sicang	han	myeng-ul
Mina-Top	yesterday	mayor	one	Cl-Acc

inthepyuha-ss-ta.
interview-Pst-Decl

onul	taythongleyng-un	*(**ku**)	sicang-ul
today	president-Top	KU	mayor-Acc

manna-n-ta.
meet-Pres-Decl

'Yesterday, Mina interviewed one mayor. Today, the president meets with **the** mayor.'

(22)

mayhay	taythongleyng-un	kak	si-uy
every.year	president-Top	each	city-Gen
(***ku**)	sicang-ul	manna-ss-ta.	
KU	mayor-Acc	meet-Pst-Decl	

'Every year, the president met with the mayor of each city.'

In a parallel fashion to German and MC, the weak D in the *part-whole* bridging relation of Korean can yield a co-varying interpretation. In (23), the tire receives such an interpretation.

(23)

cacenke-lul	tha-nun	salamtul-un	tha-ki	cen-ey
bicycle-Acc	ride-Rel	people-Top	ride-Nm	before-at
hangsang	(*ku)	thaie-uy	kongkiap-ul	
always	the/that	tire-Gen	airpressure-Acc	

cemkemha-yya ha-nta.
check should-Dcl

'People who ride a bicycle should check the air pressure of the tire.'

Quite striking is the availability of a co-varying reading to the *product-producer* bridging relation of Korean. Recall that both German and MC only opt for the strong D in this relation, but since in Korean the strong D is manifested by both the overt and covert demonstrative-marked forms, either form is realized in this relation.

(24) nonmwun-ul simsaha-taka nonmwun-i engtheli-i-myen,
draft-Acc review-while draft-Nom very bad-Copu-if
(hangsang/pothong)
always/ususally
(ku) ceca-lul pinanhakey toy-nta.
the/that author-Acc blame-come-Dcl
'If someone finds a draft very bad in the review process, he/she always/usually blames the author.'

Given the observation thus far, it is acknowledged that Korean develops a distinctive system for marking the different types of definiteness. Table 3 summarizes the different ways of encoding definiteness in Korean vis-à-vis German, MC, and Shan.

Table 4. Expressions of definiteness in German, Thai, Mandarin MC, and Shan (adapted from Moroney 2019)

Types of definite use	German (Schwarz 2009)	MC/Thai (Jenks 2015, 2018)	Shan (Moroney 2019)	Korean (Kang 2012, 2015, to appear)
Unique	Weak	Bare	Bare	Bare
Anaphoric	Strong	Demonstrative	Bare	Demonstrative/Bare
Bridging: product-producer	Strong	Demonstrative	Bare	Demonstrative/Bare
Bridging: part-whole	Weak	Bare	Bare	Bare
Donkey anaphora	Strong	Demonstrative	Bare	Demonstrative/Bare

It is worth considering the Shan language studied by Moroney (2019). This language does not employ any lexicalized element for marking definiteness. Shan can only use bare noun forms to express both unique and anaphoric definiteness, and bare nouns behave like English strong and weak D with the definite article *the*. Moroney claims that Shan can have a null anaphoric type shifter ι^x on its bare nouns. Although Korean is similar to Shan in that bare nouns can be used for strong anaphoric definites, Korean is different from Shan in that the demonstrative can function as the primary marking of anaphoric definiteness.

This typological consideration of definiteness-encoding expressions in Table 4 leads us to claim that Korean does not comply with the Blocking Principle (Chierchia 1998), which dictates that for the language having an overt determiner form of a type shifter, covert type shifting using that operator is unavailable. While like MC ones, Korean bare nouns are deployed in the environments requiring weak D's, they along with the demonstrative-marked anaphoric definites are also recruited for the environments requiring strong D's. We suggest following Moroney (2019) that in Korean, bare nouns can take the indirect strategy of employing a null anaphoric type shifter ι^x on them, thereby serving the role of strong D's.

The immediate question that arises is why Korean differs from MC in the use of bare nouns as strong D's. In other words, if Korean employs a null anaphoric type shifter ι^x for the strong D use of bare nouns, why can't MC do so? In fact, as we saw in (4) of section 1, bare nouns in the topic/subject position of MC can utilize such a null anaphoric shifter for that purpose. Thus, the most outstanding difference between Korean and MC lies in the fact that regardless of the positions they occupy, Korean bare nouns serve as an anaphoric definite; however, MC bare nouns with topic features can do so, but those lacking them cannot. Assuming that cross-linguistic variation is restricted to a narrow category of morphological properties, primarily inflectional (Chomsky 2001, 2), we advance the thesis that the difference in question between the two languages is rooted in the Case/case system: Korean entertains overt case morphology, whereas MC does not. It is striking to note that when bare nouns in Korean occur without such morphology as in (25), they cannot function as an anaphoric definite any more.

(25) **Case-less bare noun/NP in object position**:
Haksayng-i ecey ohwu yenkwusil-ey tochakhayssta.
student-Nom yesterday afternoon office-at arrived
Ku taum kim kyoswunim-i **haksayng** myentam hayssta.
and then Kim professor-Nom student interviewed
'A student arrived at the professor's office yesterday afternoon. And then Prof. Kim had an interview with a student/students in general.'

Just as overt classifier in the Cantonese Chinese nominal system contributes at the syntax-semantics interface to lexicalizing an iota operator (cf. Cheng and Sybesma 1999), case morphology in the Korean nominal system acts at the same level on lexically supporting a null anaphoric shifter, thereby bare nouns alone serving as an anaphoric definite.

4 Conclusion

To conclude, in Korean both the demonstrative-marked nominals and bare nouns can serve as an anaphoric definite. This is in sharp contrast with MC where the demonstrative-marked nominals can do so, but bare nominals can only do so in topic/subject position. This empirical generalization comes from the examination of such structural contexts as donkey constructions where anaphoric definites are called for. Since in these contexts, bare nouns are allowed in Korean, they count as an anaphoric definite. Meanwhile, in article-less languages including Korean and MC, uniqueness-denoting nominals and part nominals vis-a-vis whole nominals are realized as weak D's but never as strong D's. Thus, bare nouns in Korean can be construed as weak and strong D's, as well as being interpreted as indefinite and generic.

We have suggested that the difference between Korean and MC in the *anaphoric definite* use of bare nouns in non-topic/subject position is rooted in the different composition of a functional layer in the nominal system. Unlike in MC, in Korean bare nouns are inflected with case morphology, which in turn lexicalizes a null anaphoric type shifter inserted at the syntax-semantics interface to empower the former to serve as an anaphoric definite.

One thing we have made a generalization on at observational level is the striking parallelism in distribution and construal between bare nouns and their empty counterparts *pro's* in both Korean and MC. Specifically, unlike Korean, MC resists bare nouns and their empty counterparts *pro's* in object position when they are construed as an anaphoric definite, which calls attention to Huang's (1984) celebrated generalization on *pro*'s in MC. We leave for future work the detailed work on this important issue.

References

Ahn, Dorothy. 2017. Definite and demonstrative descriptions: a micro-typology. In Proceedings of *GLOW in Asia* XI, volume 1, ed. by Michael Yoshitaka Erlewine, 33-48.

Bi, Ruyue Agnes, and Peter Jenks. 2019. Pronouns, null arguments, and ellipsis in Mandarin Chinese. *Proceedings of Sinn und Bedeutung* 23.1: 127-14

Cheng, Lisa Lai-Shen, and Rint Sybesma. 1999. Bare and not-so-bare nouns and the structure of NP. *Linguistic Inquiry* 30:509-542.

Chierchia, Gennaro. 1998. Reference to kinds across languages. *Natural Language Semantics* 6: 339–405.

Chierchia, Gennaro. 1995. *Dynamics of Meaning*. Cambridge University Press.

Cho, Jacee. 2017. The acquisition of different types of definite noun phrases in L2-english. *International Journal of Bilingualism* 21:367–382.

Chomsky, Noam. 2001. Derivation by phase. In *Ken Hale: A Life in Language*, ed. Michael Kenstowicz, 1–52.

Clark, Herbert H. 1975. Bridging. In *Thinking: Readings in cognitive science*, ed. by P. N. Johnson-Laird and P. C. Wason, 411–420. Cambridge: Cambridge University Press.

Ebert, Karen Heide. 1971. Zwei Formen des bestimmten artikels. *In Probleme und Fortschritte der Transformationsgrammatik*, ed. D. Wunderlich, pp. 159-174. Munchen: Hueber.

Groenendijk, Jeroen, and Martin Stokhof. 1991. Dynamic predicate logic. *Linguistics & Philosophy* 14, 39-100.

Heim, Irene. 1982. *The Semantics of Definite and Indefinite Noun Phrases*. University of Massachusetts, Amherst, PhD dissertation.

Huang, C.-T. James. 1984. On the distribution and reference of empty pronominals. *Linguistic Inquiry* 15:531-574.

Hawkins, John A. 1991. On (in)definite articles: Implicatures and (un)grammaticality prediction. *Journal of Linguistics* 27:405–442.

Izumi, Yu. *The semantics of proper names and other bare nominals*. PhD diss., University of Maryland, College Park.

Jenks, Peter. 2015. Patterns of definiteness without articles. Ms., UC Berkeley.

Jenks, Peter. 2018. Articulated definiteness without articles. *Linguistic Inquiry*. 49:501-536.

Kamp, Hans, and Uwe Reyle. 1993. *From Discourse to Logic*. Kluwer, Dordrech

Kang, Arum. 2012. Semantics and pragmatics of definiteness in Korean: the case of *ku*, In *Proceedings of the eighth Workshop on Altaic Formal Linguistics* (WAFL 8), ed. by Umut Ozge., 187-198.

Kang, Arum. 2015. *(In)definiteness, disjunction and anti-specificity in Korean: a study in the semantics-pragmatics interface*. PhD diss., University of Chicago.

Kang, Arum. To appear. Marking definiteness in articleless language: The role of the domain restrictor KU in Korean. *Language and Linguistics*.

Moroney, Mary. 2019. Definiteness with bare nouns in Shan. In *At the Intersection of Language, Logic, and Information*, ed. Sikos, J. and E. Pacuit E. ESSLLI 2018. *Lecture Notes in Computer Science*, vol. 11667, 108-123. Berlin & Heidelberg: Springer.

Prince, Ellen F. 1981. Toward a taxonomy of given/new information. In *Radical pragmatics*, ed. by Peter Cole, 223–254. New York: Academic Press.

Schwarz, Florian. 2009. *Two types of definites in natural language*. Doctoral dissertation, University of Massachusetts, Amherst.

Schwarz, Florian. 2013. Two kinds of definites cross-linguistically. *Language and Linguistics Compass* 7:534–559.

Scope Rigidity of Multiple Scrambling and Economy[1]

KWANG-SUP KIM

Hankuk University of Foreign Studies

1 Puzzle

In Korean, unmarked basic word order determines the scope relations. In (1a), for instance, the object cannot have scope over the subject. If, however, the object scrambles across the subject, as in (2), it may or may not take scope over the subject (Joo 1989, An 1990, Sohn 1995, Hagstrom 2000).

(1) Nwukwunka-ka nwukwuna-lul cohaha-n-ta. (*O>S, S>O)
someone-Nom everyone-Acc like-Pres-Dec
'someone loves everyone'

(2) Nwukwuna-lul$_1$ nwukwunka-ka t_1 cohaha-n-ta. (O>S, S>O)
everyone-Acc someone-Nom like-Pres-Dec
'(Literally) everyone$_1$, someone likes t_1'

Sentences (3-4) show the same point. The direct object (DO) cannot have scope over the indirect object (IO) in (3) (L. Kim 2008), but if the DO undergoes scrambling across the IO, it can be either outside or inside the scope of the IO, as shown in (4a-b).

[1] This work was supported by the research fund (2020) of Hankuk University of Foreign Studies. I am grateful to Young-mi Song, Keiko Murasugi, and the audience at the 27th Japanese/Korean Linguistics Conference, Sogang University, 2019, for feedback and suggestions.
Japanese/Korean Linguistics 27
Edited by Michael Barrie.

(3) Susie-ka nwukwunka-eykey nwukwuna-lul sokayha-yess-ta.
S-Nom someone-Dat everyone-Acc introduce-Past-Dec
'Susie introduced everyone to someone' (IO> DO, *DO>IO)

(4) a. Susie-ka nwukwuana-lul$_1$ nwukwunka-eykey t_1
S-Nom everyone-Acc someone-Dat
sokayha-yess-ta.
introduce-Past-Dec
'Susie introduced everyone to someone' (IO>DO, DO>IO)
b. Nwukwuana-lul$_1$ Susie-ka nwukwunka-eykey t_1
everyone-Acc S-Nom someone-Dat
sokayha-yess-ta.
introduce-Past-Dec
'(Literally) everyone, Susie introduced to someone'
(IO>DO, DO>IO)

In short, unmarked basic word order exhibits the scope rigidity, and scrambling may or may not display reconstruction effects, giving rise to an ambiguity (Ko 2018, among many others).

By contrast, multiple scrambling displays a peculiar pattern. If the relative word order between two constituents is maintained after multiple scrambling, their scope relation remains the same. If (5) is not ambiguous with regard to the relative scope of α and β, (6) is not ambiguous either.

(5) … β … α … (β > α)

(6) [β [α [… ~~β~~ … ~~α~~ …]]] (β > α)

This point can be exemplified by (7b), in which both the IO and the DO are scrambled, as schematically shown in (7b). Just as (3a) is unambiguous with regard to the relative scope of the IO and the DO, (7a) is scopally unambiguous.

(7) a. Nwukwunka-eykey$_2$ nwukwuna-lul$_1$ Susie-ka t_2 t_1
Someone-Dat everyone-Acc Susie-Nom
sokayha-yess-ta.
Introduce-Past-Ind
'(Literally) to someone, everyone, Susie introduced'
b. IO$_i$ DO$_j$ S ~~IO~~ ~~DO~~ V (IO> DO, *DO<IO)

On the other hand, the word order 'DO>IO' is ambiguous.[2] If the order is maintained after multiple scrambling, the resulting structure is also ambiguous, as shown by (8a-b).

(8) a. Susie-ka nwukwuna-lul nwukwunka-eykey sokayha-yess-ta.
S-Nom everyone-Acc someone-Dat introduce-Past-Dec
(DO>IO, IO>DO)
b. Nwukwuna-lul$_1$ nwukwunka-eykey$_2$ Susie-ka t_2 t_1
everyone-Acc someone-Dat S-Nom
sokayha-yess-ta.
Introduce-Past-Dec
'(Literally) everyone, to someone, Susie introduced'
(DO>IO, IO>DO)

On theses grounds, we can make a generalization about multiple scrambling as follows:

(9) Scope Rigidity of Multiple Scrambling
If the relative word order between two expressions is maintained after multiple scrambling, the scope relation between them is maintained as well.[3]

The scope rigidity of multiple scrambling is puzzling, because it is possible that the DO has scope over the S(ubject), while the S has scope over the IO. For instance, in (10) the DO can have scope over the S, while the S can bind the anaphor contained in IO.

(10) [Caki casin-uy tongsayng-eykey]$_2$ [motun kyoswu-lul]$_1$
[Self-Gen younger brother-Dat] [every professor-Acc]
kak kak talun haksayng-I t_2 t_1 chingchanha-yess-ta.
Different student speak well of-Past-D
'a different student$_i$ spoke well of every teacher to his/her$_i$ younger brother' (DO>S and S can bind the anaphor contained in IO)

Suppose the following scenario. In the department of Linguistics, there are three professors—A, B, C, and Susie praised Professor A to her younger brother, Tom praised Professor B to his younger brother, and Mina praised Professor C to her younger brother. In this situation, sentence (10) can be used. This means it is possible that the higher copy of the DO is interpreted

[2] This suggests that the order 'IO>DO' is a basic word order and (8a) is derived by scrambling.
[3] As will be mentioned in Section 2, Japanese also displays the same pattern (Koizumi 1995, 2000, Yatsushiro 1996, Sauerland and Elbourne 2003, Arano 2017).

while the lower copy of the IO is interpreted. However, it is not possible for the DO to have scope over the IO in (7a). This puts us in a dilemma. This paper explores the possibility of providing an economy-based account of this puzzle and various other peculiar properties of scrambling.

2 Previous Approaches

Japanese exhibits the same pattern as Korean with regard to the scope rigidity of basic word order, (anti-)reconstruction effects of scrambling, and the scope rigidity of multiple scrambling. Hoji (1985) notes that the IO-DO word order displays the scope rigidity effect, while the reverse word order is ambiguous, as illustrated by (11-12).[4]

(11)	Sana-ga	dareka-ni	daremo-o	syookaisita.
	Sana-Nom	someone-Dat	everyone-Acc	introduced
	'Sana introduced everyone to someone.'			(IO> DO, *DO>IO)

(12) a.	Sana-ga	daremo-o	dareka-ni	syookaisita.
	Sana-Nom	everyone-Acc	someone-Dat	introduced
	(IO> DO, DO>IO)			
b.	Daremo-o	Sana-ga	dareka-ni	syookaisita.
	Everyone-Acc	Sana-Nom	someone-Dat	introduced
	(IO> DO, DO>IO)			

Yatsushiro (1996) observes that the scope rigidity is maintained even after multiple scrambling, as shown in (13). In (13) the relative word order between the IO and the DO is maintained, so their scope relation remains the same.

(13)	Dareka-ni$_2$	daremo-o$_1$	Sana-ga	t_2	t_1	syookaisita.
	Someone-Dat	everyone-Acc	Sana-Nom			introduced
	(IO> DO, *DO>IO)					

In short, Japanese and Korean display the same pattern. This section examines two previous approaches to Japanese multiple scrambling.[5]

---

[4] On these grounds, Yatsushiro (1998) proposes that the DO occurs in a scrambled position in (12a).

[5] There are a few previous approaches to Japanese, but there is no previous approach to this

2.1 The Shortest Move Approach

Sauerland and Elbourne (2003) make use of the principle 'Shortest Move' in an attempt to capture the pattern exhibited in multiple scrambling. In this approach, (11) is generated as follows. First of all, the IO is attracted to the edge of the clause since it is the closest constituent, and then the DO is attracted to the inner SPEC; once the IO is dislocated, the DO is the closest constituent, and the inner SPEC is the closest landing site, as shown in (14a-c).[6,7]

(14) a. Sana-Nom someone-Dat everyone-Acc introduced: Movement of 'someone-Dat'

b. Someone-Dat$_j$ Sana-Nom t$_j$ everyone-Acc introduced: Tucking in of 'everyone-Acc'

c. Someone-Dat$_j$ everyone-Acc$_i$ Sana-Nom t$_j$ t$_i$ introduced

They assume that scrambling can occur not only in the narrow syntax but also at PF, and then go on to propose that scrambling in the narrow syntax does not exhibit reconstruction effects at all, while scrambling at PF displays total reconstruction effects. If both scrambling of the IO and the scrambling of the DO take place in the narrow syntax, the IO must have scope over the DO in (14c). By contrast, the DO can have scope over the IO if the IO undergoes scrambling at PF and the DO undergoes scrambling in the narrow syntax, as in (15).

(15) Someone-Dat everyone-Acc Sana-Nom ~~Someone-Dat~~ ~~everyone-Acc~~

(Syntax)

(PF Movement)

However, the derivation in (15) is impossible; in the narrow syntax the DO *daremo-o* 'everyone-Acc' cannot cross over the IO *dareka-ni* 'someone-Dat' on account of 'Shortest Move'.[8] Therefore, (15) is not a possible derivation. The derivation in (15) is the only derivation that can produce the reading 'DO>IO', but it is not a possible derivation. Therefore, (13) is scopally unambiguous.

The 'Shortest Move' approach can capture the fact that the scope relation between two scrambled phrases must remain the same as long as the relative word order remains the same, but it fails to explain the scope relation between

---

pattern in Korean, to the best of my knowledge.

[6] In (14a-c) and similar representations, English translations of the Japanese/Korean words are used.

[7] This amounts to saying that they make use of Richards' (2001) tucking approach.

[8] PF-movement must follow Narrow Syntax-Movement. So the IO intervenes between the edge of the clause and the DO when the DO undergoes scrambling in the narrow syntax.

the scrambled phrases and the unscrambled phrase. We have seen from (10), repeated here as (16a), that it is possible that the IO takes scope under the S, while the DO takes scope over the S: that is, it is possible that the lower copy of the IO is interpreted while the higher copy of the DO is interpreted, as shown in (16b).

(16) a. [Caki casin-uy tongsayng-eykey]$_2$ [motun kyoswu-lul]$_1$
[Self-Gen younger brother-Dat] [every professor-Acc]
kak kak talun haksayng-I t_2 t_1 chingchanha-yess-ta.
Different student speak well of-Past-D
b. [~~self's brother-Dat~~ every professor-Acc [a different student-Nom
self's brother-Dat ~~every professor-Acc~~ spoke well of]]

As mentioned above, the representation in (16b) is not a possible representation under the 'Shortest Move' approach; the representation is possible only if the DO crosses over the IO in the narrow syntax and then the IO undergoes PF-movement, but scrambling of the DO across the IO in the narrow syntax is not permitted due to 'Shortest Move'. Therefore, we are led to the conclusion that Sauerland and Elbourne's approach is empirically inadequate.[9,10]

2.2 The Headless VP-movement approach

Yatsushiro (1996), Koizumi (1995, 2000) and Arano (2017) propose that if VP-fronting takes place, there is an effect of multiple scrambling. In this approach, (13) is generated if V moves to T and then the V-less VP scrambles across the S, as shown in (17).

---

[9] Later in section 3, I claim that 'Shortest Move' itself is correct. More precisely, it will be claimed that scrambling across a scrambled phrase is not permitted, and it will be shown that this follows from the Scrambling Economy.

[10] Bošković and Takahashi (1998) propose that scrambled phrases are base-generated in the scrambled position, and lower into their thematic position at LF. According to their proposal, short-distance scrambled DPs sometimes undergo LF lowering but sometimes remain in their S-Structure position, for head movement obviates the need for lowering. This approach can capture the Scope Rigidity of Multiple Scrambling, given that when multiple scrambling takes place, either all the scrambled phrases lower into their thematic positions, or all of them remain in situ. This approach, however, cannot explain (10), in which the IO undergoes lowering but the DO does not.

(17) a. [$_{TP}$ Sana-Nom [$_{VP}$ someone-Dat everyone-Acc introduce] Past]: V-movement
b. [$_{TP}$ Sana-Nom [$_{VP}$ someone-Dat everyone-Acc ~~introduce~~] introduced]: VP-scrambling
c. [$_{TP}$ [$_{VP}$ someone-Dat everyone-Acc ~~introduce~~]$_i$ [$_{TP}$ Sana-Nom t_i] introduce-ed]]]

The relative structural relation between the IO and the DO is not affected by the V-less VP scrambling. Hence, this proposal can explain why there is no change in scope relation even after scrambling.

It is predicted under this approach that if both the IO and the DO undergo scrambling, neither of them can have scope over the subject; if V-less VP undergoes scrambling, they fail to c-command the subject. However, this predication is wrong. In (18a) the IO can have scope over the S, and in (18b) the DO can take scope over the S.

(18) a. Nwukwuna-eykey$_2$ Susie-lul$_1$ nwukwnka-ka t_2 t_1
everyone-Dat Susie-Acc$_1$ someone-Nom
sokayha-yess-ta.
introduce-Past-Dec (IO>S, S>IO)
b. Susie-eykey$_2$ nwukwuna-lul$_1$ nwukwunka-ka t_2 t_1
Susie-Dat everyone-Acc someone-Nom
sokayha-yess-ta.
introduce-Past-Dec (DO>S, S<DO)

Another problem is that this approach, just like the Shortest Move Approach, fails to explain the example in (10), schematically repeated here as (19). In (19) the DO can have scope over the S, while the anaphor inside the IO can be bound by the S.

(19) [self's brother-Dat$_2$ every professor-Acc$_1$ [a different student-Nom t_2 t_1 speak well of-Past-Dec]]

This is hard to explain under the headless VP scrambling approach. To conclude this section, the Shortest Move approach and the Headless VP-scrambling approach are not viable options.

3 Scrambling Economy

There are two competing approaches to scrambling: the Free Merge Approach (Kuroda 1988, Saito 1985, 2003, Hoji 1985, Fukui 1993, Abe 1993, Cho 1994, Saito and Fukui 1998, Tada 1993, Takano 1998, 2000, R. Kim 2003, among many others) and the Feature-Driven Approach (Y. Lee 1993,

Miyagawa 1997, 2001, 2010, Karimi 1999, Grwendorf and Sabel 1999, Sabel 2001, Kitahara 2002, Lee and Cho 2003, Jung 2002, Yang and Kim 2005, Ko 2007, 2011, 2014). While adopting the free merge approach, this section attempts to show that the peculiar pattern displayed by multiple scrambling follows from the general properties of optional free merge.[11]

3.1 QR and Economy

Let us suppose that we are free to apply an operation and asked to decide whether or not we apply it. In this situation, the Economy Principle says 'if there is no effect at PF/LF, it does not take place' (Chomsky 1995, 2001, Sabel (2001), Miyagawa 2006).

(20) The Economy Condition on Optional Free Merge (Condition on Derivation):
If there is no output effect, the optional free merge does not take place.

Fox's (2000) Scope Economy is a version of the Economy Condition.

(21) Scope Economy: QR can only apply if it affects semantic interpretation. (Fox 2000)

Let us say that QR is not feature-driven. That is, QR is an optional free merge. Then, it makes sense that it does not take place if it gives no scope effect. To apply QR is a violation of the Principle of Economy if there is no semantic effect of QR. This conceptually attractive principle is empirically supported. Fox (2000) observes that (22a) is scopally ambiguous, but it is disambiguated when it is followed by *Mary does, too*, as in (22b).

(22) a. Some boy admires every teacher. (some>every, every>some)
b. Some boy admires every teacher, and Mary does, too.
(some>every, *every>some)

[11] Scrambling displays locality and anti-locality effects (Miyagawa 2001, 2010, Richards 2001, Kitahara 2002, Ko 2007, 2011, 2014, 2015). Ko (2018) argues that this constitutes evidence for the claim that scrambling is a feature-driven movement. However, I assume that optional free merge is not literally free, but constrained by the Scrambling Economy in (20) and a version of cyclicity condition like Chomsky's (2001, 2008) phase theory or Fox and Pesetsky's (2005) Cyclic Linearization. It is also noteworthy that vP may not be a phase or a spell-out domain on account of V-movement in Korean.

The ambiguity of (22a) is usually captured by QR (May 1985), as shown in (23a-b).

(23) a. [some boy admires every teacher]: QR
 b. [every teacher [some boy admires every teacher]]

Let us suppose that QR takes place in (24a). Then, there is no scope effect of QR. The Scope Economy in (21) prohibits the QR in (24a-b).

(24) a. [Mary admires every teacher]: *QR
 b. *[every teacher [Mary admires ~~every teacher~~]]

If QR is prohibited in the second conjunct of (22b), it is also prohibited in its first conjunct in accordance with the Principle of Parallelism in (25).

(25) The Principle of Parallelism: QR and reconstruction must apply in parallel in the antecedent and in the ellipsis.

Therefore, the first conjunct of (22b) is not ambiguous.

The scope economy is likely to run into a look-ahead problem in the sense that we need to calculate whether or not QR can give a scope effect before QR takes place. This problem can be avoided if it is reinterpreted from the view point of representation as follows:

(26) Revised Scope Economy
 a. QR is free to take place, but if there is no semantic effect, an ill-formed representation is generated.
 b. This problem can be repaired by ellipsis: that is, a well-formed representation can be generated if the higher copy is elided.
 c. If QR gives rise to some semantic effect, the higher copy is interpreted.

According to the Revised Scope Economy, (27b) is an ill-formed representation. I propose that this problem can be repaired by ellipsis. If the higher copy of *every teacher* is elided, a well-formed LF can be generated.

(27) a. [Mary admires every teacher]: QR
 b. [every teacher [Mary admires every teacher]]: Repair-By-Ellipsis
 c. [~~every teacher~~ [Mary admires every teacher]]

The gist of the claim is that QR is an optional free merge, so that it is free to take place. However, an ill-formed LF is generated if there is no semantic effect. This can be fixed by ellipsis.

3.2 Scrambling and Economy

I claim that scrambling obeys an analogous economy principle. Suppose that free merge takes place in the narrow syntax. Then, it must give effects at PF and/or LF and the effects made by it must not be undone by a subsequent operation; otherwise, scrambling, which is an optional free merge, should have not taken place. In short, scrambling obeys the Economy Principle in (28a-d). The principles in (28a-c) are identical to the ones in (26a-c): if 'QR' and 'semantic effect' are replaced by 'scrambling' and 'phonetic/semantic effect' respectively, (28a-c) are generated. The only addendum is (28d), which deals with multiple scrambling. In fact, (28d) is not much different from (28c) in that both of them basically say that the effects of scrambling must not be vacuous.

(28) Scrambling Economy
   a. Scrambling is free to take place, but if there is no phonetic/semantic effect, an ill-formed representation is generated. (=26a)
   b. This problem can be repaired by ellipsis: that is, a well-formed representation can be generated if the higher copy is elided. (= 26b)
   c. If scrambling gives rise to some phonetic/semantic effect, the higher copy is interpreted. (= 26c)
   d. The effect of a previous scrambling must not be undone by a subsequent scrambling.

3.2.1 Scrambling Economy and Mono-Scrambling

The scrambled phrase can be interpreted either in the landing site or in the launching site: that is, scrambling may display reconstruction effects or anti-reconstruction effect. Let us consider whether the Scrambling Economy in (28) illuminates this phenomenon. When scrambling takes place in (29a), as in (29b), a new binding possibility is generated. In this context, the copy in the scrambled position is interpreted, as schematically shown in (30).

(29) a. *caki-uy$_l$ emeni-ka motun haksayng-ul$_l$ cohaha-n-ta.
   self-Gen mother-Nom all student-Acc like-Pres-Dec
   b. motun haksayng-ul$_l$ caki-uy emeni-ka t_l cohaha-n-ta.
   all student-Acc self-Gen mother-Nom like-Pres-Dec
   '(literally) all students, his mother likes t_i'

(30) [all student]-Acc [self-Gen mother]-Nom ~~[all student]-Acc~~ like-Pres-Dec

If, on the other hand, there is no new semantic effect or the existing semantic relation is broken by scrambling, as in (31), the copy in the original position is interpreted.

(31) Caki-uy tongsayng-ul$_1$ motun haksayng-i t$_1$ ttaylye-ss-ta.
Self-Gen brother-Acc all student-Nom hit-Past-Dec
'Their brothers, all students hit'

(32) ~~[self-Gen brother]-Acc~~ all students-Nom [self-Gen brother]-Acc hit-Past-Dec

On these grounds, we make a generalization as follows:

(33) If there is a sematic effect, the copy in the landing site is interpreted. If not, the copy in the launching site is interpreted.

This generalization follows from the Scrambling Economy. In (30), repeated here as (34a), the lower copy is deleted in accordance with the Scrambling Economy in (28c).

(34) a. [all students]-Acc [self-Gen mother]-Nom [all students]-Acc like-Pres-Dec: Deletion of the Lower Copy in accordance with (28c)
b. [all students]-Acc [self-Gen mother]-Nom ~~[all students]-Acc~~ like-Pres-Dec

On the other hand, in (32) the higher copy is deleted in compliance with the Scrambling Economy in (28b): that is, it is elided as an instance of repair-by-ellipsis, as shown in (35a-b).

(35) a. [self-Gen brother]-Acc all students-Nom [self-Gen brother]-Acc hit-Past-Dec: Deletion of the Higher Copy (Repair-by-Ellipsis) in accordance with (28b).
b. ~~[self-Gen brother]-Acc~~ all students-Nom [self-Gen brother]-Acc hit-Past-Dec

Sentences (2), rewritten here as (36), can also be reinterpreted from this perspective.

(36) Nwukwuna-lul$_1$ Nwukwunka-ka t_1 cohaha-n-ta.
everyone-Acc someone-Nom like-Pres-Dec
'(literally) everyone$_1$, someone likes t_1' (O>S, S>O)

It is not the case that *nwukwuna-lul* 'everyone-Acc' always distributes over *nwukwunka-ka* 'someone' when the former c-commands the latter. For instance, (37) is ambiguous with regard to the scope relation: the subject may or may not distribute over the object.[12]

(37) Nwukwuna-ka Nwukwunka-lul cohaha-n-ta. (S>O, O>S)
everyone-Nom someone-Acc like-Pres-Dec

Likewise, *nwukwuna-lul* 'everyone-Acc' may or may not have scope over *nwukwunka-ka* 'someone-Nom' in (36) although it undergoes scrambling. If the scrambled object takes scope over the S, the higher copy is interpreted in accordance with (28c), and if not, the lower copy is interpreted in compliance with (28b).

(38) a. everyone-Acc someone-Nom everyone-Acc like-Pres-Dec:
If O>S, Deletion of the Lower Copy in accordance with (28c)
b. everyone-Acc someone-Nom ~~everyone-Acc~~ like-Pres-Dec

(39) a. everyone-Acc someone-Nom everyone-Acc like-Pres-Dec:
If S>O, Deletion of the Higher Copy in accordance with (28b)
b. ~~everyone-Acc~~ someone-Nom everyone-Acc like-Pres-Dec

Before closing this sub-section, it is noteworthy that non-scope-taking expressions cannot take scope over the other QP, so that there is no scope effect even though they are scrambled. Hence, they must be reconstructed. For instance, part of an idiomatic expression can be scrambled, but it must be interpreted in the original position. In (40) *pal-i nelp-ta* 'has many acquaintances' is an idiomatic expression, and *pal*-i 'foot-Nom' can be scrambled. However, it must be reconstructed because only a scope-taking expression can be interpreted in the scrambled position. In (40) *pal-i* cannot be a scope-taking expression if *pal-i nelp-ta* is construed as an idiom, and the non-scope-taking

[12] This follows from the ambiguity of *nwukwuna* 'everyone' and *nwukwunka* 'someone'. The former can be either distributive or non-distributive, and the latter can be either specific or non-specific. The former can take scope over the latter when the former is distributive and the latter is non-specific.

expression must not be in the scrambled position. Put differently, scrambling of the non-scope-taking expression gives no scope effect, and hence the higher copy must be deleted as an instance of repair-by-ellipsis.[13]

(40)

Pal-i$_i$	Susie-nun	t_i	nelp-ta.
Foot-Nom	Susie-Top		broad-Dec

(41)

a.	Pal-i$_i$	Susie-nun	pal-i	nelp-ta: Repair-by-Ellipsis
	Foot-Nom	Susie-Top		broad-Dec
b.	~~Pal-i$_i$~~	Susie-nun	pal-i	nelp-ta
	~~Foot-Nom~~	Susie-Top		broad-Dec

3.2.2 Scrambling Economy and Scope Rigidity of Multiple Scrambling

Let us now return to the example in (7a), repeated here as (42), in which multiple scrambling takes place.

(42)

Nwukwunka-eykey$_2$	nwukwuna-lul$_1$	Susie-ka	t_2	t_1
Someone-Dat	everyone-Acc	Susie-Nom		

sokayha-yess-ta.
introduce-Past-Dec
'(Literally) to someone, everyone, Susie introduced'

According to (28d), the effect of a previous scrambling must not be nullified by a subsequent scrambling. This can be formalized as follows: once scrambling takes place, the relative word order and the relative scope between the scrambled phrase and the rest of the constituents are determined, and it must not be contradicted by further scrambling in accordance with the Scrambling Economy in (28d).

(43) Cyclic Report of Scrambling Effects
Once scrambling of α takes place, the relative word order and the relativescope between α and the constitent(s) in the c-domain of α are determined: that is, a statement about relative word order and relative scope is generated after each scrambling.

(44) The Consistency Condition (= 28d)
The statement about the relative word order and relative scope of a previous scrambling must be consistent with the statement of a subsequent scrambling.

---

[13] The nominals in the idioms cannot co-occur with definite expressions like *ku* 'the', and their scrambling usually requires focus. This suggests that scrambling of the nominals in the idioms might be focus movement—a feature-driven movement.

According to (43), after each scrambling there is a statement about its result. Let us say that α undergoes scrambling across β, as in (45), and that α precedes β and takes scope over β, as a result of the scrambling.[14] If so, the results are stated as in (46).

(45) α [β ... ~~α~~ ...]

(46) Statement: PF: α>β, LF: α> β

The Scrambling Economy in (28d) requires that the statement in (46) must be consistent with the one that is generated after a subsequent scrambling, as stipulated in (44). This is reminiscent of Fox and Pesetsky's (2003) Cyclic Linearization. But this differs from it in that the statement in (46) reports the relation between the scrambled phrase α and the constituents in its c-domain, but not the relation between the constituents in the c-domain of a phase head.

One of the consequences of this claim is that it is forbidden to scramble across a scrambled phrase: that is, scrambling is subject to the condition 'Shortest Move', which is advocated by Sauerland and Elbourne (2003). Let us say that the IO scrambles across the S. Then the ordering statement 'IO>S, DO, V' is generated. If the DO scrambles across the scrambled IO, the order 'DO>IO, S, V' is generated. The two ordering statements contradict each other.

(47) a. S IO DO V: Scrambling of IO
b. IO S ~~IO~~ DO V: Scrambling of DO
c. [DO [IO S ~~IO~~ ~~DO~~ V]]

(48) a. The Ordering Statement after the First Scrambling: IO>S, DO, V
b. The Ordering Statement after the Second Scrambling:
DO>IO, S, V

Therefore, scrambling over a scrambled phrase is prohibited. With this in mind, let us generate (42). If the IO scrambles to the edge of the clause, the word order and the scope between the scrambled IO and the other constituents are determined. As shown by ordering and scoping statements in (50a),

[14] When α scrambles across β, α precedes β but it is not the case that α always takes scope over β.

the IO precedes the S and the DO, and the IO has scope over the DO, regardless of whether the higher copy of the IO or its lower copy is interpreted.

(49) a. Susie-Nom Someone-Dat everyone-Acc introduce-Past-Dec: Scrambling of IO
b. [Someone-Dat [Susie-Nom Someone-Dat everyone-Acc introduce-Past-Dec]

(50) Statement after Scrambling of IO: PF: IO>S, DO
LF: IO>DO, {IO>S, S>IO}

If the first scrambling in (49a-b) is accompanied by scrambling of the DO into the inner SPEC, (43) is generated, as shown in (51a-b).[15]

(51) a. [Someone-Dat [Susie-Nom Someone-Dat everyone-Acc introduce-Past-Dec]: Scrambling of DO into the Inner SPEC
b. [Someone-Dat [everyone-Acc [Susie-Nom Someone-Dat everyone-Acc introduce-Past-Dec]]

Let us now generate the ordering and scoping reports for the second scrambling. In (51b) the DO c-commands the lower copy of the IO, so it is possible for it to have scope over the IO. However, the statement in (52) must be consistent with the one in (50) in accordance with the Scrambling Economy. Therefore, the reading 'DO>IO' must be excluded. It is now not surprising that the DO cannot have scope over the IO in (43)—(7a).

(52) Statement after Scrambling of the DO: PF: DO>S
LF: {IO>DO, ~~DO>IO~~}

This approach can also explain the phenomenon that the DO has scope over the S, while the anaphor inside the IO is bound by the S. In (10), repeated here as (53), the S can bind the anaphor *caki* 'self' in the scrambled IO, and it is inside the scope of the scrambled DO.

(53) [Caki casin-uy tongsayng-eykey]$_2$ [motun kyoswu-lul]$_1$
[Self-Gen younger brother-Dat] [every professor-Acc]
kak kak talun haksayng-i t_2 t_1 chingchanha-yess-ta.
different student speak well of-Past-D
'someone$_i$ spoke well of every professor to his/her$_i$ younger brother'

---

[15] In (51a) DO is required to scramble into the inner SPEC; scrambling of the DO across the IO is a violation of (28d).

If the IO undergoes scrambling, there is a PF effect in that it precedes the S, but there is no semantic effect. Notice that the relative scope between the S and the DO is not determined when the IO scrambles; scrambling of the IO does not affect the scope relation between them. So there is no scoping statement after scrambling of the IO. If the DO scrambles into the inner SPEC, it may or may not have scope over the S, depending on whether or not it distributes over the S.

(53) a. a different student-Nom self's brother-Dat every professor-Acc introduce-Past-Dec: Scrambling of the IO
b. [self's brother-Dat [a different student-Nom self's brother-Dat every professor-Acc introduce-Past-Dec]]: Scrambling of the DO into the inner SPEC
c. [self's brother-Dat [every professor-Acc [a different student-Nom self's brother-Dat every professor-Acc introduce-Past-Dec]]

If the string in (53c) is mapped into the LF, the higher copy of the IO is deleted as an instance of repair-by-ellipsis in accordance with (28b), and the higher copy of the DO is interpreted in conformity with (28c) if the DO distributes over the S.

(55) ~~self's brother-Dat~~ every professor-Acc a different student-Nom self's brother-Dat ~~every professor-Acc~~ introduced

The ambiguity of (8b), rewritten as (56), can also be explained in a straightforward way. If the DO scrambles across the S in (57a), it may or may not have scope over the IO. This scope relation must be consistent with the scrambling of the IO in (57b-c). Accordingly, sentence (56) is ambiguous.

(56) Nwukana-lul$_j$ nwukwunka-eykey$_i$ Susie-ka t_i t_j
everyone-Acc someone-Dat S-Nom
sokayha-yess-ta.
introduce-Past-Dec

(57) a. S IO DO V: First Scrambling
b. DO$_1$ S IO t_1 V: Second Scrambling
c. DO$_2$ IO$_1$ S t_1 t_2 V

The gist of the claim is that the scope rigidity of multiple scrambling follows from the fact that the scoping report of a previous scrambling must be consistent with that of a subsequent scrambling, which originates from Scrambling Economy.

3.3 Scrambling Economy and the Scope Rigidity of Basic Word Order

This line of approach sheds light on the scope rigidity of basic word order. As mentioned above, (58-59) are scopally unambiguous, regardless of whether the sentential adverb *ama* 'probably' is present.

(58)	Nwukwunka-ka	nwukwuna-lul	(ama)	manass-ul-ke-ya.
	someone-Nom	everyone-Acc	(probably)	like-Past-Guess-Dec
	(*O>S, S>O)			

(59)	Ama	nwukwunka-ka	nwukwuna-lul	manass-ul-ke-ya.
	Probably	someone-Nom	everyone-Acc	like-Past-Guess-Dec
	(*O>S, S>O)			

This follows from Scrambling Economy. While pretending that (59) is the source sentence, let us try to generate (58). If multiple scrambling is permitted, it is likely that (60c) can be a possible representation of (58).

(60) a. (Adverb) S O V: First Scrambling
b. O (Adverb) S ~~O~~ V: *Second Scrambling
c. S O (Adverb) ~~S~~ ~~O~~ V

However, the Scrambling Economy rules out the derivation in (60a-c). After the first scrambling, the ordering statement 'O>S' obtains, and this is contradicted by the ordering statement that is generated after the second scrambling.

(61) a. Ordering Statement after the First Scrambling: O>S, (O>Adverb)
b. Ordering Statement after the First Scrambling: S>O, (S>Adverb)

This is a violation of the Scrambling Economy in (28d). Therefore, (60c) is ill-formed.[16]

---

16 Sabel (2005) argues that string-vacuous scrambling without a PF-effect is prohibited. Notice that in (60a-c), scrambling of the S and the scrambling of the O are not string-vacuous scrambling when the adverb *ama* 'probably' is present. So the derivation in (60) cannot be forbidden by simply saying that string-vacuous scrambling is prohibited.

Let us now consider the possibility in (62a-c). In (62a), the S undergoes scrambling into the edge of the clause. If so, the O cannot cross over the scrambled S as an instance of scrambling. However, it can undergo scrambling into a position that c-commands the lower copy of the S, as shown in (62b-c).

(62) a. [(Adverb) [S O V] T]: First Scrambling
b. [S [(Adverb) [~~S~~ O V] T]]: Second Scrambling
c. [S [O [(Adverb) [~~S~~ ~~O~~ V] T]]

After the first scrambling, the scope 'S>O' is determined.

(63) Statement about Scope after the First Scrambling: S>O

Thus, the scope relation between them cannot be reversed although the scrambled O c-commands the lower copy of the S in (62c). This means that if the basic word order is S>O, there is no way for the O to take scope over the S, when the relative word order is maintained.

It is noteworthy that the word order 'S O V" may be a result of no scrambling, mono scrambling, or multiple scrambling.

(64) [S O V][17]

(65) [S ~~S~~ O V]

(66) [S O ~~S~~ ~~O~~ V]

All the three representations display the same pattern: they are unambiguous with regard to the relative scope of the S and the O. Thus, the scope rigidity of the unmarked basic word order and that of multiple scrambling can be subsumed under a single constraint as follows:

(67) Scope Rigidity
If (i) the basic word order is 'α > β', every sentence maintaining the relative word order 'α > β' gives the reading 'α > β' only.

[17] If Korean T, just like English, must have an EPP, (64) is not a possible representation.

The Scope Rigidity in (67) follows from the Scrambling Economy, along with the generalization in (68).

(68) Generalization about Scrambling Languages
Scrambling languages permit optional free merge in the narrow syntax but not at LF.

In fact, the generalization follows from Gricean Maxim, as illustrated in (69a-b).

(69) a. If the speaker A intended the scope relation 'O> S', A could have scrambled the O across the S; scrambling is a free merger.
b. But A didn't scramble the O across the S, which implicates that A didn't intend 'O>S'.
c. Therefore, the hearer does not apply QR.

The upshot of the claim is that we can derive the generalization in (68) as well as the Scrambling Economy in (28) from the fact that scrambling is an optional free merge.

4 Summary and Conclusion

According to the Scrambling Economy in (28) and the Cyclic Report of Scrambling Effects in (43), the relative word order and the relative scope between α and β are fixed after the first scrambling. Let us first consider the word order. If the DO scrambles across over the IO in (70a), the word order 'DO>IO' is fixed regardless of whatever scrambling takes place later. If, on the other hand, the IO undergoes scrambling in (71a), it must precede the DO all through the derivation.

(70) a. S IO DO V
b. S DO IO ~~DO~~ V

(71) a. S IO DO V
b. IO S ~~IO~~ DO V

The scope relation is a little bit more complex because it is not the case that scrambling always gives rise to a semantic effect. However, if there is a semantic effect, there is a scoping statement, which must be consistent with the scoping statement of a subsequent scrambling.

To conclude, (i) (anti-)reconstruction effects of scrambling and the scope rigidity of multiple scrambling and unmarked word order follow from the

Scrambling Economy and the generalization that scrambling languages do not make use of QR, and (ii) the Scrambling Economy and the generalization follow from the fact that scrambling is optional free merge.

References

Abe, Jun. 1993. Binding conditions and scrambling without A/A' distinction. Doctoral dissertation, University of Connecticut, Storrs, CT.

Agbayani, Brian, Chris Golston, and Toru Ishii. 2015. Syntactic and prosodic Scram bling in Japanese. *Natural Language & Linguistic Theory* 33:47–77.

Ahn, Hee-Don. 1991. Light Verbs, VP-movement, Negation and Clausal Architecture in Korean and English. Doctoral dissertation, University of Wisconsin, Madison.

Arano, A. 2017. Multiple scrambling, headless vP-movement, and Cyclic Linearization. In *Proceedings of the Forty-Seventh Annual Meeting of the North East Linguistic Society*: Volume 1, ed. A. Lamont and K. Tetzlof, 55–64. University of Massachusetts, Amherst: Graduate Linguistic Student Association.

Bošković, Željko and DaikoTakahashi. 1998. Scrambling and last resort. *Linguistic Inquiry* 29, 347-366.

Cho, Jai-Hyoung. 1994. Scrambling in Korean: Crossover, reconstruction and binding theory. Doctoral dissertation, University of Connecticut.

Chomsky, Noam. 1995. *The Minimalist Program*. Cambridge, MA: MIT Press.

Chomsky, Noam. 2001. Derivation by phase. In *Ken Hale: A life in linguistics*, ed. Michael Kenstowicz. 1-52. Cambridge, MA: MIT Press.

Chomsky, Noam. 2008. On phases. In *Foundational issues in linguistic theory*, ed. R. Freidin, C. Otero, and M. L. Zubizarreta. 133-166. Cambridge, MA: MIT Press.

Fox, Danny and David Pesetsky. 2005. Cyclic linearization of syntactic structure. *Theoretical Linguistics* 31: 235-262.

Fukui, Naoki. 1993. Parameters and optionality. *Linguistic Inquiry* 24:399-420.

Grewendorf, Günther, and Joachim Sabel. 1999. Scrambling in German and Japanese: Adjunction versus multiple specifiers. *Natural Language and Linguistic Theory* 17:1-65.

Hagstrom, Paul. 2000. Phrasal movement in Korean negation. In *Proceedings of the 9th Student Conference in Linguistics (MITWPL 36)*, MIT Working Papers in Linguistics, Cambridge, ed. L. Veselinova et al., 127–142.

Heycock, Caroline. 1995. Asymmetries in reconstruction. *Linguistic Inquiry* 26, 153-172.

Hoji, Hajime. 1985. Logical Form constraints and configurational structure in Japanese. Doctoral dissertation, University of Washington, Seattle.

Hornstein, Norbert. 1999. Movement and control. *Linguistic Inquiry* 30: 69-96.

Hornstein, N., 2001. *Move!: A theory of construal*. Blackwell, Oxford.

Hornstein, Norbert. 2008. *A theory of syntax: minimal operations and universal grammar*. Cambridge: Cambridge University Press.

Joo, Yanghee Shim. 1989. A cross-linguistic approach to quantification in syntax. Doctoral dissertation, University of Wisconsin, Madison.

Jung, Yeun-Jin. 2002. Scrambling, edge effects and A/A'-distinction. *The Linguistic Association of Korea Journal* 10:41-64.

Karimi, Simin. 1999. Is scrambling as strange as we think it is? In *Papers on morphology and syntax, cycle one*, ed. Karlos Arregi, Benjamin Bruening, Cornelia Krause, and Vivian Lin, 159-190. MIT Working Papers in Linguistics 33. Cambridge, MA: MITWPL.

Kim, Lan. 2008. On the ditransitive construction in Korean. *Proceedings of Conference of the Student Organization of Linguistics in Europe XV*, 111-133.

Kim, Rhang-Hye-Yun. 2003. Scrambling and minimalist program. *Studies in Generative Grammar* 13:3-19.

Kitahara, Hisatsugu. 2002. Scrambling, case, and interpretability. In *Derivation and explanation in the minimalist program*, ed. Samuel David Epstein and T. Daniel Seely, 167-183. Malden, MA: Blackwell Publishing.

Ko, Heejeong. 2007. Asymmetries in scrambling and cyclic linearization. *Linguistic Inquiry* 38:49-83.

Ko, Heejeong. 2011. Predication and edge effects. *Natural Language and Linguistic Theory*29:725-778.

Ko, Heejeong. 2014. *Edges in syntax: scrambling and cyclic linearization.* Oxford: Oxford University Press.

Ko, Heejeong. 2015. On the typology of small clauses: null subject and mode of merge in resultatives. *Studies in Generative Grammar* 25: 347-375.

Ko, Heejeong. 2018. Scrambling in Korean syntax. *Oxford Linguistic Encyclopedia of Linguistics*. Oxford: Oxford University Press.

Koizumi, Masatoshi. 1993. Object agreement phrases and the split VP hypothesis. In MIT working papers in Linguistics 18, ed. Bobaljik, J. D., Phillips, 99-148.

Koizumi, Masatoshi. 1995. Phrase structure in minimalist syntax. Doctoral dissertation, MIT.

Koizumi, Masatoshi. 2000. String vacuous overt verb raising. *Journal of East Asian Linguistics* 9:227–285.

Lee, Wonbin, and Sungeun Cho. 2003b. Is scrambling EPP-driven? *Studies in Generative Grammar* 13:331-341.

Lee, Young-Suk. 1993. Scrambling as case-driven obligatory movement. Doctoral dissertation, University of Pennsylvania.

May, Robert. 1985. *Logical form: its structure and derivation.* Cambridge, MA: MIT Press.

Miyagawa, Shigeru. 1997. Against optional scrambling. *Linguistic Inquiry* 28:1–25.

Miyagawa, Shigeru. 2001. The EPP, scrambling, and *wh*-in-situ. In *Ken Hale: A life in language*, ed. Michael Kesntowicz, 293-338. Cambridge, MA: MIT Press.

Miyagawa, Shigeru. 2010. *Why Agree? Why Move? Unifying agreement-based and discourse-configurational languages.* Cambridge, MA: MIT Press.

Richards, Norvin. 2001. *Movement in language: interactions and architectures.* Oxford: Oxford University Press.

Sabel, Joachim. 2001. *Wh*-questions in Japanese: scrambling, reconstruction, and *wh*-movement. *Linguistic Analysis* 31:1-41.

Sabel, Joachim. 2005. String-vacuous scrambling and the effect on output condition, In *The free word order phenomenon:its syntactic sources and diversity*, ed. Joachim Sabel, and Mamoru Saito, 281-334. Berlin: Mouton de Gruyter.
Saito, M. 1985. Some asymmetries in Japanese and their theoretical implications. Doctoral Dissertation, Massachusetts Institute of Technology.
Saito, Mamoru. 1992. Long-distance scrambling in Japanese. *Journal of East Asian Linguistics*1:69-118.
Saito, Mamoru. 2003. A derivational approach to the interpretation of scrambling chains. *Lingua* 113: 481-518.
Saito, Mamoru, and Naoki Fukui. 1998. Order in phrase structure and movement. *Linguistic Inquiry* 29:439-474.
Sauerland, Uli, Paul Elbourne. 2002. Total reconstruction, PF movement, and derivational order. *Linguistic Inquiry* 33, 283-319.
Sohn, Keun-won. 1995. Negative polarity items, scope, and economy. Doctoral dissertation, University of Connecticut, Storrs.
Tada, Hiroaki. 1993. A/A-bar partition in derivation. Doctoral dissertation, MIT.
Takano, Yuji. 1998. Object shift and scrambling. *Natural Language and Linguistic Theory* 16:817-889.
Takano, Yuji. 2000. Illicit remnant movement: An argument for feature-driven movement. *Linguistic Inquiry* 31:141–156.
Yang, Dong-Whee, and Sung-Hun Kim. 2005. Scrambling and interpretive complex. *The Linguistic Association of Korea Journal* 13(2):169-193.
Yatsushiro, Kazuko. 1996. On the unaccusative construction and nominative Case licensing. Generals paper, University of Connecticut, Storrs.
Yatsushiro, Kazuko. 1998. Structure within VP in Japanese. In *Japanese/Korean Linguistics 8,* ed. David James Silva, 501–514. Stanford, Calif.: CSLI Publications.

Direct Object Marking and Markedness in Sika Yaeyaman

MATTHEW TOPPING

1 Introduction

1.1 Background Information on Sika Yaeyaman

This research concerns Sika Yaeyaman *=ju* and *=ba,* two marked forms of object marking described heretofore as optional elements employed only for emphasis (Miyara 1995). It explores their distribution and function within the language, in addition to their relationship to the cross-linguistic phenomena of Differential Object Marking (DOM) and markedness.

Sika is a variety of the Yaeyama language, a Southern Ryukyuan language, spoken on Ishigaki Is. in Okinawa Prefecture. Specifically, it has been grouped closely with the Kabira, Miyara, and Kohama dialects within the 'Ishigaki branch' of Nuclear Yaeyaman (Kajiku 1984, Pellard 2009, Heinrich & Shimoji 2015). Like other Ryukyuan languages throughout

Japanese/Korean Linguistics 27
Edited by Michael Barrie.

Okinawa and Kagoshima Prefectures, Sika has largely been replaced by Standard Japanese (SJ) as the language of the home and is now severely endangered. My consultants estimate that there may be around 1000 mostly elderly native speakers remaining nationwide. Ishigaki City takes up the entirety of Ishigaki Island. Its location within Okinawa prefecture is displayed on the following map.

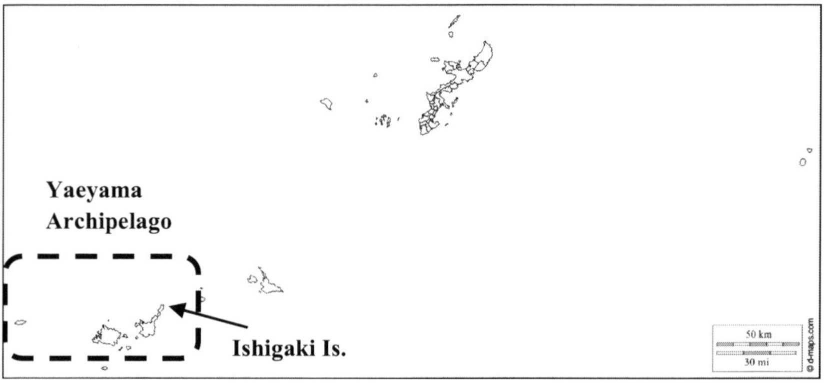

Map 1 Okinawa Prefecture[1]

Few published academic works exist for this variety of Yaeyaman, most notably Miyara (1995), a descriptive grammar, and Miyagi (2003), a Sika-Japanese dictionary. Sika is spoken in the *Shika-aza* region of Ishigaki City, which is comprised of four traditional districts. From west to east, these districts are *Arakaa* (Arakawa), *Isjanagi(ra)* (Ishigaki), *Fuugaa* (Ōkawa), and *Tunusuku* (Tonoshiro). Eleven current residents of *Shika-aza* were interviewed for this research between November 2016 and November 2018. Below is a breakdown of each district, and the ages and sexes of consultants. Data was elicited through activities such as direct translation exercises and the recording of naturalistic dialogues.

District	Pop. (as of Jan 2016)	Consultant data
Arakawa	8,734	F, 95
Ishigaki	3,888	M,88 M,87 F,83 M,79 M,57
Ōkawa	3,602	F,93
Tonoshiro	9,357	F,93 F,84 F,82

Table 1 Consultants by district

[1] Courtesy of d-maps.com 2007-2018

1.2 Sika's Direct Object Marking Paradigm

The purpose of this subsection is to provide definition and context to the markers in question. There exists a variety of clitics capable of marking direct objects (O), some of which do not possess clear analogs in SJ. It is important to delineate the accusative case particle from the various other *kakari-joshi* forms. In Ryukyuan, *kakari-joshi* comprise a class of clitic that includes topic (TOP), focus (FOC) and additive (ADD), and these may follow and fuse with the case marker of an already case-marked NP (Shimoji and Pellard 2010).

Previous literature describes accusative case as canonically zero-marked, and this assertion is validated upon close inspection of both a 1968 field recording Shibata (1972), and the researcher's own primary field data. The table below shows a tally of different types of marking on all instances of direct object in Shibata (1972) and in primary data, the latter consisting of seventeen short recordings. We see that zero-marking (=Ø) is the most common form of marking for both periods. The table also includes topic marker (TOP) *=ja,* additive marker (ADD) *=n,* and grammatical focus marker (FOC1) *=du.*

Marking		**Shibata (1972)**	**2016-2018**
ACC1	*=Ø*	34 (36.2%)	64 (34.7%)
FOC1	*=du*	8 (8.5%)	57 (31.1%)
ACC2	*=ju*	6 (6.4%)	19 (10.3%)
FOC2	*=ju*	0 (0%)	2 (1.1%)
BA	*=ba*	7 (7.4%)	9 (4.9%)
LV[2]	*(=ja)*	11 (11.7%)	13 (7.1%)
TOP	*(=ja)*	5 (5.3%)	8 (4.4%)
ADD	*=n*	18 (19.1%)	10 (5.4%)
ACC2=ADD	*=ju=n*	4 (4.3%)	0 (0%)
ACC2.TOP	*=joo*	1 (1.1%)	1 (0.5%)
BA=FOC	*=ba=du*	0 (0%)	1 (0.5%)
Total		94	183

Table 2 Prevalence of Sika direct object markers in two data sets

[2] This marker is dubbed 'long-V' (LV) for its tendency to fuse with the final vowel of the host NP. This morphophonological feature causes it to resemble the topic marker, but it has a highly restricted distribution and behaves more like a case particle. It is not the focus of the present research.

If *kakari-joshi*-suffixed forms such as *kuri=du* (this.one=FOC1) and *kuri=n* (this.one=ADD) are taken to underlyingly contain a null accusative case particle, the data in Table 2 can be further collapsed into the tallies shown in Table 3. This more clearly highlights the marked forms of marking.

Marking		**Shibata (1972)**	**2016-2018**
ACC1	=Ø	70 (74.5%)	142 (77.6%)
ACC2	=ju	6 (6.4%)	19 (10.4%)
BA	=ba	7 (7.4%)	9 (4.9%)
LV	(=ja)	11 (11.7%)	13 (7.1%)
Total		94	183

Table 3 Prevalence of Sika direct object markers (simplified)

1.3 Co-occurrence Restrictions

Introducing the co-occurrence restrictions placed on the markers in question will provide further clues about what they are, what they are not, and what they may be. Notice at the bottom of Table 2 the *kakari-joshi* combinations involving *=ju* and *=ba.* If these were case particles, we would expect combinations *=judu* (ACC2.FOC1), *=baja/=baa* (BA.TOP), and *=ban* (BA.ADD) to be attested, in addition to *=badu* (BA.FOC1), *=joo* (ACC2.TOP), and *=jun* (ACC2.ADD). In reality, only the latter three are attested, while the former three are not. In terms of classification, this fact makes *=ju* and *=ba* appear to exist in a category apart from both case particle and *kakari-joshi.* The relationship between *=ju* (ACC2) and the homophonous focus marker *=ju* (FOC2) is explored in § 3.2.

2 Theoretical Framework

2.1 Differential Object Marking

In the literature exists the concept of DOM, which refers to the acceptability of the presence or absence of a case particle on the object of a sentence. In actuality, this is a well-explored topic within literature concerning case ellipsis and information structure (Tsutsui 1984, Masunaga 1988, Yatabe 1999, etc.). Niwa (2006) examines this in his treatment of the distinction between overt and covert topic marking and case marking in SJ. He argues that bare objects in non-interrogative constructions are usually interpreted as expected or previously introduced information, and the appearance of overt case particles signals unexpected, new, or novel information, exemplified in (1) below. In Yaeyaman, this type of discourse-new verbal argument is typically introduced with FOC1 marking, as shown in (2).

(1)	manga	zjana-i=tte.	sankoosjo= ?Ø/wo
	comics	COP.NEG-NPST=QUOT	reference.book=Ø/ACC
	ka-tta=n	da.	
	buy-PST=EXP	COP	Niwa (2006)

‘(Agent) said (he actually) bought a *reference book*, not a comic book.’

(2)	usu=du	kacami-ru-n=de	arag-jen.
	cattle=FOC1	catch-NPST-IND=QUOT	attempt-EXC
	min=du	fugas-u=kajaa	
	ears=FOC1	punch.a.hole-NPST=DUB	sika180530-1b

‘(They are) trying to catch cows! (I) wonder if (they will) punch holes in (their) ears?’

Additionally, both DOM and its subject counterpart DSM have been found to arise from the need to maximally differentiate subject and object within numerous languages. Aissen (2003) notes that subjects prototypically have features that are high on the hierarchies of **animacy**, **definiteness**, and **specificity**, while objects prototypically have features which are low on these hierarchies. The following delineates two markedness scales that will be referenced in this work. Note that Aissen has combined definiteness and specificity into one scale.

a. Animacy hierarchy: Human > Animate > Inanimate
b. Definiteness hierarchy: Personal pronoun > Proper noun > Definite NP > Indefinite Specific NP > Non-specific NP

Figure 1 The animacy and definiteness scales
(Aissen 2003: 437, cf. Silverstein 1976)

In some languages, when objects (O) rank high on these scales they appear to require an atypical or “marked” form of marking, because they are the ones most likely to be confused with subjects if left unmarked (Lee 2006)[3]. This trend is known as **markedness reversal** (Batistella 1990, Croft 1990/1996, Aissen 2003, etc.) Sika OM appears to follow this cross-linguistically attested trend as well.

---

[3]Conversely, subjects which have low features are the ones most necessary to distinguish from objects because they are most likely to be confused with objects if they remain unmarked.

	Unmarked	**Most marked**
Object	Non-specific inanimate	Definite animate
Subject	Definite animate	Non-specific inanimate

Table 4 Markedness reversal for subjects and objects
(borrowed from Zribi-Hertz & Kwon 2008)

The hypothesis is that Sika *=ju* and *=ba* are "markedness indicators", signaling Os marked with respect to the hierarchies displayed in Figure 1. This hypothesis is tested in the following.

3 Analysis

3.1 Introduction to the Data

This expansive section aims to test the hypothesis of § 2 while providing examples to illustrate the other features of *=ju* and *=ba,* and begin to generalize about what meaning they might be contributing to an utterance. It will cover clause restrictions and the previously mentioned homophonous focus marker *=ju* (FOC2). Following this will be a test of their relationship to the markedness of O, and finally an exploration of their additional features.

3.2 Restrictions on Clause Type

In terms of clause type, the two markers were found to be predominately limited to infinitival and declarative clauses. Through elicitation it was found that while *=ju* may occur in interrogative (Q) and imperative (IMP) clauses, such clauses with containing *=ju* were rare in naturalistic dialogue. The marker *=ba* was found to be unavailable to mark O in Q and IMP clause types.

As noted in § 1, there is a homophonous version of *=ju* with a specialized distribution that is not limited to Os. As Miyagi (2003) demonstrates, at least in some conservative version of Sika, this marker was utilized to provide grammatical focus to case-marked NPs which are adverbial adjuncts (3) and extended arguments (4) within imperative and hortative constructions, where the focus marker *=du* cannot appear. For this reason, it is dubbed FOC2 in examples such as the following, which are adapted from Miyagi (2003).

(3) atu=kara=ju hara-Ø
later=ABL-FOC2 go-HOR
'(I) will go *later.*'

(4) gakkoo=kai=ju har-i. kuma=ngaa un-na
school=ALL1=FOC2 go-IMP here=LOC2.TOP be-PROH
'Go *to school!* Don't be here!'

Miyagi (2003)

This observation lends credence to the existence of a null case particle for ACC. It also helps explain the co-occurrence restriction on *=ju* and *=du;* At least for some instances of O, *=ju* is providing grammatical focus.

(5a) mizee irijuu=na ooba=Ø=ju / *du
water.TOP necessary=ADJZ amount=ACC=FOC2(*FOC1)
cïka-i joo
use-IMP1 DSC
'Use (only) as much water as (you) need!'

(5b) mizee irijuu=na ooba=Ø=du / ju
water.TOP necessary=ADJZ amount=ACC=FOC1 / FOC2
cïka-u doo
use-NPST DSC sika161103b
'(A will) use (only) as much water as (A) needs.'

3.3 Markedness Scales, *=ju* and *=ba*

The following tables reflect an attempt to organize all instances of O in the two sets of naturalistic data by their animacy, definiteness, and specificity status. The prevalence of *=ju/=ba* marking is contrasted as ratios with all other forms of O-marking lumped together. The animacy scale delineates 'human', 'non-human animate', and 'inanimate'. Some restrictions have been placed on the analysis. At present, the researcher does not possess the analytical tools necessary to determine definiteness in Japonic languages. Instead, the 'definiteness' column displays a scale of three 'noun classes' in 'pronoun' (PRO), 'proper noun' (PN), and 'common noun' (CN), which are taken to represent a high, medium, and low values on the definiteness scale, and which will provide a tentative framework to view this hierarchy (Christopher Davis 2019/10/16pc). In addition, only inanimates were considered for the two-way specificity scale.

		=*ju* / =*ba*	Other	Example
Animacy	Human	6/14 1 : 2.3	8/14 1 : 1.8	*faa-numee* 'children'
	N-Hum.	0/0	0/0	
	Inan.	7/80 1 : 9.1	73/80 1 : 1.1	*akkon* 'sweet potatoes'
Definiteness (Noun class)	PRO	3/10 1 : 3.3	7/10 1 : 1.4	*uri* 'that one'
	PN	0/0	0/0	
	CN	10/84 1 : 8.4	74/84 1 : 1.1	*akkon* 'sweet potatoes'
Specificity	Yes	2/34 1 : 17	32/34 1 : 1.1	*unu hanasï* 'that story'
	No	4/42 1 : 10.5	38/42 1 : 1.1	*tii* 'hands'

Table 5 Sika object markers as a function of animacy, definiteness and specificity status (Shibata 1972)

		=*ju* / =*ba*	Other	Example
Animacy	Human	0/1	1/1 1 : 1	
	N-Hum.	1/17 1 : 17	16/17 1 : 1.1	*usï* 'cow'
	Inan.	34/121 1 : 3.6	87/121 1 : 1.4	
Definiteness (Noun class)	PRO	4/14 1 : 3.5	10/14 1 : 1.4	*uri* 'that one'
	PN	0/2	2/2 1 : 1	*taiwan* 'Taiwan'
	CN	29/166 1 : 5.7	137/166 1 : 1.2	*uta* 'song'
Specificity	Yes	24/91 1 : 3.8	67/91 1 : 1.4	
	No	10/53 1 : 5.3	43/53 1 : 1.2	*fumimunu* 'shoes'

Table 6 Sika object markers as a function of animacy, definiteness and specificity status (2016-2018)

As highlighted in Table 5, the two markers in question were seen to mark human Os more often than inanimate Os, and pronouns more often than common nouns. In the present-day data of Table 6, we can see that *=ju* and *=ba* were slightly more likely to mark pronouns than common nouns, and slightly more likely to mark specific Os than nonspecific Os. These findings suggest only a weak correlation between the appearance of the two markers and these particular markedness hierarchies. After all, there is no line on the hierarchies above which *=ju/=ba* are mandatory, and no line below which they are prohibited. Reiterated, an O's prominence on these semantic scales alone does not seem to dictate the appearance of *=ju/=ba* over other forms of marking. What other factors could be at play?

3.4 Pragmatic Focus

Evoking alternatives in the discourse is the primary function of pragmatic or contrastive focus. It has been observed to be encoded in various types of linguistic prominence across languages, such as morphophonology or prosody (Gundel & Fretheim 2004). It is often triggered by topic shift, i.e. when a new topic is introduced or reintroduced, or when the meaning of one constituent is contrasted with another (Rooth 1985, Vallduví & Vilkuna 1998). An O in pragmatic focus is being highlighted out of a selection of other Os in potential nearby clauses, implying the negation of at least one of these alternatives (Molnár 2006, Vermeulen 2009). Through elicitation, it was discovered that both markers can be employed to contribute a contrastive interpretation to the utterances in which they appear. The marking on *geta* 'wood sandals' in example (6) indicates that *this* was the special kind of footwear, and not another type of shoe, which was purchased around New Year. Example (7) shows an overt alternative with which *uuki* 'washing tub' is being contrasted. Because the predicate verb is inflected for imperative here, it is ambiguous whether *=ju* is ACC2 or FOC2. Finally, it was noted by a consultant that the marking of *=ba* on *baa hanasï* 'my talk' in example (8) is only felicitous when there are other talks or speeches that the hearer may have been able to listen to.

(6) sjongazu=ngaa geta=ju kai+hj-oo-tta
New.Year=LOC2.TOP geta=ACC2/FOC2 buy+BEN-HON-PST
'On New Year's, (they) bought us *geta sandals.*'

(7) aai bakecoo aran=kuni
no bucket.TOP COP.NEG=NEG.SEQ
uuki=ju nc-as-i
washing.tub=ACC2/FOC2 fill-CAUS1-IMP
'No! Fill the *washing tub,* not the bucket!'

(8)

baa	hanasï=ba	sïki+taboori-Ø
1p.GEN	talk=BA	listen+BEN-MED1
sikaitu	nifai juu	
firmly	thank.you DSC	

'Thank you for listening to *my talk.*' (Implied: ...and not some other talk.)

3.5 Reported Speech and Storytelling

In primary data elicitation it was noted that both markers frequently appear on Os in instances of reported speech and storytelling. One elicitation method involved showing a brief clip from a silent film to one consultant, and having them explain what they saw to another consultant sitting on the other side of the room. The second consultant was then required to recall what they had just heard. In this context, some listener consultants displayed a tendency to mark several of their direct objects with either *=ju* or *=ba,* but never a mix of the two. The speaker in (9) is from Tonoshiro, and is summarizing a story she heard from her counterpart concerning cattle ranching. The speaker in (10) is from Ishigaki district, and is performing the same activity based on the same film clip. It is unclear whether the selection of *=ju* or *=ba* in this context is a matter of idiolect, topolect, or represents some other phenomenon entirely. However, the appearance of these markers does suggest some relationship to the secondary, discourse-old status of the information.

(9)

takaa=ni	usu=ju	cïkanai+oor-eer-jen	
a.lot=ADVR	cattle=ACC2/FOC2	care.for+PROG.HON-EVINFR-EXC	
raa...	...han=ju	cïk-er-u	munu=Ø
DSC	brand=ACC2/FOC2	affix-PROG-ADN	thing=ACC1
banaa	mii-da	kutu neen-aatta	
1p.TOP	see-PST.ADN	thing not.exist-PST	

'It seems that (they) are herding many cattle...I have never seen (them) branding (the cattle).'

(10)

usï+nusïturï=nu	hanasï=ba	s-ii=songa...
cow+theif=GEN	story=BA	do-PROG=ADVRS
...jar-iki	inban=ba	cïki-tte...
...COP-CSL1	brand=BA	affix-SEQ2

'(She's) telling a story about cow thieves...Therefore, they put a brand (on the cow), and...'

3.6 *=ju* as Case Marker

There is additional evidence that justifies the status of at least one kind of *=ju* as an accusative case marker. First, in a manner similar to other case particles, this homophonous marker is capable of fusing with *kakari-joshi* particles such as ADD *=n,* and the fused-vowel form of the topic marker (resulting in *=joo*), something which FOC1 *=du* cannot do. This, therefore, makes it appear more similar to a case particle and less so to a *kakari-joshi.* Second, it is prohibited from marking both overt agent and patient within causative constructions that involve transitive predicates, in a manner identical to the Double-o Constraint seen in SJ (Tsujimura 1996). These instances of *=ju* are taken to represent accusative case.

(11) joi=joo sikaitu taboor-aru-Ø=naara
festivities=ACC2.TOP firmly receive-SPON-HOR=HOR.HON
'(I) will partake of the festivities.' Shibata (1972)

(12) taroo-ngasa=kai/*ju kuri=ju noosïmee+pïsa
who-INDEF=DAT1/*ACC2 story=ACC2 fix.CAUS2+DES
a soo raa
have NMLZ DSC
'(I) want to have someone fix this.' sika180903-1b

3.7 Additional Features of *=ba*

Until this point, little has been said about how *=ba* differs from *=ju.* Firstly, this marker is prohibited from imperative and hortative/intentional clauses, and is quite rare outside of declarative clauses (Shibata 1972, Miyagi 2003, recent fieldwork). Others have noted the occasional appearance of *=ba* on the originally VP-internal theme argument of unaccusative verbs such as *naru* 'become', *foo* 'fall (of rain)' and *ncu* 'fill (intrans.)' in other varieties of Yaeyaman (Christopher Davis 2017/10/19pc). This type of construction is purportedly not found in the present-day manifestation of Sika.

In fact, so strongly does this marker appear to be associated with declarative clauses in Sika, that consultants had a tendency to modify elicitations to better accommodate it. The following involves an explanation of how to go about eating crab. When asked if *kan=nu pan* 'crab's leg' could be marked with *=ba* in this imperative construction, the consultant rejected it and instead provided a sentence in the form of a past tense declaration (13b).

(13a) meemen kan=nu pan=Ø=ju / *ba zjootoo=ni
a.little.more crab=GEN leg=ACC=FOC2 /*BA splendid=ADVR
bari+mii-ri
break+see-IMP1
'Try breaking (the) crab leg a bit better.' sika180903-1b

(13b) kan=nu pan=ba bari-tte mïï=Ø
crab=GEN leg=BA break-SEQ2 meat=ACC1
fuzuri+idasi-Ø ho-oda duraa
scoop+out-MED1 eat-PST DSC
'(A) broke the crab leg, scooped the meat out, and ate (it).'

Functionally, while *=ba* appears to overlap with *=ju* in the reported speech and storytelling domains of speech act, it does possess one unique and highly interesting feature. It seems that only *=ba* is available to mark O in clauses which denote actions that are undesirable to the speaker. In (14) below, speaker scolds someone for putting a stamp on the incorrect document. Replacing the marking on *pan* 'stamp' with *=ju* makes the utterance difficult to construe as a reprimand. Example (15) comes from a folk tale in which two birds transport a vase filled with holy water. Here, we can see examples of *=ba* for storytelling, with strongly detrimental overtones.

(14) waa=ja kanzi=nu munu=kai pan=ba / ?ju
2p=TOP this.way=GEN thing=ALL1 stamp=BA/ ?ACC2
cïkee-Ø noo=Ø=du s-ja
affix-MED1 what=ACC1=FOC1 do-WHQ
'What are you doing putting a stamp on this kind of thing?'

(15) ...nii=nu see=kai mudur-uda-a=du
baggage=GEN area=ALL1 return-PST-WHEN=FOC1
pïtu+gara=nu habu=nundu cubu=nu suba=ba
1+CL=GEN snake=NOMFOC vase=GEN side=BA
hai+u-da. kottarïmunu unu habu=ja cubu=ba
crawl+be-PST damn.it that snake=TOP vase=BA
toosi-Ø...
topple-MED1 ICCA (2016)[4]
'…and when (they) returned to where (their) baggage was, a snake was crawling beside (the) vase. Damn it, that snake (had) toppled (the) vase, and…'

---

4 Ishigaki City Cultural Association (2016)

4 Conclusions and Considerations

This research attempted to shed light on the distribution and function of two forms of direct object marking in Sika Yaeyaman, an Ishigaki Island variety of the Yaeyama language in the Southern Ryukyus. It did so from an entry point of Japonic DOM research as initially put forward by Tsutsui (1984), Masunaga (1988) and others, and postulated an intrinsic relationship to semantic scales of markedness, which have been described for a broad array of languages by numerous authors going back to Silverstein (1976) and Hopper & Thompson (1980). The analysis presented here provides a tentative conclusion to the hypothesis laid down in § 2.1.

Hypothesis: Sika *=ju* and *=ba* are "markedness indicators", signaling Os marked with respect to the hierarchies displayed in Figure 1 (animacy, definiteness, specificity)

Conclusion: Markers =ju and =ba, while displaying a weak tendency to appear on marked Os, were not limited to such semantically prominent nominals, and this suggests the strong involvement of other driving factors.

They had a tendency to mark human Os more often than inanimates in Shibata (1972). Across the data, pronouns like *kuri* 'this one' and *uri* 'that one' were slightly more likely than common nouns to receive them, and in the 2016-2018 data set, specific Os were only slightly more likely to be marked than nonspecific Os. Despite this, it was also seen than Os low on the markedness hierarchies are not barred from accepting cliticization with *=ju/=ba.*

To explain the partial failure of the hypothesis, it can first be noted that there are clitics homophonous to the two markers which are not limited to marking direct object intralinguistically within Ishigaki Yaeyaman as a whole. Even within the Sika dialect, while versions of *=ju/=ba* seem to mimic structural case particles by appearing on the VP-internal argument of transitive verbs, they refuse fusion with some *kakari-joshi* particles, a morphological process commonly observed for case particles in Ryukyuan. Their tendency to contribute contrastive focus to the pragmatics of an utterance additionally makes them appear more like *kakari-joshi* and less like case particles. Furthermore, *=ba* appears to have additional properties linking its appearance to the expression of undesirable or detrimental circumstances. This function is not shared by *=ju,* and deserves greater investigation.

It is possible that the functions and distribution of these two markers show speaker variation, generational variation, and regional variation. Importantly, they rarely occurred in the speech of the four consultants born before the mid-1930s, suggesting some kind of diachronic shift. If the distinctions explored in this work really are based in pragmatics and determined by things like information focus, untethered and purely naturalistic dialogues and basic translation exercises may not be the best methods by which to investigate them. More carefully designed fieldwork experiments are likely to be useful in getting to the heart of the matter.

5 References

Aissen, Judith. 2003. Differential Object Marking: Iconicity vs. Economy. *Natural Language & Linguistic Theory* 21: 435-483.

Battistella, Edwin. 1990. *Markedness: The Evaluative Superstructure of Language.* Albany: SUNY Press.

Croft, William. 1990. *Typology and Universals.* Cambridge: Cambridge University Press.

Gundel, Jeanette K. and Thorstein Fretheim. 2004. 8 Topic and Focus. *The Handbook of Pragmatics,* eds. L. Horn and G. Ward, 175-196. Hoboken: Wiley-Blackwell.

Heinrich, Patrick & Michinori Shimoji. 2015. *Handbook of the Ryukyuan Languages - History, structure, and use.* Berlin: De Gruyter Mouton.

Hopper, Paul J. and Sandra A. Thompson. 1980. Transitivity in Grammar and Discourse. *Language, Vol. 56, No. 2*: 251-299. New York: Linguistic Society of America.

Isigaki-si Bunka Kyōkai [Ishigaki City Cultural Association] (Sumamuni Division Training Group). 2016. *Sumamuni de yomu - Yaima nu Mukasupanasu* [Yaeyaman Folk Tales - Read in Sumamuni]. Ishigaki: Tomigawa Printing.

Kajiku, Shin'ichi. 1984. Yaeyama Hōgen Gaisetu [Yaeyama Dialect Overview]. *Kōza Hōgengaku 10 - Okinawa & Amami Tihō no Hōgen* [Course Dialectology 10 - the dialects of Okinawa & Amami], 289-361. Tokyo: National Library Association.

Lee, Hanjung. 2006. Iconicity and Variation in Choice of Object Forms in Korean. *Language Research Vol 42.2*, 323-355. SNU, Seoul.

Masunaga, Kiyoko. 1988. Case deletion and discourse context. *Papers from International Workshop on Japanese Syntax*, ed. William Poser, 145-156. Stanford: CSLI Publications.

Miyagi, Shinyū. 2003. *Isigaki Hōgen Ziten* [Ishigaki Dialect Dictionary]. Naha: Okinawa Times co. Ltd.

Miyara, Shinshō. 1995. *Minami-Ryūkyū Yaeyama Isigaki Hōgen no Bunpō* [A Grammar of the Ishigaki Dialect of Yaeyama in the southern Ryukyus]. Tokyo: Kurosio Publishing.

Molnár, Valéria. 2006. On Different Kinds of Contrast. *Architecture of Focus (Studies in Generative Grammar; 82*, eds. N. Corver and H. van der Hulst, 197-233. Berlin: De Gruyter Mouton.

Niwa, Tetsuya. 2006. *Nihongo no Daimokubun* [Topic Sentences in Japanese]. Osaka: Izumi Syoin Publishing.

Pellard, Thomas. 2009. Ōgami: Éléments de description d'un perler du Sud des Ryūkyū. Doctoral dissertation. École des hautes études en sciences sociales, Paris.

Rooth, Mats. 1985. Association with Focus. Doctoral dissertation, University of Massachusetts, Amherst.

Shibata, Takeshi (ed.) 1972. Isigaki-si Tonogusuku (Isigaki-zima) [Tonogusuku, Ishigaki City (Ishigaki Is.)]. In: *Zenkoku Hōgen Siryō: dai 11-kan Ryūkyū-hen II[National Dialect Documentation: Volume 11 Ryukyu Ed. II]* pp 227-255. Tokyo: Nihon Hōsō Kyōkai.

Shimoji, Michinori and Thomas Pellard. 2010. *An Introduction to Ryukyuan Languages*. Tokyo: ILCAA.

Silverstein, Michael. 1976. Hierarchy of Features and Ergativity. *Grammatical categories in Australian languages,* ed. R.M.W. Dixon, 112-171. New Jersey: Humanities Press.

Tsujimura, Natsuko. 1996. *An Introduction to Japanese Linguistics*. Oxford: Blackwell Publishers Ltd.

Tsutsui, Michio. 1984. Particle Ellipsis in Japanese. Doctoral dissertation, University of Illinois at Urbana-Champaign.

Vallduví, Enric and Maria Vilkuna. 1998. On rheme and kontrast. *Syntax and Semantics Vol. 29,* eds. Culicover and McNally, 79-108. Leiden: Brill.

Vermeulen, Reiko. 2009. The syntax of topic, contrast and contrastive topic. GIST / Universiteit Gent, Ghent, Belgium.

Yatabe, Shūichi. 1999. Particle ellipsis and focus projection in Japanese. *Language, Information, Text, Vol. 6*, 79-104. Department of Language and Information Sciences, University of Tokyo.

Zribi-Hertz, Anne and Song-Nim Kwon. 2008. Differential Function Marking, Case, and Information Structure: Evidence from Korean. *Language Vol. 84 No.2,* 258-299. New York: Linguistic Society of America

Part V

Phonetics/Phonology

What Does Pitch Range Tell Us About Speech and Speakers? – A Sociophonetic Study of Pitch Range Variation in Spoken Japanese [1]

CELESTE GUILLEMOT

SHIN-ICHIRO SANO

1 Introduction

The phonological organization of a language restricts the way in which pitch range can be realized lexically and/or intonationally (Ward and Hirschberg 1985; Pierrehumbert and Hirschberg 1990; Ladd 1996). Consequently, pitch range is subject to cross-linguistic variations depending on prosodic traits regarding stress, tone, and intonation, for example. Japanese is a language with lexical pitch accent, but no intonational pitch accent reported. In this study, based on the analysis of the Corpus of Spontaneous Japanese, we investigated the domain of pitch range in spoken Japanese. Specifically, we examined the effects of extra-linguistic factors on f0 range variations as well as how pitch range affects' listeners perception of speech and speakers.

Our findings sugge st that pitch range variation is allowed in Japanese, but to a restricted degree. Language-specific restrictions on pitch range can

[1] We would like to thank participants of the JK 27 conference for their comments that were helpful in developing the argumentation of this paper. All the remaining faults are, of course, ours. This project was supported by JSPS KAKENHI Grant #19K00558, #16H03426, and NINJAL collaborative research project 'A Multifaceted Study of Spoken Language Using a Large-scale Corpus of Everyday Japanese Conversation.'

Japanese/Korean Linguistics 27.
Edited by Michael Barrie.

be overridden by the influence of extra-linguistic factors such as gender and register, and influence the listeners' perception of the characteristics of speech and speakers.

The remainder of this paper is organized as follows: Section 2 introduces the definition of pitch range and the research agenda. Subsequently, in Section 3 we will present the method that this study adopted. Section 4 presents the quantitative analysis in terms of the following items: gender, register, style, spontaneity, speed, intelligibility, fluency, and self-confidence. Finally, Section 5 summarizes the discussion.

2 Background

2.1 Pitch Range

Pitch range is defined as the range between upper and lower limits of f0 value in a particular domain (such as utterance). This is illustrated in Figure 1 that represents an utterance from sample A01F0055 in the CSJ. When looking at the pitch track ①, we can identify the maximum ② and minimum ③ pitch values. The gap between ② and ③, which is represented in ④, is the pitch range of this utterance.

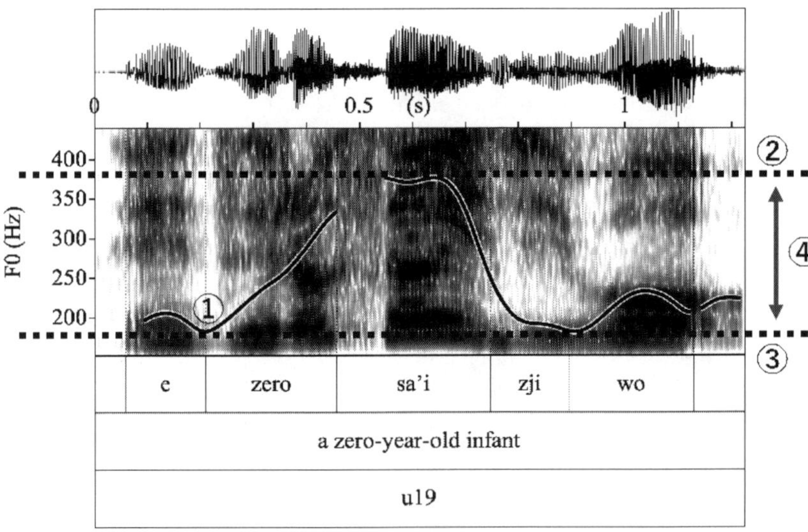

Figure 1. Example of pitch range based on an utterance from sample A01F0055 in the CSJ. (Here the original annotation in the TextGrid provided in the CSJ has been modified for expository purposes.)

The way pitch patterns are realized both lexically and in the intonation hinges on language-specific properties (Ladd 1996; Ward and Hirschberg 1985; Pierrehumbert and Hischberg 1990). What this implies is that the phonology of a language restricts the inventory of intonational tones that speakers can make use of (Grieser and Khul 1988; Fernald et al. 1989). Thus, the wideness of pitch range is subject to cross-linguistic variation; in particular, non-tonal languages, such as English, tend to show wider pitch range than tonal languages, such as Chinese.

2.2 Pitch Accent in Japanese

In this section, we will sketch the properties of pitch accent in Japanese. Pitch accent in Japanese is lexical; namely it is a property of a given word (cf. Western languages, Fernald et al. 1989). Lexical pitch accent is involved in a variety of minimal pairs, suggesting its crucial role for lexical distinction in Japanese. This is represented by the three-way contrast in pitch patterns of two mora words in examples (1) through (3).

(1) /kaki-ga/ LHH 'persimmon-NOM'
(2) /kaki-ga/ HLL 'oyster-NOM'
(3) /kaki-ga/ LHL 'fence-NOM'

A logical consequence of the important role of Japanese pitch accent is that it should therefore restrict the domain of pitch range variations in Japanese (Venditti 2005), as it might interfere with the meaning, resulting in the neutralization of contrastive items.

2.3 Previous Studies on Pitch Range

Previous studies investigating the role of gender on pitch range variations suggest that the common belief that female speakers make use of a wider f0 range than male speakers does not correspond to the reality of phonetic implementation of prosody. That is, previous findings show that male and female speakers exhibit similar pitch range patterns in English (Henton 1989). It was found, however, that speakers adjust their pitch range to different degrees of formality. For example, in Switzerland French, informal speech tends to show a wider pitch range (Sertling-Miller 2009). Gut (2009) also showed that pitch range varies based on register differences, for example in English, pitch range is wider in read speech than in spontaneous speech. Moreover, studies focusing on infant-directed speech in Japanese shed light on the fact that even in languages where f0 is used as a cue for lexical distinction, in specific pragmatic situations, speakers can make use of pitch range modulation. For example, Grieser and Kuhl (1988) for Mandarin Chinese or Igarashi et al. (2013) for Japanese found significant pitch expansion for interactions with infants when compared to those with adults.

2.4 Problems and goals

Previous studies investigated variations in pitch mainly from an experimental and qualitative point of view. Furthermore, they mainly deal with pitch range with a focus on specific pragmatic contexts (e.g. infant-directed speech). There is a need for more studies on the interaction between pitch and intonation in a spontaneous (adult) speech context. With this background, the goals of this study are as follows: to explore the variations of pitch range in spontaneous speech using corpus data; to examine how extra-linguistic factors affect pitch range variation; to identify connections between the patterns of pitch range variation and information about speech and speakers.

3 Method

3.1 Corpus and the Target Data

This study employed the Corpus of Spontaneous Japanese (Maekawa 2003, henceforth CSJ), which is a large-scale database of spontaneous speech in Japanese. We extracted data from the CSJ core, which comprises 201 speech samples (about 162,000 seconds, 111 male, 90 female speakers, age range: 25-69 years old) from four different register categories: Academic Presentation Speech (A, N=70), Simulated Public Speaking (S, N=107), Dialogue (D, N=18), and Reading (R, N=6).[2] The CSJ also comes with TextGrid files and a variety of annotations regarding speaker attributes such as gender, age, and other indexes about perceived characteristics of speech (e.g. speed, spontaneity, fluency).

3.2 Data Collection

In order to calculate pitch range, f0 data (minimum f0, and maximum f0) was extracted automatically from the TextGrid files of the CSJ using a Praat script (Boersma and Weenink 2018). We used utterances separated by 'longer-than-200 ms' pauses as units of measurements, following Maekawa's (2003) transcription unit. The raw f0 data, which includes both male and female speakers, was normalized by converting measurements from Hertz to semitones (Ward 1970) for pitch range analysis following the formula in (4).

(4) $ST = 39.87*\log(F0/50)$

---

[2] We will mention later about the characteristics of each register. See section 4.2.

The semitone scale is a logarithmic scale that divides changes in frequency on one octave in 12 equal intervals and that allows to normalize the data, so that rather than equivalent differences in absolute frequency, it is equivalent proportional differences that are evaluated. Indeed, previous research has shown that proportional variations in pitch are more related to perception than absolute changes (Ward 1970). In other words, normalizing the data using the semitone scale is effective here in balancing the inherent gender difference in f0.

The dataset is shown in Table 1. We analyzed a total of 60,045 tokens. (utterances), where average pitch range was 19.565st.

N of tokens	60,045
Average pitch range (semitone)	19.565st

Table 1. The dataset

We analyzed the data based on the CSJ annotations regarding speaker attributes such as gender, and other indexes regarding perceived characteristics of speech and speakers. We also considered the effect of register on pitch range variation. In order to test the statistical significance of distributions, a linear mixed-effects model was fitted using the R environment (R Development Core Team 2019), where the dependent variable was the normalized pitch range (st), the fixed effects were the indexes in the CSJ, and we included speaker as a random effect. Post-hoc tests were conducted using Tukey's method. We evaluated the fit of the constructed models by referring to the AIC, the BIC and the log-likelihood. The best model consisted of the variables shown in (5).

(5) Variables in the best model

dependent variable: normalized pitch range (st)

fixed effects: gender, register, style, spontaneity, speed, intelligibility, fluency, self-confidence, register:style:spontaneity (interaction term)

random effect: speaker

In the following, we will present the effects of each of these factors. Sections 4.1 to 4.3 will deal with gender and register effects, and the characteristics of speech (style, spontaneity, speed and intelligibility) will be examined in 4.4. In 4.5, we will investigate the effect of pitch range on the perceived characteristics of speakers (fluency, self-confidence). The last section summarizes and discusses the significance of our results.

4 Analysis

4.1 Gender

The first item to be examined is the gender difference in pitch range. As mentioned in Section 2.3, previous studies reported no gender difference in pitch range in English (Henton 1989). We examined whether this is also true for the case of Japanese spontaneous speech. As shown in Figure 2, results indicate that there is a significant effect of gender on pitch range in our data (t = 3.154, $p < 0.01$). In particular, male speakers exhibited a wider pitch range than female speakers (male: 20.715 st, female: 18.201st).

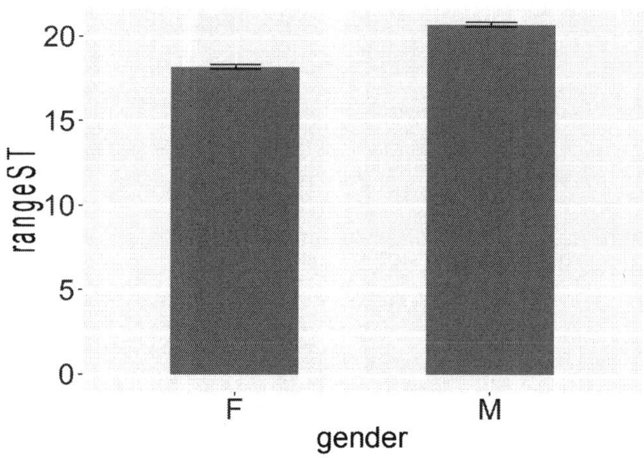

Figure 2. Average pitch range of male and female speakers in the CSJ

The gender-biased pattern observed in Japanese contrasts with previous observations about English. Furthermore, Levon (2007), another study about pitch range in English, shows that male speakers who have a wider pitch range are more likely to be identified as 'gay-like'. In other words, a wider pitch range enhances speakers' perceived femininity: It follows that if we observe any difference in pitch range, we would expect it to be wider for female speakers. Thus, the pattern we observe here in Japanese spontaneous speech is rather surprising as it is in contradiction with previous descriptions of English.

4.2 Register

The next item we considered is the effect of register on pitch range variation. The register in the present dataset consisted of four categories, whose characteristics are summarized in Table 2.

register	characteristics
Academic Presentation Speech	monolog (formal)
Simulated Public Speaking	monolog (informal)
Dialog	dialog
Reading	reading

Table 2. The characteristics of the four register categories in the CSJ

The Academic Presentation Speech category is a collection of academic talks such as conference presentations. Speech samples in this category are monologs and stylistically formal. Simulated Public Speaking consists of presentations on particular topics presented by non-professional speakers. Speech samples in this category are monologs, but relatively informal unlike those in the Academic Presentation Speech. Dialog is literally a collection of dialogs where two speakers are interacting intimately. Reading consists of read speech where participants are reading a script provided. We hypothesized that the register difference affects pitch range modulation.

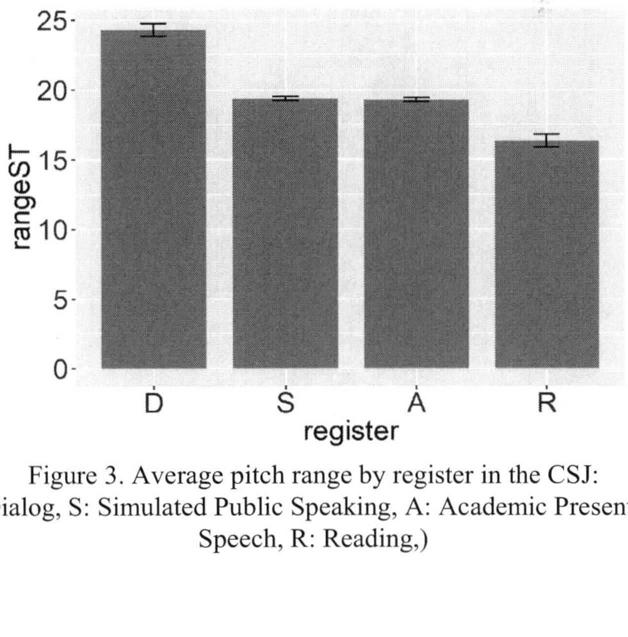

Figure 3. Average pitch range by register in the CSJ:
(D: Dialog, S: Simulated Public Speaking, A: Academic Presentation Speech, R: Reading,)

As Figure 3 shows, the average pitch range significantly differs depending on register categories (t = -2.73, p < 0.01). Specifically, we can observe the following patterns that are also consistent with the properties of each register category. First, Dialog shows the widest pitch range (st = 24.276, D > A/S: z = 22.682, 22.726, p < 0.01). This is consistent with the affective function in Dialog where two speakers are interacting intimately. The affective function is related to the solidarity or the intimacy-oriented purpose of communication. Secondly, pitch range in the Academic Presentation Speech and the Simulated Public Speaking do not significantly differ (st = 19.378 (S), 19.294 (A), z = 2.245, n.s.). Since these two categories are different in formality, we can argue that formality does not affect pitch range variation. Finally, unlike Gut's (2009) observation that read speech shows a wider pitch range in English, Reading shows the narrowest pitch range (st = 16.344, A/S > R: z = 5.503, 3.181, p < 0.01). This can be attributed to the fact that Reading does not involve any kind of interaction, and that there is no audience.

4.3 Register and Gender

This section focusses on the relationship between register and gender. The overall patterns in terms of register we just observed remain mostly the same regardless of gender (Figure 4). At the same time, however, we find some divergent patterns when comparing speech of male and female speakers.

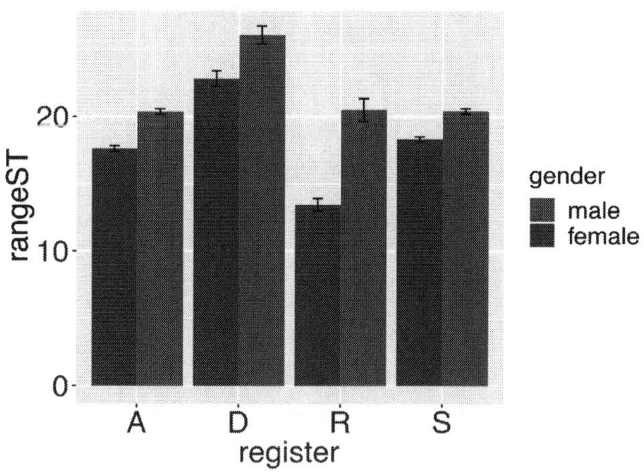

Figure 4. Average pitch range by register and gender in the CSJ (A: Academic Presentation Speech, S: Simulated Public Speaking, R: Reading, D: Dialog)

As shown in Figure 4, male speakers (right side bars) showed a pitch range expansion in Dialog (st = 26.053), but there was no significant variation in the three other categories (st = 20.349 (A), 20.491 (R), 20.402 (S)), while female speakers (left side bars) showed a pitch range expansion in Dialog (st = 22.8), and also a compression in Reading (st = 13.432). The contrasting behavior of men and women in the use of pitch range in different register categories can be imputed to their orientation in communication. Women are said to be more sensitive to the affective function, namely, they are more sensitive to the presence or absence of audience or interaction that highlights the difference between Dialog and Reading. On the other hand, men are said to be more sensitive to the referential function that bears on information-oriented purpose of communication. In other words, they are more sensitive to stylistic level or formality. This may have produced the distinction between casual Dialog and the three other (more formal) categories.

4.4 Perceived Characteristics of Speech

4.4.1 Style

In addition to the objective labels we just considered, the CSJ also comes with other indexes based on perception surveys. Here, we consider how pitch range variation is associated with the perceived characteristics of speech. In this study, 'style' refers to the degree of formality perceived by listeners. The hypothesis to be examined is if pitch range affects listeners' perception of style.

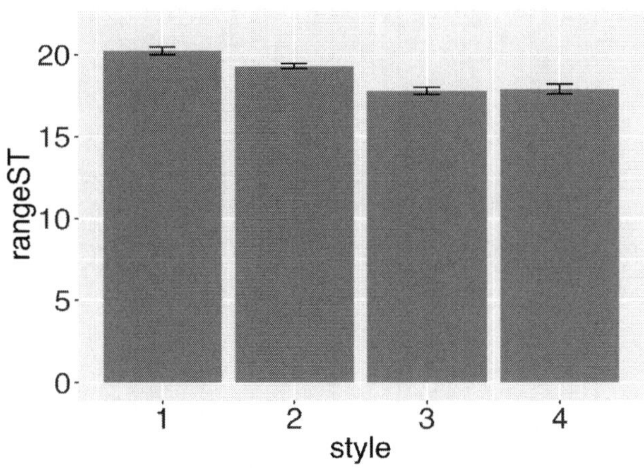

Figure 5. Average pitch range by style in the CSJ

Figure 5 illustrates the significant effect of pitch range on style ($t = 2.112$, $p < 0.05$). More formal styles categories show a narrower pitch range (st = 17.783 (3), 17.891 (4)). This suggests that speech with a narrower pitch range is likely to be perceived as more formal. Thus, we can argue that pitch range affects listeners' perception of speech formality. This result is, however, in contradiction with our observations in 4.2 and 4.3 about the characteristics of register, that Dialog (informal) has a wider pitch range when compared to more formal speech styles, which suggests a gap between production and perception.

4.4.3 Spontaneity

In this section, we examine the item 'spontaneity' in the CSJ, which is the degree of spontaneity perceived by listeners. In spontaneous speech, speakers speak on the fly without preparation, while less spontaneous speech is well-prepared, and may sound like script-reading. Based on the observation regarding register that read speech shows a narrower pitch range than more spontaneous speech styles such as dialogs, it is fair to hypothesize that a narrower pitch range is more likely to be perceived as less spontaneous; while speech with a wider pitch range is more likely to be judged more spontaneous.

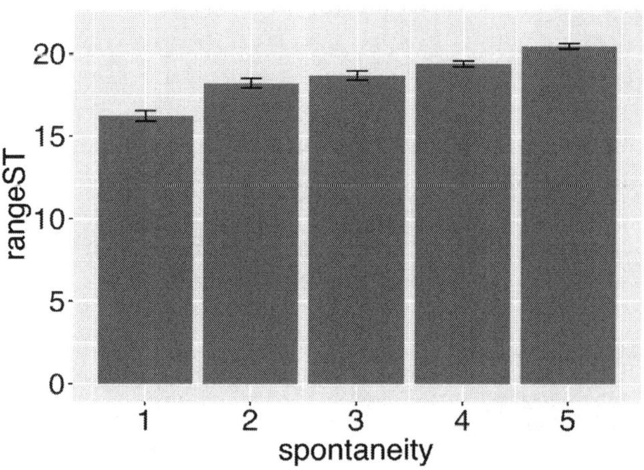

Figure 6. Average pitch range by spontaneity in the CSJ

The observation of Figure 6 indicates that pitch range significantly affects perceived spontaneity of the speech ($t = 3.472$, $p < 0.01$). More spontaneous categories show a wider pitch range (st = 19.402 (4), 20.483 (5)); while less spontaneous categories show a narrower pitch range (st = 16.217 (1), 18.223 (2)). Our hypothesis was borne out: Speech with a wider pitch range is likely to be perceived as more spontaneous, and narrower pitch range as less spontaneous. This is intuitively plausible, as monotonous voices, which lack prosodic information, are likely to be perceived as being robot- or AI-like.

4.4.4 Speed (Speech Tempo)

Next, we consider how pitch range affects listeners' perception of speed or more specifically speech tempo. Speed here does not refer to absolute velocity (i.e. speech rate) but represents listeners' feelings about the speed of elocution. The question to be examined here is whether pitch range affects listeners' perception of speed.

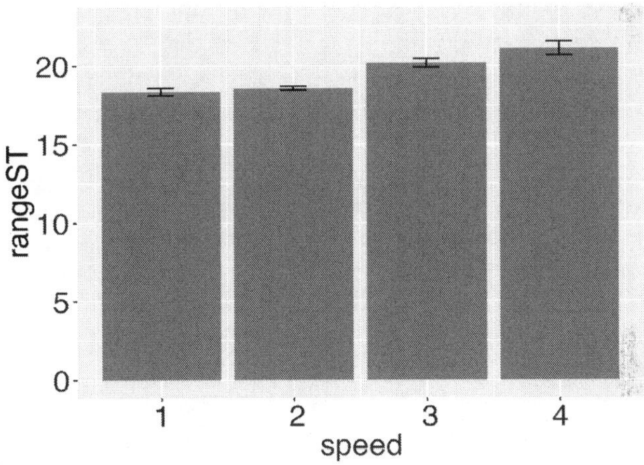

Figure 7. Average pitch range by speed in the CSJ

As Figure 7 shows, the perceived speech tempo significantly differs depending on average pitch range ($t = 2.926$, $p < 0.01$). Faster categories on the right (st = 20.163 (3), 21.089 (4)) show a wider pitch range than slower categories on the left (st = 1.359 (1), 18.579 (2)). We identified a positive correlation between pitch range and speech tempo. This suggests that speech with a wider pitch range is likely to be perceived as faster, and narrower pitch range as slower.

4.4.4 Intelligibility

The last item regarding the effect of pitch range on listeners' perception of speech characteristics is the perceived intelligibility. The question to be examined here is whether pitch range affects listeners' perception of intelligibility.

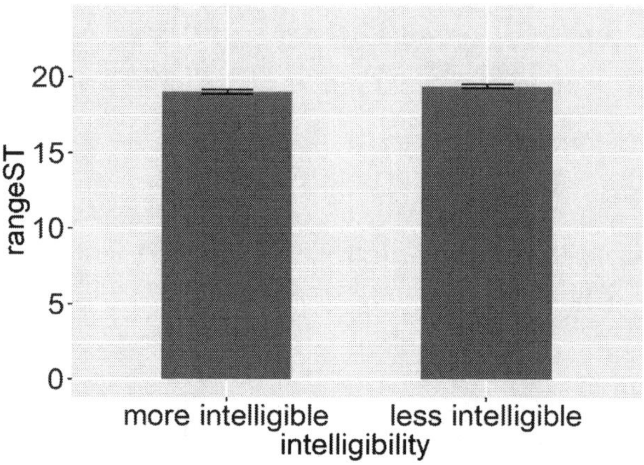

Figure 8. Average pitch range by intelligibility in the CSJ

As shown in Figure 8, we observed a significant effect of pitch range on perceived intelligibility (t = -3.409, p < 0.01). Listeners judged a narrower pitch range more intelligible (st = 19.025), while wider pitch range (st = 19.401) was associated with a lower intelligibility. This result suggests that, in Japanese, pitch range might be a crucial factor for speech intelligibility: We can argue that speaking with a narrower pitch range may enhance the intelligibility of the speech contents.

This section examined the role played by pitch range on listeners' perception of the characteristics of speech. We found that the range of f0 variations that speakers use significantly impacts listeners' impressions about the speech: Speech with a wider pitch range is perceived as casual, spontaneous, and fast, while the use by speakers of a narrower pitch range positively affects intelligibility.

4.5 Perceived Characteristics of Speakers

4.5.1 Fluency

Let us turn our attention to the items reporting the perceived characteristics of speakers. The first item to be examined is the judgement of speech fluency. This section looks at correlations between pitch range and speakers' fluency.

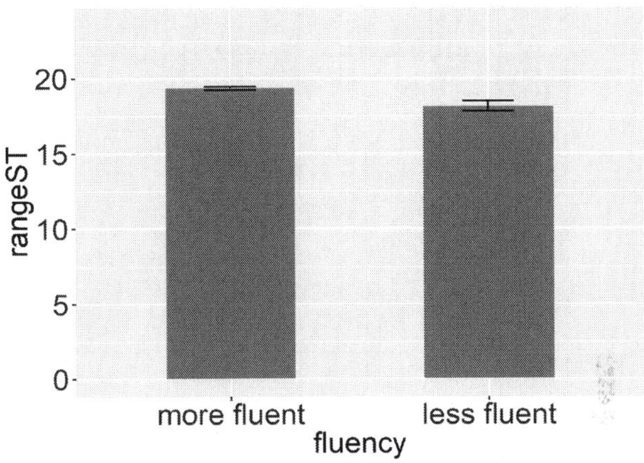

Figure 9. Average pitch range by intelligibility in the CSJ

As Figure 9 shows, there is a significant effect of pitch range on listeners' perception of speakers' fluency (t = -6.635, p < 0.01). Speeches in which speakers are judged more fluent exhibit a wider pitch range (st = 19.345) than those judged less fluent (st = 18.131). This suggests that speakers making use of a wider range of f0 variations are likely to be perceived as more fluent than those with a narrower pitch range.

4.5.2 Self-Confidence

Lastly, we looked at the item self-confidence in order to investigate whether pitch range affects listeners' perception of speakers' self-confidence.

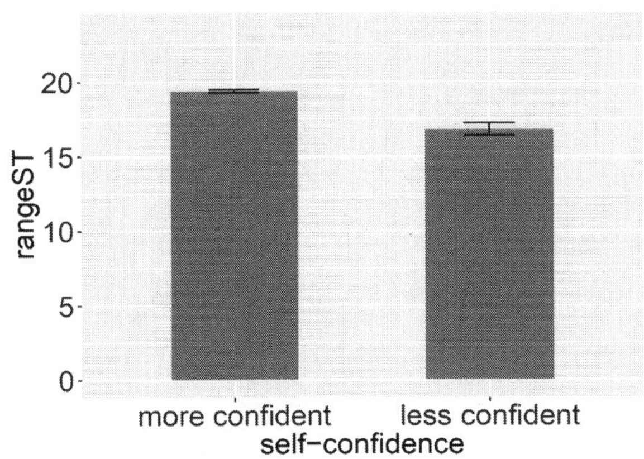

Figure 10. Average pitch range by self-confidence in the CSJ

As Figure 10 illustrates, pitch range significantly affects perceived self-confidence ($t = 4.192$, $p < 0.01$). Speeches in which speakers are judged more confident have a wider pitch range (st = 19.381) than those judged less confident (st = 16.789). This suggests that speakers who produce speech with a wider pitch range are likely to be perceived as more confident than those with a narrower pitch range.

Our results in section 4.5 suggest that pitch range also affects listeners' perception of speakers' characteristics. A speaker using a wider range of f0 variations tends to be perceived as more fluent and more confident.

5 Conclusion

This paper presented a corpus-based quantitative study of pitch range variation in spoken Japanese. In particular, we examined effects of extra-linguistic factors on f0 range variations, and how pitch range affects listeners' perception. This study confirmed that language-specific restrictions on pitch range can be overridden by the influence of extra-linguistic factors. In terms of gender, male speakers show a wider pitch range than female speakers. Regarding register, pitch range is affected by the presence/absence of interaction or audience. In addition, there was a gender difference in this pattern. Based on the patterns observed for other factors, we can make the following generalizations: A wider pitch range can give listeners a 'dynamic' impression, as in speeches are more spontaneous, speakers are more fluent and confident, and perceived as faster. On the other hand, a narrower pitch range can give listeners another type of positive impression, as in speeches are more intelligible.

Based on our results, we can argue that languages with contrastive pitch accent, similarly to tonal languages, do allow pitch range variations, but with restrictions. What the analysis of our data concerning listeners' impressions of speech and speakers suggest, is that there is a specific domain of pitch range in Japanese. When pitch range values deviate from the norm (too wide or too narrow), the speaker tends to be identified as less natural (e.g. less fluent, intelligible or confident).

Some questions, however, are left unanswered and will be addressed in future studies. Specifically, our data shed light on a surprising gender difference in the use of pitch range. Future work will investigate the nature and motivations for this pattern we observed in further detail.

References

Boersma, P. Weenink, D. 1992-2018. *Praat: Doing Phonetics by Computer.* www.praat.org.

Fernald, A., T. Taeschner, J. Dunn, M. Papousek, B. de Boysson-Bardies, and I. Fukui. 1989. A Cross-Language Study of Prosodic Modifications in Mothers' and Fathers' Speech to Preverbal Infants. *Journal of Child Language* 16: 477–501.

Grieser, D.L., P. K. Kuhl. 1988. Maternal Speech to Infants in a Tonal Language: Support for Universal Prosodic Features in Motherese. *Developmental Psychology* 24(1): 14–20.

Gut, U. 2009. *Non-Native speech: A Corpus-Based Analysis of Phonological and Phonetic Properties of L2 English and German.* Frankfurt am Main: Peter Lang.

Henton, C. G. 1989. Fact and Fiction in the Description of Female and Male Pitch. *Language & Communication* 9(4): 299–311.

Igarashi, Y., K. Nishikawa, K. Tanaka, and R. Mazuka. 2013. Phonological Theory Informs the Analysis of Intonational Exaggeration in Japanese Infant-Directed Speech. *Journal of the Acoustical Society of America* 134: 1283–1294.

Ladd, D. R. 1996. *Intonational Phonology.* Cambridge: Cambridge University Press.

Levon, E. 2007. Sexuality in Context: Variation and the Sociolinguistic Perception of Identity. *Language in Society* 36(4): 533–554.

Maekawa, K. 2003. Corpus of Spontaneous Japanese: Its Design and Evaluation. *Proceedings of The ISCA & IEEE Workshop on Spontaneous Speech Processing and Recognition* (SSPR 2003), 7–12.

Pierrehumbert, J., and J. Hirschberg. 1990. The Meaning of Intonational Contours in the Interpretation of Discourse. Intentions in Communication, eds. P. Cohen, J. Morgan, and M. Pollack, 271–311. Cambridge, MA: MIT Press.

R Development Core Team. 2019. *R: A Language and Environement for Statistical Computing.* Vienna, Austria: R Foundation for Statistical Computing.

Sterling-Miller, J. 2009. Prosodic Style-Shifting as Audience Design: Real-Time Monitoring of Pitch Range and Contour Types in Swiss French. *Sociolinguistic Variation in Contemporary French*, eds. K. Beeching, N. Armstrong, and F. Gadet, 43–62. Amsterdam/Philadelphia: John Benjamins.

Venditti, J.J. 2005. The J-Tobi Model of Japanese Intonation. *Prosodic Typology: The Phonology of Intonation and Phrasing*, ed. S. -A. Jun, 172–200. Oxford: Oxford University Press.

Ward, G. and Hirschberg, J. 1985. Implicating Uncertainty: The pragmatics of fall-rise. *Language* 61: 747–776.

Ward, W.D. 1970. Musical Perception. *Foundation of Auditory Theory*, ed. J. Tobias, 405–447. New York: Academic Press.

The Prosody of Contrastive Topic in Korean

SEUNG-EUN KIM
Cornell University

1 Introduction

This paper investigates how Contrastive Topic (CT) is prosodically realized in Korean, and also examines how the deletion of the postnominal particle =NUN interacts with prosody. I compare the prosodic pattern of CT with that of non-contrastive Topic (T) and Focus (F). I show that CT has a prosodic pattern distinct from T and F in the region where CT, T, or F occurs; yet, it is similar to F in the region following the CT as both show post-peak compression. In addition, I show that the particle =NUN is not necessary to represent the meaning of CT, and the deletion of =NUN affects the prosodic pattern of a CT phrase.

CT is defined as a phrase denoting what the question being addressed is about but implies questions about different topics (Constant 2014). Below is an example of CT adapted from Constant (2014).

(1) *A and B are at the potluck party. A showed up late, so he is asking B who brought what.*
A: What about Persephone and Antonio? What did *they* bring?
B: *Persephone* brought the gazpacho.

Japanese/Korean Linguistics 27.
Edited by Michael Barrie.

In this example, *Persephone* in B's response answers A's question, but at the same time it leaves another topic to be discussed (i.e., *Antonio*); *Persephone* is CT. In the semantic literature, CT has been discussed in relation to both T and F. Since CT answers the question being addressed (although partially), it is related to T. CT is also often compared to F because it is used to mark the presence of alternatives.

While researchers differ on how they view CT in relation to T and F, the present study follows the semantic perspective which views CT as distinct from T but similar to F (e.g., Constant 2014, Tomioka 2010). According to this view, CT and F are similar since they share the same semantic value as being F-marked; both mark the presence of alternatives. However, they undergo different semantic computations so that each achieves its own meaning. For instance, Constant (2014) argued that CT is associated with a semantic operator, CT-λ, which does not associate with F. (2) illustrates Constant (2014)'s analysis of CT in Mandarin Chinese, which is translated in Korean. CT *apeci* is marked as F, but it raises overtly to the position directly above the CT-λ, associates with it, and is thereby interpreted as CT. Although F phrases are also marked as F, they do not associate with CT-λ.

(2) *Every day, mom doesn't come home until late.*

Apeci=nun ayey oci-anhu-sin-ta
Dad=CT at all come back-NEG-HON-DCL
'(And) dad doesn't even come back at all.'

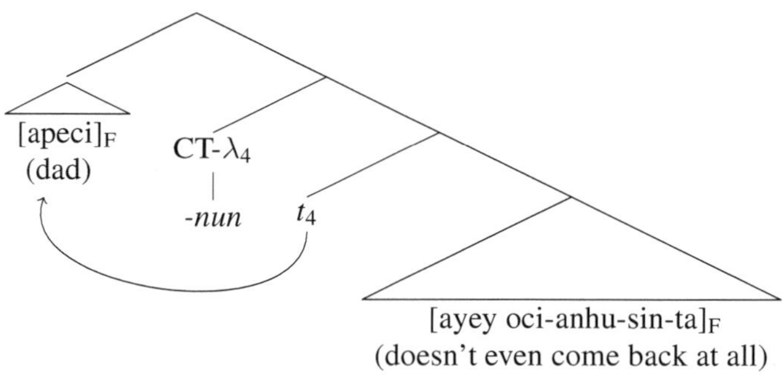

A semantic connection between CT, T, and F is reflected in their prosodic realization. Büring (2003), who argued that CT and F are semantically distinct, maintained that CT is realized as L+H*L-H% while F is realized as H*L-L%. This argument has its roots in Jackendoff (1972)'s distinction between A- (fall) and B-accent (fall-rise). Constant (2014), on the other hand, argued that the prosody of CT can be described only with a boundary tone (L-H%), and this is the realization of the semantic operator CT-λ. Contrary to

Büring (2003) and Constant (2014) who focused on the prosody only at the CT phrase, Tomioka (2010) examined prosodic patterns in phrases following the CT. He found that in Japanese, CT exhibits post-peak compression, which is also found in F. Tomioka takes this property to support his view that CT and F are semantically similar. As we see below, Korean and Japanese share this similarity between CT and F.

Although previous studies on the prosodic realization of CT have argued that the semantics of CT is closely related to its prosody, several problems remain. First, the previous studies attempted to clarify the prosodic pattern of CT based solely on introspective evidence. No experimental data were provided to support the authors' claims. Second, studies differed as to whether they examined the prosody of the CT phrase itself or the phrases following the CT. This may cause different results in comparing the prosody of CT with T and F. Lastly, not many studies explained specifically how the prosody of CT is different from that of T. Researchers argue that CT and T are semantically distinct in that CT contains the additional meaning of contrast or marking alternatives, and accordingly, they argue that their prosodic patterns are different; however, except for Lee (2008), no studies actually explained *how* the prosodic patterns of CT and T are different nor showed their difference experimentally.

In order to resolve these problems, I conducted a production experiment to examine the prosody of CT, specifically in Korean. I compared the prosody of CT with that of T and F both at the region where CT, T, or F occurs and the region following them. CT is marked morphologically and prosodically in Korean: CT is followed by the postnominal particle =NUN, and it is argued to be realized with a high tone ((L)H*) or Jackendoff (1972)'s B-accent (Lee 1999, 2003, 2008). More specifically, Lee (2008) argued that the intonational rise starts from the L tone in the final syllable of a CT phrase and reaches H* at the particle =NUN. He further argued that this prosodic pattern of CT is distinct from that of T and F as F is realized as a falling accent (H*L) and T is produced without the high accent that is present in CT. Crucially, claims about the prosody of Korean CT have not been supported by experimental evidence, and in addition, no studies on Korean have examined the prosodic patterns in phrases following the CT.

The present study also examines the particle =NUN and its interaction with prosody. Lee (2008) argued that the CT marker =NUN can be omitted, but the high tone associated with CT has to remain in order to represent the meaning of CT. The current study thus examines whether it is acceptable to delete the particle =NUN and compares the prosody of CT *with*-NUN and *without*-NUN at a CT phrase. The particle =NUN is used to mark CT as well as T in Korean. Comparing the prosodic patterns of CT and T would thus show whether the semantic difference or morpho-syntactic similarity between the two more strongly affects the prosodic pattern.

To examine these questions, an experiment with judgment and production tasks was conducted with five native speakers of Korean. Using a question-answer paradigm, CT, T, and F were elicited. Participants were asked to judge whether a given answer is felicitous to a given question, and their production of the question and answer was recorded. The experiment was designed to test the following hypotheses.

Hypothesis 1. The comparison between CT, T, and F: Although CT and T share the same particle in Korean, they will be produced differently as they are semantically distinct. Regarding CT and F, there are two possibilities: first, if the semantic value is important in prosodic realization, CT and F will be produced similarly as they are both F-marked; however, if semantic computation is important, CT and F will be produced differently since they undergo different semantic processes.

Hypothesis 2. The particle =NUN in CT: Following the argument of Lee (2008), the particle =NUN will not be necessary in marking CT; this means that the CT phrase without =NUN will be judged as acceptable. In addition, the deletion of the particle will not affect the prosodic pattern of the CT phrase.

2 Methods

2.1 Participants and Task

Five native speakers of Seoul Korean (three males, two females) participated in the experiment. There were nine blocks of 18 trials in each experimental session. On each trial, the context and question first appeared on the screen. After three seconds, the answer sentence appeared. All the answers started with a target word (i.e., CT, T, and F), but in CT, the target word was preceded by the phrase *"I don't know but..."*. This was to make the transition between the question and answer more natural in the CT context. All the questions and answers were provided in colloquial Korean. I consulted with two native speakers of Korean for the naturalness of the stimuli. Below are the example question-answer pairs each eliciting CT, T, and F (with context and question provided in English).

(3) **CT**

Context: Minsu, Ian, and Taehyun, who are friends of A and B, are going shopping this weekend.

A: What would Minsu buy?

B: (I don't know, but) Iani=(nun) kapang-ul sa-l kes kath-a
Iani=(CT) bag-ACC buy-might-DCL

'(I don't know but) Ian might buy a bag.'

(4) **T**

Context: A and B are talking about the trees planted in the school.

A: Where is the persimmon tree planted?

B: Kamnamwu=(nun) wuntongcang-ey sim-ecye-iss-e
Pers.tree=(TOP) playground-LOC plant-PASS-PRES-DCL
'The persimmon tree is planted at the playground.'

(5) **F**

Context: A is invited to B's place and they are having dinner together.

A: Who made this lotus dish?

B: Myenuli=(ka) yenkuncolim-ul mantul-ess-eyo
Daughter-in-law=(NOM) lotus dish-ACC make-PST-DCL
'Daughter-in-law made the lotus dish.'

Participants were asked to judge whether the answer is acceptable or not considering the context and question. After this judgment was given, the recording was conducted. They were asked to read out loud the question and answer, but not the context. Although the target of the analyses was the answer sentence, both question and answer were read. In addition, the recording was conducted for all trials regardless of the subjects' judgments in order to prevent them from skipping recordings by simply judging the trials as unacceptable.

There were three target conditions in the experiment: CT, T, and F. All of these conditions had the corresponding information structure (IS) category in the subject of the answer sentence (See (3)-(5)). CT and T were followed by F (i.e., *kapang* in (3) and *wuntongcang* in (4)), while F was followed by a given element already mentioned in the question (i.e., *yenkuncolim* in (5)). (6) shows the schematic structure of the answer sentence in each target condition; X represents the given element already mentioned in the discourse.

(6)
CT + F + X
T + F + X
F + X + X

In order to elicit F+F structure, the question must have two *wh*-words. An answer to that question can be understood as F+F, but alternatively as CT+F; thus, in order to avoid the semantic ambiguity, F was not followed by another F but instead was followed by the given word. Fillers looked similar to the target stimuli; for instance, they had F in the verb position or used pronouns instead of the given element.

To examine the question of the postnominal particle =NUN, all of the stimuli appeared in two variants, one *with* the particle and one *without* it. In the *with*-particle condition, the topic marker =NUN followed the IS word in condition CT and T, while the subject marker =I/KA followed the IS word in condition F. These markers were omitted in the *without*-particle condition.

2.2 Data Processing and Analysis

A total of 162 trials were recorded for each of the five participants; among them, 72 trials were CT, 18 were T, and another 18 were F, half of which had a particle, while the other half did not. Out of the 810 trials in total, 47 trials (5.8%) were discarded due to disfluencies, which left 763 trials. Among these trials, only the trials that were judged as acceptable were passed for acoustic analyses. 53 trials in CT (15.5%), 1 trial in T (1.2%), and 25 trials in F (31.3%) were excluded. A forced alignment was conducted for the remaining trials using the Korean Phonetic Aligner (Yoon and Kang 2013).

The F0 information was extracted via Matlab based on the pitch tracking algorithm in Talkin (1995). For each speaker, F0 values whose standardized values were $>$ 2.807 were excluded (0.5% of a normal distribution). After outlier removal, F0 contours were interpolated and smoothed.

For the target word analysis, the number of F0 peaks and values of those peaks as well as the mean F0, F0 range, and the duration of the target word were measured. The F0 peaks were automatically detected and went through manual inspection. The duration of the target word was measured separately for the IS word and the particle. Thus, there were three duration measurements in the *with*-particle condition, total target word (IS word + particle), IS word, and particle, while only the duration of the IS word was measured in the *without*-particle condition (which is also the duration of the total target word in this case). To characterize the global F0 contour, the max F0 difference was calculated between prosodic word (pwd) 1 and pwd2 and between pwd2 and pwd3.

For all of the acoustic measurements (except the number of peaks), a mixed effects regression with IS category (i.e., CT, T, and F) and particle (i.e., *with* and *without*) as fixed effects and speaker as a random effect was conducted. If there was a significant main effect, two-sample t-tests were conducted for post-hoc comparisons. The t-tests were conducted with the raw residuals regressed on the random effect of speakers.

3 Results

The results of the judgment task found that the *without*-NUN CTs are acceptable although some speaker variation exists. Acoustic analyses showed that the prosodic pattern of CT is significantly different from that of T and F in the target word. However, analyses of the F0 contour of the entire sen-

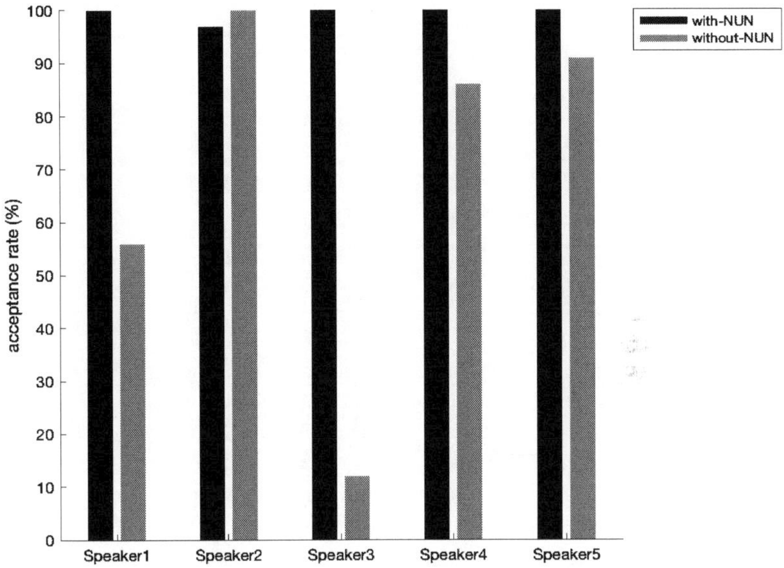

FIGURE 1 Judgment results of CT. The vertical axis is the percentage of the CT trials that were judged as acceptable. The black bar shows the acceptance rate of CTs *without*-NUN while the gray bar shows the acceptance rate of CTs *with*-NUN.

tence showed that CT and F are similar in that both lower the F0 peak of the following prosodic word. The comparison between the prosodic pattern of CT *with*-NUN and CT *without*-NUN at a CT phrase showed that they are significantly different in all acoustic measurements.

3.1 Judgment Results

The results of the judgment task showed that the particle =NUN can be omitted in CT, which supports Hypothesis 2. Figure 1 shows the acceptance rate of CTs *without*-NUN in five speakers. For comparison, the judgment results of CTs *with*-NUN are provided as well.

Although CTs *without*-NUN were not highly accepted as CTs *with*-NUN, they were judged as fairly acceptable. The CTs *with*-NUN were almost always judged as acceptable; the mean acceptance rate of the CTs *with*-NUN was 99.4%. With respect to CTs *without*-NUN, except for Speaker 3, participants judged them as fairly acceptable. Speaker 2, 4, and 5 showed over 80% of acceptance rate for CTs *without*-NUN (Speaker 2: 100%, Speaker 4: 86%, Speaker 5: 91%). In addition, Speaker 1 showed 56% of acceptance rate which was above the chance level. For Speaker 3, he moved to the United States much earlier than other speakers, and this may have affected his judg-

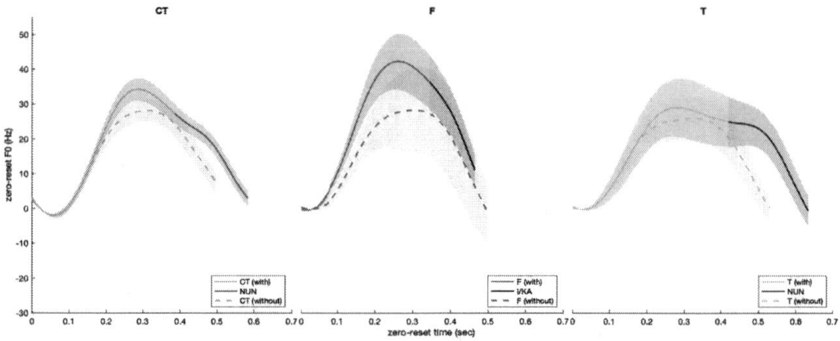

FIGURE 2 F0 contour of the target word. Time-warping was conducted separately for *with*- and *without*-particle condition and separately for the IS word and the particle. The middle lines represent the mean F0 value, and the bands indicate mean $\pm 1.96 \times$ standard error. F0 is shifted to 0 at the beginning of the target word.

ment of the less common type of CT which lacks the particle. Thus, although variation exists among speakers, the particle =NUN can be omitted in CT which comes at the subject of a sentence.

3.2 Acoustic Analyses

Regarding Hypothesis 1, it was found that CT and T are produced differently both in the target word and in the following phrases. This shows that although CT and T share the same particle, they have distinct prosodic patterns, consistent with the view that they are semantically different. With CT and F, they were produced differently at the target word, but they were similar following the target. This reflects the semantic relation between CT and F, where they share the same semantic value but undergo different semantic computations.

With respect to the prosodic aspect of Hypothesis 2, the deletion of the particle changed the prosodic pattern of the CT phrase. In other words, the prosodic pattern of CT phrase that does not have =NUN was different from the prosodic pattern of CT that has =NUN. All the acoustic measurements were significantly different between *with* and *without* condition.

CT vs. T vs. F

The target word analyses found a significant difference between CT and F in the height and number of peaks, F0 mean, and all duration measurements (i.e., total target word, IS word, particle), while CT and T were significantly different in the number of peaks, F0 mean, and the durations of the total word and IS word. Figure 2 shows the time-warped F0 contours based on the average of five speakers' data.

Analyses of the height of the peak found a significant difference between CT/T and F, but no difference was found between CT and T. A mixed-effects linear regression found a significant main effect of IS category ($\chi^2(2, N=427) = 28.74$, $p < 0.001$). Post-hoc comparisons showed that the peak height is higher in F than in CT and T (all *p*s < 0.001), but there was no significant difference between the two Topic conditions.

Regarding the number of peaks, almost all target words had either one or two peaks, and the proportion having one or two peaks was different according to IS category. (There were four trials in CT which had three peaks in the target word, but these trials were not included in the analysis.) Table 1 compares the number of trials with one peak versus two peaks in each IS condition. Among trials *with* the particle, F exclusively had one peak in the target word. In CT, there were more trials with two peaks, but still a majority of them had a single peak. The proportion of trials with two peaks increased in condition T as almost half of the trials had two peaks and the other half had a single peak. If a trial had two peaks, the second peak mostly occurred at the particle (See Figure 2). In this sense, although the same particle =NUN is used to mark CT and T, they are different in that =NUN in T is more likely to have the peak than the =NUN in CT. In sum, it can be argued that in the *with*-particle condition, F and T pattern differently in that F exclusively has one peak while T has a balanced number of trials with one peak and two peaks. CT is in between these cases, having usually one peak but some two peak trials. In the *without*-particle condition, almost 80% of the total data had a single peak although T still had some trials with two peaks. CT patterned more similarly to F in this case since it mostly had a single peak.

TABLE 1 Number of peaks in the target word

with-	1pk	2pks	*without-*	1pk	2pks
CT	131(77.5%)	38(22.5%)	CT	101(86%)	16(14%)
F	36(95%)	2(5%)	F	15(88%)	2(12%)
T	21(49%)	22(51%)	T	30(77%)	9(23%)

The F0 mean was significantly different in all IS conditions, while the F0 range did not show a difference. A mixed-effects linear regression found a significant main effect of IS category ($\chi^2(2, N=427) = 46.34$, $p < 0.001$), and the post-hoc comparisons showed that the F0 mean is highest in F, second highest in T, and lowest in CT (all *p*s < 0.01). Analyses of the F0 range however did not show a significant main effect of IS category.

The duration measurements showed a significant difference in all IS categories in the total target word (IS word + particle) and IS word, while a significant difference was found only between F and CT/T in the duration of the particle. The duration of the total target word in the *with*-particle condition was significantly longer in T than in CT, which was significantly longer than F (all *p*s < 0.001). The same result was found in the duration of the IS

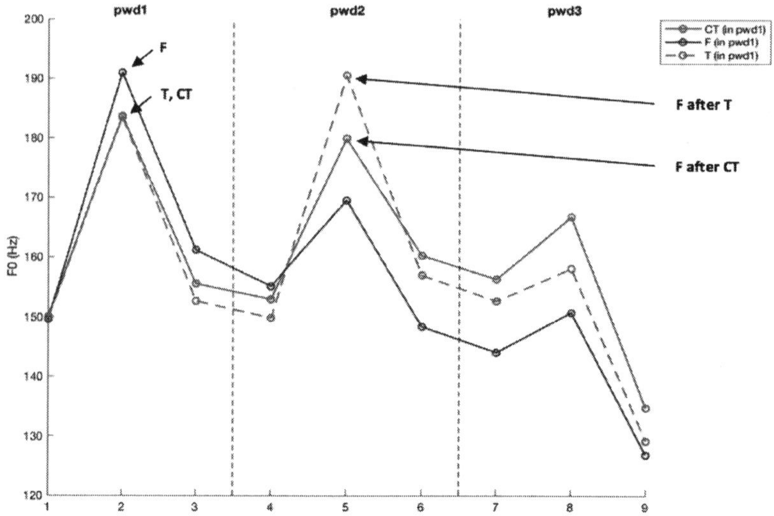

FIGURE 3 Schematic representation of the global F0 contours of the three target conditions. For each pwd, the initial, max, and end F0 values were measured. The mean F0 of the initial five samples was used as the start value, and the mean F0 of the last five samples was used as the end value in each pwd. The figure is based on all speakers' data and includes both *with*- and *without*- conditions.

word, showing T > CT > F, both in *with*- and *without*- particle conditions (all *ps* < 0.001). However, the duration of the particle was only significantly different between F and CT/T (all *ps* < 0.001), and no significant difference was found between CT and T. Unlike the analyses in the number of peaks, the =NUN in CT and T was similar in terms of duration.

While the target word analyses showed that the prosodic pattern of CT is distinct from both T and F, analyses of the F0 contour following the target word showed that CT patterns differently from T but similarly to F. Figure 3 is a schematic representation of the global F0 contours of the three IS conditions.

Analyses of the global F0 contour found that CT constrains the peak of the following pwd like F. The max F0 difference between the target word (pwd1) and the following word (pwd2) was largest in F, second largest in CT, and smallest in T (all *ps* < 0.001). In condition F, F (pwd1) was followed by a given element (pwd2), and the peak of the pwd2 was significantly lowered compared to the peak of the pwd1. In condition T and CT, both were identically followed by F (pwd2), but this F was realized differently; F following T was realized with a high peak, while F following CT did not show this property. It can be argued that the F-marked property of CT in pwd1 constrains the prosodic realization of F in pwd2, which leads to a difference between CT and T.

Further comparison between the max F0 in pwd2 and pwd3 showed a significant difference between condition T and CT ($p < 0.001$). In condition T, the peak of the given element in pwd3 was lowered following the F in pwd2; yet in condition CT, since the F in the pwd2 was not realized with a high peak, the given element in pwd3 did not show compression. This shows that in condition CT, since F in the pwd2 was not realized as F due to the influence of CT in pwd1, the peak of the pwd3 is not lowered.

Overall, the comparison of the prosodic patterns between CT, T, and F over the entire sentence showed that CT is similar to F as they both constrain the F0 peak of the following pwd. However, CT, T, and F each showed a distinct prosodic pattern in the target word.

CT *with*-NUN vs. CT *without*-NUN

Given that the particle =NUN can be deleted in CT, it was examined whether CTs *without*-NUN have the same prosodic pattern as that of CTs *with*-NUN at the target word. A comparison between the two showed that they are significantly different in all acoustic measurements (See CT in Figure 2).

First, regarding the height of the peak, CTs *with*-NUN had a higher F0 peak than CTs *without*-NUN ($p < 0.001$). Second, the number of peaks was also different in that CTs *without*-NUN had more trials with a single peak than CTs *with*-NUN. While 77.5% of CT trials *with*-NUN had a single peak, 86% of trials had a single peak in CT *without*-NUN. Additionally, both F0 mean and range were significantly different between the two conditions (all $ps < 0.01$). It was found that the F0 mean was higher and the F0 range was wider in CTs *with*-NUN than CTs *without*-NUN. Lastly, the duration of the IS word, which was the only duration measurement that could be compared between the two conditions, was also significantly different; the duration of the IS word in *without*-NUN condition was significantly longer than that in *with*-NUN condition ($p < 0.001$). It is possible that speakers compensate for the absence of the postnominal particle by lengthening the IS word.

In sum, the deletion of the particle significantly changed the prosodic pattern of a CT phrase. As the second peak usually occurred at the particle, the deletion of =NUN resulted more trials with a single peak. Furthermore, while the F0 measurements (i.e., peak height, F0 mean, F0 range) were found to be higher in CTs *with* =NUN, the duration of the CT phrase was longer when the particle was dropped. These results are different from what is argued in Lee (2008), who maintained that CTs *without*-NUN will exhibit the same prosodic pattern as CTs *with*-NUN.

4 Discussion and Conclusion

The current study investigated how the semantic category of CT is realized in Korean by conducting judgment-production experiments. The prosodic pattern of CT was compared with that of T and F, both at the target word and the entire sentence. It was found that CT is produced differently from T and F in the target word, but it is similar to F in the global F0 contour. This result supports Hypothesis 1. Although CT and T are morpho-syntactically similar, they are produced differently both locally and globally. This indicates that semantics affects prosodic realization more strongly than morpho-syntax. Regarding CT and F, it was found that they are prosodically different at the target word, but similar in the global F0 contour. This prosodic pattern can be interpreted to reflect the semantic relation between CT and F, whereby they share the same semantic value but undergo different semantic computations. This also shows that semantics and prosody are closely related to each other.

The results on the target word are consistent with Lee (2008), who argued that CT has a distinct prosody. However, CT in the current experiment was not produced with high tone or rising accent as argued in Lee (2008). On the other hand, the results for the global contour matched what Tomioka (2010) found for Japanese. As in Japanese, Korean CT also showed post-peak compression similarly to F. The results in the current study highlight the importance of looking at experimental data and examining the prosody of CT both at the target word and the entire sentence.

It should be noted that in the target word, although CT had a prosodic pattern distinct from both T and F, it was more similar to T than to F. Some might argue that the prosodic similarity between the two is due to givenness, as T appears in the previous question while CT appears in the context (See (3) and (4) above; CT *Iani* appears in the context in (3), while T *Kamnamwu* appears in the question in (4).) This however is not quite true as there were CT stimuli where CT was not previously mentioned, as in the following example.

(7) **CT**

Context: A and B are talking about pets.

A: What do dogs like to eat?

B: (I don't know, but) Koyangi=(nun) yene-lul cal mek-e
Cat=(CT) salmon-ACC well eat-INT

'(I don't know but) Cats like to eat salmon.'

In (7), CT *koyangi* is not explicitly mentioned in the previous context or in A's question; this rules out the possibility that 'givenness' drives the prosodic similarity between CT and T. However, although the CT word was not explicitly mentioned, it is not too difficult for speakers to think of the word *koyangi* since the context delimits the possible alternatives to 'pets'. We can therefore explain that CT is one of the *limited* alternatives and T is the given word, and this causes them to have a similar prosodic pattern. F is different from both CT and T as it does not have a *limited* set of alternatives. Further semantic work needs to be conducted to examine this claim.

The current study also examined the deletion of the particle =NUN and its interaction with prosody. It was found that =NUN can be omitted in CT which comes at the subject of a sentence. This result supports Hypothesis 2 regarding the deletion of =NUN. However, the prosodic aspect of the hypothesis was not supported, as CTs *without*-NUN had a significantly different prosodic pattern compared to CTs *with*-NUN.

In sum, the current study examined the prosodic properties of Korean CT using experimental data. The unique semantic properties of CT were manifested in its prosodic realization. These findings are important since they demonstrate the interaction between semantics and prosody. Furthermore, by examining the particle =NUN together with its prosody, this study contributes to the understanding of CTs in Korean. Future studies should be conducted by varying the location of CT (e.g., CTs in object position or the predicate CT) or examining CT in more complex structures such as embedded clauses. It would also be instructive to conduct a perception experiment to examine whether the acoustic differences found in the present study help speakers distinguish the different IS categories properly.

References

Büring, Daniel. 2003. On d-trees, beans, and b-accents. *Linguistics and philosophy* 26(5):511–545.

Constant, Noah. 2014. Contrastive topic: Meanings and realizations .

Jackendoff, Ray S. 1972. Semantic interpretation in generative grammar .

Lee, Chungmin. 1999. Contrastive topic: a locus of the interface–evidence from korean and english. *The semantics/pragmatics interface from different points of view* 1:317–342.

Lee, Chungmin. 2003. Contrastive topic and/or contrastive focus. *Japanese/Korean Linguistics* 12:352–364.

Lee, Chungmin. 2008. Contrastive (predicate) topic, intonation, and scalar meanings. In *Topic and focus*, pages 151–175. Springer.

Talkin, David. 1995. A robust algorithm for pitch tracking (rapt). *Speech coding and synthesis* 495:518.

Tomioka, Satoshi. 2010. Contrastive topics operate on speech acts. *Information structure: Theoretical, typological, and experimental perspectives* 115138.

Yoon, T and Y Kang. 2013. The korean phonetic aligner program suite.

Semantic Intensification and Prosodic Iconicity in Korean Colour Terms

HAE-SUNG JEON

1 Introduction

The meaning we deliver in communication comprises categorical (e.g., colour categories) and gradient (e.g., colour intensity) elements; in parallel, categorical variation and gradient acoustic parameters are exploited in spoken communication. The categorical vs. gradient distinction is often linked to the distinction between phonological categories and phonetic variation and also that between linguistic and paralinguistic information (cf. Hinton et al. 1994, Gussenhoven 1999, Ladd 2008: 34-39). In some use of paralinguistic cues, the iconic link between meaning and speech signal is assumed, and a growing body of research demonstrates that iconicity is a general and important domain of language (Shintel et al. 2006, Perniss et al. 2010, Martin 2013).

Japanese/Korean Linguistics 27.
Edited by Michael Barrie.

Although iconicity is pervasive in the sound system at the segmental level in Korean (see Sohn 1999), there is little empirical research on the phonetic iconicity and how the categorical and gradient cues are used in speech. This paper explores the mapping between gradient variations in meaning and prosodic parameters in Korean colour terms. The colour terms are of interest in that saturation or brightness can be expressed by a categorical phonemic change which can be seen as a tensification of the initial sound in some cases (e.g., /pɑlkan/ 'reddish' < /p*ɑlkɑn/ 'red') and also by prefixing the word with /sɛ(t)/. It is therefore possible to deliver, for example, four degrees of redness from 'reddish' to 'extremely red' through morpho-phonological alteration, i.e., /pɑlkan/ < /p*ɑlkɑn/ < /sɛp*ɑlkɑn/ < /s*ɛp*ɑlkɑn/. In addition, speakers can use prosodic variations to indicate the degree of 'redness'. For example, increasing duration of the colour term or raising fundamental frequency (F0, an acoustic correlate of perceived pitch) could signal an increase in 'redness'.

The aim of the experiment reported here was to examine the phonetic shape of the native Korean colour terms along a semantic intensity continuum. It was hypothesised that the colour terms with a high degree of intensity would lead to an overall increase in F0 and duration. Ko (2017) suggests that the lengthening in relation to the semantic intensification (referred to as 'expressive lengthening') occurs in the word-initial syllable but this claim has not been empirically investigated.

There are three aspects in the sound system of Korean relevant to the experiment reported here. First, the phonemic contrasts in Korean consonants are linked to symbolism (Section 2.1). Second, the type of phonemic segment in word- or phrase-initial position affects the F0 contour shape in speech (Section 2.2). Third, a prefix /sɛ(t)/ 'very' can be added to the colour terms for intensification (Section 2.3).

2 Phonetic Properties of Korean

2. 1 The word-initial consonant and sound symbolism in colour terms

There are three categories of voiceless stops or affricates (i.e., lenis, fortis, and aspirated), and two categories of voiceless alveolar fricatives (i.e., plain and fortis) in Korean, which distinguish lexical meaning (e.g., /tɑl/, 'moon'; /tʰɑl/, 'mask'; /t*ɑl/, 'daughter' and /sɑl/, 'flesh'; /s*ɑl/, 'rice', see Shin 2015 for a survey). In the native colour terms, /pɑlkan/ 'reddish', /p*ɑlkɑn/ 'red', /kɑmɑn/ 'black-ish', /k*ɑmɑn/ 'black', /nolɑn/ 'yellow' and /pʰɑlɑn/ 'blue', a lenis, aspirated, fortis or nasal consonant appears word-initially. The native terms allow alternations of vowels and consonants related to changes in connotations. The 'bright' vowels (e.g., /ɑ/ in /p*ɑlkɑn/) have a diminutive connotation of being light or bright, in contrast to the 'dark' vowels (e.g., /ɛ/ in /p*ɛlkɛn/).

Only consonantal alternation was examined in this study. Korean speakers consider the fortis consonant as a strengthened version of a lenis consonant, associating the fortis consonant with semantic intensification from its lenis counterpart, e.g., /pɑlkɑn/ 'reddish' < /p*ɑlkɑn/ 'red', /kɑmɑn/ 'blackish' < /k*ɑmɑn/ 'black' (Kim 1985). However, the consonantal alternation does not apply to /nolɑn/ 'yellow' and /pʰɑlɑn/ 'blue'; there is no possible change in the phonemic category related to diminution or intensification from the nasal or aspirated consonant.

2. 2 The phrasal F0 contour shape

The type of phrase-initial segment affects the F0 contour shape over the Accentual Phrase (AP) in Seoul Korean (henceforth Korean). In Jun's model which is widely used for prosodic analysis (e.g., Jun 1998, 2000), the AP is the smallest unit demarcated by the F0 contour. An AP tends to be approximately word-sized; it has 3-4 syllables and 1.14-1.2 content words on average (Jun & Fougeron 2000, Schafer & Jun 2002, Kim 2004).

The model assumes that the initial tone (T) of the underlying pattern, THLH, is determined by the laryngeal feature of the AP-initial segment. When the AP initial segment is in the fortis or aspirated category, /s/, /s*/, or /h/, the initial tone tends to be H, but otherwise L. Segments triggering the AP-initial H tone and segments triggering the AP-initial L tone (lenis consonants, nasals, semivowels, and vowels) are hereafter referred to as strong segments and weak segments respectively.

The number of syllables in the AP is another factor determining the F0 contour shape. When there are four or more syllables in the AP, all four tones can be realised; the second tone H is loosely associated with the second syllable in the AP and the last two tones (LH) are realised on the last two syllables. When there are three or fewer syllables in the AP, some of the tones are undershot, leading to fourteen variations in the F0 contour shape (e.g., LH, LL, LHH, LLH, HH, HLH, etc).

2.3 Morphological marker for colour intensification

A prefix /sɛ(t)/ indicating 'rich', 'sharp', or 'clear' can be attached to the native colour terms. There are four forms of the prefix, /sɛ/, /sɛt/, /si/, and /sit/ and the realisation depends on the phonological properties of the following word. /sɛ/ is followed by a fortis, aspirated consonant, or /h/, which is followed by a harmonised vowel, /ɑ/ or /o/, in the initial syllable of the following word, e.g., /sɛ-p*ɑlkɑn/ 'very red', /sɛ-pʰɑlɑn/ 'very blue', or /sɛ-k*ɑmɑn/ 'very black'. On the other hand, an alternative form /sɛt/ is used when the following word begins with a lenis stop or sonorant, and then followed by a vowel, /ɑ/ or /o/. In /sɛt-nolɑn/ 'very yellow', /t/ is assimilated to the following nasal and the phonetic output is /sɛnnolɑn/. Not all native colour terms can be prefixed. For instance, */sɛ-pɑlkɑn/ 'very reddish' or */sɛ-kɑmɑn/ 'very blackish' seems unnatural and contradictory in the meaning.

It is possible to apply further intensification from /sɛ(t)/ to /s*ɛ(t)/ to create, for example, /s*ɛp*ɑlkɑn/ 'extremely red', /s*ɛk*ɑmɑn/ 'extremely black', /s*ɛnnolɑn/ 'extremely yellow', or /s*ɛpʰɑlɑn/ 'extremely blue', following the phonetic symbolism principle. Although the categorical change between /s/ and /s*/ in the prefix is not considered standard in written Korean, the alternation related to semantic intensification is often observed in colloquial speech.

3 Methodology

3. 1 Experimental materials and procedure

The target phrases were an adjective colour term (the target word) in the categories of red, black, yellow or blue followed by a carrier noun, /tɯlɛsɯ/ 'dress'. The experimental materials were pictures of girls in a dress in the same colour category with varying degrees of saturation ordered along the saturation scale (Figure 1). One slide was created for each colour category. One each slide, nine pictures of girls appeared for red and black (e.g., three steps for /pɑlkɑn/ 'reddish', /p*ɑlkɑn/ 'red' and /sɛp*ɑlkɑn/ 'very red' respectively), whilst there were six pictures for yellow and blue (e.g., three steps each for /nolɑn/ 'yellow' and /sɛnnolɑn/ 'very yellow' respectively). The slide was designed to demonstrate a gradual increase in the colour intensification and to explicitly instruct speakers to produce three steps within each Morpho-Phonological Category (MPC, e.g., Weak: /pɑlkɑn/, Strong: /p*ɑlkɑn/ and Prefix: /sɛp*ɑlkɑn/ in Figure 1).

Four native Seoul Korean speakers (3 females and 1 male aged between 24 and 26) without speech, hearing or visual problems participated in the experiment. Although all participants were studying in the UK at the time of the experiment, none of them learned any other languages than Korean in their childhood and they were living in the UK for less than 1 year.

The speakers were shown the slides on the PC screen and asked to describe each object using the words and the sentence template on the screen, as if describing the degrees of, for example, 'redness' to a listener who could not see the slide. The experimenter prompted each speaker to produce an utterance corresponding to each step and to move onto the next slide when necessary. Speakers were reminded that the order of the pictures on a slide shows a gradual increase in the colour saturation and all instructions were given in Korean. The main experiment was preceded by a practice session, in which the colour term /hɑjɑn/ 'white' was used. The order of the slides in the main experiment was blue (6 steps)-yellow (6 steps)–red (9 steps)-black (9 steps) for all speakers. All experimental sentences were spoken five times in total by repeating from the beginning of the slide presentation (i.e., blue-yellow-red-black-blue-…). From each speaker, 30 utterances were recorded for blue and yellow (6 steps × 5 repetitions = 30 utterances) and 45 utterances were recorded for each of red and black (9 steps × 5 repetitions = 45 utterances). In total, 600 utterances were recorded [(30 utterances × 2 colour categories + 45 utterances × 2 colour categories) × 4 speakers] in the main experiment. All recording was done individually in the sound-attenuated booth in the Phonetics Laboratory at the University of Cambridge, using a Marantz PM 0670 digital recorder and a Sennheiser MKH 40 cardioid microphone. The sampling rate was 44.1KHz.

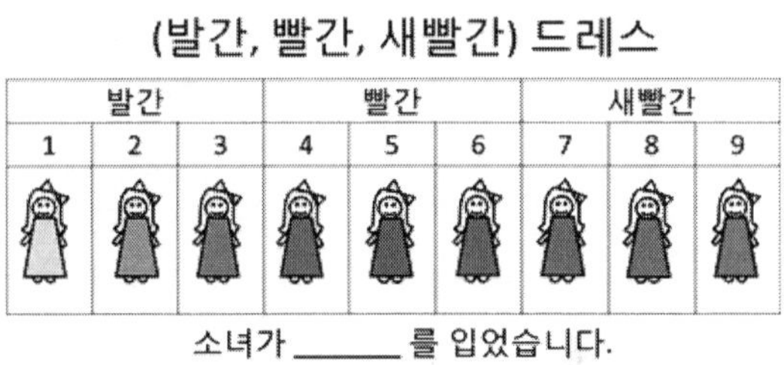

Figure 1. An example slide. The top line shows (/pɑlkan/ 'reddish', /p*ɑlkɑn/ 'red', /sɛp*ɑlkɑn/ 'very red') /tɯlɛsɯ/ 'dress'. The text below the table shows the carrier phrases, /sonjʌkɑ____ lɯlipʌs*ɯmnitɑ/ 'The girl has worn ________'. /lɯl/ following the target phrase is an accusative marker.

3.2 Measurements

In each utterance, the segment and syllable boundaries were annotated following the standard criteria in Turk et al. (2006) using Praat (Boersma & Weenink 2012). When there was a sequence of two consonants with a single closure, e.g., /nn/ in /sɛnnolɑn/ 'very yellow', the closure was halved, and each half was treated as the closure of one consonant. The duration of syllables was extracted using Praat scripts. The F0 was measured at the mid-point in each vowel, using the PSOLA method (Moulines & Charpentier 1990), and devoiced vowels were excluded from this measurement. The F0 was measured in Hz and then converted to semitones (ST) relative to 100 Hz. In the prefix /sɛ(t)/, the centroid frequency at the mid-point of the fricative noise and H1-H2 (the amplitude difference between the first two harmonics in each vowel in dB as a voice quality measure) were also measured. The centroid frequency and H1-H2 did not show systematic variation related to the experimental conditions and therefore they are not reported.

3.3 Statistical analysis

In order to examine the effects of Morpho-Phonological Category (MPC) and the intensification step on F0 and duration of all syllables, mixed effect models were fitted to the data using R ver. 3.6.1 (R Core Team, 2018) and *lme4* package (Bates, et al. 2015) for each colour category (Red, Black, Blue and Yellow). Fixed factors were MPC (Weak, Strong, and Prefix) and STEP (three steps in each MPC). For Red and Black, there were three MPCs (e.g., Weak: /palkan/ 'reddish', Strong: /p*alkan/ 'red', Prefix: /sɛp*alkan/ 'very red'), but there were two MPCs for Yellow (Weak: /nolan/ 'yellow', Prefix: /sɛnnolan/ 'very yellow') and for Blue (Strong: /pʰalan/ 'blue', Prefix: /sɛpʰalan/ 'very blue'). The initial model included both fixed factors and it was compared to a lower-order model using the log-likelihood test (*anova* function, $\alpha = 0.05/24 = 0.002$ with Bonferroni corrections, 6 Syllables × 4 colour categories). SPEAKER was always included as a random intercept.

4 Results

4.1 F0

Figure 2 shows the F0 for each syllable in the target phrase. Within each MPC, Steps are differentiated by line types (the lowest: solid, the middle: dashed, the highest: dotdash). The *x*-axis shows the syllable position in the target phrase (Syllable 0: prefix, Syllables 1 - 2: colour term, Syllables 3 - 5: /tɯlɛsɯ/ 'dress'). The error bars show one standard error; the overlapping error bars between experimental conditions indicate that their differences are not significant.

For Red and Black, for MPC-Prefix, the F0 in Syllable 0 seemed to be constant across Steps. For Syllables 1 - 2, a two-way clustering related to the type of phrase-initial segment was clear; without the prefix /sɛ(t)/, the initial F0 was relatively low for /palkan/ 'reddish', /kaman/ 'black-ish' than for /p*alkan/ 'red', /k*aman/ 'black'. For MPC-Weak, there seemed to be an expansion in the F0 range in the carrier word /tɯlɛsɯ/ 'dress', with lowering of F0 for Syllable 4 for the middle and the highest Steps. However, such trend was unclear for MPC-Strong and -Prefix. In Table 1, the effect of MPC was significant for Syllables 1 - 4. The Step effect was significant for Syllables 3 - 4 for Red and for Syllables 3 - 5 for Black. That is, Step had an additive effect to the MPC effect for the syllables in the carrier word but not for the target colour term. The detailed analysis of the F0 contour shapes over the APs are not reported here, but the averaged F0 values suggest that the representative F0 contour shape over the target phrase was HHLH with L aligned to Syllable 4 for MPC-Prefix and -Strong. For MPC-Weak, the averaged F0 values showed LHLH over the target phrase, with the second L aligned to Syllable 4.

For Blue, the target-phrase initial F0 for Syllable 0 or 1 was constantly high as predicted by the initial segment type in /sɛpʰɑlɑn/ 'very blue' and /pʰɑlɑn/ 'blue' respectively. For MPC-Prefix, the error bars across Steps overlapped for all Syllables, indicating that speakers did not systematically differentiate F0 across Steps. For MPC-Strong, a F0 range expansion of the target phrase in the middle and the highest Steps was shown with a lowering of F0 for Syllable 4. In Table 1, the MPC effect was significant for Syllables 2 - 4, and the Step effect was significant for Syllables 3 - 4. This trend is similar to Red and Black in that the target phrase-initial F0 was predicted by the type of the segment while speakers adjusted the F0 range with semantic intensification in the carrier phrase. The averaged F0 values showed HHLH over the target phrase.

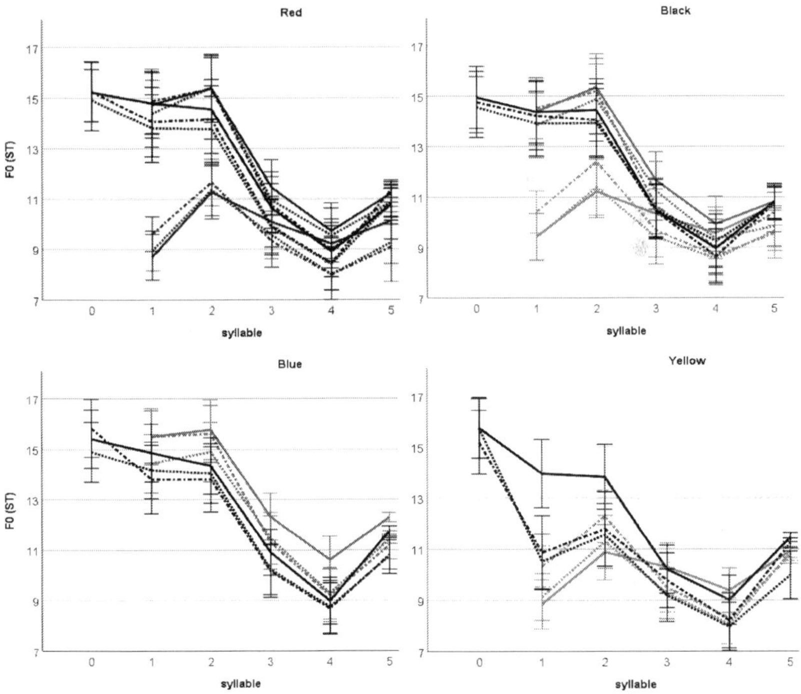

Figure 2. F0 (ST). Within each MPC, the lowest Step (solid), the middle Step (dashed), the highest Step (dotdash) are differentiated by line types.

For Yellow, the target phrase initial F0 had a low value for MPC-Weak, /nolɑn/ 'yellow' but a high value for MPC-Prefix, /sɛnnolɑn/ 'very yellow'. For MPC-Prefix, Syllable 0 had a constant F0 across Steps and the F0 showed a notable fall between Syllables 0 to 1 for the middle and the highest Steps. Table 1 shows that the MPC effect was statistically significant only for Syllable 1 and the Step effect was significant for Syllables 3 and 4. The averaged F0 for MPC-Weak showed LHLH. The tonal description for MPC-Prefix is not straightforward. The tonal pattern for the lowest step could be H#HHLH (where # indicates an AP boundary) with the prefix forming an AP on its own with a H tone. In this case, the nasal in /nolɑn/ is associated with an AP-initial high tone and this violates the AP-initial segment-tone association. Alternatively, the averaged tonal pattern could be analysed as HHLH where the first H is associated with Syllable 0 and the second H aligned to Syllable 2. For the middle and the highest steps, the tonal pattern over the target phrase could be analysed as H#LHLH, with an AP boundary between the prefix and the colour term.

	Red				Black			
	MPC		Step		MPC		Step	
	df	χ^2	df	χ^2	df	χ^2	df	χ^2
0			1	4.55			1	0.18
1	2	194.5*	1	0.16	2	216.31*	1	1.29
2	2	187.67*	1	0	2	150.63*	1	0.82
3	2	36.45*	1	22.07*	2	38.47*	1	28.12*
4	2	27.45*	1	23.11*	2	19.09*	1	24.76*
5	2	7.06	1	9.23	2	9.38	1	11.19*
	Blue				Yellow			
	MPC		Step		MPC		Step	
	df	χ^2	df	χ^2	df	χ^2	df	χ^2
0			1	1.24			1	2.55
1	1	9.21	1	4.19	1	28.64*	1	1.89
2	1	33.05*	1	1.67	1	8.10	1	0.24
3	1	33.76*	1	16.59*	1	0.01	1	19.98*
4	1	29.70*	1	19.08*	1	6.07	1	17.92*
5	1	4.66	1	4.62	1	0.16	1	1.16

Table 1. Results of the log-likelihood tests for F0, p * < 0.002

4.2 Syllable Duration

In Figure 3, a gradual increase in duration along Steps for Syllable 0 for MPC-Prefix and for Syllable 1 for MPC-Weak and -Strong is visible in all colour categories. For Syllables 2 - 5, MPC and Step did not seem to affect the syllable duration. Table 2 shows that the effects of MPC and Step were concentrated for Syllables 0 – 2 in all colour categories. Yellow showed an exception in that the effects of MPC and Step were statistically significant for Syllables 0 – 1 but not for Syllable 2.

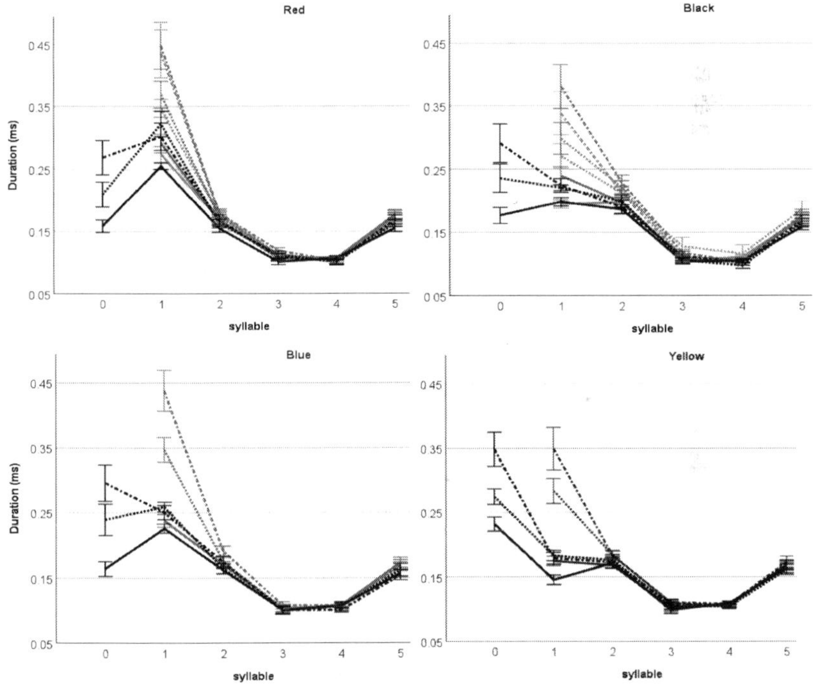

Figure 3. Syllable duration. Within each MPC, the lowest Step (solid), the middle Step (dashed), the highest Step (dotdash) are differentiated by line types.

5 General Discussion

5.1 F0

The F0 contour shapes of the target phrase shown in Figures 2 were predictable from the target phrase-initial consonant type in general; there was an association between a weak phrase-initial consonant and a low tone and that between a strong phrase-initial consonant and a high tone. In particular, for MPC-Prefix, speakers were bound to produce the constant high F0 value for the prefix (Syllable 0) regardless of semantic intensification. It seems that speakers produced F0 at the top of their normal speaking range, as the prefix /sɛ(t)/ has an inherently emphatic meaning and speakers were made aware that the MPC-Prefix conditions in the experiment were designed to have a high degree of intensification. On the other hand, there was no clear evidence that speakers' adjustment of F0 in the target words was affected by semantic intensification.

	Red				Black			
	MPC		Step		MPC		Step	
	df	χ^2	df	χ^2	df	χ^2	df	χ^2
0			1	17.86*			1	17.96*
1	2	21.81*	1	45.54*	2	34.57*	1	42.35*
2	2	18.14*	1	13.70*	2	33.47*	1	16.95*
3	2	4.09	1	8.32	2	2.42	1	1.78
4	2	0.99	1	5.64	2	6.33	1	0.79
5	2	6	1	2.96	2	4.78	1	1.57
	Blue				Yellow			
	MPC		Step		MPC		Step	
	df	χ2	df	χ2	df	χ2	df	χ2
0			1	28.51*			1	25.02*
1	1	41.10*	1	38.44*	1	43.60*	1	33.42*
2	1	12.95*	1	15.47*	1	1.92	1	2.54
3	1	4.22	1	1.66	1	3.71	1	10.96*
4	1	0.97	1	0.9	1	0.08	1	0.11
5	1	0.53	1	0.12	1	1.91	1	1.33

Table 2. Results of the log-likelihood tests for syllable duration, p * < 0.002

The statistical test results revealed that MPC affected the F0 in the target phrase. The source of this effect for Syllables 1 – 2 seemed to be the two-way distinction in the F0 related to the association between the type of the AP-initial segment and F0. Apparent in the data from Red and Black were two clusters of F0 values phrase-initially associated with lenis vs. fortis, not a gradient variation within a category. The additive effect of Step on F0 was observed in the carrier noun following the colour term. Probably speakers scaled the phrase-initial F0 depending on the segmental type and adjusted the

F0 range in the carrier word, expanding the F0 range in the higher intensification steps.

The two-way clustering for Syllables 1 and 2 was not shown for Blue and Yellow which did not have the contrast of weak vs. strong consonant for the onset of the colour term. For Blue, while the F0 values seemed to distribute gradiently, for MPC-Strong, the higher intensification Step did not systematically lead to the higher F0 in the colour term.

The results also showed how the word-internal morpho-phonological structure could influence the F0 contour. For Yellow, /sɛnnolan̥tɯlɛsɯ/ 'very yellow dress' in MPC-Prefix, speakers produced an abrupt F0 jump from Syllable 0 /sɛn/ down to Syllable 1 /no/ to mark a high degree of semantic intensification for the middle and the highest Steps (Figure 2). This could be interpreted that speakers inserted an AP boundary between the prefix and the colour term. This phenomenon was shown only for Yellow, probably due to the fact that the colour term after the morpheme boundary began with a weak segment. In contrast, for Blue, the F0 of the colour term initial syllable in MPC-Prefix was maintained high across the morpheme boundary and it did not fall as much as it did for Yellow in the MPC-Prefix condition.

5.2 Iconic lengthening at the phrase left edge

The iconic lengthening within each MPC was observed consistently at the left edge of the target phrase in all colour categories. For MPC-Prefix, the prefix showed the greatest magnitude of lengthening compared to the following syllables. For the target phrases in the MPC-Weak and -Strong conditions without the prefix, there was a clear tendency for the colour term initial syllable to be lengthened along the intensification steps.

The statistical test results indicated that the MPC and Step effects were significant for the prefix and the colour term for Red, Black and Blue; speakers adjusted the duration of the whole colour term for expressing the different degrees of colour saturation, but the effect was less visible in the colour term final syllable than in the initial syllable in Figure 3. On the other hand, for Yellow /nolan/, the lengthening effect was not significant in the colour term final syllable. For Yellow, the lengthening concentrated in the colour term initial syllable co-occurred with the abrupt lowering in F0 discussed in Section 5. 1. These could be interpreted that the prefix formed an AP on its own.

The importance of the left edge of a prosodic phrase for marking discourse functions in Korean has been reported in several studies (e.g., Cho et al. 2011, Jeon & Nolan 2017). The present study offers evidence that speakers use the phrase-initial syllable as an important information site for marking semantic intensification.

Once the iconic information is provided in the phrase-initial syllable for listeners, there would be no further need for speakers to manipulate other acoustic cues in the following part of the utterance for the same purpose. Localised phonetic cues at the phrase boundary are known to be more effectively exploited by Korean listeners than global or diffused cues in word segmentation (Kim & Cho 2009, Jeon & Nolan 2013). In this regard, speakers' active manipulation of the phrase-initial syllable seems to be an effective strategy. What is worth noting is that the location of lengthening site differs across languages, although iconic lengthening is cross-linguistically common (see Ko 2017). For example, Simard (2013) shows that iconic lengthening occurs at the right edge of a phrase in Jaminjung, an endangered language spoken in Northern Australia.

6 Conclusions

The findings reported here are from a small-scale experiment with four speakers. Nevertheless, they demonstrate how language-specific phonological properties interact with speakers' expressions of semantic intensification. The experimental results show that the phonetic adjustments following semantic intensification of the colour terms in Korean are affected by their initial consonant type. However, the effects of initial consonant and intensification were shown in different phonetic dimensions. Lengthening rather than variation in F0 was the most salient phonetic marker for semantic intensification, and the iconic lengthening localised at the left edge of the prosodic phrase.

It seems speakers' scaling of the phrase-initial F0 is not systematically influenced by the degrees of semantic intensification. In the spoken utterances, the F0 contour shapes were directly linked to the type of the target phrase initial segment. The F0 for the prefix /sɛ(t)/ which triggers an AP-initial high tone was not affected by semantic intensification within the Morpho-Phonological Category of the colour term. Weak segments were associated with phrase-initial low pitch and strong segments with high pitch even under a high degree of semantic intensification.

The division in the labour shown between F0 and duration may be related to that F0 serves as an important cue to the phonemic distinction in Korean consonants and the duration does not play a role in differentiating phonemes. That is, there is unused phonetic space for manipulating duration to be exploited for other communicative purposes whilst F0 would be more constrained as it is associated with the segmental identity AP-initially.

In addition, the experimental results revealed that the segmental composition of a word may affect prosodic restructuring under intensification. For example, an unexpected fall in F0 at the morpheme boundary which could signal an AP boundary was observed between the prefix and the colour term only when the colour term began with a weak consonant.

References

Bates, D., Mächler, M., Bolker, B., and Walker, S. 2015. Fitting linear mixed-effects models using lme4. *Journal of Statistical Software* 67(1): 1–48.

Boersma, P. and Weenink, D. 2012. Praat: Doing Phonetics By Computer [Computer program]. Version 5.3.23.

Cho, T., Lee, Y. and Kim, S. 2011. Communicatively driven versus prosodically driven hyper-articulation in Korean. *Journal of Phonetics* 39: 344-361.

Gussenhoven, C. 1999. Discreteness and gradience in intonational contrasts. *Language and Speech* 42: 283-305.

Hinton, L., Nichols, J., and Ohala, J. J. 1994. Introduction: Sound-symbolic processes. *Sound Symbolism*. eds. L. Hinton, L., J. Nichols, J. and J. J. Ohala, 1-12. Cambridge: Cambridge University Press.

Jeon, H.-S. and F. Nolan. 2013. The role of pitch and timing cues in the perception of phrasal grouping in Seoul Korean. *Journal of the Acoustical Society of America* 133: 3039-3049.

Jeon, H.-S. & Nolan, F. 2017. Prosodic marking of narrow focus in Seoul Korean. *Laboratory Phonology: Journal of the Association for Laboratory Phonology* 8(1): 2, 1–31

Jun, S.-A. 1998. The accentual phrase in the Korean prosodic hierarchy. *Phonology* 15: 189-226.

Jun, S.-A. 2000. K-ToBI (Korean ToBI) labelling conventions (ver. 3.1). *UCLA Working Papers in Phonetics* 99: 149-173.

Jun, S.-A. and Fougeron, C. 2000. A Phonological model of French intonation. *Intonation: Analysis, Modeling and Technology*, ed. A. Botinis. 209-242. Dordrecht/Boston: Kluwer Academic Publishers.

Kim, A. I. 1985. Korean color terms: an aspect of semantic fields and related phenomena. *Anthropological Linguistics* 27: 425-436.

Kim, S. 2004. The Role of Prosodic Phrasing in Korean Word Segmentation. PhD thesis. Department of Linguistics, UCLA.

Kim, S. and Cho, T. 2009. The use of phrase-level prosodic information in lexical segmentation: Evidence from word-spotting experiments in Korean. *Journal of the Acoustical Society of America* 125: 3373-3386.

Ko, E.-S. 2017. The phonology and semantics of expressive lengthening in Korean. *Studies in Phonetics, Phonology, and Morphology* 325-347.

Ladd, D. R. 2008. *Intonational Phonology*. 2nd ed., Cambridge, UK: Cambridge University Press.

Martin, P. 2013. Iconicity of melodic contours in French. *Prosody and Iconicity*, eds. S. Hancil and D. Hirst, 181-192. Amsterdam, Philadelphia: John Benjamins.

Moulines, E. and Charpentier, F. 1990. Pitch-synchronous waveform processing techniques for text-to-speech synthesis using diphones. *Speech Communication* 9: 453-467.

Perniss, P., Thompson, R. L., and Vigliocco, G. 2010. Iconicity as a general property of language: evidence from spoken and signed languages. *Frontiers in Psychology* 1: 1-15.

R Core Team. 2018. R: A Language and Environment for Statistical Computing. Vienna, Austria. URL https://www.R-project.org

Schafer, A. and Jun, S.-A. 2002. Effects of accentual phrasing on adjective interpretation of Korean. *East Asian Language Processing*, ed. M. Nakayama, 223-255. Stanford: CSLI.

Shin, J. 2015. Vowels and consonants. *The Handbook of Korean Linguistics*, eds. L. Brown & J. Yeon, 3–21. West Sussex, UK: Wiley-Blackwell.

Shintel, H., Nusbaum, H. C., and Okrent, A. 2006. Analog acoustic expression in speech communication. *Journal of Memory and Language* 55: 167-177.

Simard, C. 2013. Prosody and function of "iconic lengthening" in Jaminjung. *SOAS Working Papers in Linguistics* 16: 65-77.

Sohn, H.-M. 1999. The Korean Language. Cambridge: Cambridge University Press.

Turk, A., Nakai, S. and Sugahara, M. 2006. Acoustic segment durations in prosodic research: A practical guide. *Methods in Empirical Prosody Research*, eds. S. Sudhoff, D. Lenertová, M. Roland, S. Pappert, P. Augurzky, I. Mleinek, N. Richter and J. Schließer, 1-28. Berlin, New York: De Gruyter.

Testing Rosen's Rule Yet Again: An Experimental Study

YU TANAKA
Doshisha University

1 Introduction

Compound formation in Japanese may involve a voicing alternation known as "rendaku." When rendaku applies, the initial consonant of the second element becomes voiced, as shown in (1).[1]

(1) Compounds undergoing rendaku

maki	+	s̲usi	→	maki-**z**usi	'rolled-sushi'
ori	+	k̲ami	→	ori-**g**ami	'folding-paper'

Rendaku is quite irregular and does not apply in every compound. A number of studies have proposed phonological and non-phonological factors affecting the occurrence of this compound voicing alternation (see Vance 2015a; Kawahara 2016; Kawahara and Zamma 2016; Irwin 2016a among others for recent overviews of research on rendaku). One of such factors is the prosodic size of word elements. Rosen (2001, 2003) proposes that a non-coordinate compound composed of native nouns always undergoes rendaku if "one of its elements is three moras or longer" (unless the second element is

[1] The transcriptions of words in this paper are largely based on the kunrei romanization system. The glosses for compounds are mostly verbatim translations of their elements.

Japanese/Korean Linguistics 27.
Edited by Michael Barrie.

somehow idiosyncratically immune to voicing).[2] This condition is known as "Rosen's Rule." Illustrative examples are given in (2).

(2) Compounds showing Rosen's Rule effects

a.	hotaru	+	k̲usa	→	hotaru-**g**usa	'firefly-grass'
b.	haru	+	k̲usa	→	haru-kusa	'spring-grass'

Both compounds have /kusa/ 'grass' as their second element (henceforth "E2"). As can be seen, (2a) with a three-mora first element (henceforth "E1") shows voicing, while (2b) with a two-mora E1 does not.

Later studies confirm the validity of Rosen's Rule. Irwin (2009, 2016b) and Vance (2015a,b) conduct dictionary studies, and show that, although the rule is not actually as ironclad as Rosen (2001, 2003) has originally claimed, it does capture statistical tendencies of rendaku application. That is, generally speaking, compounds are more likely to undergo voicing when one of their elements exceeds two moras.

On the other hand, the rule's psychological reality has been called into question. Kawahara and Sano (2014) conduct a nonword experiment where Japanese speakers judge rendaku applicability in compounds with various lengths of E1. The results show that speakers do not particularly prefer voicing change when E1 is three moras compared to when it is two moras. Kawahara and Sano conclude that E1's length does not affect rendaku, further suggesting that Rosen's Rule may not be active in Japanese speakers' minds.[3]

What caused the difference between the actual data patterns reported in Irwin (2009, 2016b) and Vance (2015a,b) on one hand and the participants' behaviors in Kawahara and Sano (2014) on the other? It is possible that the tendencies seen in real words are not internalized as real phonological patterns in Japanese speakers' mental grammars, as is implied by Kawahara and Sano. Another possibility is that their null experimental results have been caused by some confounding factors, such as the length and nonword status of E2.

It should first be noted that the stimuli in Kawahara and Sano's (2014) experiment are not perfectly suited for testing Rosen's Rule from the point of view of their prosodic size. Kawahara and Sano used two-element compounds composed of two- or three-mora existing words as E1 (e.g. two-mora *mori* 'forest', three-mora *kumori* 'cloudy, cloudiness') and three-mora nonsense words as E2 (e.g. *semaro*). They predicted that rendaku application in

---

[2] See Rosen (2001, 2003) for its detailed definition. Also see Irwin (2009, 2016b) for a proposal to modify the original definition.

[3] Tamaoka et al. (2009) and Tamaoka and Ikeda (2010) conduct similar studies. Although their research is not particularly intended to test Rosen's Rule, they also conclude that there is no effect of E1's length on rendaku application.

the three-mora-E1 condition, as shown in (3b) below, would have a higher acceptance rate than that in the two-mora-E1 condition, or (3a). As stated above, the prediction was not borne out.

(3) Kawahara and Sano's (2014) experimental task
  a. mori + semaro → mori-**s**emaro or mori-**z**emaro?
  b. kumori + semaro → kumori-**s**emaro or kumori-**z**emaro?

However, Rosen's Rule, in its original definition, states that rendaku must apply if "one of the elements is three moras or longer" (see above). Notice that every stimulus word in Kawahara and Sano (2014) is already eligible for rendaku by this criterion, since E2 is trimoraic. Thus, this may have promoted their participants' rendaku responses in general, and have dampened potential effects of E1's length differences.

Meanwhile, their participants may also have been reluctant to accept rendaku application in general due to the fact that nonce words always appeared as E2. The literature shows that language speakers have a non-alternation bias (see e.g. Albright and Do 2013; Coetzee 2009): participants in an artificial language learning task tend to assume that they should not change word forms (unless they are given ample evidence telling them otherwise). It is possible that Kawahara and Sano's (2014) participants disfavored voicing change in nonce E2 items (e.g. *semaro* → *zemaro*), which they had never seen before, due to this non-alternation bias. That is, it may have played a role as a rendaku-inhibiting factor in their judgment.

It is unclear whether or how E2's length and non-word status have actually affected Kawahara and Sano's (2014) experimental results. Nevertheless, it is conceivable that these factors, which could drive rendaku application rates to the two opposite directions, have masked subtle acceptability differences among the different conditions, or in other words, potential effects of Rosen's Rule. Given these possible confounds in the previous research, a new experiment with a more controlled design is called for. This study fills the gap. I conduct a nonword rendaku judgment experiment along the lines of Kawahara and Sano (2014) while controlling for the factors discussed above. The goal of the study is thus to reexamine the psychological reality of Rosen's Rule.

2 Method

2.1 Participants

Forty-one native speakers of Japanese participated in the experiment. Most of them were college students in their late teens or early twenties who were recruited in classrooms in Doshisha University, Japan. Others were recruited through e-mails or on social media. They all took part on a voluntary basis.

2.2 Stimuli

Compounds composed of nonce and real elements were used as stimuli. For nonce elements, I created two-mora and three-mora words, randomly combining phonotactically-legal open syllables in Japanese. It was ensured that the sound sequences were not listed as lexical items on a large dictionary of Japanese (Shinmura 2008), and that, other than the length differences, they did not contain any features that could affect rendaku application (e.g. voiced obstruents, segments that are typical of Sino-Japanese words or recent loans, etc.) when appearing as E1 or E2 of a compound. Those containing features that could sound unnatural (e.g. sequences of idential moras) were also excluded. As a result, 48 two-mora words (one half for E1 and the other half for E2) and 48 three-mora words (one half each for E1 and E2) were obtained. Those to be used as E2 all had a voiceless obstruent in word-initial position, so that they would potentially undergo voicing. Examples include /heka/ and /kemosa/. (A full list of the nonce words is given in Table 3 in Appendix.)

As for existing words, I referred to the Rendaku Database compiled by Irwin et al. (2017), and adopted the 45 most frequent two-mora E1 nouns (e.g. /kusa/ 'grass') and the 49 most frequent two-mora E2 nouns (e.g. /sima/ 'island') that were not "rendaku-lovers," "rendaku-haters," or "rendaku-immune" in Rosen's (2001) terms. That is, these E2 morphemes undergo rendaku moderately, or about 33% to 66% of the time in the entire database. (Irwin 2014 call such morphemes "rendaku-waverers.")[4]

	Nonce E1 + Real E2	Real E1 + Nonce E2
2-mora Nonce	/kema-tori/ 'NONCE-bird'	/kawa-hesa/ 'river-NONCE'
3-mora Nonce	/somoka-tori/ 'NONCE-bird'	/kawa-sekora/ 'river-NONCE'

TABLE 1 Stimulus types and examples

These elements were then randomly combined to create non-existing compounds. By the length and position of the nonce elements, the words are categorized into four types: compounds composed of two- or three-mora nonce E1 and two-mora real E2 (e.g. /kema+tori/, /somoka+tori/ 'NONCE-bird'), and compounds composed of two-mora real E1 and two- or three-mora nonce E2 (e.g. /kawa+hesa/, /kawa+sekora/ 'river-NONCE'). (Recall that the real elements are all bimoraic.) The all four types are shown in Table 1 with representative examples.

[4] The reason for using the relatively large number of items, rather than selecting a smaller set, was to minimize potential effects of idiosyncratic behaviors of compound elements (see Rosen 2001; Irwin 2014; Vance 2015a,b for discussion on lexical idiosyncrasy and rendaku).

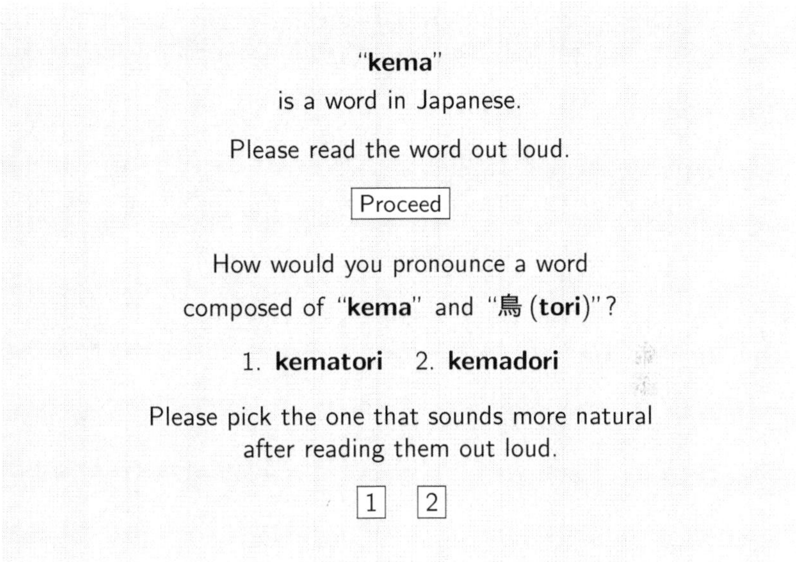

FIGURE 1 An image of the judgment task

2.3 Procedure

The experiment was run on-line on Experigen (Becker and Levine 2013). After reading a consent form and agreeing to take the experiment, participants were given general instructions. They were told that they would see some Japanese words that were obsolete or used only in some regional dialects, and that they would be answering questions about them.

Participants first completed a practice session with basic instructions, which consisted of two trials, and moved on to a main session which had 32 trials. In each trial, they were orthographically presented with a nonce word written in hiragana (phonographic letters) and were asked to read it out loud. They then clicked on a proceed button, and were asked how they would pronounce a compound composed of the word just presented to them and a real word written in kanji (Chinese characters; logograms) with hiragana in parentheses. They were given the rendaku and non-rendaku forms of the compound, and were asked to pick the one that would sound more natural after reading them aloud. To answer the question, they clicked on a button with a number corresponding to their selection. An image of the task (stylized for presentation) is shown in Figure 1. The text is translated from Japanese into English. The parts shown in boldface were presented in hiragana.

	Estimate	Std. Error	z-value	Pr(> |z|)	
Intercept: (Nonce=E1, Nonce=2μ)	0.8064	0.2240	3.600	0.0003	***
Nonce=E2	–0.7507	0.2734	–2.745	0.006	**
Nonce=3μ	0.3336	0.2374	1.405	0.160	
Nonce=E2 * Nonce=3μ	–0.6290	0.3556	–1.769	0.077	.

Signif. codes: 0 '***' 0.001 '**' 0.01 '*' 0.05 '.' 0.1

TABLE 2 Logistic regression model coefficients

The stimuli used in the 32 trials in the main session were balanced for the length and position of the nonce elements; that is, eight items were randomly selected from each of the four stimulus types in Table 1. The order of presentation was randomized for each participant.

3 Results

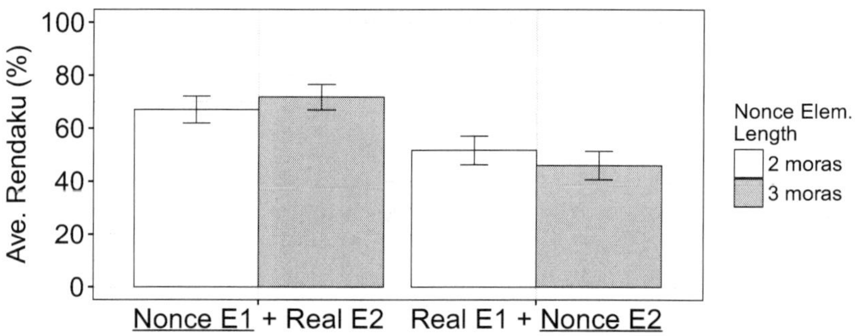

FIGURE 2 Rendaku response rates by condition (Error bars: 95%CI)

Figure 1 plots the average rates of rendaku responses by condition. The error bars represent 95% confidence intervals. For statistical analysis, a mixed-effects logistic regression model was constructed with Rendaku Response (rendaku or no rendaku) as the response variable, Nonce Element Length (two moras or three moras), Nonce Element Position (E1 or E2) and their interaction term as explanatory variables, Participant, E1 Item and E2 Item as random effects (intercepts).[5] The coefficients of the factors predicted by the model are shown in Table 2. The intercept here can be seen as corresponding to the "Nonce E1 + Real E2" condition where the nonce element is two moras.

[5] Putting random slopes for participants into the model did not improve its fit to the data according to the Akaike information criterion (AIC), and thus were removed from the final model presented here.

In the "Nonce E1 + Real E2" condition (the two bars on the left), the rendaku rate is slightly higher when E1 is 3 moras (gray) than when it is 2 moras (white); however, the effect of nonce E1's length turns out be not statistically significant (p=0.160; z=1.405). In the "Real E1 + Nonce E2" condition (the two bars on the right), the rendaku rate looks rather lower when E2 is 3 moras (gray) than when it is 2 moras (white); yet, here too, the effect of nonce E2's length is not significant (p=0.264; z=–1.117).[6] In other words, the main effect of Rosen's Rule is not attested regardless of the position of the nonce element.

The analysis also reveals that, overall, the likelihood of rendaku application is lower when the nonce element appears as E2 (the right two bars) than as E1 (the left two bars) with the main effect of Nonce Element Position being significant (p=0.006; z=–2.745). This indicates that speakers generally disfavor the occurrence of rendaku voicing in a nonce element that they have just encountered, as opposed to a real element that they already know, suggesting the existence of a non-alternation bias.[7]

The interaction term is not significant (p=0.077, z=–6.290). That is, the (non-)effects of the main predictors reported above do not change significantly when they are combined together.

4 Discussion and Conclusion

This study has conducted a nonce word experiment and has addressed the issue of whether Rosen's Rule (Rosen 2001, 2003) is psychologically real. The results do not strongly support the hypothesis that the rule is real and active in the minds of Japanese speakers. We need to be careful in interpreting these null experimental results, as they do not refute the hypothesis, either. It is possible, for example, that the rule's effects simply did not show up in the study's experimental settings due to some factors of which the author is not aware. We should also note, however, that some other experiments with similar designs (Kawahara and Sano 2014; Tamaoka et al. 2009) have equally failed to obtain robust evidence. Taken together, the current and previous studies suggest that Rosen's Rule has at best minimal effects in speakers' mental grammars.

Formalization of Rosen's Rule has been thorny (see Rosen 2003 for an attempt; Vance 2015a,b for criticism). One answer to the issue is that we

---

[6] This is not directly shown in Table 2. The values were obtained from another logistic regression analysis with the intercept being the "Real E1 + Nonce E2 (two moras)" condition.

[7] This may also be interpreted as a "rendaku promotion" effect by real E2. Not only did the participants know the real words presented to them (e.g. /tori/ 'bird'), they had most probably seen the rendaku forms (voiced forms) of those items in actual compounds (e.g. watari-**d**ori 'migrating-bird'). This may have facilitated accepting rendaku application in non-existing compounds with such E2 items (e.g. somoka-**d**ori 'NONCE-bird'). Also note, however, that the E2 items used in the experiment were all "rendaku waverers" (see §2.2), and thus the participants must have also seen them not undergoing rendaku in actual compounds (e.g. niwa-tori 'yard-bird; chicken').

may not need any theoretical treatment for it, on the assumption that theory and analysis in Generative Linguistics must be constructed based on productive phenomena. There has been much debate on whether some processes involving rendaku, or rendaku itself, should be considered to be problems in phonology due to their irregular and seemingly non-productive behaviors (see Kawahara 2015, 2016; Vance 2014 among others for discussion). With this background in mind, the non-significant results reported in this study can still be seen as "significant" in that they further our understanding of rendaku as well as Rosen's Rule, and may contribute to answering the question of what aspects of the phenomenon should be accounted for by phonological theory.

Acknowledgments

I am grateful to the audience at the 27th Conference on Japanese/Korean Linguistics at Sogang University, especially Yosuke Kubota, Haruo Kubozono, Shin-ichiro Sano, and Timothy Vance for comments and discussion.

References

Albright, A. and Y. Do. 2013. Three biases in learning phonological alternations. Paper presented at the 21th Manchester Phonology Meeting (MFM).

Becker, M. and J. Levine. 2013. Experigen — An Online Experiment Platform. Available at: http://becker.phonologist.org/experigen.

Coetzee, A. W. 2009. Learning lexical indexation. *Phonology* 26(1):109–145.

Irwin, M. 2009. Prosodic size and rendaku immunity. *Journal of East Asian Linguistics* 18:179–196.

Irwin, M. 2014. Rendaku lovers, rendaku haters and the logistic curve. *Japanese/Korean Linguistics*, eds. M. Giriko, N. Nagaya, A. Takemura, and J. T. Vance, vol. 22, 37–51. Stanford: CSLI Publications.

Irwin, M. 2016a. The rendaku database. *Sequential Voicing in Japanese: Papers from the NINJAL Rendaku Project*, eds. T. J. Vance and M. Irwin, no. 176 Studies in Language Companion, chap. 6, 79–106. Amsterdam and Philadelphia: John Benjamins.

Irwin, M. 2016b. Rosen's Rule. *Sequential Voicing in Japanese: Papers from the NINJAL Rendaku Project*, eds. T. J. Vance and M. Irwin, no. 176 Studies in Language Companion, chap. 7, 107–117. Amsterdam and Philadelphia: John Benjamins.

Irwin, M., M. Miyashita, and K. Russell. 2017. The rendaku database version 3.1. Available online at:
http://www-h.yamagata-u.ac.jp/~irwin/site/Rendaku_Database.html.

Kawahara, S. 2015. Can we use rendaku for phonological argumentation? Linguistics Vanguard, doi:10.1515/lingvan-2015-0001.

Kawahara, S. 2016. Psycholinguistic studies of rendaku. *Sequential Voicing in Japanese: Papers from the NINJAL Rendaku Project*, eds. T. J. Vance and M. Irwin, no. 176 Studies in Language Companion, chap. 3, 35–45. Amsterdam and Philadelphia: John Benjamins.

Kawahara, S. and S. Sano. 2014. Testing Rosen's Rule and Strong Lyman's Law. *NINJAL Research Papers* 7:111–120.

Kawahara, S. and H. Zamma. 2016. Generative treatments of rendaku and related issues. *Sequential Voicing in Japanese: Papers from the NINJAL Rendaku Project*, eds. T. J. Vance and M. Irwin, no. 176 Studies in Language Companion, chap. 2, 13–34. Amsterdam and Philadelphia: John Benjamins.

Rosen, E. 2001. *Phonological processes interacting with the lexicon: Variable and non-regular effects in Japanese phonology*. Ph.D. dissertation, University of British Columbia.

Rosen, E. 2003. Systematic irregularity in Japanese rendaku: How the grammar mediates patterned lexical exceptions. *Canadian Journal of Linguistics* 48:1–37.

Shinmura, I., ed. 2008. *Kōjien*. Japanese dictionary. Tokyo: Iwanami Shoten, 6th edn.

Tamaoka, K., M. Ihara, T. Murata, and H. Lim. 2009. Effects of first-element phonological-length and etymological-type features on sequential voicing (rendaku) of second elements. *Journal of Japanese Linguistics* 25:17–38.

Tamaoka, K. and F. Ikeda. 2010. Whiskey or bhiskey?: Influence of first element and dialect region on sequential voicing of shoochuu. *Gengo Kenkyū [Journal of the Linguistic Society of Japan]* 137:65–79.

Vance, T. J. 2014. If rendaku isn't a rule, what in the world is it? *Usage-based approaches to Japanese grammar: Towards the understanding of human language*, eds. K. Kabata and T. Ono, 137–152. Amsterdam: John Benjamins.

Vance, T. J. 2015a. Rendaku. *The Handbook of Japanese Phonetics and Phonology*, ed. H. Kubozono, Handbooks of Japanese Language and Linguistics 2, 397–441. Berlin and New York: Mouton de Gruyter.

Vance, T. J. 2015b. Rendaku no fukisokusei to Rosen no hōsoku [Rendaku's irregularities and Rosen's Rule]. *NINJAL Research Papers* 9:207–214.

Appendix

E1		E2	
2 moras	3 moras	2 moras	3 moras
heka	hamoro	hano	hasoki
heni	hasowa	hesa	hayora
hite	herate	hise	hekona
howa	hetuna	homa	hinose
kema	hisemo	honi	hosari
keso	kamasa	huno	hutune
kuya	kasoni	karo	kamore
meto	konati	kewa	kemosa
miri	kosewa	kima	kisana
moni	mekiwa	kino	kiwase
mose	misare	koni	korake
neku	mokise	kuna	kusuna
nemi	nakota	saro	samori
nesa	nesami	semo	sekora
newa	nimaya	siyu	siwato
notu	nisano	soke	sokume
nuwa	nisoke	suko	soneti
seyu	sayoki	suyo	sumoke
suno	semuri	tano	takune
taro	somasi	temi	tenika
tayo	somoka	teno	tewana
yuko	tanume	tike	timise
yumo	toneyo	tona	tonima
yuro	wasoya	tuni	tukoso

TABLE 3 Nonce words

Part VI

Pragmatics

A Pragmatic Account of Negative Island Obviation by *wa* in Japanese

HITOMI HIRAYAMA

1 Introduction

In this paper, I argue that negative island obviation by *wa* in Japanese is to be treated as a pragmatic phenomenon, rather than a semantic one. Specifically, negative questions accompanying *wa*, which I consider the realization of a contrastive topic (CT), are treated as marked questions, which have special discourse effects. The proposed analysis shares the idea that *wa* is a scale-aligner with that of Schwarz and Shimoyama (2010); however, I claim that the alignment is provided via pragmatic effects triggered by *wa*, and not by the semantics of *wa* per se.

This paper focuses on a phenomenon first reported by Schwarz and Shimoyama (2010). Example (1a) shows that a negative degree question in Japanese is infelicitous, as it is in English. In (1b), *wa* is added to the *wh*-phrase, *doredake nagaku* 'how long.' This question is felicitous and answerable. A possible answer to this question is given in (2).[1]

[1] In example sentences, the *wa* focused on in this paper is boldfaced and glossed as wa. *Wa* used as a topic marker, which is not of our interest, is glossed as a topic marker, TOP.

Japanese/Korean Linguistics 27.
Edited by Michael Barrie.

(1) a. * Taroo-wa doredake nagaku taizai simasen desita ka?
Taro-TOP how long stay didn't COP Q
(lit.) 'How long did Taro not stay there?'

b. Taroo-wa doredake nagaku-**wa** taizai simasen desita ka?
Taro-TOP how long-wa stay didn't Q
'What is the minimum length such that Taro did not stay there?'

(2) Taroo-wa [$_F$ tookakan]-**wa** taizai simasen desita.
Taro-TOP 10 days-wa stay didn't
'Taro didn't stay for 10 days.' (Taro stayed there for at most 9 days)

Why is (1b) felicitous? This is the first question this paper addresses. Since the only difference between (1a) and (1b) is *wa*, this particle should contribute to remedy the question. Consequently, it is necessary to understand why this particular particle can bring about this special effect, which can rescue negative degree questions.

The rest of this paper is structured as follows: The next section introduces a previous analysis, Schwarz and Shimoyama (2010), and its problem, as a background to the proposed analysis. I present my proposal in Section 3 and how it can solve the puzzle and overcome the problems of the previous analysis. This section also discusses some theoretical implications of the analysis. I then conclude in Section 4 and present the issues to be considered in the future research.

2 Background

2.1 The Previous Account

A negative degree question is, in general, infelicitous, as shown in (3).

(3) * How tall isn't John?

To account for the ungrammaticality of such a question, syntactic, semantic, and pragmatic accounts have been proposed (Kroch, 1989; Cinque, 1990; Szabolcsi and Zwarts, 1993; Abrusán, 2014). The account given in this papaer is pragmatic, but I will present a variant of the semantic account to introduce Schwarz and Shimoyama's previous approach to Japanese negative island obviation by *wa*.

According to this approach, a negative degree question such as in (3) is infelicitous, as it is semantically ill-formed. In other words, this type of question does not satisfy a presupposition that questions must satisfy. The presupposition is given as "Maximality Presupposition" as (4).

(4) Maximality Presupposition
A question presupposes that its Hamblin set has a maximally informative true element, i.e. a true proposition that entails all the other true propositions in the set. (Dayal, 1996)

If a degree phrase has the "exactly" semantics, we can easily see why (3) is infelicitous. Imagine that John's height is 175 cm. Then, the question in (3) cannot satisfy the presupposition (4). A proposition, *John is not (exactly) 174 cm tall* can be a true answer, and so can another proposition, *John is not (exactly) 176 cm tall.* Because of "exactly" semantics, there cannot be entailment relations among alternatives. Consequently, there cannot be a proposition that entails all the other true answers; therefore, the question ends up infelicitous. Note that the "exactly" semantics of degree phrases is not a problem if the question is positive. In that case, the question, *How tall is John?* has at most one true answer, namely, *John is 175 cm tall.* This proposition entails itself; therefore, the question satisfies the Maximality Presupposition.

Why can *wa* obviate the negative island effect? According to Schwarz and Shimoyama (2010), it is because *wa* can work as a scale-aligner, and adds *at least* semantics. In (5), we can see how the semantics of *nagaku* 'long' changes depending on whether *wa* is present.

(5) a. $[\![\text{long}]\!] = \lambda d.\lambda x.\lambda w.\ x$'s length is exactly d
b. $[\![\text{long+}\mathbf{wa}]\!] = \lambda d.\lambda x.\lambda w.\ x$'s length is $\geq d$

(5a) shows that as mentioned earlier, adjectives such as *long* have "exact" semantics by default. *Wa* modifies it changing the *exactly* part into *equal to or greater than*. This idea comes from the fact that when *wa* is interpreted as a contrastive *wa* (Kuno, 1973), which is *wa* attached to an item with phonological focus, it conveys the *at least* interpretation, as shown in (6).[2]

(6) [$_F$ Udon]-**wa** zettai tabetai.
udon-wa certainly want to eat
'I certainly want to eat udon **at least**.'

Using this, we can obtain the semantic denotation of (1b), which is a negative degree question with *wa*, as in (7).

(7) How long-**wa** did Taro not stay there?
$\rightsquigarrow$ $\lambda d.\ d$ is length, and Taro's stay was not d-long or longer

---

[2] This interpretation of contrastive *wa* has attracted much attention. See Hara (2006) and Tomioka (2009) for discussions.

Imagine that Taro stayed there for nine days. This time, we can find a proposition that entails all other true answers to the questions, namely, *Taro did not stay there for 10 days or longer.* This time, the Maximality Presupposition is met, and this question is felicitous.

2.2 Problems

The approach introduced in the previous section successfully explains why *wa* can obviate the negative island effect. With *wa*, the possible answers can be ordered according to the semantic strength, which eventually makes the question answerable. However, there are several problems to be addressed.

First, this account predicts that if we replace *wa* in the negative degree question with some lexical item that semantically means *at least*, the result is still felicitous. However, to my ears, it is not that acceptable. In (8), *saitee* 'at least'[3] is used to modify *nan-niti-kan* 'for how many days'.[4]

(8) *? Taro-wa **saitee** nan-niti-kan taizai simasen desita ka?
Taro-TOP at least what-days-for stay didn't COP Q
(lit.) 'For at least how many days did Taro not stay there?'

The semantic account does not explain why (8) is not felicitous or only *wa* can give this special effect.

Furthermore, the account does not provide a satisfactory explanation of why only a negative degree question in Japanese can be rescued in this way. If negative degree questions are infelicitous for the same reason across languages, maybe adding a lexical item that can order possible answers could rescue negative questions in other languages too. However, at least in English, it seems that *at least* cannot obviate the effect:

(9) * At least how tall isn't John?

Overall, we need an analysis that can explain why the Japanese *wa* is responsible for negative island obviation.

---

[3] Morphologically, this word is composed of two morphemes: *sai* makes a superlative, and *tei* means low. As a whole, it means the lowest.

[4] In (8), *doredake nagaku* 'how long' is replaced with *nan-niti-kan*, as *saitee* is not compatible with *how long* for some reason, which I do not discuss in this paper. Without *saitee*, question (8) is as bad as the negative question with *how long* without *wa*.

3 Proposal

The analysis proposed in this section is what I call the pragmatic approach. One crucial difference between this approach and the previous one is that *wa* does not have a truth-conditional effect. Rather, it is a pragmatic effect brought about by *wa* as a contrastive topic that makes negative island obviation possible. I will first present some theoretical assumptions I adopt in this analysis and then discuss how the obviation is explained within this analysis.

3.1 Assumptions

First, I assume that *wa* attached to the *wh*-phrase is contrastive *wa*. This particle, *wa*, is known as a topic marker that marks an aboutness topic in Japanese. However, in the sentences we are interested, what is marked by *wa* is unlikely to be such a topic. In addition, as briefly mentioned in the previous section, the *at least* interpretation is only available when *wa* is construed as a contrastive topic. It is difficult to determine the status of *wa* attached to a *wh*-phrase since it is inherently focused, but as long as we focus on *wa* attached to a *wh* degree phrase, it would not be unreasonable to consider it as a contrastive *wa*.[5]

Furthermore, contrastive *wa* is regarded as the realization of a contrastive topic (CT) in Japanese in this paper. It is true that as argued in the literature, such as Oshima (forthcoming), contrastive *wa* in Japanese and CTs in English or German discussed in Büring (2003) or Constant (2014) show some distinct behavior. However, they are treated on a par in this paper in terms of their role in accessing the structured discourse (Büring, 2003; Constant, 2014), which is built based on Questions under Discussion (QuDs: Roberts (1996, 2012)). Contrastive topics are tools to exhibit a certain discourse structure that the interlocutors in the discourse are trying to entertain.

Finally, degree predicates do not have *exactly* semantics but have the standard *at least* semantics here. That is, *John is 175 cm tall* is true if and only if John is 175 cm tall or taller.

3.2 A Pragmatic Analysis

As mentioned, the proposed analysis is pragmatic in that it does not give a truth-conditional difference to the denotation of *wa*. Instead, *wa* is special in a particular sense that it projects a special discourse structure. I will first introduce the contribution of *wa* and then illustrate how it triggers negative island obviation.

The function of *wa*

The analysis uses continuations (Barker and Shan, 2015; Barker, 2001). The idea is that a natural language expression can be considered a function from

[5] It would be harder to determine the status of *wa* attached to *who* or *what*. Kinjo (2017), for instance, argues that *wa* attached to those *wh*-phrases should be analyzed as thematic *wa*.

its surrounding context (continuation) to the truth value. For instance, taking up an NP, which is of type e, its continuation is et, which misses an element of type e to get a truth value. In the same way, a continuation of a verb phrase with an intransitive verb *sneeze*, for instance, is $(et)t$. A continuation of a phrase XP is also written as c_{XP}.

Within this framework, I treat *wa* as a special type-shifter, which "continuizes" an element attached to it. That is, *wa* takes an XP and makes it a function on its surrounding context to the truth-value. The ordinary semantic value of *wa* can be represented as in (10), where σ is a semantic type.

(10) $[\![\text{wa}]\!]^o = \lambda X_\sigma . \lambda c_{\sigma t} . c(X)$

Note that *wa* does not change the outcome of the semantic composition in any way. It just changes the way of the composition.

I now examine the focus semantic value, as this is where contrastive *wa* plays a crucial role in projecting a discourse structure. The process illustrated by the denotation of focus semantic value below is essentially the same as the Topic Abstraction proposed by Constant (2014). In the focus semantic value, everything is treated as a set; therefore, the semantic type of X, which is the item attached to *wa*, is σt, and the semantic type of its continuation is $(\sigma t)t$. Note that the underlined part in (11) is processed via Pointwise Functional Application (Rooth, 1985, 1996).

(11) $[\![\text{wa}]\!]^f = \lambda X_{\sigma t} . \lambda c_{(\sigma t)t} . \{\underline{c(\{x\})} | x \in D_{\sigma t}\}$

In this case too, *wa* continuizes the item attached to it, X, and this time, it makes a set of sets of propositions using the continuation and members of the set denoted by X.

Applying this semantics to a degree phrase such as *doredake nagaku* 'how long', we can obtain the semantics of *doredake nagaku wa* 'how long + *wa*'. (12) shows the denotations of *doredake nagaku* 'how long' with and without *wa*.

(12) *doredake nagaku* 'how long' with and without *wa*

a. $[\![\text{how long}]\!]^f = \lambda c_{\text{DegP}} . \underline{c_{\text{DegP}}(\{d | d \in D_{\text{Deg}}\})}$

b. $[\![\text{how long-wa}]\!]^f = \lambda c_{\text{DegP}} . \{\underline{c_{\text{DegP}}(\{d\})} | d \in D_{\text{Deg}}\}$

Here, c_{DegP} is of type $(dt)t$, which looks like $\{\lambda d.\text{Taro stayed } d\text{-long}\}$. Applying this continuation as the argument of the functions in (12), we can obtain two different focus semantic values for two kinds of questions, as in (13).

(13) a. How long did Taro not stay there?
$\rightsquigarrow$ {Taro not stayed there d-long}
$\rightsquigarrow$ {Taro not stayed there 1 day-long,
Taro not stayed there 2 day-long, ...}
b. How long+**wa** did Taro not stay there?
$\rightsquigarrow$ {{Taro not stayed there d-long}:d is duration}
$\rightsquigarrow$ {{Taro not stayed there 1 day-long},
{Taro not stayed there 2 day-long},
{Taro not stayed there 3 day-long}, ...}

The question without *wa* (13a) has a standard denotation of questions; a set of possible answers. By contrast, with *wa*, the result is a set of singleton sets of propositions. I assume the singleton set of proposition is the denotation of polar questions. Consequently, (13b) can be read as "for each d, is it the case that Taro stayed there that long?," which basically seeks the same amount of information as the question (13a) does.

Obviation of negative islands by discourse structure

In the previous section, I illustrated that the proposed denotation of *wa* creates a nested focus semantic value, albeit it does not change the amount of information it seeks. This section demonstrates how it leads to negative island obviation.

I argue here that the motivation for which a speaker adds *wa* to the question is not semantic, but pragmatic. That is, they do not add *wa* to convey that they seek different information than with the question without *wa*. Rather, the addition of *wa* throws in extra pragmatic information by projecting the discourse structure that would be useful for seeking the answer strategically. In this sense, the question with *wa* can be considered a type of biased questions, and accordingly, has a special discourse effect.

The term, *discourse effects*, comes from Farkas and Roelofsen (2017). They argue that discourse effects are of two types: basic and special. For instance, a polar question and a tag question in English (14) share the same basic discourse effect; however the latter has special effects in addition to it.

(14) a. Is it raining?
b. It is raining, isn't it?

The basic effect shared by these two questions is to make a question about whether it is raining an immediate QuD in the discourse (or to put p and $\neg p$ on the Table, using the terminology in Farkas and Bruce (2010)). However, the two kinds of questions are felicitously used in a different context. A special effect exclusive to tag questions explains why it is so. A special effect of tag questions is that the speaker has moderate to high credence to the truth of the highlighted proposition, which is in this case, *It is raining*. By contrast, a polar question (14a) does not carry such a bias. Consequently, in a context where a speaker is not supposed to have any bias, only (14a) is felicitous.

The idea is that marked interrogatives have this kind of additional discourse effect. In the case of English, an interrogative sentence in (14a) is unmarked or default, while (14b) can be considered as marked. In English, marked polar interrogatives convey evidenced commitment and the degree of the commitment simultaneously. Japanese too has a variety of marked polar questions (see Sudo (2013) and Hirayama (2019, Chapter 4)) , which convey rich information on context using particles. I argue that a negative degree question with *wa* is not an exception. Adding *wa* to a *how long* question is also a way to make a marked question and triggers a special discourse effect.

What then is the special effect brought by *wa*? I propose that it is projecting a particular discourse structure that is used to resolve the QuD in the context. Recall that when *wa* is present, a *how long* question is construed as a set of polar questions. When we have *wa* attached to a degree phrase, I assume that polar questions are ordered so that it goes from a smaller degree to a larger degree, as illustrated in (15).

(15)

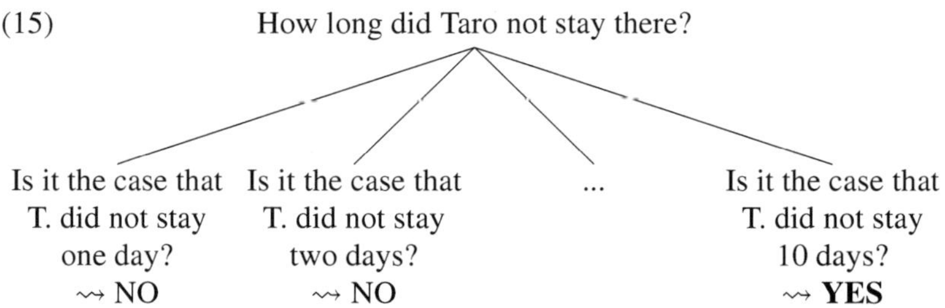

By using *wa*, the person who asks the degree question can inform the addressee that going through the polar questions one by one would be a good way to reach the answer to the question. By going over polar questions, first the addressee keeps having *no* answers. Imagine that the length of Taro's stay was nine days. The answer to the question, *Is it the case that Taro did not stay one day?* is *No*. So is the answer to the question when d equals two. When d is ten, the answer to the polar question becomes *Yes* for the first time, and by entailment, after that, the answer continues to be yes. Cooperative addressees assume that it is the most informative to give the d, from which the answer changed from no to yes, and give it as an answer to the question.

Note that the proposed analysis shares the idea that *wa* aligns answers to the question with Schwarz and Shimoyama's. In the discourse tree (15), each polar question is ordered by degrees. The difference is that the semantics of *wa* itself is not responsible for ordering. Rather, ordering is done in the process of generating a discourse structure projected by a special discourse effect triggered by contrastive *wa*.

3.3 Outcomes

Contrast between *wa* and *saitee* 'at least'

This pragmatic analysis has several good outcomes. The first and probably most important outcome is that it can account for why only *wa* but not *saitee* 'at least' can obviate negative islands. The minimal pair is given below as (16).

(16) a. ✓ Taro-wa nan-niti-kan-**wa** taizai simasen desita ka?
Taro-TOP what-days-for-**wa** stay didn't COP Q
(lit.) 'How many days-wa did Taro not stay there?'

b. *? Taro-wa **saitee** nan-niti-kan taizai simasen desita ka?
Taro-TOP at least what-days-for stay didn't COP Q
(lit.) 'For at least how many days did Taro not stay there?'

A challenge for the semantic approach is to explain the contrast between (16a-b). As mentioned earlier, the two sentences are supposed to have the same acceptability according to the semantic analysis. However, the prediction is not borne out. By contrast, the proposed analysis can explain the contrast, as *wa* and *saitee* do not have the same pragmatic effect. *Wa* itself does not have *at least* semantics and it is a discourse effect specifically associated with the lexical item that enables negative island obviation with a special discourse structure. *Saitee*, on the other hand, does not have power to manipulate such a discourse structure, and consequently, cannot obviate negative island effects. This also explains that why we do not observe a similar effect in negative degree questions with *at least* in other languages. The obviation effect is closely tied to a language-specific pragmatic effect.

In fact, suggestive evidence shows inferences triggered by contrastive *wa* and words such as *saitee* 'at least' are different. Items such as *at least* in English can convey ignorance inferences, which is an inference that the speaker does not know the exact number (Geurts and Nouwen, 2007; Nouwen, 2010). We can obtain a similar result with Japanese *sukunakutomo* 'at least' and contrastive *wa*, as shown in (17).

(17) a. [$_F$ Udon]-**wa** zettai tabetai.
udon-wa certainly want to eat

b. Sukunakutomo [$_F$ udon]-o zettai tabetai.
at least udon-ACC certainly want to eat
'I certainly want to eat udon **at least**, (but I am not sure what else I want to eat).

However, experimental results show that ignorance inferences from (17a-b) are likely to be obtained through different mechanisms (Hirayama and Brasoveanu, 2018). That is, *sukunakutomo* unambiguously delivers ignorance inferences while *wa* is sensitive to the discourse structure entertained by the interlocutors. Overall, if the negative island obviation is explained by the contribution of discourse structure, the contrast between the two in the ability to obviate negative island effects can be explained as a direct consequence of their different ability to access discourse structure.

In addition, this analysis can explain why using *saitee* or *sukunakutomo* 'at least' is infelicitous even in answering the question with *wa*. Under the semantic analysis, an answer with *saitee* is included as a member of the set of propositions denoted by the degree question with *wa*. Consequently, it would be predicted that using *saitee* would be no problem. However, if you are asked questions with *wa*, the most natural way to answer them is to use *wa* in the answer, too. Given that interrogatives with *wa* project special discourse structure, the use of *wa* in the answer can be construed as acknowledgement of the projected discourse structure. The discourse effects of *wa* proposed here can also be applied to declarative sentences with *wa* and project the similar nested discourse structure. Again, as *saitee* or *sukunakutomo* cannot project discourse structure, using them in the answer to the *wa* question would be taken to be infelicitous.

Negative island obviation in other contexts

This pragmatic analysis predicts that negative questions can be rescued as long as there is a certain scale that can guide an addressee, so that they can find a point from which answers change from no to yes and keep being yes. One example is negative questions with manner adverbials, such as in (18).

(18) Taro-wa donna-huu-ni-*(**wa**) eigo-o hanasemasen ka?
Taro-TOP which-way-in-WA English-ACC cannot speak Q
'How can Taro not speak English?'

(19) a. ✓ Taro cannot speak English [like a native speaker]-*wa*.
⇝ Taro's fluency does not exceed the level of native speakers (but better than the average Japanese)

b. ✗ Taro cannot speak English [typing on his computer]-*wa*.

Using *wa* in this question signals that there is a certain scale to be used to describe Taro's proficiency of English. As a result, it is possible to answer saying (19a), since it is easy to see the phrase *like a native speaker* is located somewhere on a scale of his English fluency. By contrast, the answer in (19b) sounds odd out of the blue since the proficiency in languages is not usually evaluated by seeing whether the speaker can speak the language typing on his computer. (19b) could be acceptable, if it is clear from the context that typing imposes a heavy cognitive load and whether a person can speak a language and type is a good indication of the proficiency of the language. From the contrast in (19), we can see that the discourse structure ordered by entailment is crucial for capturing the nature of this obviation phenomena.

With another example, we can see that pragmatic negative island obviation in Japanese is different from a similar phenomenon reported in English (Abrusán, 2014).

(20) How many apples does none of these women have?

(21) a. dono onna-no-hito-mo nanko-*(wa) ringo-o motte imasen
each women how many-WA apple-ACC not have
ka?
Q
'How many apples does no woman not have?'

b. zyuk-ko-wa motte imasen
10-CL-WA not have
'No women has 10 apples or more.

Example (20) is usually construed as an infelicitous question in English. However, Abrusán (2014, 12) reports that when a very detailed but not very plausible context is set, this question could be acceptable.[6] The context is as follows: you need to know none of the women under discussion has ten apples or more. In addition, it has to be the case that for any number smaller than ten, at least one of the relevant women has exactly that number of apples. In other words, if the answer is ten, we need to have at least nine women and each of them have a different number of apples, which is a very implausible context if this question is given out of the blue.

The example in (21a) is infelicitous without *wa*. To my ears, setting the context that can make (20) felicitous does not help make (21a) without *wa* acceptable. Adding *wa* makes the question felicitous, but we do not need such an intricate context introduced earlier. Let us say the number of apples held by each woman is at most 9. In this context, the answer to the question (21) can be given by saying (21b), using *wa* with the numeral. This answer can be given using the same mechanism proposed in the previous section. In conclusion, even when context can help negative questions, the rescue is executed differently in Japanese and in English.

[6] The sentence I use here is modified from the original. The original sentence is *How many children does none of these women have?*. I changed *children* to *apples* since it is not possible to paraphrase the sentence in Japanese using a verb that directly corresponds to *have* in English.

CTs with *wh*-questions and special *wh*-questions

Lastly, note that the proposed analysis and the result it obtained bring us interesting theoretical implications. Constant (2014) briefly discusses *wh*-questions with CTs. His Topic Abstraction is practically compatible with *wh*-questions, and he already noted that *wh*-questions with and without a CT have different focus semantic values (Constant, 2014, p.113). He notes:

> Additional research is needed to test whether languages clearly distinguish between the meanings in (73), and if so, whether such distinctions are encoded via CT marking.

His (73) is the minimal pair of *who* questions with and without a CT, as follows:

(22) a. Who came? $\rightsquigarrow$ {Fred came, Mary came, ...}
b. Who$_{CT}$ came?$\rightsquigarrow$ {{Fred came}, {Mary came},...}

The quotation from his dissertation poses two questions. The first is whether languages clearly distinguish the *wh*-questions with and without a CT. Japanese gives a partial yes answer to this question. I would say "partially" because as I have emphasized, although the two questions in (22) are used clearly differently in Japanese, the differences are not semantic. However, the pragmatic effect is sufficiently powerful to make otherwise infelicitous questions felicitous. However, the second question has a clear positive answer, examining Japanese; the presence of *wa* clearly distinguishes two kinds of questions.

Furthermore, this paper showed that not only marked polar questions but also marked constituent questions are associated with special discourse effects in Japanese. Research on marked polar questions has revealed that they convey the speakers' bias in many languages, including English and Japanese (Farkas and Roelofsen, 2017; Sudo, 2013). By contrast, marked constituent questions are not as common or popular as polar ones. Questions accompanying contrastive *wa* in Japanese can enable a better understanding of marked constituent questions in other languages (if they have any).

4 Conclusions

In this paper, I argued that negative island obviation by *wa* can be explained pragmatically. As opposed to a semantic approach, which regards that *wa* adds *at least* semantics, it was shown that it is a special discourse effect tied to this specific type of marked question that makes negative island obviation possible. The special effect of the *wa* question is, I argue, to project a nested discourse structure to be entertained by the interlocutors. The discourse structure is going to be a set of polar questions, which are pragmatically ordered by degrees. Going over such ordered alternatives makes it easier to determine the point where the answer to the question changes from negative to positive.

More research is necessary to determine if there is anything similar to negative island obviation in Japanese. In other words, a special discourse strategy that is powerful enough to rescue otherwise infelicitous questions felicitous. Constant (2014) reports that a Mandarin particle *ne* is a realization of CT of the language and is compatible with the *wh*-word. Although *wa* and *ne* do not seem to be exactly the same, examining languages that have CT particles such as Japanese is the first thing I can do to obtain a better understanding of this phenomenon.

Finally, the exact status of the focus semantic value should be explored further. It has the name focus "semantic" value; therefore, if we have two different ones, it is reasonable to think that there are "semantic" differences. However, the information sought by questions with and without *wa* is essentially the same, and the difference lies in of discourse structure. Then, is the discourse structure part of the semantics? It is well accepted that QuDs, on which discourse structure is based, affect the interpretation of various items. Further research should examine how we can assemble those pieces together.

References

Abrusán, Márta. 2014. *Weak Island Semantics*. Oxford University Press.

Barker, Chris. 2001. Introducing Continuations. In R. Hastings, B. Jackson, and Z. Zvolenszky, eds., *Proceedings of SALT IX*, pages 20–35. Ithaca, NY: Cornell University.

Barker, Chris and Chung-Chieh Shan. 2015. *Continuations and Natural Language*. Oxford University Press.

Büring, Daniel. 2003. On D-Trees, Beans, and B-Accents. *Linguistics and Philosophy* 26:511–545.

Cinque, Guglielmo. 1990. *Types of A'-dependencies*. Cambridge: MIT Press.

Constant, Noah. 2014. *Contrastive Topics: Meanings and Realizations*. PhD thesis, University of Massachusetts Amherst.

Dayal, Veneeta. 1996. *Locality in wh quantification*. Dordrecht: Kluwer.

Farkas, Donka F. and Kim B. Bruce. 2010. On reacting to assertions and polar questions. *Journal of Semantics* 27(1):81–118.

Farkas, Donka F. and Floris Roelofsen. 2017. Division of labor in the interpretation of declaratives and interrogatives. *Journal of Semantics* 34(2):237–289.

Geurts, Bart and Rick Nouwen. 2007. At least et al. *Language* 83(3):533–559.

Hara, Yurie. 2006. *Japanese Discourse Items at Interfaces*. PhD thesis, University of Delaware.

Hirayama, Hitomi. 2019. *Asking and Answering Questions: Discourse Strategies in Japanese*. PhD thesis, University of California, Santa Cruz.

Hirayama, Hitomi and Adrian Brasoveanu. 2018. Expressing Ignorance in Japanese: Contrastive *wa* versus *sukunakutomo*. *Journal of Cognitive Science* 19(3):331–355.

Kinjo, Kunio. 2017. The Wh-wa Question in Japanese -Topicalized Wh and De-stressed Focus. Talk at WAFL 13.

Kroch, Anthony. 1989. Amount quantification, referentiality, and long wh-movement. *University of Pennsylvania Working Papers in Linguistics* 5(2).

Kuno, Susumu. 1973. *The Structure of the Japanese Language*. Cambridge: MIT Press.

Nouwen, Rick. 2010. Two kinds of modified numerals. *Semantics & Pragmatics* 3:1–41.

Oshima, David Y. forthcoming. The English rise-fall-rise contour and the Japanese contrastive particle wa: A uniform account. In *Japanese/Korean Linguistics*, vol. 26. Stanford: CSLI Publications.

Roberts, Craige. 1996. Information Structure in Discourse: Towards an Integrated Formal Theory of Pragmatics. In J. H. Yoon and A. Kathol, eds., *OSUWPL Volume 49: Papers in Semantics*. The Ohio State University.

Roberts, Craige. 2012. Information Structure in Discourse: Towards an Integrated Formal Theory of Pragmatics. *Semantics & Pragmatics* 5(6):1–69.

Rooth, Mats. 1985. *Association with Focus*. Ph.D. thesis, University of Massachusetts, Amherst.

Rooth, Mats. 1996. Focus. In S. Lappin, ed., *The Handbook of Contemporary Semantic Theory*, pages 271–297. Blackwell.

Schwarz, Bernhard and Junko Shimoyama. 2010. Negative Islands and Obviation by *Wa* in Japanese Degree Questions. *Proceedings of SALT* 20:1–18.

Sudo, Yasutada. 2013. Biased Polar questions in English and Japanese. In D. Gutzmann and H.-M. Gaertner, eds., *Beyond Expressives: Explorations in Use-Conditional Meaning*, vol. Current Research in the Semantics/Pragmatics Interface (CRiSPI) 28. Brill.

Szabolcsi, Anna and Frans Zwarts. 1993. Weak islands and an algebraic semantics for scope taking. *Natural Language Semantics* 1(235-284).

Tomioka, Satoshi. 2009. Contrastive topics operate on speech acts. In M. Zimmermann and C. Fèry, eds., *Information Structure: Theoretical, Typological, and Experimental Perspectives*, pages 115–138. Oxford University Press.

Unpacking the Functions of the Epistemic Response Token *Kulekey* in Interaction

MARY SHIN KIM

SUE Y. YOON

University of Hawai'i at Mānoa

1 Introduction

In line with a growing body of recent empirical research on specific sequential and interactional contexts of Korean response tokens (Young & Lee 2004; Oh & Park 2017), this paper examines the use of the Korean response token *kulekey* in interaction. According to Rhee (2015), *kulekey* has undergone a series of semantic changes from its source meaning 'at (it) being so' to a current meaning of 'right', along with changes in its form, as in (1).

(1) Rhee 2015: 18

kulaha-ki-ey	>	kulaha-kiey>	kulek(i)ey	>	kulekey
'at (it) being so'		'because of (it) being so'	'so, therefore'		'right'

The source construction of *kulekey* consists of three elements: *kulehata*, an adjective meaning 'to be so', 'to be like that'; *-ki*, a nominalizer; and *-ey*, a locative particle.

Japanese/Korean Linguistics 27.
Edited by Michael Barrie.

Studies have proposed that *kulekey* (often translated as '(That's) right') functions to display the listener's agreement (Ahn & Yap 2013; Rhee 2015) and sympathy (An 2012; Jo 2017), as in (2).

(2) An 2012: 108

A: ya ne cincca olaykanman-i-ta!
hey you really long.time-be-DC
'Long time no see.'

B: **kulekey!**
kulekey
'Right (long time no see).'

Although prior studies have adequately shown that *kulekey* expresses a recipient's affiliative stance, the degree of commitment it indicates compared to other agreement tokens (e.g. *kulem*, *kulssey*, *kulenikka*) remains unclear. According to Rhee (2015), many agreement tokens in Korean, including *kulekey* are derived from the same adjective, *kulehata*, and they are all markers of agreement that can be roughly translated as 'right'.

(3) *Kule*-type response tokens (Rhee 2015: 14, 18)

	kulekey	
	kulssey	
kulehata	*kulem*	'right'
'to be so'	*kulenikka*	
	kulehkomalko	

However, these tokens are not interchangeable, which raises the question of how they differ. Of particular interest are the differences between *kulekey* and *kulssey*, as both are derived from the combination of the adjective *kulehata* with a nominalizer (*ki*, *ssay*).

Furthermore, some studies have claimed that rather than being purely affiliative, *kulekey* can also serve to display a hesitant or evasive stance (An 2012; Jo 2017). An (2012) provided the example in (4), where *kulekey* allows B to avoid apologizing or accepting blame for being late.

(4) An 2012: 113

A: ne-n onul-to tto cikak-i-kwuna.
you-TOP today-also again be.late-be-UNASSIM
'You are late again today.'

B: **kulekey-yo.**
kulekey-POL
'KULEKEY'

Utilizing a conversation analytic perspective and analyzing naturally occurring instances of *kulekey*, this paper seeks to provide a clearer picture of when and how *kulekey* is used in interaction and to reconcile the diverging views of its functions.

2 Data and Methodology

The analysis is based on twenty-seven instances of *kulekey* found in nineteen different telephone calls (570 minutes) from the Linguistic Data Consortium Korean Corpus of Telephone Speech, nineteen instances of *kulekey* found in seventeen broadcast interviews (177 minutes), and five instances from five video recorded multiparty interactions (134 minutes) among speakers of Korean from the authors' own data collections. The study's conversation analytic approach focuses on examining how participants in interaction compose and position turns at talk so as to realize specific actions (Schegloff 2007).

3 *Kulekey*'s Sequential and Interactional Environments

An examination of the data shows that *kulekey* commonly occurs in two environments. First, it routinely occurs in response to a speaker's assertion that describes a state of affairs or makes an assessment, which makes acknowledgement or agreement in the next turn relevant. Second, *kulekey* is frequently produced as a response to a double-barreled question. In both environments, *kulekey* serves as more than a mere marker of agreement. We will show how *kulekey* is used in these two environments as a resource for indexing and/or negotiating the recipient's epistemic and affiliative stances.

3.1 Assertion Sequences

Excerpt 1 comes from a face-to-face talk between Mia (M) and Jun (J), who are watching a soccer match between Germany and Sweden on TV. The segment begins with the sportscaster (S) providing a detailed description of the German players' technique.

Excerpt 1 Soccer

1 S: ca tokil-un khulosu-ka koyngcanghi nac-ko
DM Germany-TOP cross-NOM very low-and

2 ppalu-key phaysuha-tusi ollawa-yo.
fast-ADV pass-as.if go.up-POL
'See, German players cross the ball very low and fast as if they pass it.'

3 kuke-l cosimhay-ya toy-yo.
that-ACC careful-should-POL
'One needs to watch out for that.'

4 nophi an ha-pnita.
high NEG do-DEF
'They don't pass it high.'

5 weynmanhayse-n nophi an [ttaylye-yo.]
unless.necessary-TOP high NEG hit-POL
'Unless absolutely necessary, they don't pass it high.'

6 M: [kulekey:.]
'KULEKEY:.'

7 sweydeyn-hako toykey talu-**ta:.**
Sweden-with really different DC
'(Oh) Their style is very different from Sweden.'

8 J: ung.
'Yeah.'

9 M: heli wi-lo cal an ollaka-n-**ta:**. kong-i.
waist above-to well NEG go.up-PRS-DC ball-NOM
'(Oh) It does not go above their waist. The ball.'

As the sportscaster describes the German players' technique (lines 1–5), Mia responds with *kulekey* (line 6). The use of *kulekey* here displays not only her agreement, but a change in her epistemic stance. A rough translation of this instance of *kulekey* might be: 'Oh, yeah, they don't pass the ball high.' Thus, *kulekey* here displays that, while listening to the sportscaster's comments, Mia is in the process of registering or realizing the matter of these comments to be true. What follows *kulekey* further demonstrates that a change occurred in the recipient's knowledge state. Mia continues with her own observation and assessment that the German and Swedish players' techniques are indeed different (lines 7, 9). Further, in these lines she uses the sentence ending *-ta*, which, according to Lee (1991), is often deployed in delivering newly perceived information in the immediate environment.

Taken together, the resources Mia deploys in her turn suggest that *kulekey* displays agreement while also marking the speaker's epistemic position as lower than that of the prior speaker, as she has just realized something of which she was not previously aware.

It is important to note that, unlike the English 'oh', *kulekey* is not simply a change-of-state token (Heritage 1984). It has the lexical meaning of 'Yeah (that's right.)', displaying the recipient's agreement toward the matter at hand, and it simultaneously indexes the recipient's epistemic and affiliative stances.

Excerpt 2 also shows the function of *kulekey* of displaying agreement from a lower epistemic position. Here, A and B are talking about a mutual friend's marital problems.

Excerpt 2 [KO_5637]

1 A: kuleh-key hay-se com ccacungpwuli-myen:
be.so-ADV do-and a.little annoyed-if

2 namphyen-i sepsephay-se:,
husband-NOM disappointed-and
'If she gets annoyed (with her husband for giving her mother-in-law money), then her husband gets disappointed, and.'

3 B: ung.
'Yeah.'

4 A: ung? kuleko. mak kulen yayki [( ) --]
right and DM such story
'Right? And, such story-'

5 B: [kuke] mwe yensokkuk kathu-ta?
that DM soap.opera like-DC
'It is like a soap opera.'

6 A: kulekey::
'KULEKEY::'

7 B: ung.
'Yeah.'

8 A: kulaykaciko nay-ka kuke ttak tut-kose,
so I-NOM that exactly listen-after
'So, after I heard that,'

While A, as the story teller, is still in the course of telling the story, B, as the story recipient, makes an assessment of the situation: 'it is like a soap opera' (line 5). This assessment is slightly disaligned from A's main storytelling in several aspects. First, A is still in the midst of the storytelling, and the assessment occurs a bit earlier than expected. An assessment makes an agreement or disagreement in the next turn relevant, and this one therefore makes A suspend her unfolding story. In addition, while A tells the story from the friend's perspective, emphasizing how troubling and stressful it is for her, B's assessment ('like a soap opera') views the matter from a different angle. In line 6, A responds to this assessment with *kulekey*. This *kulekey* is delivered with marked prosody (:: marks a rising intonation contour), which not only displays A's consensus with B's assessment, but also A's subordinate epistemic position, as it indicates that she only came to understand this aspect of the story after B brought it up. Once the assessment sequence closes, A resumes her suspended story from line 8.

Although in lines 1–2 and 4, speaker A plays the role of primary informer (i.e., the speaker with epistemic primacy), when A responds with *kulekey* to B's assessment, their epistemic positions are reversed in that moment of the talk. Thus, while Excerpt 1 shows a case of given asymmetric epistemic positions between an expert and a nonexpert, Excerpt 2 demonstrates a case wherein the epistemic positions of the speaker and the recipient shift in the course of the interaction. This difference between the two excerpts demonstrates that *kulekey* does not simply mark the given knowledge state of the participants, but can be actively used by participants to adjust their epistemic stance according to emerging variables in the course of an interaction.

To consider how *kulekey* can fulfill these two functions (marking agreement and at the same time indexing a lower epistemic position), we looked at its source construction. The nominalizer *ki* describes an action, event, or situation yet to be realized (Sohn 1999: 321), and the locative particle *-ey* marks a movement toward a goal or destination.

-ki
an action/event yet to be realized

-ey
goal marker

↘ ↙

-key
denotes a realization in the speaker's knowledge state

The combined form *-key* represents a realization in the recipient's knowledge state: The matter a prior speaker just brought up is now becoming a factual piece of information to the recipient. It is through this denoting of that process of realization in the recipient's knowledge state that *kulekey* conveys the recipient's subordinate epistemic position compared to the prior speaker. Simultaneously, the deictic *kule-* 'to be like that' takes up the assertion of the prior turn anaphorically, expressing agreement with it.

Note how such usage of *kulekey* distinguishes it from another agreement token, *kulssey*, as shown in Excerpt 3, which comes from a telephone call between two friends.[1] The segment centers on visa problems when entering the US. Note how speaker B repeatedly deploys *kulssey* whenever she discloses her knowledge of what speaker A is talking about.

Excerpt 3 [KO_6773]

1 A: o: kuttay ettehkey nawa-ss-e? =
oh that.time how come-PST-Q
'Oh, how did you enter (the US) last time?'

2 = salam-tul ta: [pica-] ceki mwe-ya?
people-PL all visa DM what-be:Q
'All the people, (due to) visa, what is it?'

3 B: [e.]
'Yeah.'

4 **>kulssey** pica ttaymwuney< [mwe ku] tongney mos nao-n
kulssey visa due.to DM that neighbor NEG come-RL
'KULSSEY, due to visa (problems), many of the neighbors could not enter (the US),'

5 A: [e::]
'Yeah.'

6 B: [salam manh-tamay?]
people many-you.said
'You said (that).'

7 A: [yeki wuli kyohoy]. sopra- soprano:,
here our church sopra- soprano
'Yeah, the sopra- soprano in our church here,'

8 **B:** **<kulssey**, ku pwun acikto mos nawa-ss-e?
kulssey that person still NEG come-PST-Q

9 kuttay yaykihay-ss-canh-a caki-ka.
that.time talk-PST-you.know-IE you-NOM
'KULSSEY, that person still could not enter (the US)? You told me about her last time.'

[1] HyeYoung Smith and Mary Shin Kim (2019) discussed the function of *kulssey* in this data segment at the 2019 IPrA conference.

In lines 1–4, while A is still searching for words to explain others' visa problems, B formulates the utterance A is having trouble with. B can do so because A has already told her about the matter (line 6, 'You said that.'). Here, B prefaces her response with *kulssey* (line 4). Again in line 7, when A begins to provide a more detailed example of someone who had a visa problem, a soprano in her church, B rushes (as shown by the angle bracket at the beginning of line 8) to disclose that she already knows about the soprano's case, again because A herself had told her about it. Sure enough, B prefaces her turn with *kulssey*. Both of these *kulssey*-prefaced turns serve to alert the prior speaker that the recipient knows about the matter the prior speaker is referring to, so she can *get to the point* and leave out unnecessary preambles (e.g. explaining her neighbors' situation). As Excerpt 3 shows, unlike *kulekey*, *kulssey* is used when the recipient claims and competes for epistemic rights over the matter at hand (Smith & Kim 2019).[2]

3.2 Double-barreled Question Sequences

As previously mentioned, some prior studies have claimed that *kulekey* displays an evasive stance. However, in Excerpts 1 and 2 there is no sign of evasiveness:

Excerpt 1

S: 'Unless absolutely necessary, (Germans) [don't pass (the ball) high.'
M: ***[kulekey:.***

Excerpt 2

B: 'It is like a soap opera.'
A: ***kulekey::***

Kulekey in these two cases displays agreement to what was said in a prior turn from a lower epistemic position, but does not convey an evasive stance. Where then does this idea of this response token's evasiveness come from?

What we found is that it is not so much *kulekey* itself but a specific sequential and interactional environment in which *kulekey* occurs that contributes to the sense of evasiveness: in response to a double-barreled question.

According to Schegloff (2007: 76–77), questions may simply request information, but they serve to conduct other actions as well. For instance, 'Would you like a cup of coffee?' does not merely ask, but also offers:

---

[2]Questions remain regarding whether the functional differences between *kulekey* and *kulssey* (*kul(ehal)-ssay-ey*) derive from the differences between the two nominalizers *ki* and *ssay*.

Q: Would you like a cup of coffee?
A: **Yes,** **thank you.**
(Format) **(Action)**

In the response, 'yes' answers the question (format), while 'thank you' responds to the offer (action). Such double-barreled questions commonly elicit responses in this order; that is, first the format, and then the action.

Let's look at another example of a double-barreled question in an interaction between a director and an actor,[3] in which the question receives an answer but the underlying action does not get a response.

DIR: 'Hey, why are you still holding me?'
ACT: ***kulekey-yo*** **Ø.** ((The actor continues to hold the director in his arms.))
(Format) **(Action)**

'Why are you still holding me?' is not simply a question that seeks information, but a request that the actor completes a specific action: letting the director go. The response of *kulekey-yo* (*kulekey*-politeness marker) displays the actor's realization of the director's point (meaning something like, 'Oh, yeah, I am still holding you'), but the actor does not take the physical action of letting the director go. With *kulekey*, the recipient endorses the proposition in the prior speaker's utterance, but without necessarily endorsing the action or project that underlies the utterance. We suggest that such responses—that is, of *kulekey* by itself with no further response to the underlying action—may be one of the reasons *kulekey* has been proposed to display an evasive stance.[4]

Excerpt 4 provides an example of how *kulekey* is used in response to a double-barreled question during a face-to-face talk between the same couple in Excerpt 1. Mia is in the room next to the room where Jun is watching a soccer game on TV.

---

[3]This segment is from a 29-second film called *Kulekeyyo*. Although this is scripted data, we include it as an example of a double-barreled question in which the underlying action is a request for an embodied action.

[4]Although *kulekey* conveying an evasive stance mainly occurs in response to double-barreled questions in our data, it can also be observed in statements that perform another layer of action, as in Example (4). When the recipient in (4) responds with *kulekey*, she concurs with the simple informational statement (i.e. that she is late), rather than responding to the underlying action of complaint (e.g. by apologizing or pledging not to be late again); thus, overall, her response conveys evasiveness.

Excerpt 4 Shelf

1 M: ceke way an hay cwu-nya?
that why NEG do.something.for.me-Q
'Why haven't they installed the (shelf) for us?'

2 J: kulekey. ((Jun looks at Mia while he responds.))
'KULEKEY.'

3 ((Jun continues watching the soccer game.))

In line 1, Mia makes a negative observation, using a question as a way of initiating a complaint that the landlord has not yet installed a shelf. Jun responds, neutrally, with *kulekey*. By doing so, he concurs with what Mia has noticed (the shelf remains uninstalled) without joining her in the action of complaining or providing any explanation for why the shelf has not been installed. He continues to watch the soccer game with no further response.

Excerpt 5 provides another example of the use of *kulekey* in response to a double-barreled question. The question occurs during an interview between a reporter and a singer who is known for singing for many of her celebrity friends at their weddings.

Excerpt 5 News Interview: Marriage

1 IR: ponin-to icey chwukha-lul
self-also now congratulations-ACC

2 pat-aya toy-canh-a-yo:?
receive-should-you.know-IE-POL
'Isn't it your turn to receive congratulations?'

3 IE: kulekey-yo. hh hh
kulekey-POL
'KULEKEY.'

4 IR: ku-chyo:?
be.so-COMM:POL
'That's correct, right:?'

5 ilehkey aykyo-to manh-kwu:,
like.this cuteness-also much-and

6 e ilehkey salangsulewu-ntey mal-i-cyo:.
uh like.this lovely-but saying-be-COMM:POL
'Uh, (when) you are so charming and lovely.'

The reporter elicits confirmation from the singer that it is her turn to be receiving congratulations, implying that she, like her friends, should get married. In response to this somewhat personal question, the singer neither confirms nor disconfirms it, but responds with *kulekey-yo* and laughter. With this answer, the singer endorses the general idea of it being her turn, but neither promises nor suggests that she is about to get married. As such, with *kulekey*, a recipient can endorse the proposition in a prior speaker's utterance at the surface level without endorsing the action or project that underlies the utterance.

Our data show that *kulekey* is often observed in interviews when an interviewee is faced with a question to which she or he does not want to give a full or straightforward answer, as above, or when the interviewer seeks to maintain neutrality. The following segment from an interview between a news broadcaster and an actor shows another similar case. In this case, the interviewer (IR) and the interviewee (IE) are both cautious about displaying their stance as they share their concerns about typhoon damage in Busan, where an international film festival is scheduled to open the following day.

Excerpt 6 News Interview: Film Festival

1 IR: nayil-pwuthe way ce:
tomorrow-from DM DM

2 pwusan kwukcey yenghwacey nayil ka-si-cyo?
Busan international film.festival tomorrow go-SH-COMM:POL
'The Busan International Film Festival (begins) tomorrow. You are going, aren't you?'

3 IE: ney.
'Yes.'

4 IR: kuntey keki cikum thayphwung phihay-ka iss-[ese.]
but there now typhoon damage-NOM exist-because
'Because there is typhoon damage now,'

5 IE: [ney.]
'Yes.'

6 IR: yenghwacey-ey-to com chacil-ul picul kes-i-ta
film.festival-LOC-also a.little problem-ACC cause thing-be-DC

7 ilen yayki-to nao-ki-nun ha-[nuntey.]
such talk-also come.out-NML-TOP do-but
'People say that the festival will have a setback, too.'

8 IE: [ney.]
'Yes.'

9 IR: e pwusan simin yelepwun-tul-to
uh Busan citizen many.people-PL-also

10 kekceng-ul manhi ha-si-l kes kat-ko.
Worry-ACC much do-SH-RL thing like-and
'Uh, the people of Busan are probably very concerned.'

11 IE: **kulssey** cehui-to ama hayngsacang-ul
kulssey we-also probably event.location-ACC

12 olmki-ko kule-na pwa-yo. =
move-and be.so-seem-POL
'KULSSEY it looks like we will be moving to another location for the event.'

13 IR: = yey yey.
'Yes, yes.'

14 IE: keki chimswu-toy-n tey-to iss-ko kulayse:.
There flood-become-RL place-also exist-and since
'Since some places are flooded.'

15 IR: yey.
'Yes.'

16 IE: kulayto ( ) hayngsa-nun tto cinhaynghay-ya toy-keyss-cyo? =
nevertheless event-TOP DM proceed-should-DCT:RE-COMM:POL
'Nevertheless, I guess we need to proceed with the event, right?'

17 IR: = kulekey-yo.
'KULEKEY.'

18 IE: yey.
'Yes.'

The interviewee is conflicted, as she is expected to attend the film festival as a judge while there is an ongoing crisis at the festival site. Her question in line 16 displays how she cautiously elicits the interviewer's support in proceeding with the film festival despite the crisis. *Kulekey* is used when the interviewer answers this somewhat sensitive question. The interviewer cannot firmly argue for the need to hold a film festival during a crisis. So, in line 17, the interviewer simply responds with *kulekey*. In this way, he does not take a clear stance on whether it should be held or not, but rather minimally complies with what is being said.[5]

We have observed that interviewers often deploy *kulekey* in interviews. News broadcasters need to keep a neutral stance, and *kulekey* is a resource for maintaining that neutrality. Its use allows interviewers to distance themselves from the views being expressed while still maintaining a degree of alignment with the interviewee.

As Excerpts 4, 5, and 6 demonstrate, *kulekey* allows recipients to tailor their affiliative stance. If recipients wish only to endorse a proposition at the surface level (and not endorse the action or project underlying the utterance), they can do so by limiting their response to *kulekey*. However, if recipients wish to fully endorse both the proposition and the entailed action, they need to endorse both. Excerpt 7 is from a reporter's interview with an actor who has just received an award. Note how this interviewee's response differs from the case in Excerpt 5.

Excerpt 7 News Interview: Bonus

1 IR: mal-man ani-ko com ponesu com
word-only not-and a.little bonus a.little

2 cwu-sy-eya ha-nun ke aniey-yo?
give-SH-should-RL thing be.not-POL
'Shouldn't (the head of your agency) give you a bonus, not just words (of gratitude)?'

3 IE: ku(hh)lekey-yo. **ponesu hh com cwu-sey-yo**.
kulekey-POL bonus a.little give-SH-POL
'KULEKEY. Give me a bonus.'

4 ah ponesu-ka eps-ess-e-yo. ((smiling voice))
ah bonus a.little give-SH-POL
'Ah, there was no bonus.'

Just prior to this segment, the reporter mentioned that the head of the actor's agency had publicly congratulated the actor and thanked him for making the agency proud. In line 1, the reporter is conducting two actions. First, she is making a complaint with the claim that the head of the agency should do more than offer empty words of gratitude. Second, she is suggesting that the actor deserves a bonus. Note how in line 3, the actor

[5] The epistemic differences between *kulekey* and *kulssey*, which we saw in Excerpt 3, are reconfirmed in Excerpt 6. When the interviewer suggests the possibility of a setback for the film festival (lines 6–7), the interviewee contributes her own knowledge of the matter in lines 11-12, prefacing this display of her epistemic rights over the matter with *kulssey*.

responds to both actions. He first endorses the complaint with *kulekey* (meaning something like, 'Oh, yeah, he shouldn't be giving me just empty words (of gratitude)'), and he then explicitly addresses the utterance's underlying action by demanding a bonus. In this case, even though the recipient responds with *kulekey*, there is no sense of evasiveness because he follows his *kulekey* by immediately addressing the underlying action.

We often focus on the function of certain words or expressions—what has been verbalized—but, in fact, what is not verbalized in interaction can be equally important for understanding the interlocutors' actions.

4 Discussion and Conclusion

The analyses in this study show that *kulekey* not only conveys a recipient's agreement, but also functions as an epistemic response token that indexes a recipient's subordinate epistemic position compared to the prior speaker. And this is what separates *kulekey* from other agreement markers, in particular *kulssey*, which is used when a recipient claims and competes for epistemic rights over the matter at hand. In addition, the analyses show that recipients deploy *kulekey* to adjust and tailor their affiliative stances when they are facing double-barreled questions. With *kulekey*, recipients can choose to endorse the proposition in a prior speaker's utterance, without necessarily endorsing the action or project that underlies the utterance. This shows that the use of *kulekey* does not position recipients as passive participants who simply concur with what has been said in a prior turn, but is a resource for active coparticipants to control and adjust the degree and scope of their commitment to a prior utterance in interaction.

References

Ahn, M., & Yap, F. H. 2013. Negotiating common ground in discourse: A diachronic and discourse analysis of *maliya* in Korean. *Language Sciences, 37*, 36–51.

An, Y. M. 2012. A study on the discourse marker '*kulehge*'. *Korean Linguistics,* 56: 91–118.

Heritage, J. 1984. A change-of-state token and aspects of its sequential placement. *Structures of social action: studies in conversation analysis*, eds. J. Maxwell Atkinson and John Heritage, 299–345. Cambridge: Cambridge University Press.

Jo, M. 2017. A study on the interactional functions of 'verbal backchannel'. *Hanmal Yenkwu,* 44: 175–206.

Lee, H. S. 1991. *Tense, aspect, and modality: A discourse-pragmatic analysis of verbal affixes in Korean from a typological perspective*. Unpublished Ph.D. dissertation, University of California, Los Angeles.

Oh, S-Y. & Park, Y-Y. 2017. Interactional uses of acknowledgment tokens: '*ung*' and 'e' as responses to multi-unit turns in Korean conversation. *Enabling Human Conduct. Studies of Talk-in-interaction in Honor of Emanuel A. Schegloff*, eds. G. Raymond, G. H. Lerner and J. Heritage, 145-166. Amsterdam: John Benjamins.

Rhee, S. 2015. On the emergence of Korean markers of agreement. *Journal of Pragmatics,* 83: 10–26.

Schegloff, E. A. 2007. *Sequence organization in Interaction: A primer in conversation analysis*, Volume 1. Cambridge: Cambridge University Press.

Smith, H. Y. & Kim, M. S. 2019. Turn-initial and turn-final Korean discourse particle *kulssey*. The 16th International Pragmatics Conference, Hong Kong Polytechnic University.

Sohn, H. 1990. *The Korean Language*. Cambridge: Cambridge University Press.

Young, R. F. & Lee, J. 2004. Identifying units in interaction: Reactive tokens in Korean and English conversations. *Journal of Sociolinguistics* 8(3): 380-407.